Entrepreneurial Marketing

Entrepreneurial Marketing

A Blueprint for Customer Engagement

Beth Goldstein

Los Angeles | London | New Delhi
Singapore | Washington DC | Melbourne

FOR INFORMATION:

SAGE Publications, Inc.
2455 Teller Road
Thousand Oaks, California 91320
E-mail: order@sagepub.com

SAGE Publications Ltd.
1 Oliver's Yard
55 City Road
London EC1Y 1SP
United Kingdom

SAGE Publications India Pvt. Ltd.
B 1/I 1 Mohan Cooperative Industrial Area
Mathura Road, New Delhi 110 044
India

SAGE Publications Asia-Pacific Pte. Ltd.
18 Cross Street #10-10/11/12
China Square Central
Singapore 048423

Acquisitions Editor: Maggie Stanley
Editorial Assistant: Janeane Calderon
Production Editor: Kelle Clarke
Copy Editor: Diane DiMura
Typesetter: C&M Digitals (P) Ltd.
Proofreader: Caryne Brown
Indexer: Kathleen Paparchontis
Cover Designer: Janet Kiesel
Marketing Manager: Sarah Panella

Copyright © 2021 by SAGE Publications, Inc.

All rights reserved. Except as permitted by U.S. copyright law, no part of this work may be reproduced or distributed in any form or by any means, or stored in a database or retrieval system, without permission in writing from the publisher.

All third party trademarks referenced or depicted herein are included solely for the purpose of illustration and are the property of their respective owners. Reference to these trademarks in no way indicates any relationship with, or endorsement by, the trademark owner.

Printed in the United States of America

Library of Congress Cataloging-in-Publication Data

Names: Goldstein, Beth, author.

Title: Entrepreneurial marketing : a blueprint for customer engagement / Beth Goldstein, Babson College.

Description: Thousand Oaks, California : SAGE, [2021] | Includes bibliographical references and index.

Identifiers: LCCN 2019035165 | ISBN 9781544320434 (paperback) | ISBN 9781544397436 (epub) | ISBN 9781544397443 (epub) | ISBN 9781544397429 (pdf)

Subjects: LCSH: Marketing. | Consumer satisfaction | Branding (Marketing) | Internet marketing.

Classification: LCC HF5415 .G592 2021 | DDC 658.8—dc23
LC record available at https://lccn.loc.gov/2019035165

This book is printed on acid-free paper.

20 21 22 23 24 10 9 8 7 6 5 4 3 2 1

BRIEF TABLE OF CONTENTS

Preface	xvi
Acknowledgments	xxv
About the Author	xxvii
CHAPTER 1 • Marketing Using an Entrepreneurial Lens	1
CHAPTER 2 • Understanding Your Ecosystem	28
CHAPTER 3 • Identifying Your Customers' Journey	64
CHAPTER 4 • Listening to the Voice of the Customer	96
CHAPTER 5 • Managing Competition and Inertia	117
CHAPTER 6 • Creating Brand Engagement	138
CHAPTER 7 • Designing Marketing Partnerships That Empower Growth	161
CHAPTER 8 • Creating Sales Processes and Systems	184
CHAPTER 9 • Solution Selling	211
CHAPTER 10 • Doing Well While Doing Good	242
CHAPTER 11 • Deploying Omnichannel Marketing to Create Customer Engagement	261
CHAPTER 12 • Leveraging Old School Marketing Tactics	289
CHAPTER 13 • Using Data and Passion to Move From Idea to Market	311
References	332
Index	337

DETAILED TABLE OF CONTENTS

Preface	xvi
Acknowledgments	xxv
About the Author	xxvii

CHAPTER 1 • Marketing Using an Entrepreneurial Lens — 1

An Entrepreneurial Approach to Marketing	1
New Tools—Same Old Rules	4
Designing a Business Model That Creates Value	8
▸ VIEW FROM THE TRENCHES: PhiloSophie's®: From Mass Market to Tying the Knot	9
Reality Check—The Truth About Business Success and Failure	12
The Importance of Setting S.M.A.R.T. Goals	14
▸ ACTION CREATES TRIUMPHS (ACT): Interview an Entrepreneur	16
Entrepreneur Interview	16
Sample Questions and Script	17
▸ ACTION CREATES TRIUMPHS (ACT): Idea Generation	18
▸ FOCUS ON APPLICATION: WAKU The Entrepreneurial Journey	20
▸ AHAs: Lessons and Takeaways	21
Toolkit	22
Worksheet 1.1: Setting S.M.A.R.T. Goals	22
Worksheet 1.2: Sample S.M.A.R.T. Goal	23
Worksheet 1.3: Business Launch Plan/Road Map	24
Worksheet 1.4: Completing an Ethnography Study	26

CHAPTER 2 • Understanding Your Ecosystem — 28

Introduction to Market Research	28
Defining and Understanding the Ecosystem You Operate Within	28
Primary Versus Secondary Data Sources	29
Understanding Evolving Market Trends	29
Defining Your Market	31
Building Your Business Model	32
Sources of Data and Trends	33
Tools for Understanding Trends	35
The Value of Industry Association Data	35

Market Size	36
➡ **ACTION CREATES TRIUMPHS (ACT):** Your Market	38
Your Business Relative to Others in the Industry: SWOT Analysis	38
Strengths	39
Weaknesses	40
Opportunities	41
Threats	41
PESTLE Analysis	42
Positioning Map	44
➡ **ACTION CREATES TRIUMPHS (ACT):** Country Entrepreneurship Opportunity Challenge	45
Your Challenge	45
Sources of Country Data	45
Country Data to Analyze	46
➡ **VIEW FROM THE TRENCHES:** Marabots Technology Corporation	47
In Their Shoes	50
➡ **HIGHLIGHTS OF MARABOTS RESEARCH FINDINGS**	50
➡ **MARABOTS FINAL RECOMMENDATION**	54
➡ **FOCUS ON APPLICATION: WAKU** The Entrepreneurial Journey	55
➡ **AHAs:** Lessons and Takeaways	57
Toolkit	58
Worksheet 2.1: SWOT Analysis	58
Worksheet 2.2: Strategic Plan to Address SWOT	60
Worksheet 2.3: Market Size Analysis	63

CHAPTER 3 • Identifying Your Customers' Journey   64

The Journey of Customer Discovery	64
Turn Data Into Knowledge	65
The Importance of Saying No: Knowing Which Customers Are Not the Right Match for You	65
Ask the Right Questions	67
Methods of Discovering Customer Needs	67
Ethical Issues in Customer Research	68
Getting to Know Your Customers	68
Value Proposition Canvas	71
Select Your Questions Wisely	72
➡ **ACTION CREATES TRIUMPHS (ACT):** Select Your Questions	72
Building Your Business Model	72
Four Methods of Customer Discovery Research	74
Survey Design	74
Ethnographic Studies	80

➡ ACTION CREATES TRIUMPHS (ACT): Ethnography Challenge	82
Part One: Observation and Note-Taking	82
Part Two: Insights and Recommendations	83
Focus Groups	83
One-on-One Interviews	85
➡ ACTION CREATES TRIUMPHS (ACT): Customer Discovery Analysis Assignment	86
What Questions Do You Need to Ask?	86
How Do You Begin to Discover the Answers?	86
Deliverables	88
➡ VIEW FROM THE TRENCHES: Chewie's Colossal Cookie Company Survey	88
Chewie's Colossal Cookie Company Survey: Version One	89
Chewie's Colossal Cookie Company Final Survey: Version Two	92
➡ AHAs: Lessons and Takeaways	93
Toolkit	94
Worksheet 3.1: Resources for Proper Survey Design	94

CHAPTER 4 • Listening to the Voice of the Customer — 96

How Do You Hear the Voice of Your Customer?	96
Prototypes to Help Identify Profiles	97
The SunChips® Package Story	99
Prototyping the Google Way	100
Beyond Physical Products: Prototyping Services and Apps	101
Storyboards	101
Role-Plays	102
Website and Social Media Test Sites or Landing Pages	102
➡ VIEW FROM THE TRENCHES: Meet Aimee: The Aimee Bio Story	103
➡ ACTION CREATES TRIUMPHS (ACT): Now on to Your Prototype	108
Building Your Business Model	108
Going From Prototype to MVP	109
➡ FOCUS ON APPLICATION: WAKU The Entrepreneurial Journey	110
How Did Waku Launch Its Crowdfunding Campaign?	111
Identifying Suspects, Customers, and Prospects	112
B2B Versus B2C Profiling	113
➡ ACTION CREATES TRIUMPHS (ACT): Designing Customer Profiles	114
Ideal Customer Profile (Persona) Description	115
➡ AHAs: Lessons and Takeaways	115
Toolkit	116
Worksheet 4.1: Ideal Customer Profile (Persona) Description	116

CHAPTER 5 • Managing Competition and Inertia — 117

Competitors Don't Always Look Like You	117
Clearly Defining Competition	117

How Substitute Products Impact Revenue Potential	118
➡ **ACTION CREATES TRIUMPHS (ACT):** Friend or Foe?	119
The Right Perspective	119
➡ **ACTION CREATES TRIUMPHS (ACT):** Whom Do You Really Compete With?	120
Sources of Competitive Data	121
The Myth of First Mover Advantage	122
Second Mover Advantage	123
What Is Inertia?	124
Leapfrog Your Competition	125
➡ **FOCUS ON APPLICATION: WAKU** The Entrepreneurial Journey	126
➡ **VIEW FROM THE TRENCHES:** Go Nuts for Gonuts Donuts and Coffee	129
In Their Shoes	132
Building Your Business Model	132
➡ **AHAs:** Lessons and Takeaways	133
Toolkit	134
Worksheet 5.1: Competitive Assessment	134
Worksheet 5.2: Competitive Differentiator Analysis	136

CHAPTER 6 • Creating Brand Engagement — 138

Building a Strong Brand	138
Don't Let Your Brand Be a Lizard	138
➡ **ACTION CREATES TRIUMPHS (ACT):** Your Favorite Brands	140
Consistently Communicate Your Brand Position	140
Why Do People Buy a Brand?	141
➡ **EXPERT INSIGHT: Developing Powerful Brands:** Dale Bornstein, **CEO at M Booth**	142
You Don't Control Your Brand Reputation	143
➡ **ACTION CREATES TRIUMPHS (ACT):** What's Your Brand Value?	143
Components of a Successful Brand	144
How Do You Create a Unique Brand?	144
➡ **ACTION CREATES TRIUMPHS (ACT):** Creating a Strong Brand: 8 Key Actions to Take	145
Building Your Business Model	146
➡ **VIEW FROM THE TRENCHES:** Bali Banana	148
Bali Banana: In Their Shoes	151
Master Your Brand Delivery Skills	151
What Are the Lessons Learned?	152
Make Your Elevator Pitch Soar Out of the Park	152
➡ **EXPERT INSIGHT: Art of the Pitch, Paul Horn**	154
➡ **ACTION CREATES TRIUMPHS (ACT):** Creating Your OWN Pitch	156
Remember to Start at the End	156
Your Pitch	156

▶ FOCUS ON APPLICATION: WAKU	
The Entrepreneurial Journey	157
▶ AHAs: Lessons and Takeaways	159
Toolkit	159
Worksheet 6.1: Creating a Winning Elevator Pitch	159

CHAPTER 7 • Designing Marketing Partnerships That Empower Growth — 161

Finding Partners That Fit	161
The Right Partnership	161
Using Your SWOT and PESTLE Analyses to Identify the Right Partner	162
▶ ACTION CREATES TRIUMPHS (ACT): Step-by-Step Process to Creating Winning Marketing Partnerships	162
Marketing Alliance Benefits	164
Risk–Reward Balance	165
▶ ACTION CREATES TRIUMPHS (ACT): Canine Connections: Partners in Action	165
▶ VIEW FROM THE TRENCHES: The Lasse Paakkonen Olympic Story	166
A Word About Business Values	168
Creating a Win–Win Scenario	169
Green Light Ahead	170
What Could Go Wrong?	171
Building Your Business Model	172
▶ VIEW FROM THE TRENCHES: Artistia—Connecting Customers With Artisans	172
In Their Shoes	175
▶ FOCUS ON APPLICATION: WAKU	
The Entrepreneurial Journey	175
▶ AHAs: Lessons and Takeaways	177
Toolkit	178
Worksheet 7.1: Getting Partnerships Right	178
Worksheet 7.2: Partner/Alliance Analysis and Strategy	179
Worksheet 7.3: Individual Partnership Assessment	180
Worksheet 7.4: Partnership Checklist	183

CHAPTER 8 • Creating Sales Processes and Systems — 184

Sales Is All About Building Relationships	184
Sales and Marketing Data Flow	184
Different Worldviews	185
Sales and Marketing Collaboration	186
Sales and Marketing Collaboration Model	187
▶ ACTION CREATES TRIUMPHS (ACT): Sales and Marketing Collaboration Model	188

B2B or B2C or Some Combination of the Two?	188
➠ FOCUS ON APPLICATION: WAKU	
The Entrepreneurial Journey	190
Designing Sales Processes and Systems	191
➠ ACTION CREATES TRIUMPHS (ACT): Sales Goals	192
Sales Analysis and Projections	192
Prospect/Sales Cycle	192
Customer Revenue and Profit Analysis	193
Marketing Tactics	193
Data Capture Plan	194
Managing Customer Relationships	194
Knowledge Is Power	195
Managing Your Team's Sales Cycle	197
Chewie's Colossal Cookie Company: Letting the Data Inform Your Next Steps	197
Building Your Business Model	200
➠ VIEW FROM THE TRENCHES: DetraPel—Repelling Stains One Customer at a Time	201
In Their Shoes: Achieving DetraPel's Sales Goals	202
➠ FOCUS ON APPLICATION: WAKU	
The Entrepreneurial Journey	203
In Their Shoes: Creating a Customer Sales Database	204
➠ AHAs: Lessons and Takeaways	204
Toolkit	205
Worksheet 8.1: Sales Conversion	205
Worksheet 8.2: Sales Time Analysis	206
Worksheet 8.3: Sales Prospect Calculator	206
Worksheet 8.4: Sales Analysis Projection	207
Worksheet 8.5: Customer Profit and Time Analysis	208
Worksheet 8.6: Data Capture Plan/Dashboard	210

CHAPTER 9 • Solution Selling — 211

Sales Is About Listening	211
Sales for Those Who Hate Selling	211
Ready to Start Selling?	214
Communication and Listening Skills	214
Analytical Skills	214
Organizational Skills	215
Time Management and Discipline	215
Keen Interest in Learning	216
Passion	216
Do Your Homework	216

Five Stages of the Sales Process ... 218
    Stage One: Preparation ... 218
    Stage Two: The Introduction ... 220
    Stage Three: Preparing for the In-Person Appointment ... 221
    Stage Four: The Meeting ... 222
    Stage Five: Follow-Up and Servicing the Account's Needs ... 224

Dealing With Objections ... 225

Sales Tips for Building Relationships ... 225
    Contact Times ... 225
    Hot Buttons ... 226
    Open Versus Close-Ended Questioning Techniques ... 226
    ▶ **FOCUS ON APPLICATION: WAKU**
        The Entrepreneurial Journey ... 227
        Waku Sales Process and Product Pitch ... 227
        In Their Shoes ... 231
    ▶ **AUTHOR'S NOTE: Trust and Building Relationships As Seen Through the Eyes of a Car Buyer** ... 231

Building Your Business Model ... 232

Networking to Jump-Start and Grow Your Business ... 233

It's Not About Making Friends ... 233
    ▶ **EXPERT INSIGHT: Paul Horn: Golden Rules of Networking** ... 233
        Rule # 1: Networking Is Reciprocal. ... 234
        Rule # 2: Opportunities Are Unlimited ... 234

Conferences as a Great Opportunity to Build Your Networking Skills ... 235

Holding Your Own Seminars and Webinars ... 237

Still Not Convinced ... 237
    ▶ **AHAs: Lessons and Takeaways** ... 238

Toolkit ... 239
    Worksheet 9.1: Sales Stages Checklist ... 239
    Worksheet 9.2: Selling to Difficult Customers ... 241

CHAPTER 10 • Doing Well While Doing Good ... 242

Aligning Your Messaging to Underscore Your Social Value ... 242

Are YOU a Social Entrepreneur? ... 242

Warby Parker ... 243
    Revolutionizing an Industry ... 243

Editing Others Into the Conversation About Your Mission ... 245

The Ad Council: Inspiring Change, Improving Lives ... 245

Five Fundamentals for Making Social Impact on YouTube ... 246

Corporate Social Responsibility ... 247

Taking the Next Step in Corporate Social Responsibility ... 248

Think Like a Donor ... 250

- ▶ **ACTION CREATES TRIUMPHS (ACT):** Finding Passion Around a Mission — 251

Passionate Entrepreneurs Can Make a Difference — 251

- ▶ **VIEW FROM THE TRENCHES:** Kees Chic—Saving the Planet . . . One Plastic Bag at a Time — 252
  - In Their Shoes — 254
- ▶ **VIEW FROM THE TRENCHES:** Artyfactos—Helping Women— One Orange Peel at a Time — 255
  - Earthy Yet Innovative — 256
  - Understanding Your Customer Base — 257
  - In Their Shoes — 258
- ▶ **FOCUS ON APPLICATION: WAKU**
  - The Entrepreneurial Journey — 258
- ▶ **ACTION CREATES TRIUMPHS (ACT):** Mission-Focused Brands — 259
- ▶ **AHAs:** Lessons and Takeaways — 260

CHAPTER 11 • Deploying Omnichannel Marketing to Create Customer Engagement — 261

Let the Games Begin—Time to Focus on Your Marketing Campaign Design — 261

Getting Your Customers Engaged Through an Omnichannel Marketing Approach — 262

Think Like Starbucks — 263

- ▶ **ACTION CREATES TRIUMPHS (ACT):** Creating Seamless Experiences — 265

Creating Brand Engagement and Buzz — 265

Disruptive Brand Marketing Campaigns — 267

Ceding Control of Your Brand — 267

Return to Your Research Findings to Get Customer Touch Points Right — 268

- ▶ **VIEW FROM THE TRENCHES:** Clothing Consignment: Research First—Channels Second — 268

Omnichannel: Combining the Best of Old School Marketing With New School Channels — 269

Let's Talk Social — 270

Content Is King — 271

Public Relations and Creating Thought Leaders and Influencers — 272

- ▶ **EXPERT INSIGHT:** Becoming a Thought Leader and Influencer—Lisa Murray — 272
  - Find a Voice — 273
  - Course Correct (if needed) — 274

What if You're Not an Expert — 274

Creating and Delivering Content — 275
  - Blogs — 275
  - Webinars — 276

Podcasts	276
Videos	277
Exploring Top Social Tools	**279**
YouTube	280
Facebook	280
Instagram	280
Pinterest	281
Snapchat as a Marketing Tool	**281**
Email Marketing	**283**
Email Marketing Tips to Get You Focused	283
Tools, Tips, and Training Resources	**284**
▶ **ACTION CREATES TRIUMPHS (ACT):** Social Media Critique and Campaign Development	**285**
Part One: Social Media Critique	285
Part Two: Social Media Campaign	286
Information to Include in Your Social Marketing Campaign Presentation	287
▶ **AHAs: Lessons and Takeaways**	**288**

CHAPTER 12 • Leveraging Old School Marketing Tactics — 289

Old School Never Goes Out of Style	**289**
Old School Methods of Reaching Your Customers	**289**
Brochures	289
Direct Mail	290
Get Them to Act	291
Traditional Advertising	291
The Power of Networking: Making the RIGHT Connections at the RIGHT Events	**292**
Where Else Can You Meet the RIGHT People?	**294**
Developing Your Network: You Can't Succeed Alone	**296**
▶ **ACTION CREATES TRIUMPHS (ACT):** Create a Networking Plan	**297**
▶ **VIEW FROM THE TRENCHES:** Stallion Deliveries	**297**
Mother's Day Campaign	299
Send a Smile: Eid (Celebration) Day Campaign	299
In Their Shoes	300
▶ **FOCUS ON APPLICATION: WAKU**	
The Entrepreneurial Journey	**300**
Your Marketing Campaign Rollout	**303**
Channels and Tools	303
▶ **AHAs: Lessons and Takeaways**	**304**
Toolkit	**305**
Worksheet 12.1: Marketing Channel Projections and Analysis	305
Worksheet 12.2: Omnichannel Marketing Campaign	306
Worksheet 12.3: Marketing Campaign Strategy Outline	307
Worksheet 12.4: Networking—Making the Right Connections	309

CHAPTER 13 • Using Data and Passion to Move From Idea to Market — **311**

- Understanding the Customer Journey Through the Data — 311
- Channeling Your Passion to Fuel Success — 312
- Watch the Flames — 312
- Learning to Accept Failure — 313
  - ➡ **ACTION CREATES TRIUMPHS (ACT): Test Your Readiness to Commit to Your Venture** — **314**
    - Scorecard Instructions — 314
- Cut Once, Measure Twice — 317
- Just the Facts: Getting the Right Data and Getting the Data Right — 318
- Where to Begin Your Analysis — 319
  - Measuring Your Input and Outcomes — 320
  - Sales Analysis and Projections — 320
  - Prospect and Customer Sales Cycles — 320
  - Employee Analysis — 320
  - Customer Revenue and Profit Analysis — 321
  - Product/Service Analysis — 321
  - Marketing Tactics — 321
- Customer Lifetime Value — 322
- Selecting the Right Customer Mix — 324
- Your Data Capture Plan — 325
- Ready, Set, Launch: Your Marketing Road map — 325
- Navigating Your Path to Success — 328
- A Journey of Exploration — 328
  - Oh! The Places You'll Go — 328
  - Oh! The Places You'll Go! — 328
- Toolkit — 329
  - Worksheet 13.1: Data Capture Plan — 329
  - Worksheet 13.2: Measuring Your Input and Outcome — 329
  - Worksheet 13.3: Customer Lifetime Value — 331

References — **332**

Index — **337**

PREFACE

The landscape for marketing has changed dramatically over the past decade, and social media has become a strong force impacting business decisions related to customer knowledge and acquisition. However, many students arrive on campus with an understanding of social media from the "consumer" perspective and don't realize that, as a business owner, the use of social media is quite different and is not always the best nor only tool to engage customers and grow an organization. By engaging in the activities throughout this book, students will be in a stronger position to understand, differentiate, and select among the variety of marketing options available to them, ranging from customer discovery and research tools to sales, social media, and other methods of creating traction that impact profit and revenue.

Throughout the book, students will learn how to

- deploy appropriate customer discovery tools to identify customer and market needs, problems, and entrepreneurial opportunities.

- define customer profiles and create personas to align customer outreach methods and messaging with identified behaviors, interests, and attitudes.

- respond to evolving unmet customer needs using personal, digital, social, and mobile spheres.

- develop, manage, and measure the success of an omnichannel marketing campaign that creates traction and engagement for entrepreneurial organizations.

- develop content that directly addresses consumer needs and creates brand engagement.

- analyze various market opportunities and assess risks with the focus on meeting customer needs.

- develop (and adjust when necessary) key performance indicators (KPIs), metrics, and milestones for their campaign and evaluate their success based on achieving these metrics.

- effectively allocate limited resources and budgets across diverse marketing channels.

Entrepreneurial marketing, like entrepreneurship itself, involves a journey where students begin to identify customer needs and unravel opportunities with the goal of creating a new business or developing a new product or service based on an identifiable need in the marketplace. Marketing is about the relationship between customers and products, and this book helps students maintain a strong focus on the role customers play in helping them develop a business where product–market fit is the centerpiece of their business design. This hands-on entrepreneurial marketing textbook allows students to gain practical experience in the world of marketing by helping them to first understand and then apply key marketing frameworks with the goal of creating a customer-centric, omnichannel marketing program for a for-profit or nonprofit business or organization. They will learn how to view the customer engagement experience through the eyes of their target market to effectively build a sustainable brand. The book walks them through the process of creating a marketing campaign, allowing them to implement and measure the campaign's impact in a safe classroom environment. This book will also help them understand the journey that entrepreneurs undertake as they launch their businesses with a strong focus on developing products and services based on identified customer needs in the market. Throughout the book, students will explore topics ranging from customer discovery to social media campaign design, exploring businesses in nine countries around the world: Colombia, Ecuador, Finland, Indonesia, Kuwait, Lebanon, Pakistan, Kingdom of Saudi Arabia, and the United States.

OUR APPROACH/VISION— WHAT MAKES THIS BOOK UNIQUE

As an educator, teaching on campus, online, and around the world, I have encountered no greater challenge than identifying marketing tools that engage students in applying key marketing concepts and tools directly to real-world business problems, ones they can easily relate to. Through the practice of learning, then testing, these marketing tools, students experience firsthand which solutions best address customer problems. This knowledge will empower them to not only own the learning and improve their marketing self-efficacy but also help them gain a new skill set that allows them to apply the learning to solve future challenges. Combining the framework plus an experiential pedagogical model is a primary design concept used throughout the book.

The book is written using a very friendly and approachable writing style, ensuring students can apply the tools and knowledge immediately to the business or product that they are thinking about launching. The cases share the same approachable style, featuring business owners who were students when they launched their business. This accessible style allows the reader to recognize that the marketing tools and business ideas that they are reading about are within their grasp.

The book is designed to create student awareness about the fact that marketing principles and techniques transcend city, country, and regional borders. Whether students are sitting in a classroom in the United States, Latin America, the Middle East, or any place else around the world, they will find these business owners featured in the book to be individuals whom they can easily relate to, as many started their companies when they were college students, like them. Since I split my time between the world of academia and the business world, my frameworks are not purely theoretical but are designed around experiences I have had working with thousands of companies around the world. Interspersed throughout the book are stories of success and failure, chronicling business owners' experiences from Lebanon and Saudi Arabia to Colombia and Ecuador, countries rarely featured in U.S.-based textbooks. Oftentimes, textbooks focus on Western business founders, creating a distortion that influences how students view entrepreneurship opportunities. Featuring students and business owners from cities around the globe ensures all students see themselves in these cases and helps them gain an understanding that entrepreneurial journeys are universal. A global approach to problem solving is important because it helps students relate to the challenges faced by the entrepreneur in Boston as well as the one in Beirut, finding value in how that person used marketing to identify, define, and seize an opportunity. More than one million international students are enrolled in U.S. universities, and many of these non-American students can't relate to or don't see themselves in cases that they read about in textbooks.

The featured cases of business owners applying marketing best practices in various parts of the world will help prepare them, as future business leaders, to understand how to think and act with a global mindset. For example, in the Colombian case study featuring Artyfactos, students learn about a jewelry business launched by Colombian native Angela Sanchez. The story of Artyfactos demonstrates how entrepreneurs can do good by helping poor women in South America, and concurrently do well, measured in terms of economic value created by her firm. In the Kuwait story about GoNuts, students learn how Abdulrahman Al Rabah launched his donut business in Kuwait City, Kuwait, and the competitive challenges he faced as he grew his business. In the story from Finland, they hear about Olympic athlete Lasse Paakkonen's entrepreneurial journey and his discovery of the power of business and marketing partnerships to fuel his success. The book opens with a case about a U.S.-based entrepreneur, Joanna Alberti, where students will learn about her 15-year journey to develop PhiloSophie's®, a line of greeting cards and stationery based on the stylish and witty illustrated character, Sophie. Her company experienced numerous obstacles and pivots, yet Joanna has remained steadfast in her pursuit of success.

While the book shares an abundance of advice and experiential learning opportunities, one important feature is the application of these marketing concepts to one company whose story is shared throughout the book. The reader will walk alongside two entrepreneurs as they launch a healthy-drink business in the United States. Students will be introduced to Juan Giraldo and Nicolás (Nico) Estrella, two young entrepreneurs who launched Waku in Boston, Massachusetts. Waku is an alternative tea drink based on the "healing waters" of Ecuador, Juan and Nico's home country. They'll hear about Juan and Nico's journey, struggles, wins, and losses as they launched their infused drink with two goals in mind: (1) create economic value as a U.S.-based business and (2) help the farmers in Ecuador maintain a livelihood.

Other unique features of the book that bring the frameworks to life, keep the reader engaged, and help them own the learning include the following:

- Toolkit at the end of many chapters featuring worksheets that support the experiential nature of the pedagogy

- ACT (Action Creates Triumphs) section offered throughout the book that presents a challenge to the students to answer questions or engage in an activity to make the lessons stick so they own the learning

- Tables, charts, and graphs to reinforce the material, including photos and artwork that bring the cases to life

- Case studies titled View From the Trenches that feature business owners whom they can relate to followed by a section, In Their Shoes, that asks the students to consider how they would address the challenge or opportunity that the entrepreneur in the case study is facing

- Advice From the Experts features pearls of wisdom from business experts focusing on enriching the students' understanding of key concepts and frameworks

- Chapter openers to describe what students will learn

- AHAs: Lessons and Takeaways offered at the end of each chapter highlighting and reinforcing the chapter's learning

Combing all of these features helps students understand and experience the frameworks in the book by creating real-world experiential learning activities that allow them to apply the material immediately. For example, we will give the students an approach to customer discovery using a specific framework that helps them identify potential customer needs. Next, they use the worksheet in the "field" to observe and conduct firsthand research through interviews with potential consumers of their product or service. Each worksheet will describe the steps they need to take to develop the skills and expertise described in the framework. These worksheets are available as separate PDF documents at **study.sagepub.com/goldstein1e**, which students can use in the classroom now and later on in their career.

CONTENT AND ORGANIZATION—
WHAT TO EXPECT IN EACH CHAPTER

Students will learn marketing techniques that have been deployed by individuals and companies around the world. CEOs, managers, founders, and business experts have contributed their expertise from a variety of organizations, including small and midsize, as well as for-profit and nonprofit companies. Best practices as well as strategies that have gone awry are discussed, including key takeaways and lessons learned. By the conclusion of the book, students will not only understand the variety of approaches to growing and launching a marketing campaign but will also have had the opportunity to practice the techniques presented, with the goal of creating an integrated, customer-centric, omni-channel marketing plan. This will not be the type of plan that resides in the cloud or on a shelf collecting dust, but one that is a living document charting a course to success for them to use now, and in the future.

Here's an overview of the knowledge that the students will discover in each chapter. Beginning with the first chapter of the book, Marketing Using an Entrepreneurial Lens, we introduce students to the concept of marketing as applied with an entrepreneurial lens. We'll help them understand the key differences between more traditional marketing approaches and those that truly integrate an entrepreneurial mindset, and the impact that has on business success. As they become comfortable with this notion, we will introduce a framework known as the Business Model Canvas (Osterwalder & Pigneur, 2010), which emphasizes the importance of having their value proposition (why customers care about their solution) at the heart of their business. They will see that they do not need to own a company to apply these frameworks, nor do they need to be the person responsible for marketing.

In Chapter 2, Understanding Your Ecosystem, we focus on helping students understand the importance of their ecosystem to ensure that their concept has merit and is realistic given the needs in the marketplace and their ability to deliver the value their customers want. We will discuss the importance of identifying target market needs, trends in the industry that impact their opportunity, and factors like environmental and government regulations plus changes in market channels or business models that influence how they can successfully test the feasibility of their concept.

Chapter 3, Identifying Your Customers' Journey, focuses on clearly identifying the specific needs of the customers who will buy from the businesses the students propose to create. Students need to understand not only who their customers are (i.e., demographics like age, gender, and location) but also customer behaviors, interests, and attitudes. Primary market research, also known as customer discovery, will help students get into the minds of their customers and, if conducted properly, put them in a stronger position to confirm if there is indeed a market for their proposed solution before they launch the business.

In Listening to the Voice of the Customer, the fourth chapter of the book, students will learn how to secure critical information about their customers to create a prototype of their product or service by actively listening to stakeholder feedback based on their interactions with their product or service, designing simple prototypes of the products and services that they want to deliver, and creating customer profiles (also referred to as customer personas) that reflect their customers' values, beliefs, and decision-making processes.

In Chapter 5, Managing Competition and Inertia, we debunk the myth that too many entrepreneurs have and this is the belief that they do not have competitors because they don't see "others" who look like them. While believing they have no competition might be considered a "rookie mistake," it's not uncommon to hear seasoned business owners make this claim because they haven't identified anybody in the market that produces the same product (or service) that they do. In this chapter, students learn how to define competition and substitute products, conduct a thorough competitive analysis, use a positioning map to understand where their product stands in the market, and create strategies that overcome the competitive power of inertia.

Chapter 5 is a great segue to Chapter 6, Creating Brand Engagement. Now that students have carefully listened to the voice of their customer, they should have a solid understanding of their customers' needs. This chapter helps students understand how to effectively communicate how their business meets or exceeds customer needs. This chapter emphasizes the importance of creating a winning pitch that succinctly describes their company's value proposition and creates brand engagement. We cover what it takes to build a strong brand and consistently communicate its value to customers, prospects, and all stakeholders. Students will learn how to define branding as it applies to their company or to themselves, differentiate between attributes of a brand (i.e., logo, taglines) versus a well-branded organization, consistently communicate their brand, describe why stakeholders value different aspects of a brand's benefits, and create a powerful elevator pitch that describes their brand value to key stakeholders.

In Chapter 7, Designing Marketing Partnerships That Empower Growth, we review the pros and cons of partnerships and alliances to help students identify which might be the right fit. Then, we examine the steps to take to develop a positive working partnership. In this chapter, students learn how to identify the right organizations that can support their marketing and business goals, use a SWOT analysis to identify partnerships that strengthen their company's ability to grow, assess which companies target similar markets with related products so they can develop synergistic sales growth opportunities, and develop a balanced partnership structure to ensure the risk–reward ratio is relatively equal for each organization.

Chapters 8 and 9 focus on selling and the sales process. In chapter 8, Creating Sales Processes and Systems, we focus on how the sales process is critical in building relationships. Recognizing that sales and marketing departments, even in small companies, do not always spend the time required to ensure they understand each other's goals to successfully align their activities, we show students how to develop sales processes and systems to analyze their current data and track future data so sales tactics are aligned with marketing goals. Students will learn how to define the differences and similarities between sales and marketing goals; identify the processes that need to be created so sales, marketing, and product development collaborate to address customer needs; differentiate between B2B (Business to Business), B2C (Business to Consumer), and C2C (Customer to Customer) sales and marketing strategies; and analyze the data they have to project sales targets, goals, and other information required to make informed business decisions. In Chapter 9, Solution Selling, we explore the importance of sales skills for every entrepreneur, regardless of the students' interest in pursuing a career in sales. While many entrepreneurs are comfortable and familiar with the sales process, there are just as many who dread networking or see sales as self-promotion. Selling is not about forcing a service or solution upon somebody who doesn't want or need it. It's about actively listening to prospective customers, identifying their key needs, and determining how they can meet their needs. Students needs to understand that selling is an essential part of marketing their business. In this chapter, we cover the sales process from networking and planning sales calls to cultivating business relationships. Students learn and practice the various techniques for improving and gaining comfort with their ability to sell, discover important tactics to manage their sales efforts, understand how to prepare for the various stages of the sales process, and embrace the importance of networking as a way to grow their business.

In Chapter 10, Doing Well While Doing Good, we explore businesses with a social mission, including for-profit and nonprofit businesses and organizations. We focus on organizations that create social value as well organizations whose mission is to create economic value but who are also committed to fulfilling a social mission. We show students how similar their marketing and customer outreach efforts are. Plus, we will discuss the differences that they need to understand related to their journey to create social value. Students will learn how to define the characteristics of business models that are designed to create social value, understand the importance of creating economic value along with social value to sustain a business or organization, define the similarities and differences between socially driven businesses and economically driven businesses, and understand the importance of being authentic to engage customers.

The next two chapters, 11 and 12, focus on helping students develop an omnichannel marketing program for their business. Chapter 11, Deploying Omnichannel Marketing to Create Customer Engagement, discusses how to select the right marketing channels to connect with customers, prospects, and other business stakeholders (e.g., potential partners, future employees, investors). It's likely that most of the students have been thinking about getting their message out since the first day they started thinking about their business. However, the process of identifying the best way to get a message out to target markets requires that the students first have a solid understanding of their customers' needs and decision-making processes before they can begin to approach them. This chapter covers the importance of creating an omnichannel, versus multichannel, approach and defines what the difference is. This includes traditional, old-school methods of communicating with customers as well as mobile, social, and other technology-driven methods. We show students how to deploy these channels so online efforts align with offline strategy, thereby creating a seamless experience—hence the term *omnichannel*. This chapter shows students how to use their customer profiles to develop an integrated online and offline marketing program, define what an omnichannel versus multichannel marketing approach is and how to deploy this strategy, identify the aligned online and offline channels that will target the right customers and build brand engagement, and develop content that resonates with their customers' needs.

Chapter 12, Leveraging Old-School Marketing Tactics, builds upon the conversation about omnichannel marketing, with a focus on more traditional methods of engaging with customers. We call them *Old School* but they clearly never go out of style and can be leveraged to deepen customer relationships. In this chapter, students learn how to differentiate between traditional and current methods of communicating with customers and prospects, develop an understanding of when to apply different communication strategies with customers and prospects, develop important networking skills to help them succeed in business, and design a marketing campaign strategy that aligns with their customer and business goals.

The final chapter of the book, Chapter 13, Using Data and Passion to Move From Idea to Market, positions students to use and act on the hard work that they've completed to identify their customers' needs and understand their business's value proposition as it aligns with the needs of the marketplace. This chapter begins with an understanding of the importance of having passion about their business, even when things don't go as planned and their business stumbles or fails. Then we focus on how students can define the metrics and key performance indicators required for success so that they, acting as the CEO or marketing manager, can determine if they are achieving a realistic and sustainable return on their marketing investment. This includes the ROI on each marketing campaign as well as understanding the lifetime value of key customer groups to ensure they are attracting the right customers using the most effective and efficient marketing channels. This chapter ties all of the pieces together with a discussion about the importance of SMART goal design to ensure students are able to create a customer-centric, omnichannel marketing plan. This plan must be fluid and flexible, allowing them to make changes and adjustments throughout their journey. Their SMART goals and the dashboard will inform their plan and allow it to be a living document that can change as market conditions and customer needs evolve over time.

We have designed this book to support students' vision and entrepreneurial journey. With your support, they can take advantage of the variety of exercises to help move their business vision forward. As you are working with your students, it's important to remind them that the entrepreneurial process is iterative. Therefore, they will likely need, and hopefully want, to revisit many of the exercises in this book as they address different market opportunities throughout their career, embracing the notion that each market is forever evolving. Growing a business is a fluid process that simply never stops. We hope that they will think of this book as a toolkit that they will use throughout their entrepreneurial journey, deploying the tools they need at various times throughout their entrepreneurial journey.

ACKNOWLEDGMENTS

Whoever said writing a book, getting your doctorate, and working full time was a piece of cake was out of their mind. Oh, wait, nobody said that! Nonetheless, writing this book has been an impassioned journey, allowing me to secure an even deeper level of understanding of the marketing domain that I've worked in for over 30 years. It has also reinforced the importance of having a supportive network. My friends and family have been there for me throughout this exploration, and I thank them profusely for their continuous advice, and guidance, and patience. Let me begin by thanking my mom, who has always been there for me, checking in to see how things are going and providing unconditional love that has helped get me through many of life's adventures. To my children, who always have a kind word and smile, Jacqui, Ben, Greg, and Jennifer, cheers to you and thanks for your love and humor throughout the past 2 years. I can't forget the furry members of the family whose kisses and wags made those frustrating times a little less stressful. Chewie, Twizzler, Callie, and Bandit—extra biscuits, on the house, for each of you. Finally, a special thanks to my life partner, David, who sacrificed much to ensure I was able to make my deadlines and has always been there with a hug, bouquet of flowers, and a much-needed neck massage.

To all of the individuals who contributed their ideas, expertise, and advice throughout the book, my eternal thanks and appreciation for your contribution to the book. A shout-out to Joanna Alberti, Abdulrahman Al Rabah, Lulwa AlSoudairy, Dale Bornstein, Stephen Brand, Caroline Daniels, Wisnu Dewobroto, Melinda Emerson, Nicolas Estrella, Tony Feghali, Juan Giraldo, Paul Horn, Muhammad Hassan Khan, Dany Khoury, Cheryl Kiser, Anita Juho, Katie Martell, Lisa Murray, Lasse Paakkonen, Diana Rayyan, Angela Sanchez, Jessica Syella, and David Zamarin.

I would like to thank the following experts who have generously given their time to provide valuable insight and guidance by reviewing the content of the book. I truly appreciate the support provided by:

Corinne Bodeman, Northern Michigan University

Martin Bressler, Southeastern Oklahoma State University

Violet Zalatar-Christopher, California State University at Northridge; Antelope Valley College

Caroline Daniels, Entrepreneurship Division, Babson College

Ali Kara, Penn State University, York Campus

Jen Linck, Pepperdine Graziadio Business School

Justin O'Brien, Royal Holloway University of London

Joseph C. Picken, The University of Texas at Dallas

Reza Rajabi, University of Massachusetts, Amherst

Ayisha Sereni, Community College of Philadelphia

Barry S. Slaymaker, Jr., Dalton State College

Sam Vegter, Western Piedmont Community College

Jennifer Yurchisin, Catawba College

Gregory F. Zerovnik, California State University, Monterey Bay

ABOUT THE AUTHOR

Beth Goldstein has spent the last 30+ years helping entrepreneurs, executives, small business owners, educators, and students around the globe launch and grow their businesses and organizations. She founded her consulting firm, Marketing Edge Consulting Group, in 1999 and established the company's training division, Edge Institute (www.edge-institute.com), in 2013 with a focus on helping entrepreneurs better understand how their key stakeholders and customers think, what they value, and what influences their purchasing decisions. She then works with them to ensure they know how to apply this knowledge to create targeted business growth programs that drive revenue growth while increasing profitability and customer loyalty.

Beth is currently pursuing her doctorate in education from Johns Hopkins University with a focus on understanding how entrepreneurship educators can activate entrepreneurial self-efficacy, confidence, and grit in students, business owners, and managers in global and emerging markets. She teaches entrepreneurship and marketing courses at Babson College and at the Isenberg School of Management at UMass, Amherst. She is also a visiting professor at Tecnológico de Monterrey in Mexico. Beth works closely with the Lewis Institute for Social Innovation at Babson College, helping them design and deliver educational programs for the Youth Impact Lab, activating youth changemakers through entrepreneurship. She serves as business advisor in Babson's Summer Venture Program and taught marketing and consulting courses at Brandeis University. Beth also spent 13 years at the Boston University Questrom School of Business, where she ran their New Venture Competition for 10 years and served as the faculty director for the university's top ranked online graduate certificate in entrepreneurship program from 2005 to 2014.

Beth's first book, *The Ultimate Small Business Marketing Toolkit* (McGraw-Hill, 2007) has been used in 30+ cities around the United States to teach business owners the critical skills they need to accelerate growth. In her second book, *Lucky By Design* (Dog Ear Publishing, 2011), Beth examined the fallacies and dangers of underestimating your own ability to control the destiny of your company and create powerful business opportunities. The book is being published in Chinese by Peking University Press. Beth's marketing advice was also featured in the *McGraw-Hill Small Business Resource Guide for QuickBooks Users* (2009) distributed to over 100,000 QuickBooks users.

Beth conducts business growth workshops throughout the United States for organizations ranging from publicly funded groups like the MA Supplier Diversity Office to Fortune 500 companies like Fidelity Investments and Carrier Corporation. She served as the lead instructor for Interise's nationwide training program, run in conjunction with the U.S. SBA: Small Business Association's Emerging Leaders (e200) Initiative, providing training to hundreds of business owners throughout the United States. She was also the managing director for the BU Urban Business Accelerator Program, an educational program that brought students to economically disadvantaged neighborhoods in Boston with the goal of improving financial capacity and business.

Beth specializes in custom-designing classroom and online business growth training programs ranging from 1/2-day workshops to intensive 9-month programs for companies as well as government agencies and organizations. She was on a three-person MBA design team that created an innovative MBA program for the Mohammad Bin Salman College of Business and Entrepreneurship, Saudi Arabia. She also led the design teams for the master's in entrepreneurial leadership and the 4-year undergraduate marketing degree. Beth has taught in the United States and abroad, including China, Costa Rica, Egypt, Germany, Indonesia, Kuwait, Lebanon, Mexico, Nigeria, Oman, Saudi Arabia, Thailand, and the United Kingdom. Beth holds an MBA from Boston University and a BA in economics and sociology from Brandeis University.

CHAPTER ONE

MARKETING USING AN ENTREPRENEURIAL LENS

AN ENTREPRENEURIAL APPROACH TO MARKETING

In this first chapter, we introduce you to the concept of marketing as applied with an entrepreneurial lens. Marketing has evolved significantly over the past 30 years with much of the control about a company's brand value switching from the hands of the business owners into the hands of consumers. This is a positive if you're the consumer, but more challenging, hence the entrepreneurial approach that is needed, when you're the business owner trying to get your brand recognized and embraced by consumers. We'll help you understand the key differences between more traditional marketing approaches and those that truly integrate an entrepreneurial mindset, and the impact that has on business success. As you become comfortable with this notion, we will introduce a framework known as the Business Model Canvas (Osterwalder & Pigneur, 2010), which emphasizes the importance of having your value proposition (why customers care about your solution) at the heart of your business. You do not need to own the company to apply these frameworks, nor do you need to be the person responsible for marketing. Throughout the book you will begin to embrace the notion of designing a business around consumer needs versus creating a product or service in search of a customer. We conclude with a discussion about setting S.M.A.R.T. (Specific, Measurable, Assignable, Realistic, Time-Related) (Doran, 1981) goals that will allow you to align your marketing plan with your strategic business objectives.

Marketing has been in a state of fluctuation over the past decade and will continue to evolve as we identify different channels and methods for communicating with prospects and customers.

Learning Objectives

In this chapter, you will learn to

- differentiate between entrepreneurial marketing and traditional marketing tactics.

- apply the concept of S..MA.R.T. (Doran, 1981) goals to a goal you plan to achieve.

- identify how the principles of Business Model Canvas (Osterwalder & Pigneur, 2010) design apply to a concept you are interested in exploring.

Millennials (anyone born between 1981 and 1996) are the largest generation in the United States, and the way they make decisions is different from that of any generation that came before them. For example, Pew Research Center's Study (2018a) on the influence of social media found that 23% of 18- to 29-year-olds changed their views on a social or political issue because of something they saw on social media versus only 13% of 50- to 64-year-olds making the same claim. Engagement is critical, and millennials have led the charge in terms of interacting with the brands they love. Let's look at Coca-Cola's "Share a Coke" campaign that launched in the United States in 2014 where they swapped out their logo on bottles of coke and replaced it with 250 of America's most popular first names such as John and Sarah. In 2015, they increased the number of names to 1,000 and created an option for individuals to order personalized bottles or six-packs (Moye, 2015). For consumers, this allowed Coke to become a part of their daily life experiences in a more personal way. According to a *Wall Street Journal* article, this led to a 2% increase in 2014 of Coca-Cola's carbonated-soft drink sales (Esterl, 2014).

In future chapters, we will explore further research on the impact of social media on decision making. However, for now it's important to understand the importance of changes in behavior and decision-making processes as they impact business and marketing decisions. In this book, we will spend time explaining important marketing frameworks and show you how to apply them to a variety of evolving opportunities to successfully grow a business or organization. We will show you how to apply marketing principles to solve a problem or seize an opportunity using an entrepreneurial approach. If you are successful at learning the frameworks, you will be able to address business challenges with greater comfort. This is because the basic principles and rules of customer engagement will not change in the same manner as the tools you use to reach customers will. Therefore, if you understand these basic frameworks of customer engagement and acquisition, you will be in a stronger position to select and deploy the right tools, as they evolve over time and apply them appropriately to whatever situation you find yourself and your company in. This is the essence of entrepreneurial marketing.

Let's begin with a definition of what an *entrepreneurial marketing approach* is, as opposed to traditional marketing methods. This sets the stage for the work you will do throughout the book. We begin this first chapter with a definition of *entrepreneurship* and then show you how to apply this to the practice of marketing.

When many people think of entrepreneurs, they think of people who own businesses. However, we challenge you to rethink this definition. Babson College, ranked the number one undergraduate school for entrepreneurship in the United States for over 21 consecutive years (as of the publishing of this book) by *U.S. News & World Report* has a different view of entrepreneurship (Babson, 2018). Professor Heidi Neck, along with her colleagues Christopher Neck and Emma Murray, explain in their book, *Entrepreneurship: The Practice and Mindset* (2018), that

> Entrepreneurship is complex, chaotic, and lacking in any notion of linearity. The entrepreneurship practice requires creative and nimble thinking leading to a heightened level of experimentation where numerous iterations represent stages of learning rather than a series of starts and stops or even successes and failures.

In this definition of *entrepreneurship*, there is no mention about owning or running a business. Therefore, what does this mean and what is the implication for your work in designing an entrepreneurial marketing initiative? Basically, this means that there is no one simple linear or straight line that will guarantee your connection with customers who are interested in your products or services. There are a multitude of methods that can be tried and tested to determine how to get your product in the hands of prospects and paying customers. Through a series of iterative tests, you will learn which approach is best to get to market. Keep in mind that this approach must reflect customers' evolving needs and will therefore need to change and evolve over time as customers respond differently to different outreach methods. What worked yesterday may not work today and will likely not work tomorrow.

According to research conducted by the Pew Research Center (2018b), 89% of all U.S. adults used the Internet in 2018. There are also differences by age, race, gender, education and income that might impact the decisions you make related to connecting with customers. You might be surprised (or not) to learn that 66% of individuals 65 and older (perhaps, your grandparents) are online compared to 98% of 18- to 29- year-olds (we suspect that statistic does not surprise you). Therefore, it's incumbent upon the individuals responsible for the growth of a business, organization, or product line to learn the various experiments necessary to identify the best methods for reaching their customers. Only by learning these frameworks about customer discovery can one have a chance of being successful in the long term.

How do entrepreneurial best practices apply to customer discovery? Some business owners believe that the hardest part of business growth is product or service design and once they have the product created, then they simply need to figure out which channels to use to get it in customers' hands, and they're all set. But business growth and marketing are much more complex than that, as you may have experienced or are beginning to realize. Ideas iterate as new knowledge is accumulated about the market, customers, competitors, and your internal skills and capabilities. As these new ideas—sometimes challenges and other times opportunities—become apparent, entrepreneurs need to understand how to change and pivot from their original thinking and embrace this circular, entrepreneurial process as a given, not the exception to the rule. Business growth and design are never linear, and the most successful business owners and entrepreneurs learn how to evolve their ideas, thinking, products, and business model around the new information. Therefore, it's important to have a structure in place that allows you to secure this new information and be able to respond and react in a positive manner to impact change and growth.

Your framework must support the evolution of your product or business idea with a focus on having a strong value proposition that revolves around the customer and his or her changing needs. One model that works very effectively for this is the Business Model Canvas. The canvas, explained here based on the book *Business Model Generation: A Handbook for Visionaries, Game Changers, and Challengers*, by Osterwalder and Pigneur (2010), provides an excellent framework for entrepreneurs to begin to think about their business as it relates to the value they create and deliver to key stakeholders—ranging from customers and prospects to partners, investors, and employees. In addition, there are numerous videos that explain how the canvas works. Here are two sources that you might want to review:

1. Strategyzer resources page at https://strategyzer.com/canvas
2. *The Business Model Canvas—9 Steps to Creating a Successful Business Model: Startup Tips* at https://www.youtube.com/watch?v=IP0cUBWTgpY

Below are a series of questions that you can apply to your idea that will help you address the many parts of the model as it relates to your marketing plan initiative. This will allow you to better understand and access your customers. In this chapter, we outline the questions you will need to answer to help you address customer value propositions and to support your ability to think and act like an entrepreneur. We will occasionally revisit these throughout the book to help you use entrepreneurial thinking to solve sticky problems and address how you can seize opportunities you see in the marketplace. Keep in mind the fact that *entrepreneurial thinking* is about taking a creative and nimble approach to opportunities and problems that you see in the market and then experimenting with a variety of approaches to seize the opportunity or solve the problem. This is an iterative approach that requires that you continuously learn from the experiments that you perform such as interviewing customers or prototyping a product. Then you take this learning and apply it to your evolving business.

As you begin to think like an entrepreneur and recognize that a linear way of thinking about business growth is not a realistic way to organize a business, you will be one step closer to creating a business that focuses around your customers and their current and evolving needs.

NEW TOOLS—SAME OLD RULES

As you are beginning to understand, marketing revolves around the customer and not the product or solution that you want to bring to market. Therefore, we must apply customer discovery tactics to the practice of marketing, focusing first on defining the

Table 1.1 Questions to Address Based on the Business Model Canvas Framework

1. **Customer Segments**
   - For whom are you creating value?
   - Who makes up the potential and target audience that you are addressing?
     - What are their key defining characteristics, that is, demographics, behaviors?
     - What is their compelling problem or need or pain?
     - Which segment(s) are most attractive? Why?
     - Do your target customers care about how you create or offer social value?
   - How large is this market?
     - How many people and/or companies and organizations?
     - What evidence do you have to support this estimate?
     - What assumptions did you make? How might you confirm them?
     - How easy is it to target the market?

2. **Value Proposition**
   - What is the problem you are trying to solve or the opportunity you are attempting to seize?
   - What value do you deliver to the customer?
   - How are you creating social value?
   - Which customer needs are you satisfying?
   - What bundle(s) of products and services are you offering to each segment?
   - Are you providing social value to the communities you serve?
   - What are you specifically offering?
     - What are the most important benefits to your target audience?
     - Is value sufficient to adopt your product or service?

3. **Channels**
   - How is your target audience currently addressing the problem or need?
     - What alternatives (substitute solutions) do they have? Who's your competition?
   - Through which channels do your customer segments want to be reached?
   - How will you reach them?
   - Are your channels integrated?
     - Do some work better than others?
   - Which channels are most cost-efficient?
   - Will you integrate your channels with customer routines and behaviors?

4. **Customer Relationships**
   - What type of relationship does each customer segment expect you to establish and maintain?
   - How expensive is ethically acquiring, maintaining, and retaining this relationship?
     - What is your customer lifetime value?
   - How is this relationship integrated with the rest of your business model?

(Continued)

Table 1.1 (Continued)

5. **Revenue Streams**
   - What are your customers willing to pay?
   - What do they currently pay?
   - How are they currently paying?
   - How would they prefer to pay?
   - How much does each revenue stream contribute to overall company revenue?
   - How will you charge for your product or service?

6. **Key Resources**
   - What key resources does your value proposition require?
   - What are your needs in terms of physical, intellectual, and financial resources?
   - What needs do you have to ensure you can ethically distribute through identified channels?
   - What resources do you need to acquire and maintain customer relationships?
   - What resources will you need to launch and how do you plan on accessing them?
     - What resources are required by any business operating in this space?
     - What resources are unique to your solution or competitive position?
     - What do you still need to research?
   - What are the most critical skills and people resources needed to successfully launch the business?
     - What are the values that you and your team expect to exemplify and communicate in this venture? What kind of culture do you want to create?

7. **Key Activities**
   - What activities are required to deliver your value proposition?
   - How do these activities support the social value you will create or build into your business model?
   - How do these activities impact the following areas: production, problem solving, network, distribution channel, customer relationships, and revenue stream?

8. **Key Partnerships**
   - Who are your key partners?
   - Who are your key suppliers?
   - Which key resources or expertise or experience do you need from partners—optimization, economy of scale, reduction of risk, access to customers, and/or markets?

9. **Cost Structure**
   - What are your key costs? Are they primarily fixed or variable?
   - Which key resources are most expensive?
   - Which key activities are most expensive?
   - Are you focused on minimizing your cost or maximizing your value?

10. **Is the Venture Feasible?**
    Based on your answers to the questions here about your business model:
    - Does your proposed business model and strategy work?
    - Are you able to support a model that creates and/or supports social value?
    - Do you need to explore changes to any element of your business model to increase your chances of success?
      - What additional research do you need to conduct?

needs and interests of consumers and then determining how to align your solution with those needs. Sometimes this requires that your solution change or evolve to avoid obsolescence and business failure. This clearly reinforces the importance of taking an entrepreneurial approach to creatively reviewing customer needs on an ongoing basis and applying new learning to sustain a product through multiple business cycles.

Marketing programs that can be sustained through the constantly evolving ways in which businesses engage with customers always begin with a clear understanding of potential and current customer needs. Then, the business uses this data to determine how to approach its target market with a continuous cycle of improving your message, channel selection, and ultimately your product or service solution to ensure you align your product with customer needs. With the target market in focus as the primary driver of your business, this reinforces the importance of developing synergistic business strategies that align with the needs of the consumer.

Hopefully, we haven't terrified you about the seemingly complex set of steps required to design a marketing plan with actions that will get you to market and engaging with customers. The goal of seeing your customer as an entrepreneur does require a change of focus, leading to a change in your marketing efforts.

> Instead of designing a product or solution in search of a customer, you must flip your business model and first identify the needs of your target markets and then design the products, services and business model to address and deliver your unique solution.

Throughout this book, we provide you with a variety of tools that are required to flip your model and way of thinking about your product or service. The frameworks are designed to be used in start-ups, growing organizations, and even large, well-established firms. Once again, we would like to reinforce the fact that you do not need to own the company to apply these frameworks, nor do you need to be the person responsible for marketing. However, without the perspective of "customer first" followed by product design and delivery, the organization will likely find itself in a precarious position where sustaining brand loyalty and market share will be very difficult. The larger a company gets, sometimes the further away it gets from understanding its customers' and prospects' needs. That's why the entrepreneurial mindset is so important. It requires numerous iterations that are constantly evolving to ensure organizations view their products and solutions through the eyes of their target customer.

We live in a time when entrepreneurs and small businesses with limited budgets have access to a myriad of marketing channels to reach customers around the globe. It appears that the playing field has been leveled and small businesses can now compete with behemoth companies. However, many businesses continue to struggle and find it hard to compete because while they now can access channels that were previously outside of their reach, they still face limitations related to money, people, and time. The constraints include the amount of money they can spend on customer outreach campaigns, a lack of people (human resources) such as a dedicated team of marketers who can focus on deploying and tracking marketing campaigns, and the time required to launch a targeted campaign before their funds dry up. They have to come out of the "proverbial gate" with a campaign that is focused squarely on their customers' identified needs since they might not get a second opportunity to target their customers. The pre-work required before launching a campaign is more critical for these business owners because their larger competitors typically have more manpower and money to use for campaigns. Therefore, if their first marketing attempt doesn't work in their favor, it won't be the end for them. Having an entrepreneurial mindset to ensure you do the work right (measure twice, cut once) before you determine your marketing channels is essential for increasing your odds of success.

Therefore, the approach that is required to successfully target customers when time, money, and human capital are scarce must be entrepreneurial in nature. Now that we've defined what this mean, let's talk about how to apply it to a business to create value for the company and consumer.

DESIGNING A BUSINESS MODEL THAT CREATES VALUE

While the focus of this book is to show how to apply entrepreneurial marketing principles to solve a consumer-centric problem or seize an opportunity, we need to focus on how to design a business model that creates value before we get into the detail of how to design your marketing approach.

To secure sustainable business growth throughout multiple business cycles, it's important to design a business model that supports the continuous changes that occur over time, with a focus on the customer and not the product. While many of the methods and channels we use have evolved (such as social media and virtual customer acquisition), the principle of making business decisions related to customer needs remains constant.

Therefore, while you may think of marketing as advertisements you see in your community or online messages you receive in your Facebook feed, the heart of marketing remains focused on understanding and satisfying the needs of your customers. You currently experience marketing as a consumer, but as this book progresses, you will understand the importance of putting on your "proverbial" business owner or product manager hat and seeing and experiencing products and services through the eyes of consumers. In this light, marketing focuses first on identifying customer needs and then determining which marketing tools to deploy to grow a business.

The stronger your skills become at differentiating and selecting among the myriad of marketing options available to you, the better you will be at creating customer interest in the solution you provide. Let's illustrate this with an example of a young entrepreneur named Joanna Alberti.

VIEW FROM THE TRENCHES

PhiloSophie's®: From Mass Market to Tying the Knot

PhiloSophie's® (www.celebratewithsophies.com) was launched in 2005 by Joanna Alberti, a few years after getting her undergraduate degree from The Boston University Questrom School of Business. Joanna created a line of greeting cards and stationery based on the stylish and witty illustrated character, Sophie. With wide-ranging appeal, Joanna's trendy designs and motivational messages on topics such as work challenges, friendship, and special occasions have attracted a fan following as well as licensing deals. Joanna even landed a major distribution agreement that featured her greeting cards in Target stores.

Like many entrepreneurs, Joanna began philoSophie's® out of her Boston, Massachusetts, apartment, single-handedly illustrating and managing the printing and negotiations involved in building the business. In 2005, Joanna was featured on the CNN segment "Young People Who Rock" and was later rated by *Business Week* as one of the top five entrepreneurs under the age of 25. In 2007, she decided to move her company from Boston to her hometown of Rochester, New York, taking the business from her apartment to a dedicated studio workspace. Two years later, Joanna opened a storefront and hired two freelance graphic designers. This allowed her to focus on what she enjoys most—the creation and marketing of her products.

However, these achievements were not without challenges. As a relative unknown in the industry, Joanna had a hard time persuading manufacturers to sign on to the Sophie character. Rather than work with a newcomer, manufacturers preferred dealing with a more established brand that they believed would be more likely to move products quickly off the shelves. In addition to this challenge, Joanna's lack of business experience was problematic. There was nothing the young entrepreneur believed she could not do. That resulted in her trying to manage all aspects of her growing business without seeking proper support. Joanna comments: *I think when I first started I probably was just so eager that I just asked a lot of questions and I never really felt like I couldn't do anything. And when you keep going and hit a lot of snags in the road or "no's" and things like that, you get a little discouraged.*

Despite the company and the owner's youth, philoSophie's® was able to overcome the obstacles it faced to grow into an established player in the greeting card market. A friend who studied at BU with Joanna saw the illustrations that she had created and nominated her to be featured in *Business Week*. It also turned out that one of the customers from her Rochester store was a representative for the Recycled Paper Greetings line of cards owned by American Greetings. It's through this meeting that philoSophie's® was able to get a small line of greeting cards into Target.

(Continued)

(Continued)

Even with a growing presence in the market, Joanna, like all entrepreneurs, struggled at times to define the right strategy for her business to ensure its sustainability. She was continuously developing new concepts and products and evolving her artwork. While she made early business decisions "from the heart," she quickly realized the value of more strategically approaching the growth of her business to identify which products would not only attract the most customers but also create positive profit centers for her company.

Joanna talks about what goes into making philoSophie's® successful: *It's learning to grow with consumers—so I try to take advantage of Facebook, Instagram, and other social media tools and keep up to date with blogs. The public relationship side of the business is a big part of growing the brand because then people create a personal attachment with you and they see that there's a person behind the brand and it not just a big corporation that created this. I have always taken a more grassroots approach. I don't really spend any money on advertising. I think it's so important to send a handwritten note and do those small things that will lead to bigger opportunities. It didn't just happen. At a certain point in time, either certain things stick or they don't. And when they don't and you feel like they're not really moving where you want to be, you try a different approach.*

As a one-woman operation, Joanna realized the critical importance of pursuing the product lines that would make the most efficient and effective use of her limited resources (her time and money) while ensuring that her focus always remained squarely set on her customer. In other words, the company needed to do things in a much smarter and more strategic manner. In order to figure out which solutions to offer, she did a complete financial analysis of her products, channels of distribution (online versus offline), and profit margins per product. Using this data, she had an eye-opening experience because she began to acknowledge that

Please join us for a Celebration of
Love, Laughter, Friendship, and Family as

Jacqueline Amanda Weiner

and

Gregory Kinsella Hartwich

Join Hands In Marriage
Saturday, the Twenty Eighth of October
Two Thousand Seventeen
At Six O'Clock in the Evening
Temple Concord of Syracuse
10 Madison Street
Syracuse, New York 13210

Join Us For

Cocktails, Dinner & Dancing!

7 O'Clock in the Evening

The Sherwood Inn
26 W Genesee Street, Skaneateles New York
Visit our wedding website for more details:
WWW.HAPPILYEVERHARTWICH.COM

Let Us Know…

Kindly Reply By

September 28, 2017

M_____

_____ Wouldn't Miss It For the World

We promise to dance if you play this song:
_____ By: _____

_____ Regretfully Decline

_____ Number of Guests Attending

philoSophie's®

the cards she sold in stores and online were not actually creating the most profit for her company. The most profitable product line was her bridal products. In addition, this is where the demand for additional products was originating.

Brides buy with passion and were more willing to spend money on the special day than her average holiday or special event card customer. They also tell their friends, creating a word-of-mouth marketing effort that had become a very powerful source of business for Joanna. Armed with this newly recognized information, Joanna turned her focus to creating bundled packages for brides. She also created a strong alliance with "The Knot," a popular online site that is a virtual, one-stop shop for everything related to wedding planning.

With a new strategic approach, Joanna created a "Wedding Shop" tab at the top of her website and launched product lines ranging from bridal shower and wedding invitations to gifts and everything paper related a bride could need for her wedding. She contemplated creating a stand-alone website but explained, *"Once my brides start having babies it's more convenient for them to have one website to remember and visit for baby announcements, holiday cards, and other gifts."* Plus, managing two sites simply didn't make sense in terms of Joanna's limited time and focus. Joanna refocused her business model by focusing on her customers and not the products she produced. This allowed her to create a more sustainable business model because her passion for designing cards needed to evolve into a more specific market niche—brides who are passionate and interested in buying her brand.

We know from the case that Joanna was quite adept at recognizing customer needs. Her products and the complementary services she created evolved based on what she heard and verified that her customers needed. She understood that THEY defined her business value more than she did, and by allowing them her

key customers this level of "decision making" in the product lines she offered, she was able to position herself to be more profitable.

This might seem obvious to somebody reading the case, but giving control of the products and solutions you offer to your customers is really hard to do. Joanna struggled for many years to achieve a level of growth and profitability that aligned with her goals. She originally viewed her value proposition as the cards and messages that her character Sophie espoused. However, this was not what her customers valued the most, and she recognized this only by allowing herself to see her business through a different lens, that of her customer. At the same time, she had to acknowledge that not all of her customers had the same value to her. Her target market was the higher, more luxury-focused end of the bridal market spectrum where value was measured by providing brides with one-of-a-kind, custom-designed bridal invitations. Price was not a major obstacle, and focusing on this end of the market allowed her to offer a solution at a higher price point and margin than her other cards and products. This

(Continued)

(Continued)

gave her the ability to grow her business and continue to offer all levels of products but primarily focus on growing the luxury sector of the market.

In Their Shoes

Let's explore what you have learned from philo-Sophie's® evolving path to success.

1. How might you have approached the original design of this business as a young entrepreneur who recently graduated from college?
2. What types of customer discovery activities should Joanna complete on an ongoing basis to ensure she continues to create solutions that customers want?
3. What would you recommend to Joanna in terms of next steps for growth?

REALITY CHECK—THE TRUTH ABOUT BUSINESS SUCCESS AND FAILURE

Following on Joanna's story, it's important to understand the truth about business success and failure rates in the United States. According to the U.S. Small Business Association: Small Business Facts Reports (2012), "About two-thirds of businesses with employees survive at least 2 years and about half survive at least 5 years. As one would expect, after the first few relatively volatile years, survival rates flatten out."

What does this data tell us about business? Should we not even bother trying since our chances of success are 50:50? Definitely not! But with only half of businesses still operating after 5 years, it might make you ask, "What did the survivors know that helped them succeed?" It's a fair question that doesn't have a simple answer. If there was an easy way to ensure business success, then clearly more people would jump in, knowing what the predictable outcome would be. While success hinges on many different factors, you can improve your chances of developing a sustainable company by first recognizing the importance of evolving your business model around the needs of the customer and the marketplace.

According to the 2018 Global Entrepreneurship Monitor (GEM) Report, the world's foremost study of entrepreneurship, co-founded by Babson College and London Business School and representing a consortium of academic institutions worldwide, there are a multitude of reasons that businesses fail or discontinue.

> Some reasons could be seen as positive, such as the opportunity to sell, pursuing another opportunity or planned retirement. On the other hand, discontinuation may be due to lack of business profitability, problems with accessing finance and running out of working capital. Figure 1.1 shows

some of the identified reasons why businesses discontinue. Clearly, a lack of business profitability is consistently cited as the major reason for business discontinuance, with a third of business exits due to this reason, on average, across all three development phases. (Singer, Herrington, & Menipaz, 2018)

However, selling retiring, exiting and pursuing another opportunity accounts for a significantly important factor in the discontinuation of a business. Therefore, not being in existence is not necessarily representative of a failure.

What does this data mean for the individual interested in pursuing a business opportunity? It shows that being a business owner is not an easy role to assume. There are many risks that need to be assumed, and being prepared to pivot and continuously evolve with your customer base is paramount. Nonetheless, there can be a very positive

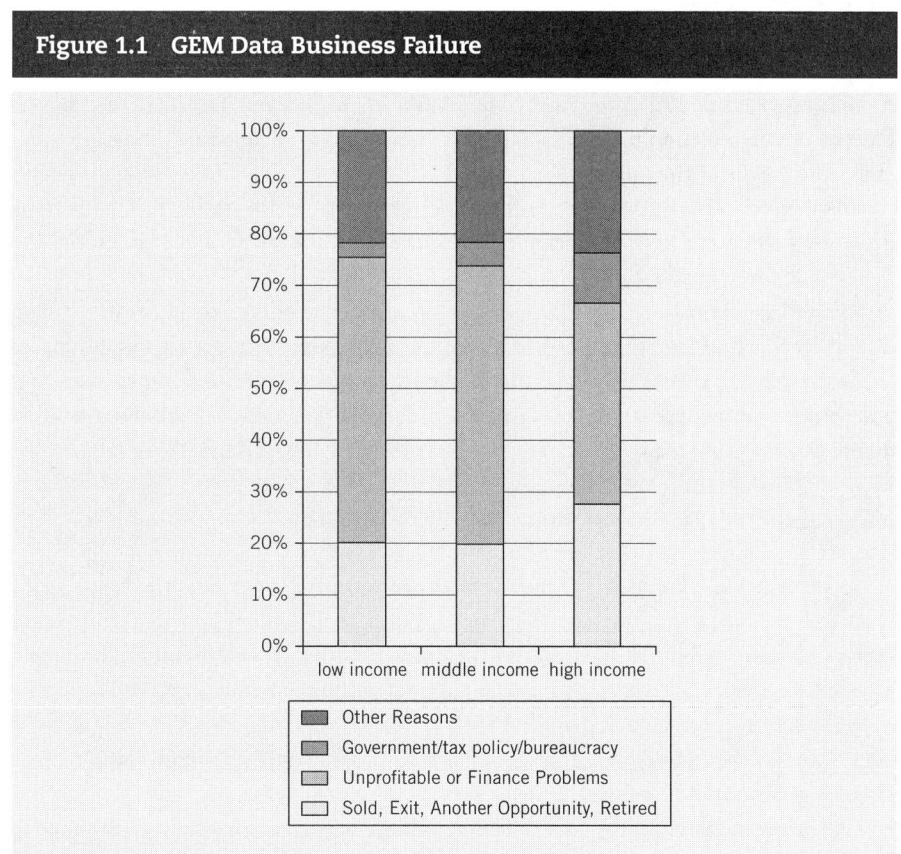

Figure 1.1 GEM Data Business Failure

Permission to use data from GEM 2018, which appears here, has been granted by the copyright holders. The GEM is an international consortium and data was collected in 49 economies in 2018. Our thanks go to the authors, national teams, researchers, funding bodies and other contributors who have made this possible.

return on your time, money and resources if you accept the risks and succeed. However, if you decide to discontinue your business you can take those lessons learned with you and apply them to your next business opportunity.

Owning a business does not make you an entrepreneur and is definitely not the only way to act and think like one. This is a misnomer that we have tried to dispel. Many individuals are entrepreneurial in their approach to problem solving and don't own their own company. Likewise, many people who have responsibility for growing a company may not be the owner or even a part of the senior management team. Nonetheless, the way they view problems and approach situations in a nonlinear way with a focus on their customers' needs, as opposed to just their products, makes them entrepreneurial thinkers.

THE IMPORTANCE OF SETTING S.M.A.R.T. GOALS

You may be wondering what the first steps are in terms of creating a successful entrepreneurial marketing plan for your business. We must begin by clearly defining your business goals, which in turn will support your ability to create a marketing plan that aligns these goals with your customers' needs.

As mentioned in the preface, there are a variety of tools and worksheets in the book designed to help you design your marketing plan. Our first worksheet is an exercise to help you learn or improve your S.M.A.R.T. goal setting skills.

What's a S.M.A.R.T. goal? If you're not familiar with this concept, let me explain how it works. Each letter represents an important aspect of the goal. The examples below are related to business goals. You might not be ready to do this for a business, but you will first get an opportunity to set a personal goal so you can understand the process. Then, when you are ready, you can focus on creating S.M.A.R.T. business goals.

S: Specific: This may seem obvious, but you'd be surprised how often goals are set that are so wishy-washy that the entrepreneur who set it won't know if the goal was achieved or if it had an impact on the business. A nonspecific goal is something like, "I want to increase sales in the next year." or "I want my customers to be happy with my service." These are both common responses, and typically my question to the business owner is this: So, you're saying you'll be happy if you increase sales by just one dollar even if your costs increase by two dollars?

Naturally they think that's absurd but that's the goal they set because they weren't specific about the terms. Here's an improved goal: "I want to increase my profit (not sales) by $50,000 in the next six months." That's better, right? The customer satisfaction (happiness) question is a little more complicated because you have to measure customer satisfaction (or happiness) in order to know if you're achieving it. A goal might be to launch a survey to measure specific customer satisfaction levels with various areas of your business and set target figures (i.e., all factors must achieve at least a 4.3 out of a 5.0 score).

M: Measurable: Measuring goals is a fundamental part of being specific. If you can't or don't measure a goal, you can't manage toward it and are that much less likely to achieve that goal. Again, setting a benchmark that you hope to achieve is important. Let's look at a goal that might appear to be easy to measure on the surface but, in fact, is difficult. "I want to increase my profit margin on all of my products by 3%." Here's the catch—Do you know what your current profit margins are? Some of you may say, "of course I do" and good for you. However, I've worked with many business owners over the years who have a general sense of their profit margins but don't REALLY know the margins since they have been estimating costs and applying them across all products.

The positive aspect of setting a margin-driven goal, like profit margin, is that it will very likely shed light on what data you know and what you thought you knew but in reality don't have a handle on. This plays into the *A* of the S.M.A.R.T. goals: who will be assigned to ensure it is completed?

A: Assignable: Now is the time to figure out who will be responsible for achieving the goal you set. Let's say you're running a bakery and your goal is to "Increase production of biscotti, the most popular item you sell, by 30% in the next 60 days." Can you actually achieve this given the team you have onboard? How will you do it, and, most important, who will be responsible? In addition, it's important how this activity will impact the rest of your operation if you assign one or more people to also complete these tasks.

One of the key elements of having an achievable goal is ensuring that you truly have the people onboard who have not only the expertise required but the time to commit to the initiative as well. This tends to be where great ideas end up in the trash—it works on paper but if there isn't a dedicated individual or individuals responsible for making it happen (and this doesn't have to be the business owner), then it usually won't get very far off the ground.

R: Realistic: Realistic refers to the fact that while you might be able to achieve this goal given all the resources needed, it may be totally unrealistic in terms of your overall business focus, manpower, or priorities. For example, let's say your big picture goal is to "Increase sales by 20% each year." Does this align with how your company operates or how you're structured? Will achieving this cause internal problems that conflict with the goal because in order to increase sales you have to double your team? You might be able to achieve this goal, but the reality of its impact on other actions and strategies might cause major conflicts with your top and/or bottom line.

On the other hand, articulating this goal will give you the opportunity to look at your business and the industry you operate within and determine what changes need to be made to achieve this. Do you need to target new markets? Do you need to develop products for the same customers but with higher profit margins? By taking the time to think about the implications of the goal, you will be working ON your business and not simply doing the daily grind while ignoring the big picture (working IN the business).

T: Time-related: Time-related always seems to be the simplest aspect of goal-setting, yet one that people simply forget about. "Increasing sales by 30% in the next year" needs some more dates around it. Are you increasing sales for specific products by specific periods in time throughout the year or simply by the end of your fiscal year? Do you have a variety of dates to benchmark results against, or is "whenever" good enough for you? (We certainly hope not!)

Are you ready to try this? Go to Worksheet 1.1: Setting S.M.A.R.T Goals and write down your #1 most important personal goal for the next 6 months (or business goal if you are ready). By focusing first on using the S.M.A.R.T technique with a personal goal, it will be easier to do this when you begin to focus on your company's goal.

ACTION CREATES TRIUMPHS (ACT)
Interview an Entrepreneur

How do you embrace what it means to have an entrepreneurial mindset? We are providing you with two activities that you can engage in that will help you understand how entrepreneurs think and evaluate your perspective on problem solving as compared to theirs.

Entrepreneur Interview

This exercise allows you to explore the challenges and opportunities faced by individuals who are responsible for business growth for their own business or for another company or organization. This can be a for-profit or non-profit organization. You should identify an entrepreneur with a minimum of 10 years of business experience for your interview and carefully analyze your findings. We suggest you identify an entrepreneur who is working in a field or industry that interests you. For example, if you care about the environment, try to identify somebody who is working in the cleantech field or perhaps working for a clean energy organization. Likewise, you might have an interest in finance or sales as a career goal. Try to identify an entrepreneur whose role in an organization focuses on financial analysis or managing a sales team. Remember that entrepreneurs and those who possess entrepreneurial thinking skills should not be identified simply by their job, role, or title. Entrepreneurial thinking crosses many boundaries because it's a way of approaching problems that makes it entrepreneurial in nature, not the problem or job itself. Therefore, the person you interview might be responsible for customer service for the company. This might not seem "entrepreneur" based on his job title, but perhaps he thinks like an entrepreneur (is creative and nimble and experiments with a variety of approaches to solving problems) and has implemented some new policies to better serve the needs of the customers his company serves. He might be a great person to interview.

Next is a list of questions (along with an introduction) that you **could** use to learn more about the interviewee. However, you are free to ask any questions that you like. The key criterion is that you want to identify an individual who deploys hands-on, entrepreneurial practices, like those that we have discussed in this chapter.

The goal of this assignment is to have you analyze and explain what you have learned about being an entrepreneur, what you want to understand more about, and how being an entrepreneur will impact your future career decisions. Therefore, when you pose questions, always ask if the person can share a specific story that further explains her response. For example, if she tells you that she has many ideas that failed before starting her current business, probe further into this and ask her to specifically tell you at least one story about one of the business ideas and why it didn't work. Plus, ask her if they can share what she learned. The more stories you hear firsthand from individuals who have tried and failed, the more comfortable you will be embracing the notion that failure isn't an end; it's simply a process that leads to the "next" outcome.

When completing the assignment, do not create a transcript that is a simple write-up of the interview or provide only details about what the entrepreneur's responsibilities are. **This assignment must reflect insight and analysis about the interview.** This should include a reflection of what you have learned through lectures, readings, and any work experience that you have.

Sample Questions and Script

Thank you for your time today. I have a series of questions that I'm going to ask you about your business/organization and your role. I appreciate your honest feedback and hope that you're comfortable sharing specific stories that describe what you've learned and experienced.

1. How and why did you choose your career?
2. How do you define entrepreneurship?
3. Do you consider yourself to be an entrepreneur? Why?
4. How is your success measured?
5. Do you have a business or growth plan in place? If not, how do you plan for the next 1 to 3 years?
6. Do you tend to rely on your gut to make growth decisions or conduct research? How has this impacted your success?
7. How do you identify new opportunities? What activities have you or your company recently implemented to seize these opportunities?
8. How do you identify changing customer (target market) needs? Do you survey or interview your customers or prospects?
9. How has business changed for your specific organization in the past 5 years? Do you see those changes as positive or negative? Why?
10. What do you think about risk as it relates to achieving goals?
11. What do you think about failure?
12. What is the greatest challenge that your company faced? How did you handle or overcome that challenge?
13. We recognize that things don't always turn out despite our best efforts. Are you willing to share a story about a challenge where the outcome was less successful or at least unexpected from what you planned?
14. Are you willing to share some of your current challenges or barriers and how you are dealing with these?
15. What is the most important lesson learned from your experience?

ACTION CREATES TRIUMPHS (ACT)
Idea Generation

One of the primary goals of this book is to show you how to take the discussions, frameworks and cases and apply them to a business concept that you are working on. In order to do this, you need to have a business idea that you can apply the learnings to throughout the book, keeping in mind that this idea will definitely change and evolve as you practice the entrepreneurial marketing lessons shared. The idea might get stronger as you better understand the market, or you may discover that, while your idea is interesting to you, there's no "ready" market or customers who are interested in the solution you offer, requiring that you change, pivot, or simply start over. Don't worry, there's nothing wrong with having to begin again. You will always own what you learned from practicing the frameworks and determining that the current iteration of your idea is a no-go solution. This will prepare you for the next version of idea generation that you conduct and get you closer to learning how to address customer needs in an entrepreneurial manner.

There are many ways you can approach idea generation. For this exercise, based on an exercise created by Dr. Caroline Daniels at Babson College, we are going to use the practice of ethnography to help you generate business ideas. *Ethnography*, according to Merriam-Webster, is "the study and systematic recording of human cultures." Basically, it's observing and recording what we see about various groups. As used in this book, you will take your observations and your unbiased recording and begin to create ideas around it that can be the basis of a new business concept.

You can do your own ethnographic study by observing people in a location or "space" such as a shopping mall, campus bookstore, main street, waterfront area, or basically any place that interests you. Alternatively, you can list a number of problems or opportunities that intrigue you and then purposefully go out and observe situations where the problem or opportunity can be objectively observed and recorded with the goal of better understanding how it occurs. You will complete an ethnography study multiple times throughout the course of developing your business concept. We introduce it in this first chapter, but we will also provide you with an opportunity in Chapter 3 to do a deeper dive with a focus on learning more about your potential customers with the goal of creating a Customer Profile (Chapter 4).

Ready? Let's begin this exercise. You can do this alone, but since you are likely part of a class, we suggest you create teams of six to eight people and, as a team, do the following:

1. Decide which option you will begin with:
   a. opportunity space to identify people in a specific setting that interests you, or
   b. problem or opportunity that you want to observe.
2. Once you have decided which approach is the best for your team, then select a specific location or space to complete your ethnography study. In the case of option #2, you will first need to agree on the problem or opportunity you want to observe before you identify the space.
3. Now that you have agreed on the location, divide your larger group into smaller subgroups to complete the observation.
   a. In smaller subgroups of two to three people, go to your selected space.

b. Spend at least 30 minutes recording your observations—basically facts of what you are seeing. Remember to only observe. Do not judge or formulate any conclusions yet about why these things are happening. Things to write down include the following:

   i. What are people doing?
   ii. What is their behavior?
   iii. Do they seem to have a motive or goal?

c. Take pictures (when appropriate) to present to your larger team and eventually to the class.

d. After your initial observation, return to a centrally agreed-upon location and regroup with your larger team.

e. Share observations for 30 to 40 minutes with your team.

4. Now, brainstorm insights for 30 minutes. Basically ask questions focused on the "Why" and the "What" of the observations.

   a. Why do these facts exist?
   b. What are the motives of the people you observed?
   c. What do motives tell you about needs and opportunities?

5. Develop three to five well-articulated insights about the reason that you observed what you did. For example, perhaps young people are gathering in one location because the WiFi is better or there's a store that is very popular.

6. Select the best insight for the team to work on.

7. Finally, develop a business concept around it. What business idea could you come up with that would allow you to further explore how to turn a problem or opportunity into a business?

The best way to generate ideas for a business begins with a question: "How can we . . ." For example, you might have observed that there are a lot of plastic bags floating in the marina by your house. Or, perhaps you observed that students are sitting together outside of the classroom but not talking to each other because they are all using their phones to communicate. You might start your idea generation session by asking these questions:

- ✓ How can we get rid of the excess plastic bags in the marina?
- ✓ How can we discourage people from letting plastic bags get in the water?
- ✓ How can we encourage students to talk more to each other in person versus texting or using social media?

Once you have formulated your "How can we . . ." question, you need to brainstorm solutions that could lead to the development of a business concept. IDEO (2019), a design and innovation consulting firm, suggests seven rules for teams working with observations to gain insights about designing innovative products and services for customers.

Remember that brainstorming allows everyone to have time to share their thoughts, so make sure you allow enough time to formulate lots of great business concepts.

1. Defer judgment: Don't judge the insight about others involved in an observation. There are no wrong ideas.

(Continued)

(Continued)

2. Encourage wild ideas: It's important to think creatively. You're trying to figure out how to solve problems and think beyond the world that you already know.
3. Build on the ideas and observations of others: If one person has the same idea that you do, that's fine but don't simply repeat their idea . . . take it to the next level.
4. Stay focused on the topic: Don't get distracted by three other ideas that popped into your head about another problem. Try to stay close to the original question, "How can we . . ."
5. One conversation at a time: Don't talk over each other. Remember to listen to what others are saying.
6. Be visual: Make sure you take pictures or can draw ideas that you have based on your observation. A picture might clarify your ideas or what you observed.
7. Go for quantity: The more ideas you have, the better the process. At this point, try to get as many ideas out there before you start to narrow them down.

One method for sharing observations and insights is allow each team member to suggest his top two to three ideas. You can also spend a few minutes writing your ideas on sticky notes and then posting all of them to a poster board. The goal is to accumulate as many ideas as possible that address the "How can we . . ." question.

Once all of your ideas are recorded, you can allow everybody to get three votes (you might use something like stickers to vote with) and then rate the group's favorite ideas. Once you have your top three ideas, vote on them so you can focus on one business concept to work on with the goal of determining how feasible your idea is (basically, are there customers and markets that are interested in your solution?).

FOCUS ON APPLICATION: WAKU

The Entrepreneurial Journey

Curious about how a company used this brainstorming technique and the other entrepreneurial marketing tactics that we will discuss to create their business? Throughout this book you are going to read about the creation of Waku. In 2017, two friends, Juan Giraldo, an MBA student at Babson College in Massachusetts and his friend Nicolás (Nico) Estrella went on a road trip to the southern part of Ecuador. There they met Don Miguel, an indigenous farmer who introduced them to a local herbal drink known as "el agua que cura," which means "the healing water." This is a drink infusion made up of more than 20 herbs and flowers from the Andes Mountains. Don Miguel shared his story with Juan and Nico and explained how hard it is to make a living as a producer of these medicinal herbs used for the "healing water." He and his fellow farmers struggled with low incomes because they lacked access to large markets and

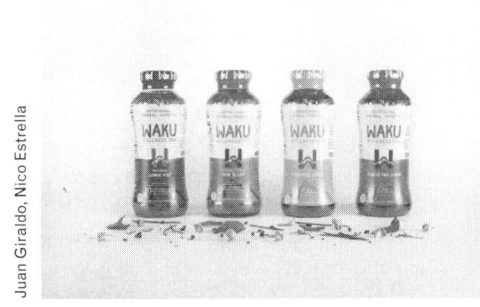

Juan Giraldo, Nico Estrella

locally could not sell their product at prices that would support a profit margin to keep them in business. Learning this inspired Juan and Nico to create a market-driven solution for this social problem. Juan explained, "We want to share this amazing drink with the world, and by doing this, we are going to be able to help Ecuadorian independent farmers improve their quality of life."

They returned from their trip inspired to achieve the following two goals: (1) help small farmers continue to produce this infusion and maintain a livelihood and (2) bring this delicious and healthy drink to the world. They brainstormed ways to address the "How can we . . ." question, and eventually the idea of Waku was born. Within a year, they had developed their first herbal tealike drink based on an ancestral recipe containing the herb and flower infusion that has been consumed for centuries in the Andes Mountains of Ecuador. It has a fruity and aromatic flavor with a hint of lemon and is sourced with purely organic ingredients directly from Ecuadorian farmers at fair trade prices, with the goal of helping them improve their quality of life. You will continue to read about their journey throughout the book.

AHAs

Lessons and Takeaways

Let's recap highlights of this first chapter.

1. Entrepreneurship is not about owning a business but an approach to solving problems and seizing opportunities. When deploying an entrepreneurial mindset, one needs to be creative and nimble and apply what one learns from the market to achieve successes

2. Entrepreneurial thinking applied to marketing requires that you learn what your customers need and want on a continuous and ongoing basis to ensure you solve their evolving needs. Marketing is not a static activity because it requires constant awareness of changes in the marketplace. As new ideas—sometimes challenges and other times opportunities—become apparent, entrepreneurs need to understand how to change and pivot from their original thinking and embrace this circular, entrepreneurial process as a given part of business.

3. The Business Model Canvas provides a solid framework that supports the evolution of your product or business idea. With its emphasis on having a

(Continued)

(Continued)

value proposition that revolves around the customer and his or her changing needs, it provides a perfect backdrop to design a business and marketing initiative to seize customers.

4. Instead of designing a product or solution in search of a customer, you must flip your business model and first identify the needs of your target markets and then design the products, services, and business model to address and deliver your unique solution. This will provide you with a unique opportunity to achieve sustainable success.

5. To secure sustainable business growth throughout multiple business cycles, it's important to design a business model that supports the continuous changes that occur over time, with a focus on the customer and not the product. While many of the methods and channels we use have evolved (such as social media and virtual customer acquisition), the principle of making business decisions related to customer needs remains constant.

6. Being a business owner is not an easy role. There are many risks that need to be assumed, and being prepared to pivot and continuously evolve with your customer base is paramount. Nonetheless, there can be a very positive return on your time, money, and resources if you accept the risks and succeed. However, if you decide to discontinue your business, you can take those lessons learned with you and apply them to your next business opportunity.

7. Setting S.M.A.R.T. (Specific, Measurable, Assignable, Realistic, Time-Related) goals will allow you to align your marketing plan with your strategic business objectives. Once you have defined your S.M.A.R.T. goals, then you can begin to design your marketing plan to ensure it meets customer goals, now and for the future.

TOOLKIT

Worksheet 1.1: Setting S.M.A.R.T. Goals

Please describe your single most important business goal to achieve in the next 6 months (Make sure this is **S.M.A.R.T.**: *Specific, Measurable, Assignable, Realistic,* and *Time-Related*)

What makes it . . .

Specific?

Measurable?

Assignable?

Realistic?

Time-Related?

Worksheet 1.2: Sample S.M.A.R.T. Goal

SAMPLE: Goal #1—Increase number of sales leads to 90 per month by May of 20xx. We need to average at least a 45% closing ratio and an $850 average sale amount.

<u>Action #1:</u> Design a marketing plan that targets our customers demographically and geographically and creates sales leads that generate required closing ratio.

- Deadline
  - Dec. 20xx
- Impact on resources
  - Time to create plan and do research required
  - Cost to narrow focus of whom to target
  - Cost of actual advertising and other outreach methods
  - Time and cost to track effectiveness on a weekly and monthly basis
- Responsible: Olivia

Action #2: Create a Facebook and YouTube channel that is updated and managed weekly.

- Deadline
  - Aug 20xx
- Impact on resources
  - Time and cost to design
  - Time and cost to manage and measure impact
  - Time and cost of social media optimization
- Responsible: Abdul

Action #3: Implement and measure the RESULTS of a training program that supports a lead-generating environment. This includes office staff to field workers and is for existing employees and new hires.

- Deadline
  - March 20xx
- Impact on resources
  - Cost and time to design, implement, and measure
  - Cost and time to shadow other successful businesses of similar size regarding what we are wanting to achieve (other geographical areas)
  - Cost and time to continuously train and monitor
- Responsible: Jonathan and Olivia

Action #4: Create a process and procedure that creates a "WOW" buying experience whose impact is measured in sales results.

- Deadline
  - Jan. 20xx
- Impact on resources
  - Time and cost to design, implement, monitor, measure, and train
  - Time to understand competitors' "WOW's"
  - Cost and time to shadow other successful businesses of similar size and understand what they are doing to achieve their goals (outside our geographic areas)
- Responsible: Omar

Worksheet 1.3: Business Launch Plan/Road Map

Please describe your three most important business goals for the next 12 months (Make sure these are **S.M.A.R.T.**: *Specific, Measurable, Assignable, Realistic* and *Time-Related*). Use a separate page for each goal.

Business Goal #1

Now, list critical actions required to achieve the goal above including the deadline, the person responsible, and the Impact on Resources (i.e., people, time, money).

Actions to Achieve Goal	Deadline	Person(s) Responsible	Impact on Resources
1.			
2.			
3.			
4.			
5.			

Worksheet 1.3: Business Launch Plan/ Road Map

Business Goal #2:

Now, list critical actions required to achieve the goal above including the deadline, the person responsible, and the Impact on Resources (i.e., people, time, money).

Actions to Achieve Goal	Deadline	Person(s) Responsible	Impact on Resources
1.			
2.			
3.			
4.			
5.			

Worksheet 1.3: Business Launch Plan/Road Map *continued*

Business Goal #3:

Now, list critical actions required to achieve the goal above including the deadline, the person responsible, and the Impact on Resources (i.e., people, time, money).

Actions to Achieve Goal	Deadline	Person(s) Responsible	Impact on Resources
1.			
2.			
3.			
4.			
5.			

Worksheet 1.4: Completing an Ethnography Study

Create teams of six to eight people to complete your ethnography study.

1. Decide which option you will begin with:
   a. opportunity space to identify people in a specific setting that interests you, or
   b. problem or opportunity that you want to observe.
2. Once you have decided which approach is the best for your team, then select a specific location or space to complete your ethnography study. In the case of option #2, you will first need to agree on the problem or opportunity you want to observe before you identify the space.
3. Now that you have agreed on the location, divide your larger group into smaller subgroups to complete the observation.
   a. In smaller subgroups of two to three people, go to your selected space.
   b. Spend at least 30 minutes recording your observations—basically facts of what you are seeing. Remember to only observe. Do not judge or formulate any conclusions yet about why these things are happening. Things to write down include the following:

          i. What are people doing?
          ii. What is their behavior?
          iii. Do they seem to have a motive or goal?
       c. Take pictures (when appropriate) to present to your larger team and eventually to the class.
       d. After your initial observation—return to a centrally agreed-upon location and regroup with your larger team.
       e. Share observations for 30 to 40 minutes with your team.
4. Now, brainstorm insights for 30 minutes. Basically, ask questions focused on the "Why" and the "What" of the observations.
    a. Why do these facts exist?
    b. What are the motives of the people you observed?
    c. What do motives tell you about needs and opportunities?
5. Develop three to five well-articulated insights about the reason that you observed what you did. For example, perhaps young people are gathering in one location because the Wi-Fi is better or there's a store that is very popular.
6. Select the best insight for the team to work on.
7. Finally, develop a business concept around your insight: What business idea could you come up with that would allow you to further explore how to turn a problem or opportunity into a business?

Developed by Dr. Caroline Daniels

CHAPTER TWO

UNDERSTANDING YOUR ECOSYSTEM

Learning Objectives

In this chapter, you will learn to

- assess the ecosystem that your business operates in.
- evaluate market trends as they relate to your business concept.
- analyze the various sources of data to determine which will provide you with the greatest insight about your industry.
- understand how entrepreneurs use secondary research to evaluate their business concepts.

INTRODUCTION TO MARKET RESEARCH

No company operates successfully without understanding the business ecosystem that its organization operates within. This chapter focuses on helping you understand the importance of your ecosystem to ensure your concept has merit and is realistic given the needs in the marketplace and your ability to deliver the value customers want. We will discuss the importance of identifying target market needs, trends in the industry that impact your opportunity, and factors like environmental and government regulations plus changes in market channels or business models that influence how you can successfully test the feasibility of your concept.

DEFINING AND UNDERSTANDING THE ECOSYSTEM YOU OPERATE WITHIN

Before you dive headfirst into the proverbial deep end of the pool to launch your business, let's get a scan of the marketplace to see what is happening. You will have a much stronger understanding of the environment that you will be operating in if you begin your research by conducting what is referred to as secondary market research, basically researching data about the market that is one step removed from the firsthand research that you will conduct with potential customers and others in the market. Oftentimes, this is the more easily accessible data available and a good starting point. You will want to understand what this data tells you prior to focusing directly on target customers, which we will discuss in the next chapter.

Secondary market research involves uncovering clues about industry practices and norms and gathering data about target markets, market size, and the marketplace in general. The word *general* is the key here, since these data will most likely not be specific enough to allow you to make any critical business decisions, resulting in your need to confirm its relevance to your business through firsthand or primary research, which we will discuss in the next chapter. The sources of secondary research, in most cases, are online and offline publications, documents (government and nongovernment), newspapers, magazines, association research, journals, and articles. This type of research might include government studies, chamber of commerce statistics, surveys conducted by trade associations or industry-affiliated organizations, or research carried out by reputable organizations. Since you won't be conducting the research yourself, you want to ensure that the standards the source used to uncover data are top quality. Therefore, ensure that the source, be it a research company or perhaps an industry leader, has a solid reputation. Learn as much as you can about their research methodology and use common sense in terms of determining if this source should be trusted. Otherwise, you can easily be led down the wrong path if you rely heavily on them for early cues about the potential for your business concept since skewed or error-prone data cannot only be quite misleading but might easily take you down the wrong path entirely.

PRIMARY VERSUS SECONDARY DATA SOURCES

Perhaps you are wondering if you still need to conduct primary market research if you do a great job uncovering secondary market research data. The answer is absolutely. While secondary research is valuable, it is critical that you speak with customers and prospects directly since every business is unique. Below are the differences between primary and secondary research sources, highlighting the importance of both to understand your ability to successfully launch a business.

UNDERSTANDING EVOLVING MARKET TRENDS

It is critical that you establish a baseline of knowledge about the markets you anticipate you will operate within before you begin to develop your product or service. This knowledge includes market trends that influence and impact the success of a business. Let's explore one example. Imagine that you've been running an antiques shop in your local town for the past 20 years. Business has always been good, and you depend on a mix of local clientele and out-of-towners who travel to visit your shop. However, in the past several years, you have begun to notice that some of your regular customers are spending more time browsing and less time buying. When they do make a purchase, they're negotiating harder, cutting your profit margin dramatically. You're not sure what's causing these changes, but they are starting to have an enormous impact on your inventory level and the profit that you're generating. You know that you've got to remedy this situation

Table 2.1 Primary vs. Secondary Data Sources

	Primary	Secondary
Source of Data	Conducted by you, your team, or somebody you hired for YOUR specific needs	Conducted by a third party for general needs or the needs of another company (not yours)
Research Methods (More details in Chapter 3)	Surveys, focus groups, ethnographic studies, interviews with YOUR specific market	Can be any of these methods but not necessarily with your specific market
Type of Data Collected	Qualitative and/or Quantitative	Qualitative and/or Quantitative
Relative Cost	More expensive	Less expensive
Relative Time Required to Complete	More time required	Less time to access data
Uniqueness and Relevance	Designed around your company needs, now	Not specific and not always relevant to your company. Content might be outdated
Relevance for Start-Ups	You might have limited or no access to customers or prospects making this harder to complete (but not impossible)	Easier to access since this does not require that you have access to customers or prospects to get a highlighted view of similar needs

quickly, or you won't be in business much longer. As profits continue to plummet, you begin to feel panic set in, and you ask yourself, "What is happening, and what could I have done to prevent this situation?" Pause for a minute and consider what type of data you need to uncover to understand why these changes are occurring in your business. What type of research and what sources would you use to understand market trends that impact you?

You might have heard the phrase, Hindsight is 20/20. While it's a bit cliché, it's an important truth: You can always see the past better than you can see the future. However, if this antiques shop owner had paid more attention to the decrease in local demand and the softening of prices a few years ago, she might have realized that these changes subtly began to occur around the same time that the Internet became more easily accessible and her older clientele became more comfortable using the web to make purchases. The decrease in demand and prices is strongly related to the availability of antiques online (creating global competition at a very local level).

If you, as an antiques shop owner, had seen the trend earlier, you might have had the opportunity to react by changing your inventory levels or the products you offered (perhaps by offering heavier pieces of furniture that are expensive to ship, deterring buyers from purchasing from nonlocal sources). You could have even decided to go online to expand your customer base. Regardless of the actions you would have taken, you'll probably agree that it's always better to be prepared with information about external forces such as supply, channel access, competition, or changes in interest in certain products that can affect your business, from a positive as well as a negative perspective. This will allow you to be proactive and make more informed decisions, rather than being forced to scramble to react to market changes after they have already had a negative impact on your revenue stream.

You don't have to look too far to witness how the web and other powerful distribution channels have upended business models and put successful companies out of business while creating opportunities for new market entrants. Let's look at two companies in the video rental space: Blockbuster and Netflix, as a primary example. Blockbuster, a brick-and-mortar retailer that launched in 1985, was known for its video rental stores. At their peak in 2004, they had over 84,000 employees and operated more than 9,000 stores. By 2010, it filed for bankruptcy, and in July 2018, its last two stores (in Alaska) finally shuttered their doors to customers (Collective Campus, 2017). Blockbuster failed to seize the massive wave of changes going on in consumer demands for convenience and immediate, on-demand access to everything, ranging from shoes and clothing to pizza and ah, yes, videos. Their customers no longer wanted to go to a store, once perceived as convenient, to rent a video. However, Netflix, an up-and-coming player in the video rental space launched in 1998 by delivering DVDs by mail, later evolving to streaming videos. Netflix continued to transform its business model to meet customer demands and flourished, claiming over 137 million worldwide subscribers by the end of 2018 (Statista, 2018). Lesson learned: You must not only be aware of changes in consumer demand but you must also be able to change your business model, when necessary, to remain relevant and in business. That lesson has been learned by numerous businesses, especially brick-and-mortar stores over the years that were not able to change their business model to address changes and no longer exist. In this category are stores like Kodak, Woolworth, Borders Book, and Toys "R" Us.

DEFINING YOUR MARKET

Before we present sources of data, let's talk about the various metrics and specific type of data that you will want to secure so you can analyze market conditions to inform your decisions moving forward. These include the following:

1. Defining size of the market

2. Strength of players in the market (we will cover more about competitors in Chapter 5)

3. Trends and regulations in the industry

It's important to understand how paradigm changes or shifts in market channels or business models such as the growth in shared economy models influence how customers think about accessing products and services. These shifts can provide a variety of opportunities for a new business. Common examples of this include renting your home à la Airbnb or ride sharing models like Uber. However, these models can be seen on college campuses where students are launching businesses to share bikes, their own cars, and even sports equipment or other items lying around their dorm rooms. This is an exciting area to explore since it requires understanding needs within specific communities and figuring out how you can capture a share of the market.

BUILDING YOUR BUSINESS MODEL

Let's revisit the Business Model Canvas framework that we discussed in the first chapter and focus on the Customer Segments analysis required to understand your business model. The first questions about the "who" are important to understand and will be addressed in the next chapter as we get closer to defining your specific target customer through primary research. However, as we do a deep dive in this chapter into the overall marketplace that you will be operating within, you will want to ask certain questions:

- Who makes up the potential and target audience that you are addressing and creating value for?
    - What are their key defining characteristics—that is, demographics, behaviors?
    - What is their compelling problem, need, or pain?
    - Which segment(s) are most attractive? Why?
    - Do your target customers care about how you create or offer economic as well as social value?
- How large is this market?
    - How many people or companies or organizations are seeking the solution you offer?
    - What evidence do you have to support this estimate?
    - What assumptions did you make? How might you confirm them?
    - How easy is it to target and access the market?

Keep these questions in mind, since a primary activity for this chapter involves you using the sources of data, described next, to answer these questions.

SOURCES OF DATA AND TRENDS

Below is a list of sources of data that you should consider accessing through your school library, business library, or online. While this list is not exhaustive in any manner, it is a good starter for securing data that will help you address questions about industry dynamics. This will allow you to focus your idea as you attempt to nurture it into a feasible business based on current and evolving market conditions.

1. Key associations and publications in your industry (more on this below)
2. Websites and social media pages of companies that belong to these associations
3. Surveys or research these associations conduct
4. Value proposition/messaging from companies affiliated with the industry
5. Annual industry statistics
6. Conferences well respected by the industry
7. Hot topics and trends being discussed at conferences
8. Speaker presentations and white papers from the conference sites
9. Consulting and research firms respected in the industry
10. School library's online business and industry databases that are a great resource
11. Newspapers, reports, journals, magazines, books

In addition to the industry-specific associations, publications, newsletters, and consulting and research firms' reports, a slew of organizations (public and private) offer general business data. Below is a starter list of general business resources and publications that you might review, especially if you are trying to understand the U.S. market. If your scope is outside the United States, the data might be more challenging to secure, but with a solid effort, you can often locate what you need. When students or business people are searching for trends, oftentimes a good starting point is to look at the data for the U.S. market since it's more readily available for most industry sectors. Then extrapolate those findings and apply to your country. It's not a perfect science, but is a good starting point and is better than simply guessing.

- Annual Reports Service and OrderAnnualReports.com (www.orderannualreports.com/)
- Bureau of Labor Statistics (www.bls.gov)

- The Business Technology Network (www.brint.com)
- CEO Express (www.ceoexpress.com)
- Edgar Online (www.edgar-online.com)
- Global Entrepreneurship Monitor: GEM (www.gemconsortium.org/)
- Nationwide Public Record Search (www.searchsystems.net)
- Kauffman Center for Entrepreneurial Leadership (www.entrepreneurship.org)
- Service Corp. of Retired Executives (SCORE) (www.score.org)
- Small Business Administration (SBA) (www.sba.gov)
- Thomas Register of American Manufacturers (www.thomasnet.com)
- U.S. Census Bureau (www.census.gov)
- U.S. Dept. of Commerce Country Commercial Guides (www.export.gov)
- U.S. Dept. of State Country Reports (https://www.state.gov/misc/list/index.htm)
- U.S. Government's official web portal (firstgov.gov)
- *Wall Street Journal* small business marketing website: (www.wsj.com/news/business/small-business-marketing)
- World Economic Forum Reports (https://www.weforum.org/reports)

In addition to researching industries online, you should also try to find out which companies are actively involved with research or provide consulting or advisory services within these industries. For example, if you're in the technology field, you should definitely review what major consulting/research firms like Gartner and Forrester Research have to say about the industry and the trends that they are seeing. Keep in mind that the information gleaned by these firms might be expensive to purchase. It's important to know that many businesses like these produce press releases or reports that highlight important findings or statistics about the industry, based on surveys or research that they conducted. Since their goal is to sell their reports, they want to call attention to the firm's latest report by providing interesting "teaser" facts. These facts may be enough to help you identify key trends and information about important businesses and partnerships in the market. But depending on the price of the report, it could be a worthwhile purchase and may be considerably less expensive than hiring a market research firm or spending hundreds of hours trying to obtain the same data on your own.

TOOLS FOR UNDERSTANDING TRENDS

There are also numerous online tools that will help you identify trends in the market. Below are some that you might want to consider using or at least checking out.

1. Google Trends (https://trends.google.com/trends/): Type in a word and see what it reveals. For example, if you type in healthy drinks—you can see interest by region, related queries (i.e., energy drinks, healthy food), related topics (drink, health, Starbucks). You can even compare this to related topics like healthy food.

2. Serpstat (https://serpstat.com.): This site provides you with a plethora of information about websites that you don't manage including search volume, competition, cost per click, and so on. For example, if you type in a specific website or a topic such as dog biscuits, you would be able to see things like organic keywords, total number of possible versions of a given keyword (dog biscuit recipes, homemade dog biscuits), paid keywords (peanut butter dog biscuits, biscuits for dogs), keyword trends over time, competitors in organic search, ratio of the number of keywords to the popularity of the keyword that the top 20 search results yield. There are even examples of ads (https://www.milkbone.com/products).

3. Hubspot's Website Grader (https://website.grader.com/). The site is a free online tool that grades any website against key metrics like performance, mobile readiness, SEO, and security. You can see how companies in the industry you are interested in are performing in terms of attracting customers to their sites.

4. SEMrush (https://www.semrush.com): This site allows you to view images of organic vs. paid search, CPC distribution, trends over time, phrase match and related keywords, organic search results and ads. Once again, this is an opportunity for you to see how other companies are performing in sectors that interest you.

THE VALUE OF INDUSTRY ASSOCIATION DATA

To better understand the scope of a market that interests you, you might begin looking at the key associations in the industry and the companies that belong to these associations. Questions that you should try to answer include these:

1. For each association, what are the most active companies on the association site? (You can tell this from their support of the site or perhaps their appearance at industry conferences.)

2. Does the association conduct an annual survey of its members or the industry? If yes, can you get access to it? What information does it tell you about the industry that will impact your business concept?
3. Is anybody advertising on the industry or association web site? If yes, who are they, what is their value proposition and how are they differentiating their value?
4. What annual industry statistics can you find? What trends does the data reveal?
5. Are there annual surveys about the industry that you can secure?
6. What conferences or events are important to the industry? Can you attend any of these? What are the hot topics being discussed?
7. Can you download presentations (YouTube or Brainshark) or white papers from the conference sites that will give you a better understanding of the market?
8. Which companies are sponsoring these conferences? Visit their websites to learn more about them and their role in the industry.
9. Who are the top (3 or 4) competitors in the industry? How do they position themselves in the industry in terms of their value to their customers?
10. What consulting and research firms are respected in the industry? What information do they reveal that is important?
11. Are there any meet-ups happening that would allow you to network with individuals in the sector?

MARKET SIZE

Next, we want to understand how large the market is. One simple approach to doing this is called a TAM-SAM-SOM approach. This begins with defining the Total Available Market (TAM). TAM is calculated by identifying the total revenue or sales within the market in the last year or projections in the near future (next 2 to 3 years). You will find this data in the research sources described previously in the chapter. For example, if you are hoping to launch a dog biscuit company in a small town in New Jersey, then you will might begin by understanding the size of the market in terms of sales for the state. Don't state how large the market is in the United States because this provides you with an inflated view of the size of YOUR market. Next you will want to look at your Serviceable Available Market (SAM). SAM refers to the geographic region or perhaps a segment of the market that you will have access to. Your SAM might be a range of 50 miles from your home. Perhaps that is 20% of the state. Now your SAM is 20% × TAM. Finally, you want to calculate your Share of the Market (SOM) assuming that there are others in the market and you will not likely have 100% of the market. You are confident that you can capture 20% of the serviceable market.

Let's walk through this example using the same concept of launching a dog biscuit company (these numbers do not represent actual figures, so if you're really interested in launching a dog biscuit company in New Jersey, please make sure you do your own research).

1. Dog biscuit sales in the United States in 2018 = $50,000,000
2. TAM: Dog biscuit sales in New Jersey in 2018 = $1,000,000
3. SAM: Dog biscuit sales in your target reach in 2018 (TAM × 20%) = $200,000
4. SOM: You plan to capture 20% of the market (TAM) = $40,000

We hope you can now see how important it is to get a clear picture of the actual market size. If you had looked at dog biscuit sales in the United States and believed that the market size was $50 million and stopped your analysis with this figure, you would not have realized that in your world, the actual market size is a more realistic $40,000. If we take this one step further and decide that you are going to launch this only on your college campus and sell to students who have dogs at home, your market size will be even smaller. Having a small market size is not necessarily a negative since it gives you an opportunity to learn about the market and customer needs and when you are ready, expand beyond the reaches of your dorm or local community.

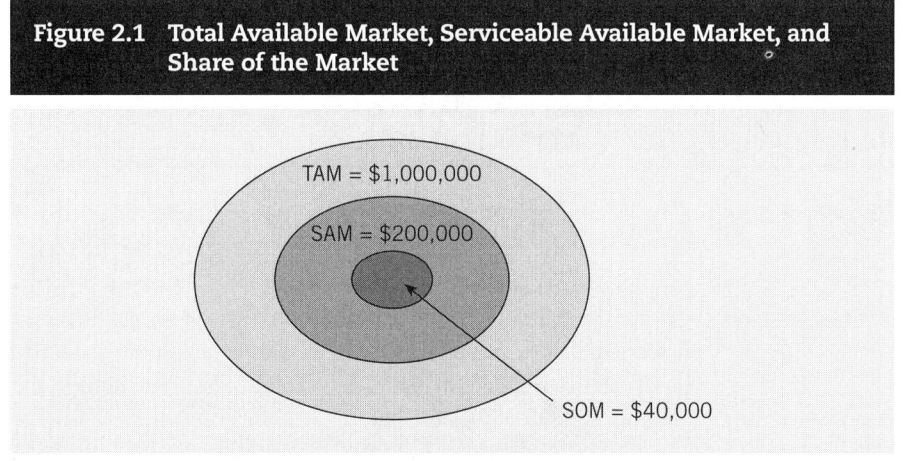

Figure 2.1 Total Available Market, Serviceable Available Market, and Share of the Market

ACTION CREATES TRIUMPHS (ACT)

Your Market

Before you go any further with the concept you are thinking about, it's important to ensure you understand the market forces that will impact your ability to succeed. Remember, ideas without customers and a market that provides an opportunity to succeed are not businesses; they are merely dreams. No matter how great your idea may seem to be in your mind, it cannot survive without a business environment that demonstrates a need for new solutions, like the one you are considering. Please address the questions below that will fit into the Business Model Canvas that you are designing for your concept. You should begin by selecting a few of the data sources described so far in this chapter. Then, completing the research required, address the following questions:

- Who makes up the potential and target audience that you are addressing and creating value for?
    - What are their key defining characteristics, that is, demographics, behaviors?
    - What is their compelling problem, need, or pain?
    - Which segment(s) are most attractive? Why?
    - Do your target customers care about how you create or offer economic as well as social value?
- How large is this market?
    - How many people or companies or organizations are seeking the solution you offer? Basically, what is your Share of the Market (SOM)?
    - What evidence do you have to support this estimate?
    - What assumptions did you make? How might you confirm them?
    - How easy is it to target and access the market? (You may not yet be able to address this, but it's worth beginning to think about.)

YOUR BUSINESS RELATIVE TO OTHERS IN THE INDUSTRY: SWOT ANALYSIS

As we have been discussing, understanding the market needs and condition that you will operate in is critical to your success. Even the best business ideas will not flourish if several conditions are not met: (1) there must be a proven need in the market, (2) there must be an ability to pay for the solution you offer, and (3) market conditions must allow for you to access your market. Those are some of the key external conditions that must be met. However, there is an internal factor that cannot be underscored enough, and that is the ability to organize your own resources and partners to deliver on the value that your target market requires. Therefore, even if all market conditions are met, if your company is not positioned to support this and scale, your success will be limited even if you can achieve early success.

Therefore, a critical step in completing your market and industry research is to determine how you align or stand out from others in the industry. You should examine your company and teams' core competencies and strengths and your overall competitive position using a popular business framework called SWOT Analysis: Strengths, Weaknesses, Opportunities, and Threats. Strengths and weaknesses refer to traits like flexibility, a special expertise or lack thereof, and other internal factors that you have some level of control over. On the other hand, opportunities and threats are environmental factors like energy prices, changes in consumer preferences, rising interest rates, and other external events that are much more difficult, or even impossible, to control (but clearly impact your ability to succeed in the market).

Strengths

Strengths, also known as core competencies, are areas where your organization stands out from others in your industry. These can include technology (special code or patents that only you possess), marketing/sales savvy, personnel, experience, or cost advantages. When you're trying to figure out what your strengths are (and those of your entire team), some questions you might want to ask yourself include the following:

- What unique advantages does or will my company have in the marketplace or industry?
- What does or will my company do very well?
- What does or will my company do that surpasses our competitors?
- Do we have access to resources, distribution channels, or technology that is unique to my company?
- How do or will individuals within the organization contribute to our success?
- What expertise or unique experience do I or my employees have that will have a positive impact on our business growth?
- What other strengths does my company have that provide it with a unique advantage in the market?

The strengths that you and your company have are relative to the entire industry. Therefore, if all of your competitors have the same cost position or access to the same distribution channels, then you cannot consider that a strength; it simply becomes a minimum requirement. A good example of this is in the banking industry, where exceptional service is critical to keeping customers (especially as banks find it harder to compete on interest rates alone). Using a customer relationship management (CRM) system to communicate with your clients is a nice-to-have asset, but it is not necessarily something that would be considered a strength, since it has become a minimum requirement rather than an exception for most banks. However, if a bank does something different with the software that allows it to better serve its customers, then the use of this specialized program is turned into a strength or core competency.

Weaknesses

Obviously, weaknesses are areas in which your company fails to excel or lacks expertise altogether. Therefore, not possessing some of the qualities noted in the strength category can be considered weaknesses if your major competitors have these abilities. But if your competitors don't have these skills either (perhaps everybody's poor at managing changing customer demand), then this may not be a mortal weakness—yet. Important questions to ask yourself to determine your weaknesses include the following:

- Relative to our competitors, what areas are we simply not proficient at?
- Do we lack experience in a vital area such as sales, or do we lack the ability to develop new products that will contribute to our growth?
- Do we have a shortage of people with the right experience, skills, or expertise?
- How much knowledge do we possess about certain markets or industry sectors that are relevant to our business?
- Do we lack technical skills or need improvements in our ability to operate smoothly?
- Are we experiencing production capacity problems because our systems are not working at peak performance?
- Are our manufacturing/production costs too high, yet we are not able to lower them in the near future?
- What other areas need improvement?

It's far easier to admit to your strengths, but a candid appraisal of your weaknesses is important. If you have colleagues or friends whom you trust, ask them if they think your assessment is accurate. If you have employees, their input is vital, too. If you personally are not good at selling, don't delude yourself into believing that you can overcome this simply by being passionately committed to your business. Talking to others may help you see that your competition might be just as passionate—and have a talented sales force as well. However, if everybody in the industry is weak in a certain area (such as limited distribution channels), you may see that this may not be a major weakness *yet*, since it puts you on a level playing field with your competitors. Once you have clearly defined your areas of weakness, then you will be in a better position to determine if they can be turned into strengths.

Opportunities

It's always fun to daydream about business opportunities—a new location, a possible new product line, an expansion through acquisition, or discovering an underserved market.

Opportunities are external factors in the marketplace that you do not control yet that present you with the ability to grow your business if you position yourself correctly. Opportunities can include strong demand for certain products, lack of satisfaction with available product options, or limited competition. Below are some questions to help you identify opportunities in your market. However, do not rely on your gut instinct to answer these. You will need to complete market research to understand and clearly define this.

- Is there strong customer demand in the market for our products or services and the value that we provide to our customers?
- Is there a lack of satisfaction with the products that are currently offered or available?
- Is our competition limited or weak in certain areas that we have not yet addressed or attacked with full effort?
- Is there a lack of competitors or substitute products or services that currently satisfy customers' needs?
- Are there readily available or easily accessed distribution channels (e.g., the Internet or the opening of a new trade channel) that we can take advantage of?
- Are there opportunities to easily enter a new or related market?
- What other opportunities are there in the market that will help me launch my business?
- Are switching costs (perceived or real) low?

Threats

By threats, we refer to conditions in the marketplace that make entry or growth less desirable, more difficult, or even risky, including competitors, regulation, tax law changes, new technologies, cheaper overseas labor, and litigation. Threats include obstacles that stand in the way of your company's achieving success because you lack control over them. An example of a threat that is being faced by many businesses today is the movement of production facilities to low-cost countries like India and China. If your competitors now begin to benefit from significantly lower production costs, this could have a major impact on your organization, your pricing scenario, and the industry as a whole. To identify threats to your business, begin by asking yourself questions like these:

- Do barriers to entry, such as limited distribution channels or the closure of certain channels for importing or exporting products, affect my business?
- How much competition is there in the market?
- Are there a lot of substitute products, making it difficult for me to differentiate my value?
- Is my company affected by an increase in the price of supplies or lack of availability of certain supplies required to develop or deliver my product?
- Does inertia affect my business (i.e., people are "happy enough" with the present solution to their problem)?
- What regulations affect my business, now and in the future?
- Have there been any changes in customers' interest in my product or service?

PESTLE ANALYSIS

In order to ensure you have a complete understanding of the environment that you plan to operate within, another tool that you can use to understanding the OT portion of the SWOT (Opportunities and Threats) is called a PESTLE Analysis (2019).

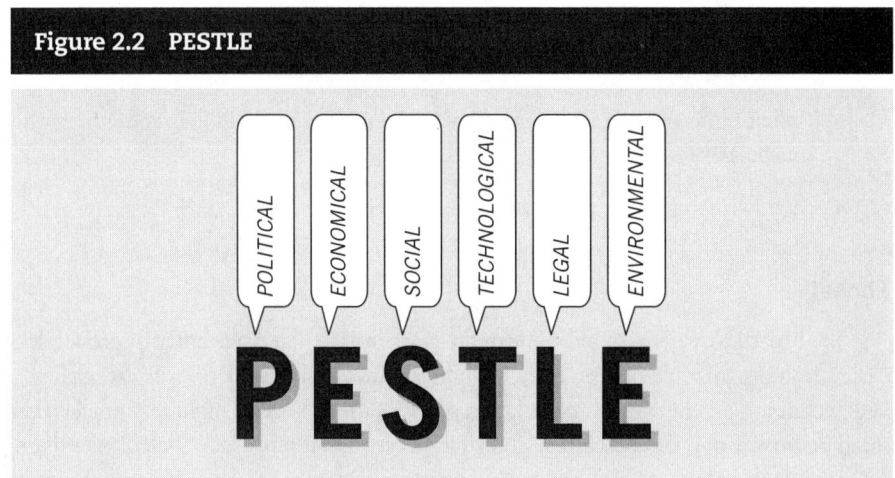

Figure 2.2 PESTLE

These are factors that you cannot control but need to be aware of to understand your ability to launch and grow your business in a region or within a sector of the market. PESTLE is an acronym that represents the following:

- **P:** Political—These include governmental policies such as taxes, tariffs, and trade that impact your ability to conduct business in a region and to be profitable. Areas to consider are government stability, regulation as it relates to competition, import-export regulations, political committees, freedom of the press, and deregulation.

- **E:** Economic—These include economic factors that you need to be aware of, such as inflation rates, interest rates, and foreign exchange rates. Areas to consider are growth rate, availability of credit, GDP, stock market trends, and price fluctuations.

- **S:** Social—These factors focus on the cultural mindset of a region or an industry. This might include demographics like gender and age, sociocultural beliefs and practices. Areas to consider are social classes, diversity and racial equity, attitudes toward a variety of business-relevant factors, and lifestyle factors.

- **T:** Technological—This factor focuses on the impact of technological advances or lack thereof in a region or within a sector. Areas to consider are technology R&D, automation, innovation, Internet infrastructures, and technology use and awareness.

- **L:** Legal—Legal factors focus on the laws and legislature in a region or market that impact your company's ability to grow. Areas to consider are laws that focus on discrimination, antitrust, employment, consumer protection, education, and copyright and patent protection.

- **E:** Environmental—This factor relates to the geography and environmental issues that impact your business. Areas to consider are recycling, renewable energy, attitudes about green products, natural disasters, pollution, and climate change.

As you study the impact of these factors on your business and build them into your SWOT Analysis, remember that not all of these factors will impact your ability to grow. However, it's important to understand which areas you need to think about, now and as situations change and evolve over time. This will help ensure you acknowledge the role that external (OT) factors play since you will likely have very limited or no control over them and will need to align your team's strengths to address these factors.

POSITIONING MAP

Now that you're familiar with the SWOT Analysis, let's compile the research that you conducted, create a SWOT Analysis for your company, and then create a visual of your position in the market. This is called a Positioning Map (it is also referred to as a Perceptual Map). Basically, the goal of this type of visual demonstration is to show how you will be positioned in the market relative to two factors that are important to stakeholders. It could be factors like price, quality, innovation, performance, customer service, or something else that is valued by your potential customers. This is a good way to not only view your potential competitors but to also identify your brand distinction. Here's an example to get you started. You decide that you want to create a sneaker that has innovative features such as the ability to be designed to contour to your feet, power laces, special wicking material to keep wearers dry even in the pouring rain and really easy to keep clear with special dirt protection woven into the fabric. You look at the price points of competitors and realize that even at the luxury/high end of the price, nobody is offering anything truly innovative. You also see that the more traditional sneakers are priced lower, what we call *value priced*. Perhaps there's a gap in the market for you to create a truly more innovative product but also price it below the luxury brands. Obviously, you will need to complete a significant amount of research to determine customer needs and values (e.g., will perception of the value be lowered if you price it too low?), but this visual has given you enough data to feel confident that there might be an opportunity,

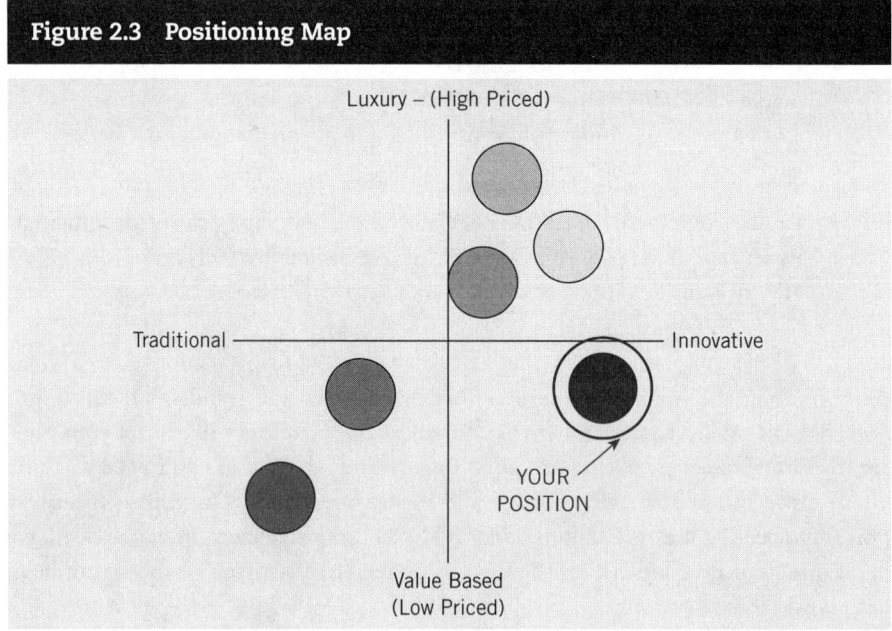

Figure 2.3   Positioning Map

and you are ready to explore that through secondary research, as discussed in this chapter, as well as primary research, which we will discuss in the next chapter.

Now, it's your turn. Before you continue, select two factors (examples include price and ability to innovate) that are important to your customers and identify the other players in the market to see what your value proposition needs to align with the needs of the market to be unique.

ACTION CREATES TRIUMPHS (ACT)
Country Entrepreneurship Opportunity Challenge

Next, we'd like you to develop a solid understanding of the challenges and opportunities individuals face in launching a business in different countries around the world. This could be countries or regions that you are familiar with or ones that you are not. You will complete this project in teams of two to five people with the goal of analyzing two different countries.

As you have learned through the discussions in this book, entrepreneurs don't wait for perfect or ideal conditions to start a business. They learn to navigate the landscape and leverage the positives (opportunities) while overcoming barriers (threats) using their strengths and figuring out ways to address their weaknesses in order to make their entrepreneurial vision a reality. As you select the two countries, keep in mind the fact that some countries may seem more attractive than others but all have constraints that you will need to address.

Your Challenge

Your team has launched a consulting firm that specializes in helping entrepreneurs start businesses in countries around the world. Congratulations! You've landed your first client, Amanda Wingate, a seasoned entrepreneur who graduated from your school 15 years ago. She cares deeply about the environment and has started multiple businesses in retail, manufacturing, and health services. She cares deeply about giving back to society and wants to ensure that her next company supports a healthy and diverse work environment. Amanda has just returned from her first visit to two different countries, and she is inspired to start a business in ONE of the two. However, she is having a hard time deciding which will allow her to further her values of creating economic as well as social value without harming the environment.

Your job is to thoroughly research each country and provide recommendations to her in terms of what she needs to consider to start a business in each of these countries. You do not need to tell her which country your research shows will meet her criteria. You simply need to complete a solid analysis of both opportunities as well as explain the challenges that she will face, allowing her to select the country that is right for her.

Sources of Country Data

You must use published, credible sources in your research, and we encourage you to interview experts from the countries, when possible. ONE of your primary research sources must be the Global Entrepreneurship Monitor (GEM) Report, a leading study of entrepreneurship around the world. It includes 18+ years of data compiled

(Continued)

(Continued)

through 200,000+ interviews a year in over 100 economies. The GEM Report studies the entrepreneurial behavior and attitudes of individuals in each country and analyzes how the national context impacts entrepreneurship opportunities and challenges. GEM began in 1999 as a joint project between Babson College (United States) and London Business School (England). The latest edition of the report must be used and can be found online at https://www.gemconsortium.org/report. You can also use the appropriate National or Special Topics Report, if they are relevant.

In addition to the GEM Report, you must use at least two other reliable sources of data, remembering to cite your sources in your Endnotes. Your school university will likely have a variety of sources you can use. We recommend you ask your librarian about some of the following reports:

- BMI Research: Country risk, industry reports, and company coverage in global markets; includes news, reports, and data
- EIU.com—Economist Intelligence Unit: Profiles of countries' finance sector and detailed reports about all aspects of doing business in a country
- Emerging Markets Information Service: News, company and industry information, and financial and economic data for emerging markets/countries
- Continuum Economics (formerly Roubini Global Economics): Useful for understanding the global economy and for tracking the impact of political and economic policies in various countries
- Euromonitor Passport: Find international market intelligence, including economic statistics, on industries, countries, and consumers
- Global Competitiveness Report (World Economic Forum)
- U.S. Dept. of Commerce Country Commercial Guides: Guides cover leading sectors, trade regulations, market research

Country Data to Analyze

In your research, you must consider the following for each country:

1. What is the environment like for entrepreneurship?
2. What are some key characteristics of entrepreneurship in each country? In what ways is entrepreneurship in these countries distinct from that in other countries?
3. What are the challenges of doing business in these countries as it relates to the country's unique cultural, social, economic, and environmental practices?
4. How easy is it to get a business started? What are the constraints to starting a business?
5. What factors are most critical for success?
6. What type(s) of businesses might be feasible?
7. How do self-perceptions and attitudes about entrepreneurship in each country impact the opportunity to launch a business?
8. What considerations are important for an expat (foreign) entrepreneur starting a business in this country?

9. What actions would you recommend an entrepreneur take to increase his or her chances of success in each country?

10. Other questions relevant to each country's unique circumstances to support (or not support) entrepreneurship

You can select countries with which you are familiar (perhaps the countries you call home), or you can select other countries that interest you. Please make sure you review the GEM report before commencing the project to ensure the countries you have selected are part of the report. Your deliverable will consist of one report (not two individual reports). This should be a well-written report, 10 pages, double-spaced, using 11-point Times New Roman font. You will be able to include an additional three pages of exhibits, graphs, and charts that support your findings. This should be included in the appendix that follows the main body of the report.

VIEW FROM THE TRENCHES

Marabots Technology Corporation

Next, let's turn to a fictional company, Marabots, a small growing firm that entered the underwater drone market as it was in the process of evolving, providing the company with a mix of challenges. On the positive side, it had the ability to shape the direction of the industry as it grew the business but, as an early entry into the market, it also faced the challenge of ensuring its solution wasn't too early or not the right fit for a market that was rapidly evolving.

Marabots manufactures commercial-grade, portable underwater vehicles, basically unmanned underwater drones from a small office on the east coast of the United States. The company's focus is Business-to-Business (B2B) with a strong track record in serving the marine and military markets. Its vehicles are priced to be more affordable than other inspection/observation class Remotely Operated Underwater Vehicles (ROVs). It is proud of the fact that its vehicles are simple to use yet powerful enough to accomplish complex missions. It positions itself as a company that transforms technologies, previously used below the water, into products with aerial (above-the-water) functions.

Its portfolio of products included ROVs, a hybrid vehicle (a mixture of autonomous and remote) underwater vehicles (AUVs), and underwater camera systems utilized in commercial, educational, industrial, government, military, and recreational applications. Its goal is to help anybody who has an interest in exploring what is beneath the water.

Marabots has solid sales success and market penetration in the B2B space, but as they looked to expand its suite of product offerings, it has decided to explore the B2C (Business to Consumer) market with a product offered at a relatively low price point. The question it needs to address before going into full product development mode is "Is there a market for an underwater drone in the $1,000 price-point range?"

(Continued)

(Continued)

To address this opportunity, Marabots decides to conduct industry research to better understand need, distribution, and willingness to pay for a lower priced B2C product. It doesn't want to simply "build it" and hope that customers "will come." It also wants to understand the potential for cannibalization, basically creating a sales problem for its higher priced market position by offering a significantly lower priced ROV with fewer features.

The company hires a marketing consultant who brings two of his undergraduate student interns to work with him on the project. They begin the initiative by outlining their project goals:

- ✓ Identify growth sectors and opportunities for recreational (consumer-facing) products around the $1,000 price point.
- ✓ Understand competitive forces that impact their business's opportunity for growth within the recreational market.
- ✓ Understand how competition, market trends, climate change, environmental concerns, and the economy impact its business decisions as well as its growth opportunities, both locally and globally.
- ✓ Define the following about customers:
  - o Understand how they're finding solutions or products to meet their current needs (e.g., safety, exploration).
  - o Define which products are perceived as "need-to-have products" in the relevant sectors.
  - o Determine what criteria are used during the purchasing process (e.g., price, features, access).
  - o Recognize where any challenges may reside in converting prospects to paying customers and how price impacts purchasing decisions.
  - o Identify the differences, as well as similarities, between the decision-making process for various buyers (e.g., end users, marine shops, marine safety officials).

The student interns, directed by their boss, begin to conduct secondary market research using online business sources and reference material from a list similar to the one discussed earlier in this chapter. They decide to create very specific research questions to guide them as they work toward understanding the larger strategic questions outlined for the project:

1. What are the trends in the market?
   a. Has an interest in ROVs and drones grown, stayed the same, or declined?
      i. What proof exists?
      ii. What factors have impacted this (e.g., environment, economy, green trend, climate change)?
   b. Has there been similar or opposite shifts in trends for other types of remotely operated vehicles?
2. How is the market size assessed?
   a. How large is this market?
      i. How many people or companies/organizations in the industry?
      ii. What evidence exists to support this estimate?
      iii. What assumptions were made, if any? How might you confirm them?

iv. How easy is it to target the market?
b. What are the ROV and drone markets?
  i. What is market share of ROVs or drones by country?
  ii. What is market share of ROVs or drones by brand?
  iii. Are there one or two dominant brands or a lot of small brands?
  iv. What is market share of ROVs or drones by price point?
     < $500, $500–$1,000, $1,000–$2,000, > $2,000

3. How do consumers make buying decisions in this market?
a. Who makes up the potential and target audience that they are addressing?
  i. What are their key defining characteristics, (i.e., demographics, behaviors)?
  ii. What's most important to customers in transacting business with an ROV or drone company?
  iii. Which segment(s) are most attractive? Why?
  iv. What are most common needs that customers share?
  v. What are their customers' decision-making processes (meaning, what issues do they consider before they purchase products or services from Marabots or from a competitor)?
b. How do customers find out about ROVs or underwater drones?
c. How important is location in transacting business (is being local critical to purchasing?)
d. What influence does price have in customers' decisions to purchase?

4. What are the marketing channels and distribution options?
a. What are the channels of distribution for recreational submersible underwater drones/ROVs in the United States and around the world?
  i. Are there a few large master distributors or many smaller distributors? If the latter, which have leading market share?
b. Since Marabots is a U.S. firm, does it make sense to launch in the United States?
  i. If so, what supportive evidence or facts does it know about market demographics and needs?
c. How is the company's target audience currently addressing the problem or need?
  i. What alternatives (substitute solutions) do they have? Who's the competition?
  ii. Through which channels do customer segments want to be reached?
  iii. Which channels are most cost-efficient?
  iv. Will the company integrate its channels with customer routines and behaviors?
d. What is the retail distribution?
  i. What are the retail outlets for recreational ROVs and drones?

(Continued)

(Continued)

    ii. What does the research on marine retailers, marine electronics retailers, and associations show?
1. What does the company know about the products it sells?
2. Can it describe its customers?
3. Are marine-focused retailers a good distribution option?

    iii. What percentage of recreational ROVs are sold via the following?
1. Small dive shops
2. Specialty marine retail shops
3. Superstores
4. Online
5. Other (please define)

5. What is the competition and unique value proposition?
    a. What is the messaging and value proposition for similar recreational ROV products? What can the company learn from this?
    b. Compared to the competition, what attributes does the product need to offer to make it unique or more valuable to customers?
    c. What competitors exist in the recreation market in the < $2,500 price point?

In Their Shoes

Before you continue reading, imagine that you are one of the student interns completing the industry research. How would you address these specific questions? Think about the different research channels you would use to answer these questions.

- Write down five to eight channel or sources you would research to answer the questions outlined.
- Would you want to interview anybody at key organizations, associations, or companies?
- What questions would you ask?
- What information would you ask Marabots to provide you with?
- How would you locate competitor information?
- Describe your market research process.

HIGHLIGHTS OF MARABOTS RESEARCH FINDINGS

Below we have provided you with highlights of the students' key findings. This data combined primary research interviews with secondary market research designed to understand competition and changes in the market. There was also a focus on the impact the massive growth in the drone market would have in the recreational (B2C) submersible drone market. They decided to study "Underwater Drone Campaigns" on Crowdfunding Sites Indiegogo and Kickstarter to see what activity was occurring in the start-up space to ensure they covered current and future trends. Did you think about doing this?

Review the summarized data and think about what you would recommend to Marabots and why you could justify that recommendation. After you have read the findings, then proceed to read the final recommendations the consultant and students gave to Marabots.

1. The Role of Price

- Now that action cameras are waterproof and people can throw them below the boat and take pictures, they are not spending a lot of money in the $1,000 price range.

- If there was a $1,000 unit it might be desirable, but it must be very high quality or it could turn people away because they don't want to keep upgrading it. If it breaks after a week or two, then the reviews go bad online and people get turned off.

- Price is a big driver; keeping it low is important; keeping it small is important. There are so many applications; adaptability is also important—depends on which customers you talk to. Some want to take it fishing or check reefs or boat.

- There are a number of small competitors whose primary value proposition is to lower the traditional high price point of ROVs. They priced theirs between $1.5K and $1.8K.

- Average boater finds $1,000 too high: would need compelling interest or event like going to the Caribbean and diving.

- Be careful—it would be hard to produce a decent product at this price; most drones have 10% margin; a low cost couldn't survive with that margin; have to produce at a much lower cost; volume isn't there. Others sell in volume; you would have to sacrifice many components and features or quality to do that, and you can't make up for it in volume because the market demand simply isn't there. There aren't enough people in the market who want it.

  o 10 or 15 companies have products announced at the $1K price point; companies are excited about it.

  o Small margin on $1K and the crowdfunding campaigns for underwater units raise a lot less than aerial units.

  o People don't understand what they're going to see in the water; with aerial units, there's more to see; core difference in what you're filming.

2. Impact of Aerial Drone Market on Submersible Drone Market

- There is demand for $1,000 price point due to the interest in drones, but it's a one-time purchase—unlike aerial drones. People don't start with a cheap one and move up; they buy what they need.

- The growth in the aerial market helped gain exposure, but it's a different customer due to geography.

- The main use for an aerial drone is to take pictures of cool things people see on the water surface and then post pictures to social media; there is minimal demand to see things under the water that a camera can't provide.

- Aerial drone market is much larger than underwater. People are more focused on marketing to businesses and improving the environmental efficiency and ultimately, more profit for the company.

(Continued)

(Continued)

- Trend in market is down overall in the United States for robotics; however, marine robotics are growing because of this year's uptake with infrastructure and exploration (mostly educational research). International markets are increasing because of wind farms and concerns for environment.

- There is a large range of prices in the drone market:
    - Under $100 = very limited features
    - Several hundred = more specialized (infrared, radar, sensors)
    - Tens of thousands = large devices, industrial use

3. Market Size and Growth Sectors

- Expansion into the UUV (unmanned underwater vehicles) market shows growth in the B2B space as opposed to the B2C space.
    - The UUV market is about to ramp as the aerial drone market did during the 1990s. There are several market drivers to accelerate this ramp. These include military applications, seabed mining, oil and gas applications, and telecommunications.
    - Research forecasts the UUV market will grow from $1.2 billion in 2014 to $4.8 billion in 2019. There are also clear estimates that the global AUV market will expand from $457 million in 2014 at almost 32% CAGR through 2019.
    - Underwater drone news has increased, although little is occurring within the consumer sea drone space. The military and industrial sectors have seen heavy news flow validating the value and utility of UUVs.

- Substantial growth prospects of the market can be attributed to surging eminence of drone flying as hobby initiatives such as UAV photography and racing.

4. Customer Alignment

- The market for marine robotics/ROV's is the 30+ male with money, with a 30+ foot boat, and making US$200K+ with disposable income; family sector and fishing guy; likes boating.

- The underwater market it is more oriented toward research. With the underwater market, this is NOT a hobbyist market and is very fractured and specialized.

- Consumers are less likely to purchase semiprofessional drones at higher price point.

- Consumer use is a much smaller market, but is heavily influenced by the diving industry, which is growing rapidly and constantly seeing a use for marine robotics.

- Marine drones are less well-known, but there is increasing use for environmental and commercial use.

- Can absolutely see the explosion for drones increasing demand for underwater drones. However, the aerial market is fueled by the hobby market and folks who specialize in a focused area such as research.

- Inspecting merchant ships—done by divers and video camera—is how it's done now; done in drydock and inspection is annual so it's tough to justify the cost when it's once year. This is another reason underwater drones are harder to sell.

5. Understanding the Marine Market

- The market in recreational boating has been decreasing with recreational fishing and for accessory purchases made by owners of recreational boats. There is hope for more households buying a boat within the next year; however, it is not a significant enough amount to raise the industry sales in the billions. It also does not consider the size of the boat that will be purchased or the price point at which it will be sold; therefore, we cannot assume those individuals will be buying drones in addition to a boat within the next year.

- Market for recreational boating in 2001 to 2014 decreased beginning in 2013.

6. Understanding the Drone Market

- You can currently buy a drone online starting as low as $50 and up to $4,499 on Amazon.

- The global market for commercial applications of drone technology, currently estimated at about $2 billion, will balloon to as much as $127 billion by 2020.

- The global consumer drone market is projected to grow at a CAGR of 23.40% from 2016 to 2020 and at an estimated CAGR of close to 30%, from 2016 to 2024. It is expected to reach $4.19 billion by 2024.

- Substantial growth prospects of the market can be attributed to surging eminence of drone flying as hobby and initiatives such as UAV photography and racing.

- Yacht owners will pay $4K to $5K for a marine electronic/robotic. However, there are individuals who own smaller boats who are more price sensitive so it's become more important to sell at a more reasonable price point ($1,000 to $1,500).

- Consumer use is a much smaller market, but is heavily influenced by the diving industry, which is growing rapidly and constantly seeing a use for marine robotics.

7. Features Desired

- The features that people care about are quality of the picture, lights and thrust—can it go against the current: 2 or 3 knot currents—that's important.

- In terms of offering a unique value proposition, price is part of this but the user experience is critical. Theirs has a patent pending modular system offering a top-notch experience so individuals from 5 to 95 can use it; it's very intuitive, even Grandma can use it.

- There are new features: They don't tether but, technologically, this isn't an option; more sensory integration. Customers want products that don't tether but from a technology perspective, this is not an option. Customers also want more integration of the sensors, but the company doesn't offer support for this. To resolve this, a tool that manipulates movement would be acceptable. Grabbers or manipulators would be great.

- Consumers want better sensors, more flexibility, and a longer battery to continue research in the field instead of stopping and coming back to finish. There's a high chance for more development in the industry to improve these features—specifically, programming manipulators hardware for use of data to be applied to the environment on the spot.

Before you read the recommendation presented to Marabots, please write down what you would recommend based on the highlighted summary above. In addition, create a Positioning Map for Marabots to visually display its place in the market.

MARABOTS FINAL RECOMMENDATION

Based on our extensive primary and secondary research, the opportunity for underwater drones in the B2C space is not the optimal strategy for a company like Marabots. You currently have a business model built around the B2B market where you rely on high margins, lead generation programs, and sales activities to grow your business. The B2C market requires a different customer acquisition strategy and market approach—one that focuses on brand loyalty, awareness, and engagement campaigns that are expensive and require securing different channels of customer interaction.

You are a small business with limited human capital and a restricted marketing budget, so staying focused with your marketing channels as well as targeting specific sectors of the market where you have strong connections and penetration is key to your survival. At this time, the market for underwater submersibles is becoming saturated with start-ups and venture-backed businesses that are trying to produce an underwater drone at a low price point with narrow margins. The primary customers are hobbyists, and this is not your focus in the market. It would be expensive to gain traction in this area by launching B2C marketing campaigns to secure new customers, especially given the low margin on these products.

Another concern with the B2C approach focused on developing products with a significantly lower price point is that you could find yourself in a position where you are cannibalizing your own B2B market, competing directly with your higher priced ROVs. This can work, for example, with products like Apple's iPad/Mac because it is targeting the same customer with similar marketing tactics and focusing on purchasing multiple products. However, if you are going after a different market, you risk eroding your profit margin in the B2B market and concurrently not realizing enough of a profit margin with the gain in your share of the competitive consumer market. Therefore, the perceived ROI for Marabots would not be appealing and could have a severe impact on your ability to grow since your resources are limited and staying focused is critical to your success. The B2C space is traditionally more difficult to capture so, with tight margins and a misalignment with your current target customer, this is not the best use of your limited resources in terms of human capital, time, and money.

In conclusion, your focus and success in the B2B market has allowed you to get to a critical point in your business where you are ready to identify new products and business collaborations to realize the next stage of growth. Switching your focus to a B2C product with a low-margin, low-price-point product does not fit into a logical business strategy and is not recommended.

Did you come to the same conclusion as the research team or were you considering a different approach? What data helped you formulate your recommendation? How will this help you in the future as you begin to consider product launches for a business that intrigues you?

FOCUS ON APPLICATION: WAKU

The Entrepreneurial Journey

Juan Giraldo, Nico Estrella

Finally, let's take a quick look at the research that Waku conducted to better assess what the demand in the healthy-beverage market looked like in the United States (the market they elected to launch their business). They used a variety of sources to understand the market, and below we have highlighted a few that they found to be most valuable:

Google Beverage Trends Report 2017 (Horwitz & Zimmer, 2017). This report used Google data to identify and compare nonalcoholic beverage trends across four different markets: United States, United Kingdom, Spain, and Mexico. The goal of the report was to understand which beverage trends represent the largest opportunity. What the research revealed was process, flavor, and premium are critical factors in the beverage demand sector.

- Major increases in demand for beverages that are cold brewed (beverages brewed used room-temperature or cold water) demonstrated that how beverages are processed is growing in demand. The experience of making and enjoying the tea has become more important to the consumer.

- Top searches grow significantly based on earthy flavors associated with plants and herbs. Food that are functional and associated with health benefits and earthy flavors are more popular. For example, "Prior to 2016, interest in matcha flavored foods was almost nonexistent across the four markets. While matcha drinks continue to grow at a strong rate of 64% year over year across the four markets, matcha associated foods such as cake, cookies and ice cream have been gaining interest at a rate of 62% year over year" (Horwitz & Zimmer, 2017). In addition, the research shows that the buzz or conversation about matcha focuses on its antioxidant qualities, rich and smooth consistency, and its affiliation with boosting metabolism. This was based on "caption" data that analyzes the language of top influencers content related to matcha qualities.

- Growth in water is fueled by an interest in more enhanced or premium water that goes beyond simply quenching one's thirst. Again, the process that was used to make it and even the container has become an important factor in terms of searching for the product. YouTube influencers were talking about taste, safety, carbonation, and accessorizing (more interesting packaging).

(Continued)

(Continued)

- Infusions (soaking plant leaves or herbs in hot or cold) and tea are growing in terms of search, with the tea-drinking experience becoming a more important part of the consumption of the product (versus simply being functional, i.e., to quench thirst).

Beyond Google analysis, Waku looked at major research that had been conducted to ensure they understood the trends in the market:

- Mintel Group research shows that "Beating out juice and plain sparkling water, tea took the lead as a healthy beverage choice, with 49% of consumers agreeing that they consider tea (hot or iced) to be a healthy option when dining out. Plain sparkling water follows closely behind at 43%. While tea can have hidden sugars, in an unsweetened natural state it's known for offering a variety of health benefits that's likely driving the association."
- According to Mintel's *Coffee and Tea on Premise—US, December 2016* Report, 27% of consumers would pay more for coffee/tea beverages with added health benefits. Plant-based water, such as coconut water, is growing in popularity in retail settings, but is still fairly limited in restaurant settings. Nevertheless, 32% of consumers correlate plant-based waters with health, demonstrating its increased growth in health segments. According to Mintel's GNPD database, coconut water noted a 39% increase in product launches from 2015 to 2016.
- The trend for healthy hydration is driving growth in plant-based waters with global sales growing 21% in 2016 to reach sales of more than $2.7 billion USD. According to Zenith Global, the market by 2020 will have doubled in size to reach $5.4 billion (Zenith, 2017).
- Unilever research of 20,000 adults in five countries showed that sustainability is critical when it comes to food and beverage products. Seventy-eight percent of U.S. consumers feel better when they buy products that are sustainably produced. "Sustainability was voted 'most important' in the food and beverage trend for 2017. 1 of 3 global consumers choose to buy brands that they believe are doing social or environmental good. More than one in five (21%) of the people surveyed said they would actively choose brands if they made their sustainability credentials clearer on their packaging and in their marketing" (Unilever, 2017).

Implications based on this research helped Waku understand the importance of premium drinks infused with natural ingredients that create an experience for the user. They saw a growth in plant-based waters moving beyond coconut. Yet, they understood that this was a crowded space with many massive market share holders competing for customers. This supported their interest in further pursuing their idea and decided that it was time to look even more closely at the market in the United States for their new concept. In the next chapter, we will discuss what they learned when they talked to potential customers.

AHAs

Lessons and Takeaways

It is critical that you establish a baseline of knowledge about the markets you anticipate you will operate within before you begin to develop your product or service. This knowledge includes market trends that influence and impact the success of a business. In this chapter, we focused on secondary market research tactics that involve uncovering clues about industry practices and norms and how to gather data about target markets and the marketplace in general. The sources of secondary research vary tremendously, and it's critical that you ensure that the data is solid and well researched before you attempt to use it to make business decisions.

There are also numerous online tools that will help you identify trends in the market. The specific type of data that you will want to secure includes (but is certainly not limited to) the following:

1. The size of the target markets that seek your solution, now and as they evolve and change over time
2. Your ability to access these markets, now and as they evolve over time
3. The strength of direct competitors (organizations that offer solutions that are similar to yours) as well as indirect competitors (also known as substitutes) that provide a way to address the customers' current needs that may be quite different from your solution
4. Trends in the industry that impact your opportunity, in either a positive or negative manner
5. Factors like environmental or government regulations that impact your business model, in a positive and/or negative manner

Finally, you should examine your company and teams' core competencies and strengths and your overall competitive position using two popular business frameworks called SWOT Analysis and Positioning (Perceptual) Map. These will allow you to combine your strengths with the opportunity in the market to combat threats from competitors that do not possess the same skills and expertise that you do. You can then use what you learned to project this information into a visual map to see how you might position your business against others in the market based on two qualities or traits that are valued by customers.

TOOLKIT

Worksheet 2.1: SWOT Analysis

Name _____ Company _____

Strengths—Consider these areas:

- What unique advantages does or will my company have in the marketplace or industry?
- What does or will my company do very well?
- What does or will my company do that surpasses our competitors?
- Do we have access to resources, distribution channels, or technology that is unique to my company?
- How do or will individuals within the organization contribute to our success?
- What expertise or unique experience do I or my employees have that will have a positive impact on our business growth?
- What other strengths does my company have that provide it with a unique advantage in the market?

Name three Strengths unique to your company:

1.

2.

3.

Weaknesses—Consider these areas:

- Relative to our competitors, what areas are we simply not proficient at?
- Do we lack experience in a vital area such as sales, or do we lack the ability to develop new products that will contribute to our growth?
- Do we have a shortage of people with the right experience, skills, or expertise?
- How much knowledge do we possess about certain markets or industry sectors that are relevant to our business?
- Do we lack technical skills or need improvements in our ability to operate smoothly?

- Are we experiencing production capacity problems because our systems are not working at peak performance?
- Are our manufacturing/production costs too high, yet we are not able to lower them in the near future?
- What other areas need improvement?

Name three Weaknesses unique to your company:

1.

2.

3.

Opportunities—Consider these areas:
- Is there strong customer demand in the market for our products or services and the value that we provide to our customers?
- Is there a lack of satisfaction with the products that are currently offered or available?
- Is our competition limited or weak in certain areas that we have not yet addressed or attacked with full effort?
- Is there a lack of competitors or substitute products or services that currently satisfy customers' needs?
- Are there readily available or easily accessed distribution channels (e.g., the Internet or the opening of a new trade channel) that we can take advantage of?
- Are there opportunities to easily enter a new or related market?
- What other opportunities are there in the market that will help me launch my business?
- Are switching costs (perceived or real) low?

Name three Opportunities that you can take advantage of:

1.

2.

3.

Threats—Consider these areas:

- Do barriers to entry, such as limited distribution channels or the closure of certain channels for importing or exporting products, affect my business?
- How much competition is there in the market?
- Are there a lot of substitute products, making it difficult for me to differentiate my value?
- Is my company affected by an increase in the price of supplies or lack of availability of certain supplies required to develop or deliver my product?
- Does inertia affect my business (i.e., people are "happy enough" with the present solution to their problem)?
- What regulations affect my business, now and in the future?
- Have there been any changes in customers' interest in my product or service?

Name three Threats that you need to be cautious of:

1.

2.

3.

Worksheet 2.2: Strategic Plan to Address SWOT

Strengths (S): List your top three strengths/core competencies.

1.

2.

3.

In the left column, list the top three opportunities and threats that you encounter as a company. In the right column list the strategies you will deploy using your strength to maximize your opportunities and minimize your threats.

Opportunities (O)	Strategies for using strengths that maximize opportunities
1.	1.
2.	2.
3.	3.

Threats (T)	Strategies (S) for using strengths to deal with external threats
1.	1.
2.	2.
3.	3.

Strategic Plan to Address SWOT continued

Weaknesses (W): List your top three weaknesses as a company.

    1.

    2.

    3.

In the left column, list the top three opportunities and threats that you encounter as a company. In the right column list the strategies you will deploy to overcome weaknesses to maximize your opportunities and minimize your threats.

Opportunities (O)	Strategies for overcoming weaknesses to ensure maximization of opportunities
1.	1.
2.	2.
3.	3.

Threats (T)	Strategies for overcoming weaknesses to minimize threats
1.	1.
2.	2.
3.	3.

Worksheet 2.3: Market Size Analysis

Step One: Calculate your Total Available Market (TAM). TAM is calculated by identifying the total revenue or sales within the market in the last year or projections in the near future (next 2 to 3 years).

Step Two: Calculate your Serviceable Available Market (SAM). SAM refers to the geographic region or perhaps a segment of the market that you will have access to.

Step Three: Calculate your Share of the Market (SOM) assuming that there are others in the market and you will not likely have 100% of the market.

Step Four: Create a visual representation of your TAM-SAM-SOM. Using a series of circles show your estimated market size below.

CHAPTER THREE

IDENTIFYING YOUR CUSTOMERS' JOURNEY

Learning Objectives

In this chapter, you will learn to

- identify the variety of tools available to uncover customer needs.
- explain the importance of different research tools to prepare your marketing plan.
- prepare interview questions to be used in a survey or focus group.
- diagnose customer needs using ethnographic methods.
- analyze customer survey questions to determine which are most valuable in decision making.
- evaluate how entrepreneurs have used research tools to launch their business.

THE JOURNEY OF CUSTOMER DISCOVERY

Now that we have established an understanding of what's happening in your ecosystem, we turn our focus to clearly identifying the specific needs of the customers who will buy from you. You need not only to understand who they are (i.e., demographics like age, gender, and location), but you also need to understand their behaviors, interests, and attitudes. Primary market research, also known as customer discovery, will help you get into the minds of your customers and, if conducted properly, put you in a stronger position to confirm if there is indeed a market for your solution before you launch the business.

Think about how valuable it would be if you could experience what your customers experience and think as it relates to the solutions you offer. Do they have a strong need for your product or service? Is there something missing in their current solution that you could offer or feature? "Getting inside their heads" will help you make really well-informed business decisions and ideally get your business started in the right direction. Then, using this acquired customer knowledge, you will be able to state, with confidence, that there is (or is not) a market willing and interested in purchasing your product or service. If there is, then you can use the research to determine how to best deliver the product and value your potential customers have stated they want.

Are you ready to learn how you can deploy a variety of customer discovery tools to accurately create customer profiles (Chapter 4) that will inform your overall business decisions and, more specifically, your marketing efforts?

TURN DATA INTO KNOWLEDGE

In Chapter 2, you learned how to identify general (secondary source) information about your potential target markets. However, it is important to note that one essential element that separates successful companies from those who are struggling is their ability to turn information about customers' needs into knowledge that can be used to make sound business decisions. Information and knowledge are vastly different. Simple facts alone cannot help you grow your business. You need to turn those facts—the raw data—into knowledge by adding your own analysis and primary research, and then use this to create value for your business. If you cannot use the knowledge effectively, then conducting the research is not worth your time and effort because it won't help your business grow. In fact, it might actually harm your business because raw data used improperly can lead to very poor business decisions. This is not stated here to discourage you from conducting research and creating knowledge but to emphasize the importance of both conducting research and, of equal importance, applying the lessons learned to benefit your business.

THE IMPORTANCE OF SAYING NO: KNOWING WHICH CUSTOMERS ARE NOT THE RIGHT MATCH FOR YOU

Let us start by sharing an example of a business owner who used research findings from a survey conducted by a small-market research firm to keep his business from going under. During the height of the Great Recession in the United States (late 2007 to 2009), VacuumCo, a manufacturer of vacuum chambers (a rigid enclosure from which air and other gases are removed by a vacuum pump creating a low-pressure environment within the chamber) was gravely concerned that his prices were too high. Jim, the founder, chief engineer, and president, had drawn this conclusion based on the fact that sales were down for the past 6 months, and he heard grumblings from his sales team that they needed to lower prices during the recession. Jim was quite hesitant to lower prices and decided to hire a small-market research firm, ResearchIsUs, to help him determine what his next steps should be to get his business back on track and ideally increase revenue (and profit).

ResearchIsUs explained that they could not rely on sales results alone to explain the cause of the downturn in sales. They recommended launching a survey of their client's customer base. They decided to ask a series of questions to VacuumCo's customer base ranging from satisfaction with their current services to understanding their needs for products like the vacuum chamber that their client was selling. One of the most important questions that they included in this brief survey was "If you could choose ONE factor only, what is most influential in your decision to purchase a vacuum chamber from VacuumCo?" Their options were (in this order) the following:

- Price
- Product quality
- Customization of product
- Customer service
- Other (this was a fill-in-the-blank).

The results may surprise you. Forty percent of VacuumCo's customers stated product quality was their number ONE criterion for buying, 33% stated customization of product, and only 16% stated price. The research firm decided to further investigate the composition of the 16% who did state price was a leading criterion for buying a vacuum chamber. They learned that VacuumCo actually had two very different types of customers. One target market was sophisticated science- and technology-driven businesses where scientists with large budgets influenced purchasing decisions for products they needed to test and run their own products. On the other hand, VacuumCo's other target market was composed of small crafters. These are individuals who design jewelry and other products that require a chamber to get rid of air and liquid gases as their products are designed. They had very low budgets and were extremely price sensitive.

Let's think about the implications here. The primary customers VacuumCo worked with who had solid budgets were clearly not using price as the primary factor in their buying decision. They valued the high-quality product VacuumCo created and the fact that the products could be customized. Quality and price are very tightly integrated, especially in these sophisticated markets, so there's a danger of causing a negative reaction to the price cut because it could easily create an atmosphere of suspicion that quality may have also been cut. Therefore, if VacuumCo had cut its prices not only would it have lost profit margin but might very well have harmed its reputation with its most important customers for offering a high-quality product. Given that customization and quality were significantly more important than price to the customers he valued the most, Jim proceeded to do the opposite of his original intention . . . he actually raised his prices. In the end, he didn't lose a single customer, and, as he changed his message to focus more on quality and customization, his business began to grow again.

VacuumCo used this as a valuable lesson in not only asking customers, on a regular basis, what matters to them but also in understanding what the profiles of customers look like and in understanding if there are differences that impact how they position their product. Research needs to be conducted during activities that are not related to the sales process.

However, it is also important to note that that if VacuumCo had been in a meeting with these customers, they almost certainly would have told him price was a critical factor in the decision-making process. That's part of the negotiating process but NOT part of the research process. However, due to the fact that the survey was anonymous and run by a third-party research firm, the answers received were not part of a sales negotiation exchange. How's VacuumCo doing? Jim survived the downturn in the economy and, raised his prices, and his cash flow and balance sheet propelled him into developing more products and services based on customer needs.

ASK THE RIGHT QUESTIONS

We hope this brief case helped you understand the importance of "not" making business decisions in a vacuum, pun intended. You must clearly ask customers and prospects what they value before you leap into designing a product or service that "you" believe is valuable but have not yet confirmed that the market agrees with you.

How do you begin the process? You start by figuring out what knowledge you need to gain so that you ask the right questions. As described in the previous chapter, you should conduct secondary research as a starting point so that you have a clear sense of the information you're trying to obtain and then phrasing your questions specifically to elicit the information that you need to further understand market needs. This will help you avoid securing inconsistent or erroneous responses that might lead you to make disastrous business decisions. This is true with every type of research that you conduct, from running a survey and interviewing prospects to conducting online and offline written research. In fact, making a decision based on gut instinct or no information at all is as dangerous as making a decision based on research secured from primary research where your research process is flawed. The reason for this is because you might feel quite confident that the findings are accurate because you secured them yourself and without relying on a secondary data source. However, this false sense of confidence can lead you to false conclusions about the market or customer need. This is something you want to avoid at all costs since critical business decisions will be made based on your findings.

But this is not a reason to panic. The good news is that it isn't that difficult to ask the right questions. We shared the VacuumCo story to ensure that you understand how vital it is to think about the knowledge that you are seeking before you make any major business decisions that will dramatically change the way you launch a business or impact your customers' perception of your brand. Begin with the end in mind and ask yourself, "What is the purpose of obtaining this information?" and "How will I use the answer to improve my business?" If you constantly ask those questions and can honestly provide a response that makes logical business sense, then you're heading in the right direction.

METHODS OF DISCOVERING CUSTOMER NEEDS

Before we leapfrog into developing questions that you will ask, let's examine the various methods you can use to obtain customer information. They are not limited to simply asking questions; they include other research such as observing behavior. If your business is very early stage, meaning you have few or no customers or prospects, then the following methods are a good starting point. These are not in order of how they should be conducted. Depending on your situation, you may find that a survey is easier to conduct or you might decide to begin with a focus group to get a better understanding of your target customers' needs.

1. Survey design
2. Ethnographic studies
3. Focus groups
4. One-on-one interviews

If your business is more advanced and has customers or engaged prospects (perhaps individuals who are testing your prototype), then you should also include the following methods to secure more data about the behaviors of your target market(s):

- website activity
- social media exchanges
- e-mail, text, and other communication

ETHICAL ISSUES IN CUSTOMER RESEARCH

Regardless of the methods that you select, it's important to keep in mind that everything you do in terms of securing customer data be guided by ethical business practices. Participants or respondents should be aware of the content and goal of your research. If the information is going to be confidential and names will not be disclosed, clearly state this and adhere to this policy. This allows respondents to make informed decisions as it relates to their participation in your research. If you have any questions about this, please discuss your concerns with your professor.

GETTING TO KNOW YOUR CUSTOMERS

There are three categories that reflect important characteristics that you need to be aware of as they relate to your customers' needs. Some of these may be relevant to your business while others may not. The categories include (1) demographics, (2) psychographic/behavioral influences, and (3) life-cycle events. Your goal will be to come as close as

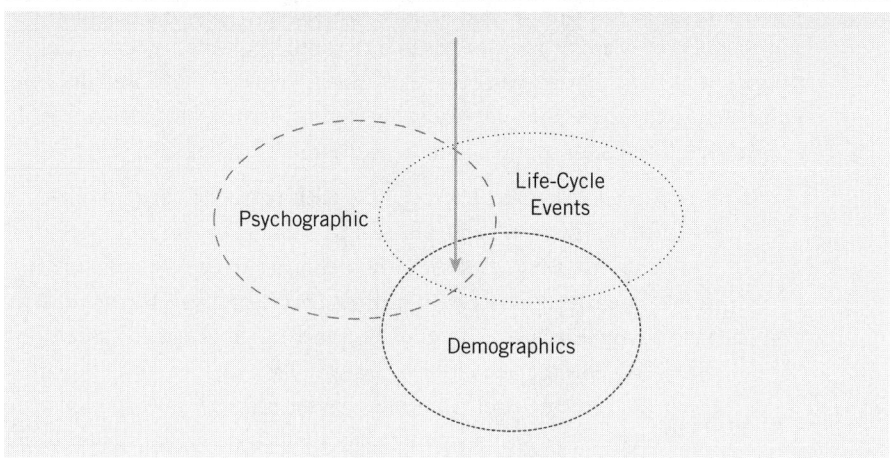

Figure 3.1 Target Market/Customer Persona Sweet Spot

possible to locating the intersection or sweet spot where these characteristics intersect and determine how to target these customers.

1. Demographics

    These are fact- (versus opinion-) driven data points. Depending on your customer base, you might need to know only a few, or perhaps you will want to be prepared to uncover more than we have included in this list. For example, are your customers single, women with a college degree, ages 35–50 who live in Florida in the United States, or are they 45- to 60-year-old married men with two children, and a master's degree who live in Egypt?

    - Age (range)
    - Gender identification
    - Family status (single, married, etc.)
    - Ethnicity
    - Education
    - Location—Where are your customers located, and how do they find you?
    - Businesses (industry, title, company size, previous products purchased)

2. Psychographic and Behavioral Influences

    You need to understand what psychographic or behavioral influences or habits impact customers' purchasing decision-making process. This includes attitudes, values, and beliefs such as how important health is to them or do they care about the environment or their status in a community (they want only the best and most expensive items). Questions you will ask them to discover this will focus on their past behavior and the types of companies and products they are or want to be affiliated with. A question focused on this might be "In the past year, how many times have you purchased or been influenced to purchase a product from a company because the company had a positive reputation of supporting the environment?"

    a. Pain points/challenges. Except in the health care industry, *customer pain* does not refer to a true physical pain, but refers instead to a problem or challenge that the customer needs to fix. What issues or problems challenge your customers and influence their behavior? Think about the answer an ideal customer might give if you asked them, "What is the one problem that you have that we solve for you better than anyone else?" Reflecting on the answer, now compose a question that you would ask them to identify if they have this problem.

    b. Opportunities being sought. What gain or opportunity is your customer in search of? If your product offers them the ability to seize this opportunity, perhaps further grow their business, then you need to identify customers looking for these opportunities.

    c. Purchasing location. Where do your customers look for your solution or similar solutions to meet their needs? Do they shop only onsite or online? Do they use Google to find the solution or Amazon or the local store? Sometimes businesses open a storefront because they got a really good deal on the monthly rent or because it's the only location they can afford, only to discover that customers aren't looking for them at this location. If your customers can't find you, whether you're on the street or in the virtual community of the Internet, then it doesn't matter how targeted your products and services are. You need to discover where they are looking for solutions before you choose your location(s).

    d. Behavior and decision-making processes. What behaviors or habits influence your customers' purchasing process? Do your customers need specific information before they make a decision? Do they conduct a lot of research before they purchase your type of product, or is this an impulse purchase? Is timing a factor? Who is involved in the purchase decision?

    e. Spending patterns. Do certain times of year influence your customers' spending patterns? For example, is your product most popular when students are heading back to school but not a big "need" any other time of the year?

f. Price sensitivity. How much does price influence your customers' decision? How important is their perception of the value of your product linked to the price? You can price too high or too low, so you need to be careful in asking this question. What are the trade-offs among price, features, and performance?

g. Lifestyle, interests, and attitudes. How does their attitude and the way they choose to lead their life impact their decisions? For example, is being green and environmentally sensitive reflect who they are and does it impact their purchasing decisions?

h. Brand loyalty. Are your customers more concerned about price, value, reliability, or something entirely different, such as status or brand appeal?

3. Life-Cycle Events

    In addition to understanding their behaviors, one final overlay in the customer profile development process is understanding life-cycle events. These are timely events or activities that happen to a group of people or organizations that impact their purchasing decisions. For consumers, this might be an event like getting married, purchasing a home, starting a new job, or having a baby. However, when you consider business life cycles, these are activities like launching a business, getting or seeking funding, or being impacted by a new law or regulation. It's something that impacts the business as a whole. Nonetheless, you can't survey a whole company, which means you will need to identify the role of the person who is most influential or impacted by this event.

VALUE PROPOSITION CANVAS

A popular framework for understanding customer needs is the Value Proposition Canvas designed by Strategyzer (n.d.). They focus on the jobs that customers need to accomplish, along with the gains and pains they experience. This is quite similar to our previous discussion about looking at the problems that you solve for customers and the opportunities that you create. Let's review the Value Proposition Canvas framework since this will likely help to reinforce the importance of truly understanding what customers care about.

In the Value Proposition Canvas, Strategyzer discussed the jobs that customers need to accomplish. Jobs might be functional like trying to "create healthy meals for their family" or socially or emotionally oriented like "trying to secure a better status in their community." Once you have identified the jobs to be accomplished, then you think about the pains and gains associated with getting these jobs done. Pains, for example, are negative outcomes that customers are trying to avoid and are typically found in the current solutions. If they are trying to create healthy meals, then a pain or challenge with the current solution might include not being able to easily buy quality healthy food at an affordable price. The gains, on the other hand, are positive outcomes of having achieved the job, such as their children having more energy or feeling better because they are eating healthier foods. Check out their video to learn more about this method at http://blog.strategyzer.com/posts/2017/3/9/value-proposition-canvas-a-tool-to-understand-what-customers-really-want.

SELECT YOUR QUESTIONS WISELY

To begin determining which questions and method(s) will be most effective for your customer discovery analysis, it's best to start with what you don't yet know about your potential customers, but need to learn to launch or grow your company. Imagine that you are in a room with your top prospects or customers and you have the opportunity to ask them anything you need to know about how they make purchasing decisions. What 10 questions would you ask them? Think about the type of data outlined so far in this chapter. What questions come to mind?

Next, how do you want to receive the responses? Do you want them to test a prototype before they answer the questions, or do you prefer this to be a one-on-one discussion? Perhaps it's easier to have them complete a survey online because you want to collect data from hundreds of different types of prospects so one-on-one interviews won't work. Think about what's critical to you in terms of your next steps. Are you ready?

ACTION CREATES TRIUMPHS (ACT)

Select Your Questions

Write down the 10 questions that you determined are important to obtain answers to using the worksheet at the end of the chapter. Then next to each entry, answer the following two questions:

1. What is your goal in gathering this information—basically, how will the knowledge help your business grow?

2. What method(s) is best to secure the answer? Methods could include surveys, ethnography studies, focus groups, or interviews.

Building Your Business Model

As you think about the questions you need to have answered, let's look back at the Business Model Canvas Framework to ensure these questions are front and center and, when appropriate, can be answered using one of the research methodologies discussed in this chapter:

1. **Customer Segments**
   - For whom are you creating value?
   - Who makes up the potential and target audience that you are addressing?
     - What are their key defining characteristics (i.e., demographics, behaviors)?
     - What jobs do they need to get done?
       - What is their compelling problem or pain?
       - What gains do they seek from a solution?
     - Which segment(s) are most attractive? Why?
     - Do your target customers care about how you create or offer social value?
   - How large is this market?
     - How many people or companies or organizations?
     - What evidence do you have to support this estimate?
     - What assumptions did you make? How might you confirm them?
     - How easy is it to target the market?

2. **Value Proposition**
   - What is the problem you are trying to solve or the opportunity you are attempting to seize?
   - What value do you deliver to the customer?
   - How are you creating social value?
   - Which customer needs are you satisfying?
   - What bundle(s) of products and services are you offering to each segment?
   - Are you providing social value to the communities you serve?
   - What are you specifically offering?
     - What are the most important benefits to your target audience?
     - Is value sufficient to adopt your product or service?

3. **Channels**
   - How is your target audience currently addressing the problem or need?
     - What alternatives (substitute solutions) do they have? Who's your competition?

- Through which channels do your customer segments want to be reached?
- How will you reach them?
- Are your channels integrated?
  - Do some work better than others?
- Which channels are most cost-efficient?
- Will you integrate your channels with customer routines and behaviors?

FOUR METHODS OF CUSTOMER DISCOVERY RESEARCH

It's time to review, in detail, the four methods of completing customer discovery research:

1. Survey design
2. Ethnographic studies
3. Focus groups
4. One-on-one interviews

1. Survey Design

We previously reviewed what you would ask your key customers if they were sitting in a room with you. Now, imagine that you once again have this opportunity to question your customers, but this time through an online survey where you won't be around them when they are responding to the questions. Therefore, your questions have to be absolutely clear and concise. There's no room for ambiguity, since you won't be able to clarify what you *really meant to ask*. If there is any vagueness in your questions, your responses will be meaningless, since your respondents might have misinterpreted the question, responding in a manner that didn't address the question, and you won't know it.

It's also critical that you focus your questions so that you ask only the most critical ones. Of course, we'd all love to have 100 questions answered by our potential customers. But if you create a survey with 100 questions, it's likely that your response rates will be so low that your results will be useless. If you can get between 10 to 15 focused, key questions answered by 100 of your key prospects, then you are quite likely to have enough data points to be able to understand customer needs and trends that will affect your business. Therefore, review each question that you wrote down and now, ask yourself, "What will I do with this answer?" If you cannot think of a good use for the response, then eliminate the question.

Before you launch the survey, test it with people who match the criteria of your key target audience. Ask them to complete the survey and then have them describe to you what they believe you are trying to understand from each question. If there is ambiguity, you need to change the style or wording of the question. You should also test the survey with somebody who knows little about your business. If such a person can understand the questions (even if he's not qualified to answer them), then you very likely have a clear, precise series of questions. Send it to your friends, your teachers, or even your mother. This is an inexpensive, simple, and usually effective way to determine if you're asking the questions as clearly as possible.

Remember, the goal of designing a survey is to be able to identify primary and secondary target audiences. You should focus on creating a brief survey (with approximately 12 to 15 questions including demographic data) that will help you define the needs of your prospective customers. If you have too many questions, your response rates will decrease, so you want to avoid asking too many initial questions. You can always follow up the survey with one-on-one interviews, a focus group, or even another survey.

As a result of your firsthand research, you should be able to clearly describe the demographic, psychographic/behavioral, and life-cycle characteristics of your target audience(s). Keep in mind the fact that your decision makers and/or purchasers may be a subgroup from the user profile and/or a totally different group. In this case, you might need to survey or interview them separately.

Your goal is to have your survey answered by at least 100 prospective customers who provide you with enough data to create a customer profile. We will discuss how to do that in the next chapter.

Your draft survey or script should be submitted to your professor or another expert for review and approval before you launch it to ensure that it is objective and will provide you with the answers that you need to uncover customer needs.

Question Format

It's important to understand the different formats for survey question design. The most common ones are described below. We recommend no more than two open-ended questions with the remainder closed. That will give you the opportunity to compare responses by demographics, psychographic, and life-cycle events. For example, it will be important for you to understand if the customers most interested in your solution are 25- to 35-year-old single women who score high in terms of their concern about the environment as opposed to 45- to 55-year-old married men with no interest in the environment. Your goal from the survey is to narrow your focus on what your customers care most about.

Therefore, format of question design is just as important as the questions themselves because it will be the fuel you need to analyze the survey results and design an ideal customer profile that allows you to target specific target markets.

Below are different question formats that you need to understand:

1. <u>Open Ended</u>: An open-ended question is one in which you give the person the opportunity to write down their input on a topic at length. This type of question allows them to freely respond in their own words to a question such as, "What is your greatest business challenge?" or "Given today's economy, what keeps you up at night?" While these can give you great, unbiased insight about the customers' needs, you don't want to have more than one or two of these in a survey or you may discover you are spending an incredible amount of your time analyzing what they are saying and not achieving any significant insight about your customers to be able to put them into "target groups."

2. <u>Closed ended</u>: A closed-ended question is one that seeks a short response. These are questions that you can use to compare responses across your entire base of survey respondents. Examples include the following:

   - Yes or No: This type of question is used to get a very specific answer about a need or interest. An example of this would be
     - In the past 2 years, have you purchased a bike for a child under 10 years of age?

     Yes/No

   - Rank Value: These questions ask the respondent to evaluate the importance or their agreement about the topic posed based on a scale (typically 1–5, sometimes 1–7). For example, you might ask the respondent, "On a scale of 1 to 5, with 1 being completely disagree and 5 being completely agree, please answer the following question:
     - Learning to ride a bike is an important part of growing up.

   - Multiple Select Response: This allows the respondent to pick from a variety of options and allows them to select more than one response. For example, if you are trying to understand what somebody looks for when they purchase a new bicycle, you could ask these:
     - Which of the following features are important to you when selecting a new bike for your child? (select ALL that are important)
       - Color
       - Size
       - Safety features
       - Price
       - Customer service
       - Easy repair options

- Single Select Response: This allows the respondent to pick only one feature from a variety of options. It would look exactly like the previous question except that the respondent can only select ONE of the options, not as many as they like.
  - Which of the following features is MOST important to you when selecting a new bike for your child? (select ONE only)
    - Color
    - Size
    - Safety features
    - Price
    - Customer service
    - Easy repair options
- Order Items: This type of questions asks the person to order the importance of different options. Keep in mind, this can be harder to complete because you are asking them to order them in terms of their importance and people can struggle determining which is a 2 and which a 3. This question could appear to be similar to the previous but with different results.
  - Rank the importance of the following features when selecting a new bike for your child. Rank these from 1 to 6 with 1 being most important and 6 being least.
    - Color   Rank _____
    - Size   Rank _____
    - Safety features   Rank _____
    - Price   Rank _____
    - Customer service   Rank _____
    - Easy repair options Rank _____

Tools

There are a variety of free or low-cost tools that you can use to launch your survey. You might have taken a survey in the past where the tool was used or perhaps you have even created a survey in the past. We suggest you look at the following tools and decide which is the easiest for you to use:

- Google Forms: https://docs.google.com/forms/
- Survey Monkey: https://www.surveymonkey.com/
- Qualtrics: https://www.qualtrics.com/ (Many schools already have this available for student use.)
- Typeform: https://www.typeform.com/

Introductory Cover Letter

Don't forget the importance of your cover letter, whether it's an e-mail or an actual letter that accompanies your request to complete the survey. Make sure you put the time into creating a well-written and targeted letter that speaks directly to your audience and clearly explains the value of the survey to that audience. This is as important as your elevator pitch for your company. Along with your introduction, the strength of your cover letter to convey your message will help determine the success of the survey.

Net Promoter Score

While your business is not likely ready to determine its Net Promoter Score® (NPS), it's important to understand what this metric represents. Satmetrix designed NPS as a brand loyalty measurement tool that focuses on customer experience and may be a factor in predicting growth and sustainability (n.d.). Basically, you ask customers, "On a scale of 1 to 10, how likely are you to recommend this company to a friend or colleague?" Then you calculate the percentage of loyal enthusiasts or Promoters (9 and 10 raters) minus the percentage of unhappy customers or Detractors (0 to 6). Those individuals who provide a score of 7 or 8 are considered passive and are not included in this calculation. Satmetrix defines the respondents as follows:

- **Promoters** (score 9–10) are loyal enthusiasts who will keep buying and refer others, fueling growth.
- **Passives** (score 7–8) are satisfied but unenthusiastic customers who are vulnerable to competitive offerings.
- **Detractors** (score 0–6) are unhappy customers who can damage your brand and impede growth through negative word-of-mouth.

You might have seen these questions on surveys you have participated in and wondered what they were doing with this metric. It's considered an important factor in understanding how well a business is satisfying the needs of its customers based on how likely customers are to recommend the company to a friend or colleague. Some people say it's the only question to ask in a survey. We suggest you use a variety of questions, but, when appropriate, consider this question since it describes a customer's action that can be a powerful indicator of loyalty, satisfaction, and eventual growth for a company. Many small businesses use this metric to track customer sentiment year after year to ensure they continue to satisfy customers and are aware when the numbers are going in the wrong direction so they can take action as quickly as possible to course-correct a disastrous outcome.

Let's look at an example to better understand the importance of this score. Let's say you own a chocolate shop downtown and your cousin owns a similar shop in the suburbs. You are trying to understand how loyal your customers are. You both conduct a survey, and your scores are as follows:

- **Promoters** (score 9–10): 50%
- **Passives** (score 7–8): 40%
- **Detractors** (score 0–6): 10%

Your cousin, on the other hand, receives the following scores:

- **Promoters** (score 9–10): 50%
- **Passives** (score 7–8): 2%
- **Detractors** (score 0–6): 38%

Your net promoter score is a 40, while your cousin's score is a 12. What does this say about your businesses? If you only looked at your promoters, then you might think that you are equal in terms of customer satisfaction. However, your cousin has a lot of customers who are really unhappy, with over a third of them providing low scores. Your business has fewer customers who are really unhappy, but you have a significant number who are not loyal, and if you don't make some changes, might be likely to become loyal to another chocolate company. This number alone doesn't tell you the whole story of how you are doing or how your cousin is doing, but it does shed some light on the fact that you both have customer satisfaction challenges that could lead to problems in the long term. Therefore, you will want to further investigate other questions in your survey to pinpoint what is happening with your customers and how you can course-correct.

Finally, I'd like to provide you with a variety of ways that you can improve your response rates while conducting a survey. Below is a list of proven methods that work to get you the data you need.

Boost your survey response rates

1. **Keep it simple.** Don't confuse your respondents by asking them to do anything other than complete the survey. This will dilute your message and have a negative impact on your response rates.

2. **Use clear and concise questions**. Make sure that the survey is easy to complete and understand. As with every marketing tool that you create, it's essential that you speak directly to your audience in an easily understandable tone and style. The easier the survey is to complete, the better the response rates will be.

3. **Offer a gift or premium for participating**. Make sure you're offering an item that will be an incentive to your target audience.

4. **Assure confidentiality.** This is essential. Respondents will be more willing to share honest responses with you if you let them know that what they say will be confidential.

5. **Thank them.** This basic lesson, which my parents taught me long ago, applies to all business communications. Thanking respondents for their time can only help to further promote your image as a company that cares about its customers.

6. **Tell them why.** Why is it important for you to hear from your audience? Why is it important to your customers to complete the survey? If the survey results are going to help you make decisions that will improve your customers' lives or help you develop products that are specifically designed to meet their needs, let them know that. They can't read your mind, so make sure they know why they're spending their time doing this for you.

7. **Highlight what they will get for responding.** It's important that you not only offer a gift but also clearly explain when, why, and how the winning respondent will receive it, and then follow through on your promises. For example, this can be a gift for all respondents, or for a selected winner drawn from survey respondents.

8. **Send your request from the highest or most appropriate level in the organization.** If receiving a letter from the company president or customer service director will have a strong impact on response rates, then use this strategy.

9. **Include a space for comments.** People may want to share additional thoughts with you. You never know what other information the respondents will want to tell you. I've seen these responses turn out to be the most interesting data gathered from the survey because they're unsolicited and provide you with information that you might never have thought of asking for. Customers can have the best suggestions for products and sometimes advertising venues.

10. **Allow them to respond in a variety of ways.** Many times you are tempted to request one method of communication, especially if you are conducting an online survey and your database is set up to receive information and sort it automatically. But the more options you can offer for response, the higher your response rate will be.

11. **Give them something unexpected.** Underpromise and overdeliver works in every venue of business life. If you promise them 10 methods to increase response rates, then give them 11 ways!

2. Ethnographic Studies

The world-renowned anthropologist, Dr. Margaret Mead, said, "What people say, what people do, and what they say they do are entirely different things." Understanding this is important because observation can be a very powerful tool in understanding human behavior. We introduced you to the concept of ethnography in our first chapter. Let's review what this means: Ethnography is the study and recording of human culture where a researcher observes a group that he or she is studying. The simplest way of describing an ethnographic study is to think of it as an opportunity to go to the place where you want to see and experience what your "subjects" or potential customers are doing and watch them. Hopefully you tried this when you were first identifying a problem or opportunity. Now, you should be using this to further explore the market that you have identified as having a pain that your business concept addresses. For example, let's say you are trying to understand the buying habits of 18- to 25-year-old women who frequent shopping malls to verify if your new shopping app might solve a problem you believe they are experiencing: finding the exact product they want in a large shopping mall. To observe this problem, you would go to a shopping mall to experience, with all of your senses, how they engage with the environment. You will want to take written notes and consider using video or audio recording tools or even photographing the activities.

Dr. Stephen Brand, educator at the Isenberg School of Management at the University of Massachusetts, Amherst, shared his insight around ethnography and provided us with a template for an ethnographic study that you can conduct to get comfortable with the practice. Dr. Brand explained,

> The most important power of ethnography is to not always trust what people tell you but to observe what they actually do. Traditional ethnography requires the ethnographer to live in a culture to better understand how those being studied live, work and exist as a culture and society. This is a tool that has been reinvented as an approach to understanding business, customers and service delivery. However, many people aren't familiar or necessarily comfortable with the practice of observing others and recording what they observe, without judgment.

Here's an activity that Dr. Brand shared that you could complete to get comfortable with the practice. It can be quite valuable in defining customer needs and values, and if you really pay attention, you might discover the hidden obvious. What do we mean by this term *hidden obvious*? It basically refers to something that only becomes *obvious* after you learn the answer. It's hidden in plain sight. Here's an example:

> Jacqueline and Amanda were born on the same day of the same month of the same year to the same mother and the same father—yet they are not twins. How is that possible?
>
> Solution: *They are triplets.*
>
> See how obvious the answer is, once you know it.

ACTION CREATES TRIUMPHS (ACT)
Ethnography Challenge

There are two parts to your ethnography challenge.

Part One: Observation and Note-Taking

Remember, you are in data-collection mode; do not make judgments or generate new ideas. Simply collect and document what you observe and what happens. Basically, stay naïve. Note: Not forming judgments or opinions is likely going to be harder than you might imagine.

- Deliverable: Create observation notes during a 2+ hour observation at a restaurant—anyplace where you live, work, or travel. If you decide to be more ambitious, you can visit a few locations to make comparisons. If you are really ambitious, you can observe a number of other restaurants. You might even ask friends and family members in other countries to conduct some observations for a more diverse set of data points.
- The process is quite simple. Choose a restaurant to observe.
    - If you feel comfortable, you may want to let the manager know that you will be observing employees and customers for a class project—your work will not be published or posted on the Internet.
    - Bring some way to take notes—or even take pictures—please be respectful of others.
    - Take notes as you provide thick and rich descriptions of what you observe—colors, sounds, smells, conversations, types of people, types of interactions, inside/outside, for instance.
    - Observe customers and employees. What are they doing? Do they look happy, sad, mad? What is their experience?
    - What is the infrastructure like—lighting, flooring, layout, seating, for example.
    - Look for the obvious in new ways; look for the unobvious for interesting insights.
    - You are observing with new eyes, ears, and a mindset for uncovering things that others don't realize or articulate.
- Your observations should reflect what people are saying, doing, thinking, and feeling. To better understand what they are thinking and feeling, be bold and reach out to some individuals for an interview to better understand their or their family's relationship with a specific restaurant, eating out, or other areas of inquiry that spark your interest. Remember to NOT ask them WHY they acted or engaged as you observed but ask them to retell WHAT they did. People oftentimes think they act or respond one way but, in reality, their actions are different than they realize.

> **Part Two: Insights and Recommendations**
>
> Write a memo to the management team at the restaurant. You should reflect on your observations, impressions, and thoughts. This should be in-depth and present insights and recommendations based on your ethnographic study. Your paper should include the following:
>
> - a description of how you conducted your research;
> - highlights of some of the more interesting and curious elements of your observations, including excerpts from your notes, and explaining them;
> - what you now understand and what you want to learn more about following the observation;
> - what story you can tell about the restaurant and its brand based on your observation;
> - what you have learned about how customers and employees engage.
>
> A summary of the implications of the observation activity should be presented in a format that you could review with the restaurant's executive team. The goal would be to advise them about what happens at their store and what actions or innovations they could consider, if appropriate. For example, what could the restaurant do to create a better work-place for employees or perhaps a better study environment for customers or students?
>
> For more insight, watch ethnographer Ellen Isaacs's TEDxBroadway Talk about the hidden obvious at https://www.youtube.com/watch?v=nV0jY5VgymI&feature=youtube

3. Focus Groups

A focus group can build upon what you learn in the survey or be completed before you run a survey. It can help answer specific, focused questions, especially questions that require visual aids to understand (such as evaluating a product or design). This is more subjective and open ended in nature, but it will allow you to compare the responses to your survey or interviews in order to validate the results. This is similar to the ethnography exercise because you are hearing what people are saying but also observing their reactions to your questions as well as to the comments of other individuals in the group.

Oftentimes, you will hear things that you would not have imagined as participants spark new ideas among each other and ask you and others questions that you had not considered. The goal is to allow them to build on each other's ideas, spark new ideas, and engage in what can seem like a brainstorming session. Oftentimes they will give you (the business owner) new ideas related to the product or solution that you had not thought were important or had not seriously considered. The physical nature of this allows you to watch emotions and body language to better understand customer needs and interests.

In an ideal world, you would have an unbiased facilitator run the session comprised of approximately six to 12 targeted individuals. The facilitator would be somebody who has no vested interest in the result and ideally experienced in running focus groups. Nonetheless, this is something that you can do, keeping mind the fact that groups can be subject to groupthink (one person makes a statement and others jump in and agree), so you should try to hold several focus groups to ensure that your results are valid and reliable.

Rules for running successful focus groups

- Try to include between six to 12 individuals who are part of your target market. Fewer than six and you won't have a good dialogue among the group and more than 12, it becomes hard to manage

- You will want to prescreen the participants to ensure they are individuals who fit into your customer profile, or their input won't be as valuable.

- The focus group should last approximately 45 to 90 minutes. Less than that and you won't have enough time for participants to share their views. More than 90 minutes and participants might become less engaged in the dialogue.

- You should have at least one member of your business taking very careful notes. Two is better, in case there is a lot of conversation and something important is missed or misinterpreted.

- If the group agrees, make an audio or video recording of the session(s) so that you and others can review them later for clarity. Let them know that it's being recorded only to ensure you capture everything that is being stated. This can backfire if participants are not comfortable being recorded and feel less comfortable sharing their input. Be sensitive to this.

- Start with very basic and broad questions before you begin to narrow the focus around your product. You want to make the participants comfortable with the open nature of the session.

- If you have a prototype or sample of what you are planning to offer, the ideal time to share it with the group is about halfway through the focus group. You don't want to bias the group with the "solution" before ensuring you understand their needs, values, and interests.

- The types of questions you will want to encourage are open ended and nonthreatening, encouraging the participants to share. Consider questions like the following:
  - *Tell me more about _____.*
  - *How would you improve this?*

- *When you first see this product, what is your reaction?*
- *What else comes to mind when you think about _____?*
- *How does this compare with others you have used?*

When you have completed at least one round of focus groups, carefully write the results and the recommendations, in the same way you did for the ethnography study. This information will help you build your customer profile or address issues that you need clarified from your other research methodologies.

4. One-On-One Interviews

This is a great method to use if you want to further explore the information revealed in your other research methods. Sometimes businesses start with a limited number of interviews to get a general understanding of the challenges being faced by their target market. Then they use the findings to develop the survey or focus group questions. There is no "right way" to do this. The interviews can be done before surveys or focus groups, afterward, or both. It depends on your needs and your time. Interviewers will typically use the same questions or a subset of the questions that were included in the survey or focus group and are appropriate to be conducted in person or by phone (although you cannot watch body language over the phone unless you are using Skype, FaceTime, WhatsApp, or another video chat tool). The goal is to give you a deeper level of feedback to develop your customer profile. Again, make sure that the questions are focused and unbiased so that you create knowledge.

We realize that you probably do not have a lot of experience conducting interviews. Don't panic. This is a great opportunity to learn. So while this might seem scary at first, you will likely be surprised to learn that it's not as difficult as it might appear. We suggest you start the process by identifying people you know (if appropriate) for the first round of questions. That will allow you to get comfortable with the process itself. However, if these individuals are not representative of the type of customer whom you need to capture data about, don't use the findings in your analysis. Simply think of this as a practice exercise in conducting interviews. Once you are comfortable with the process (likely after two or three completed interviews), look outside your scope of friends and family to individuals who are actual customer targets. You might need to ask for recommendations from your network to identify these people and then e-mail them requesting a brief interview. You might even find them on LinkedIn or another business network. If you are polite and explain that you are a student conducting research for a school project, they might be more willing to help you. Remember to express your appreciation for their time and reassure them that the interview won't last more than 10 to 15 minutes.

We have now spent a fair amount of time reviewing four unique yet related methods to uncover key customer data and turn that data into knowledge that helps you navigate your path to success.

ACTION CREATES TRIUMPHS (ACT)

Customer Discovery Analysis Assignment

To develop a solid marketing campaign strategy for a business, you need to be able to identify the needs of your prospect or customer base. The **Customer Discovery Analysis** assignment requires you to create a brief written survey or script for a focus group or one-on-one interviews that you can deploy with at least 100 prospective (or current, if available) customers. Your draft survey or script should be submitted to your professor for approval before you begin. You will submit a two-page, single-spaced summary of your findings, including how the results impact your business and your marketing campaign.

The goal of this assignment is to be able to identify primary and secondary target audiences. As a result of your firsthand research, you should be able to clearly describe the demographic, geographic, psychographic, and behavioral characteristics of your target audience(s). Please note that your decision makers or purchasers may be a subgroup from the user profile or a totally different group. In this case, you might need to survey or interview them separately.

What Questions Do You Need to Ask?

Below are examples of information that you need to understand before creating a marketing program. You may not be able to find answers to all of these, and you will likely have your own unique questions. Use this as a guide to begin to craft your survey and interview questions:

1. What's most important to your customers in transacting business with your company?
2. Compared to what your competition offers, what makes your products or services unique or more valuable to your customers?
3. What jobs do your customers need to get done?
4. What are the top pains or problems they now have finding a solution?
5. What gains are they looking for to address these jobs?
6. What are your customers' decision-making processes (meaning, what issues do they consider before they purchase products or services from you or from a competitor)?
7. Why do your customers value your products or services?
8. How do your customers find out about your products or services?
9. What influence does price play in your customers' decision to purchase products or services from you?
10. What role does brand loyalty play in their purchasing decision?

How Do You Begin to Discover the Answers?

You need to ask the **right** questions to reveal:

1. **Customer Gains and Pains**. Start by describing what the customers you are targeting are trying to get done. It could be the tasks they are trying to perform and complete, the problems they are trying to solve, or the needs they are trying to satisfy.
    a. **Pain points/challenges**. Except in the health care industry, "customer pain" does not refer

to a true physical pain, but refers instead to a problem or challenge that must be fixed. What pain can you resolve for your customers? Next describe the negative emotions, undesired costs and consequences, and risks that your customer experiences or could experience before, during, and after getting the job done.

b. **Gains/opportunities**. Does your product open doors for your customers or offer them the ability to further grow their business? Are you creating an opportunity for them to improve their lives? What are you helping them do better? How can you move up the value chain? Describe the benefits your customer expects, desires, or would be surprised and delighted by. This includes functional utility, social gains, positive emotions, and cost savings.

c. In Chapter 4, we will take this information to the next level and create your value proposition by addressing the following:

   i. Your products and services alleviate customer pains. How do they eliminate or reduce negative emotions, undesired costs and situations, and risks your customer experiences or could experience before, during, and after getting the job done?

   ii. Your products and services create customer gains. How do they create benefits your customer expects, desires, or would be surprised by, including functional utility, social gains, positive emotions, and cost savings?

2. **Location**. Is your business located in a place that's convenient for your customers or makes sense for their lifestyle? Sometimes businesses open a storefront because they got a really good deal on the monthly rent or because it's the only location they can afford. If your customers can't find you, whether you're on the street or in the virtual community on the Internet, then it doesn't matter how targeted your products and services are.

3. **Behavior and decision-making processes**. What behaviors or habits influence your customers' purchasing process? Do your customers need specific information before they make a decision? Do they conduct a lot of research before they purchase your product, or is your product an impulse purchase? Is timing a factor? Who is involved in the purchase decision? Do you know who their customers are?

4. **Spending patterns**. Do certain times of year influence your customers' spending patterns? Does a lifestyle change, such as getting married or having a baby, influence their decision?

5. **Price sensitivity**. How much does price influence your customers' decision? How closely is their perception of the value of your product linked to the price? You can price too high or too low, so you need to be careful in answering this question. What are the trade-offs among price, features, and performance?

(Continued)

(Continued)

Deliverables

- Survey or Script Draft: You will submit a brief survey or script (with approximately 12 to 15 questions, including demographic data) that will help you define the needs of your prospective customers. These will be reviewed and approved/finalized by the professor within 48 hours of submission. You are encouraged to submit these as soon as possible to ensure you have time to complete the survey or interview. You will then have 2 weeks to get responses to your survey or to conduct focus groups or interviews (at least 100 prospective customers must complete the survey or be interviewed by you to obtain the answers).

- Analysis and Findings: You will submit your analysis of your findings and be prepared to discuss in class how these apply to your brand and value proposition. You should identify what you have learned about customer needs on a firsthand basis, how that supports or contradicts what you have learned through secondary research (online, data sources), and what the implications are for your business goals and marketing campaign strategy. This information will be presented in a two-page write-up (single spaced) that summarizes customer needs based on the research conducted by your business team.

VIEW FROM THE TRENCHES

Chewie's Colossal Cookie Company Survey

Credit: Greg Goldstein Hartwich

While getting her MBA, Jacqueline Wingate was launching a business that provides fresh, all-natural, homemade dog food—a venture inspired by her own dog, Chewie, who needed an alternative food to treat a skin condition that he developed as a puppy.

Jacqueline could not find any fresh dog food, so after thorough research and working with an animal nutritionist, she created a balanced food that helped Chewie. Of course, Jacqueline realized that just because this product worked for her dog did not mean that there was a market for it. She understood that there's a huge difference between a bona fide business idea and simply a good idea, and she needed to conduct research to determine the feasibility of her concept.

Jacqueline began researching the pet food industry to understand where there were product gaps that she could fill. She also spoke with a variety of dog owners to try to assess their level of interest in a homemade dog food. Early results showed an interest in the product. But this secondary research was not enough. Before she invested a significant amount of money into launching this product, Jacqueline wanted to better understand her potential customers' needs. Therefore, she, along with two fellow dog-loving students, decided to conduct research that included a formal survey and a focus group.

Her initial survey is provided here. While you are reading the questions, think about whether the survey passes the "What will I do with this answer?" challenge.

In addition, consider the following:

1. How easy is the survey to complete?
2. How valid are the survey questions?
3. Were all of the questions clear?
4. Were any questions vague or misleading?
5. Do any of the questions assume knowledge that the respondent might not have?
6. Are there questions that you think should be added or eliminated?

Chewie's Colossal Cookie Company Survey: Version One

Target Audience: Dog lovers of any type conducted at pet stores—large chains & small boutiques

Product

- Would you buy this product?
- If so, would you feed this to your dog as an occasional treat or as an everyday meal?
- How often would you buy this product and at what quantities?
- What do you like/not like about the product (i.e., texture, smell, etc.)?
- Do you think your dog would like this food?
- Do you perceive any health benefits to your dog from eating a natural dog food? Any health risks?

Price

- How much would you spend for a 16 oz. container of this product?
- How much more expensive than canned dog food/dry dog food would you expect a product like this to be?
- Do special price promotions drive your purchases?

Packaging (Show them the package)

- Does this package communicate what the product is?
- Is there enough/too much color?
- Would you prefer different packaging?
- What else would you include to communicate what the product is?

Consumer Behavior

- How often do you buy dog food?
- How much do you spend per month on dog food?
- Where do you purchase dog food? Specialty pet store; natural foods store such as Whole Foods or Trader Joe's; grocery store; mass retailer such as Walmart; major pet retailer such as PetCo
- Do you have freezer space constraints?

(Continued)

(Continued)

- ✓ Would you dedicate freezer space for Chewie's Colossal Cookie Company products?

Demographics

- ✓ Age and Household Income
- ✓ Main household purchaser—who makes buying decision
- ✓ How many kids are there in the house
- ✓ How many animals/dogs—big dog/small dog

Contact/Follow-up

- ✓ Can we call you to follow up?
- ✓ Would you be interested in participating in focus group?
- ✓ Name/E-mail/Phone

Now that you've reviewed the survey, what are your thoughts? What would you change or add to make this survey more valuable for the business owner, Jacqueline, in terms of determining next steps with Chewie's Colossal Cookie Company? Below we have provided you with some things to consider to make the survey a more effective and powerful tool.

Product

1. Would you buy this product?

    Comment: Asking prospects if they would buy the product, as one of your first questions, is premature and doesn't provide you with any insight into customer interests and buying behavior. You haven't even established if this person has a need for the product, and you're asking them if they would buy it. Even if they all said *yes*, it doesn't really tell you anything valuable because it's a response made under pressure. However, if you ask them about their current buying habits, their need for specific products for their dog, and the likelihood (on a scale) of purchasing this type of product, then you will have results you can work with.

    Given the scale concept, we would suggest changing the wording:

    "On a scale of 1 to 5 (1 being very unlikely, 5 being very likely), how likely are you to buy this product in the next 3 months?"

2. If so, would you feed this to your dog as an occasional treat or as an everyday meal?

    Comment: This is your second question after showing them the product. At this point in the survey, you have not even established what they currently feed their dog, how this product might meet their needs, and if they are even your right target audience. In addition, they might want to feed this to their dog as a treat and a meal, but you've limited their response to one or the other. We are not sure this question is valid at this point in the survey process and should be eliminated.

3. How often would you buy this product and at what quantities?

    Comment: To begin with, these are two different questions. Even if they're broken into separate questions, the respondents' frequency of purchase may not mean anything since they do not have enough information about the product to know what size it comes in, how long it lasts, and so forth. They need a lot more information before they can answer this question with any data that will help you make a decision.

4. What do you like/not like about the product (i.e., texture, smell)?

Comment: This question also requires a scale system and relevance to their purchasing decision. Perhaps they dislike aspects but they're not important in the decision-making process. Just because it smells and you do not like the smell does not necessarily mean you won't buy the product. A better way to state this would be to separate product features and ask this: On a scale of 1 to 5, how important is texture to you when you purchase dog food? Then ask about smell or other details. The responses to these types of questions will give you more data to work with that will help you determine which features of the product are critical in the purchasing decision.

5. Do you think your dog would like this food?

   Comment: Honestly, how will the owner know if the dog will like the product? Is that answer going to give you any relevant information to use? If it doesn't, it should be eliminated since there are many questions in this survey, and you want to be sure your respondents answer all of the important ones and don't get bogged down with meaningless questions.

6. Do you perceive any health benefits to your dog from eating a natural dog food? Any health risks?

   Comment: How important are health benefits or risks to dog owners? We believe that's really what you want to know and if these perceptions play a role in the decision-making process. If that's the answer you need, then you should change the wording of the question to read, On a scale of 1 to 5, how important are health benefits in determining which dog food you purchase?

Price

7. How much would you spend for a 16 oz. container of this product?

   Comment: Pricing questions are very difficult. At this point in time, it's more important for you to understand how much they currently spend on their dog food purchases versus asking them how much they would spend on this one item. Your responses will likely range from 50 cents to $15, providing you with completely useless information.

8. How much more expensive than canned dog food/dry dog food would you expect a product like this to be?

   Comment: Are you expecting a percentage, a dollar amount, or something else? What will you do with these responses in a way that will provide you with any relevant data? Price is a combination of cost, perception, what the market will bear, competition, and other factors. Why ask how much more they would expect this to be if they don't know enough about the product to make that decision?

9. Do special price promotions drive your purchases?

   Comment: Very few people will state, "No, I never buy products on sale." Again, you could use a scale 1 to 5 and ask, How much does price influence your purchase? You're trying to determine how these factors (price, smell, texture, health benefits, etc.) are important to the decision-making process. In addition to using a scale, another way to uncover this answer is to have them rank these qualities in order of importance.

(Continued)

(Continued)

Chewie's Colossal Cookie Company Final Survey: Version Two

Here are the revisions Jacqueline made to the survey to help her determine next steps for her company.

We represent a local company starting a business making all-natural homemade dog food. This new dog food is **fully cooked**—it is not a raw or "barf" diet. It is made from all-natural ingredients including ground turkey or beef, beef liver, spinach, carrots, broccoli, barley, brown rice, and oats. This is a fresh product—it's not canned or dry. It will be sold frozen in packaging that can be quickly defrosted in the microwave or refrigerator. We thank you for your time and value your comments and suggestions.

****

1. How many dogs do you have?

    1   2   3   More than 3

2. Who makes the pet food buying decision in your household?

    Myself   Spouse   Children   Vet   Other _____

3. What type of dog food do you buy? (Check all that apply)

    Dry   Canned   Other _____

4. How often do you buy dog food?

    Once per month   2 X per month
    3 X per month   More than 3 X per month

5. Where do you primarily purchase dog food? (Check only 1 box)

    Small, independently owned pet stores
    Natural foods store (such as Whole Foods)
    Grocery store   Mass retailer (e.g., Walmart)
    Mass Pet Retailer (e.g., PetSmart)
    Online   Other _____

6. Name of store(s) where you purchase dog food _____

7. How much do you spend per month on dog food?

    Less than $10 $10 to $50
    $51 to $100 $100 +

Please indicate the extent to which you agree or disagree with each of the following statements (1 = completely disagree and 5 = completely agree)

8. Money is no object when it comes to my dog.   1 2 3 4 5

9. I think of my dog as a member of the family.   1 2 3 4 5

10. My dog's health is as important as my own.   1 2 3 4 5

11. My dog deserves only the best quality food.   1 2 3 4 5

12. I am knowledgeable about current dog-related issues in the news   1 2 3 4 5

13. Have you ever fed your dog fresh dog food (not canned or dry)?

    Yes   No

14. Do you perceive any health benefits to your dog from eating a fresh, natural dog food?

    Yes   No   Don't know

On a scale of 1 to 5 (1 = definitely not likely and 5 = very likely), how likely are you to

15. Buy fresh, all natural dog food as an alternative to   1 2 3 4 5

    dry or canned dog food *within the next 6 months?*

16. Dedicate freezer space to frozen dog food? 1 2 3 4 5

Please rate the following considerations in terms of buying fresh, all-natural dog food. (1 = not important at all and 5 = extremely important)

17. Price 1 2 3 4 5
18. Availability 1 2 3 4 5
19. Nutritional value 1 2 3 4 5
20. Dog's preference 1 2 3 4 5
21. Vet recommended 1 2 3 4 5
22. Health considerations of your dog (such as allergies, etc.) 1 2 3 4 5

You're almost done. Please share a little about yourself to help us analyze the data.

23. Your age

    Under 18   18–24   25–39   40–55   Over 55

24. Gender

    Male   Female   Non-binary/transgender   Prefer Not to Answer   Other _____

25. Marital status

    Single   Married

26. Do you have children?

    Yes   No

27. Can we contact you to follow up?

    Yes   No

    Name_____

    Phone Number_____

    E-mail address_____

28. Would you be interested in participating in a focus group?

    Yes   No

29. Comments or suggestions?

AHAs

Lessons and Takeaways

Let's recap highlights of this third chapter, focused on customer discovery:

An essential element that separates successful companies from those that are struggling is their ability to turn information about customers' needs into knowledge that can be used to make sound business decisions. You need to turn those facts—the raw data—into knowledge by adding your own analysis and primary research, and then use this to create value for your business.

You must clearly ask customers and prospects what they value before you leap into designing a product or service that "you" believe is valuable but have not yet confirmed that the market agrees with you.

(Continued)

(Continued)

Four key methods to learn more about customer needs include surveys, ethnographic studies, focus groups, and one-on-one interviews.

There are three categories that reflect important characteristics that you need to be aware of as they relate to your customers' needs. These are (1) demographics, (2) psychographic/behavioral influences, and (3) life-cycle events.

Strategyzer's Value Proposition Canvas reinforces the notion that there are jobs that customers need to accomplish. Jobs might be functional like trying to "create healthy meals for their family" or socially or emotionally oriented like "trying to secure a better status in their community." Once you have identified the jobs to be accomplished, then you think about the pains and gains associated with getting these jobs done.

Question design format is just as important as the questions themselves because it will be the fuel you need to analyze the survey results and design an ideal customer profile that allows you to target specific target markets.

TOOLKIT

Worksheet 3.1: Resources for Proper Survey Design

Here are valuable resources to help you design your survey along with a checklist to measure your achievement of the survey goals.

Sample Survey Questions, Answers, and Tips

- ✓ http://www.constantcontact.com/aka/docs/pdf/survey_sample_qa_tips.pdf
- ✓ http://blogs.constantcontact.com/category/surveys-and-feedback/

Google Analytics Solutions: Surveys

- ✓ http://www.google.com/insights/consumersurveys/how

Survey Template Library

- ✓ http://www.questionpro.com/a/showLibrary.do?categoryID=5&mode=1

Survey Checklist

After you have drafted your first survey, use the checklist below to make sure you've met these critical objectives:

- ✓ The survey is the message.
- ✓ Use clear and concise questions.

- ✓ You know what you will do with each answer.
- ✓ A gift or premium is offered for participating.
- ✓ A thank-you for participating emphasized.
- ✓ Explain why it's important to complete the survey.
- ✓ Highlight what people get for responding.
- ✓ The request is sent from the highest or most appropriate level in the organization.
- ✓ Space for comments is included.
- ✓ A gift is offered in advance.
- ✓ Confidentiality is assured.
- ✓ A variety of response methods is offered.
- ✓ A bonus or unexpected item is offered.
- ✓ You have tested your survey with friends or colleagues to ensure that it's clear and concise.
- ✓ Do any of the questions assume knowledge that the respondent might not have?
- ✓ Are any questions vague or misleading?
- ✓ Are there questions that you can eliminate without negatively affecting the survey?
- ✓ Are there additional questions that you should ask?
- ✓ Do questions include a ranking or scale system to ensure that you receive responses that force the respondents to evaluate the likelihood or importance of each question?
- ✓ Survey follow-up has been prepared for, including possible interviews, focus groups, or meetings.

CHAPTER FOUR

LISTENING TO THE VOICE OF THE CUSTOMER

Learning Objectives

In this chapter, you will learn to

- secure critical information about your customers to create a prototype of your product or service with them.
- actively listen to stakeholder feedback based on their interactions with your product or service.
- design simple prototypes of the products and services that you want to deliver.
- create customer profiles (also referred to as *customer personas*) that reflect your customers' values, beliefs, and decision-making processes.

HOW DO YOU HEAR THE VOICE OF YOUR CUSTOMER?

While it's obviously important that you understand the benefits and value of the products and services that you offer customers, it's even more critical that you understand the benefits your customers experience from engaging with your company. We acknowledge the fact that many companies have launched their businesses focused entirely on their product (versus customer). However, it is a rare company that can launch a business this way and create a sustainable business model. Without clearly focusing on how your customers' needs are being addressed, now and into the future, your growth will be stunted. This is because customer needs evolve over time, and if you focus only on your products or services you will diminish your ability to recognize new, changing opportunities that align with your value proposition—which must reflect customer needs and not simply product features.

Why is it critical to understand and hear customers' motivations and needs? Let's consider a very simple business model. You are running a small café, and you believe that the reason customers frequent your shop is that you have the best coffee in town. However, the real reason they visit your café is that they love the croissants you serve. Unfortunately, you didn't realize this critical fact because most customers come in and buy coffee and croissants together. Therefore, if you decide to switch bakers to save money, your revenue would likely decrease dramatically and you'd be at a complete loss for an explanation—all because you didn't truly understand your customers' needs—what motivated them to buy from you. On the other hand, if you understand how important the croissants are and recognize the lesser role the coffee plays, you might be able to save money by switching to a less expensive or perhaps more desirable coffee brand and avoid damaging your profit margin (you might even increase it if the new coffee is a hit). Alternatively, you could provide other baked goods or even consider a whole new line of food items. Clearly identifying customers' true needs is critical throughout the life cycle of any business.

PROTOTYPES TO HELP IDENTIFY PROFILES

Rapid Prototyping is . . . a mindset for how own approaches learning. Doing is the best type of thinking.

Tom Chi, Former Head of Experience, Google X

Studying and responding to customers' needs early on in the development phase is easier than trying to redesign products or services at some point in the future when you are already rolling out your new products. Therefore, it's important to begin this process by using prototypes and MVPs (minimum viable products) to demonstrate the value of your solution. This will help you confirm its validity or provide insight so you can adjust early on in the process, aligning your customers' needs with the value you provide.

Before we begin to align prototypes with customer needs, let's start with a definition of a *prototype*. A prototype, in its simplest form, is basically a model of a product or a service that shows some (but not necessarily all) of the features of the envisioned final deliverable. Oftentimes, companies will create a prototype so they can share their vision with others and get feedback. There are many useful benefits associated with creating prototypes because it allows your potential customers and other stakeholders to interact with the product or service. Benefits to designing prototypes include the following:

1. <u>Customer Validation</u>: Helps validate if the customer is indeed interested in the product or service by allowing them to see what "you" the business owner sees. This is important because many times you will hear somebody describe a product, but without seeing it, your vision is quite different from the one the other person has.

2. <u>Customer-Product Interaction</u>: Allows you to experience it and interact with the product beyond the description somebody shared with you (as we explained above). Depending on the end product, you might be able to use the following senses to experience the product:

    a. Sight: examples include most products that you only previously heard about. For services, you can visualize how the flow of the service might be experienced.

    b. Smell: examples include food products, beverages, soaps.

c. Auditory/Hearing: examples include music, kitchen appliances, food packaging. (We'll explain this one later in the chapter.)

d. Taste: examples include food, beverages, vitamins.

e. Touch: examples include linens, pillows, mobile devices.

3. <u>Customer Interaction With Services</u>: It's equally important to understand how customers engage with services that are clearly intangible. Using the SERVQUAL model designed by Parasuraman, Berry, and Zeithaml (1988, 1991), the following factors are important elements to measure, and you can gain valuable insight from asking questions about these when designing a prototype:

   a. **Reliability:** the ability to perform the promised service dependably and accurately

   b. **Assurance:** the knowledge and courtesy of employees and their ability to convey trust and confidence

   c. **Tangibles:** the appearance of physical facilities, equipment, personnel, and communication materials

   d. **Empathy:** the provision of caring, individualized attention to customers

   e. **Responsiveness:** the willingness to help customers and to provide prompt service

4. <u>Funder Buy-In</u>: You might require funding to go from idea to final product ready for market entry. If you need to engage funders, having a prototype to show them will strengthen your ability to convey the value of your product.

5. <u>Management or Team Buy-In</u>: Oftentimes, different members of a team have a different vision for a product—even if you have all been discussing the product for months. Creating a prototype will provide the sensory experience that allows you to see what you are talking about and confirm if you are all indeed on the "same page" or if you have quite different visions of the end product.

6. <u>User Feedback to Refine</u>: It's rare that you will create a product in isolation. It will require a variety of models that continue to evolve to meet customer needs based on continuous feedback that you receive.

Getting feedback from customers using a prototype may seem obvious, but unfortunately many companies simply skip this step in developing their organization. Some simply are so passionate about their solution that they are convinced that they do not need to ask prospects what they think. Others believe that prototyping is too expensive for them. However, prototypes do not require an enormous budget that only Fortune 500 companies can afford. The reality of prototyping is that it is designed to be rapid in nature and use material that is readily available or not too difficult to access. While prototypes can be made out of ordinary household products like cardboard (cereal boxes) and string, you should explore the use of 3D printers, when available. These machines provide a relatively fast, easy, and relatively inexpensive way to create an example of the physical product that you want to design. This gives your prospects, investors, and even members of your own team something they can hold, interact with, and comment on. Your school might have one that is available to use, so it's worth exploring this option further. Remember, however you design your prototype, you are not attempting to sell this product—only provide users with an experience so you can watch them engage with the product and secure feedback.

Businesses do not operate in isolation, and asking for feedback from stakeholders who "are not in love with the product" can make the difference between success and failure. Do you remember that we mentioned that food packaging was on the list of auditory or hearing experiences? Here's our example of a company, SunChips®, that produced a snack item that was quite popular, but it misfired on the packaging of the product as it went to market.

The SunChips® Package Story

SunChips® is a brand of fried, ripped, multigrain chips that was launched in 1991 by Frito-Lay (a unit of PepsiCo). In April 2008, Frito Lay introduced a compostable package for the SunChips® product line. The bag was made from plant-based material designed to decompose within 14 weeks in a hot, active compost pile. Unfortunately, Frito-Lay had to take the package off the market because of the excessive noise it created. The company even posted the following on its own Facebook page on February 24, 2011:

> You asked for a quieter bag and we heard you loud and clear. Original SunChips® snacks now come in a new compostable bag that's twice as quiet as our last one. Filled with the same SunChips® taste you've come to love, our new bags are rolling out in stores as we speak so grab one soon and tell us what you think. We're listening!

The noise was so loud and irritating that a Facebook group titled "Sorry, But I Can't Hear You Over This Sun Chips Bag" was created. As of the writing of this book, this group had over 41,000 likes. While the bag was clearly environmentally friendly, it turned out that this benefit wasn't valued enough by consumers who would not tolerate the noise created by the plant-based material.

Want to hear the "noise" yourself? Check out this 2010 YouTube video, *Super-Noisy Sun Chips*: www.youtube.com/watch?v=kki32mt8p6w&t=20s

While we have no inside knowledge about the research conducted by Frito-Lay in advance of launching this compostable package, an article published by ABC News, written by Charisse Jones and *USA Today* (n.d.) implies that research about the importance of packaging as it relates to concerns for the environment was conducted (although perhaps not directly for Frito-Lay).

> A January report by The Hartman Group, a market researcher, found that packaging was key for consumers who are concerned about the environment.
>
> "It was almost like a marker or indicator as to how good or bad a company may be," says Laurie Demeritt, the agency's president. "And in most cases, when they thought about packaging (they asked), 'What can happen to it after I get it home? Is it recyclable? Is it biodegradable?'"
>
> Of the 1,600 people surveyed for the report, 75% said it was at least somewhat important that packaging be recyclable, while 51% felt it was at least somewhat important that it be compostable, meaning it breaks down with the presence of oxygen and water.

There's no arguing with the fact that consumers care about the environment and Frito-Lay was focused on addressing these needs. It gets lots of accolades on that front. However, it does lead one to question IF it actually tested the package with consumers before introducing it to the market. Did consumers have the opportunity to interact with a prototype (through touch, sight, and hearing) prior to the product launch? It's hard to believe that this happened, since it seems as if the reaction to the product would have sent them back to the labs to create a quieter version of the eco-friendly package.

PROTOTYPING THE GOOGLE WAY

Another great example of rapid prototyping in action is the way Google designed the Google Glass.

During his TEDYouth Talk in 2012, Tom Chi explained how his team at Google X built 150 hardware prototypes in 3 months for Google Glass with a $20,000 budget and a three-person team. Google X is a semi-secret division of Google that is responsible for projects like Google Glass, autonomous driving vehicles, contact lenses that monitor glucose through tears, and lots more, You can watch his TEDEd Talk at https://ed.ted.com/lessons/rapid-prototyping-google-glass-tom-chi.

One important follow-up note about Google Glass is that from the consumer perspective, the product was far from a success. From an early adopter perspective, Google Glass was seen as rather creepy, raising concerns about privacy, aesthetically unappealing, and didn't have a clear function (job) that would support consumer interest in buying the product (at a steep price point). However, Alphabet (Google's parent company) didn't abandon the product. Instead, it recognized something important from this failure; it was targeting the wrong market. When it began to explore options for industrial use, it recognized that there was great value in this market. For companies like GE, Boeing, and DHL, the glasses helped with productivity and quality on their manufacturing floors (Levy, 2017). In many ways, the rollout in the consumer market was similar to a prototype exercise for the business and industrial market. Google took the lessons learned about challenges with the product experience and used them to more clearly define their market.

BEYOND PHYSICAL PRODUCTS: PROTOTYPING SERVICES AND APPS

You may be wondering if prototyping is applicable to you if you are considering launching a service business or perhaps creating a mobile app. Yes, those things that you can't reach out and touch can definitely be prototyped. In many cases, it's even more important to prototype these intangibles because by their very nature, they are much harder to understand since they are limited by one's inability to touch and see them. How you would best approach a prototype for a service or a mobile app? There are several ways you can achieve this:

1. Storyboards
2. Role-plays
3. Website and social media test sites

Storyboards

Storyboards are visual displays that tell the story (in sequence) of your business or the product. It's basically taking your words and putting them into pictures to tell a story. Many people think of these for films and videos, and that's a very common use. They allow you to stretch your imagination and put on paper what you see in your head. Beyond creating a movie, this is a great way for you to convey what you are imagining for your business or product. For example, let's say you have a business idea and you need some initial funding from friends or family. You are thinking about offering a service that delivers snacks to students on campus starting a 7 p.m. and running until 3 a.m. (when many students are working on homework and papers). You've decided to call this business NightNRG (pronounced Night Energy). To create a storyboard you could create a series of images showing how customers would order the snack, how they would pay, and then how the service is delivered to them. You can even include how you would get your supplies, how customers would find out about your business, and how easily they can refer new business to you by sharing with their friends. A picture is worth a thousand words, so creating a visual that explains this clearly to others beyond just telling them can be a powerful way to persuade potential investors (think Mom and Dad).

Role-Plays

Role-plays, from a business perspective, are ways of acting out scenarios that would occur in your business. For example, you believe that NightNRG is going to be a winner, but you're having a hard time explaining the process to somebody else. A role-play would be an opportunity to practice your pitch (business explanation) with potential customers. You could ask a few friends to play the role of hungry students who are working on a presentation due the next day in class. It's 11 p.m., and the only option is a vending machine full of unhealthy options. A fellow student, Amanda, has heard about your service from another friend and has called you to find out how it works. The role-play would involve you answering her questions and describing the service. You might even ask Amanda to ask tough questions and really push you into justifying *why* she should order from you. This would allow you to practice your pitch or business explanation and answer questions and concerns from prospective customers. It will likely lead you to review how you present the business and might even lead to changes to the business. For example, Amanda might ask about healthy food options or why you charge so much. You need to be prepared to answer these questions, and if you learn from enough students that healthy snacks at night are most desirable, you might change your product mix and how you describe the benefits of your products.

Website and Social Media Test Sites or Landing Pages

One of the most powerful ways to test a new product or service is to allow prospects to "play" with it in an interactive manner. Let's continue to use the NightNRG example. Perhaps you have confirmed that students are interested in ordering late snacks from you. However, they've made it clear that they don't want to call you to do this. They want to have the ability to order it from a website or mobile app with the goal of having it delivered in 30 minutes or less to their dorm room. The good news is that they're interested. The challenge is that you're not sure if you can create an easy-to-use app or website that meets their needs and allows you enough time to deliver the snacks to them in time. However, your best friend is a programmer, so you want to give it a try. Therefore, you hire your friend to create a simple home page (it doesn't have to be a fully designed website) and a complementary app that can be used on a mobile device. You let her know that the major features (ordering and paying) need to work, but the layout doesn't have to be fully functional for your prototype site because you're still in the testing phase. Hopefully, she can create this quickly (less than 2 weeks as opposed to a 3- to 6-month development time for the full site or app). Then you can share this with prospects and get their reaction to using the site or app before you begin the longer process. This could save you time and money in the future because users will likely point out things that they like and find easy to use and areas that need improvement. This is really critical because many times individuals design a significant part of a site or app and then test it, only to discover that they need to scrap 80% of the project. At that point, they have likely lost time and lots of money because they didn't get enough customer feedback in advance of moving to the next stage of the process. This is also known as an agile development process. Agile is a style of managing projects that divides the development steps into phases of work. It is oftentimes associated with software development but can easily be applied to other ways of working. Using Agile methodology, you would use the feedback and learning secured at the end of EACH phase to reassess the process before moving onto the next phase.

VIEW FROM THE TRENCHES

Meet Aimee: The Aimee Bio Story

Aimee Bio (Aimee) is a tech start-up launched by Tony Feghali in Beirut, Lebanon. Tony came up with the idea of Aimee in 2014 with the goal of providing youth the ability to showcase their experience, skills, and expertise, academically and through non-school-related activities. Think of it as a LinkedIn for individuals 13 to 21 years old. To keep the idea alive, Tony competed and won a seat in the UK Lebanon Tech Hub 2015 accelerator program. Aimee went through a series of iterations before it was soft-launched to the public in October 2017.

So, you're probably asking yourself, "What is Aimee?" Tony likes to describe Aimee in a variety of ways using a unique customer persona for each market he was targeting. He did this because he understood that the value proposition for Aimee varied by the user, and he wanted to ensure that users understood what Aimee would mean to them. For example, assuming Aimee was a person and he was talking to the student target market he would say, "She is the young, friendly, laid-back lady in charge of student affairs—the one whose office you visit on your own time to chat, the one you confide in, and the one who drives you to maximize your potential." If he was describing Aimee to parents, he would say, "Aimee is your kids' home away from home—someone who spends her days with them, gets to know them closely, understands and guides them." Finally, if Aimee were being introduced to teachers, he would explain that "She's the colleague who's likable and seasoned in the workings of the world, whose opinions and advice are valued. She is knowledgeable and wise."

But Aimee Bio is not a person. It's a mobile and web-based app that has a compelling purpose at the core of its mission: to take teenagers and young adults seriously and revolutionize the way they are publicly perceived, academically and beyond. Want to hear more?

Aimee Bio is designed to empower youth to be themselves, to do the things they put their heart into, to share that persona with others, and connect with those who are not only like-minded but also different. Aimee recognizes that youth have more to offer than the

(Continued)

(Continued)

academics described on their CV or résumé or through a LinkedIn profile, which is why Aimee's goal is to shine the light on the areas of their life that include their interests, activities, hobbies, and volunteer work, in addition to their academic performance. It's a more holistic approach to describing who each person is who creates a bio with Aimee.

Aimee empowers youth to do a variety of important tasks:

1. Keeping track of their activities, achievements, and awards—from cross-country training to attending a workshop, volunteering for an organization, or getting lifeguard certification.
2. Connecting with students from all corners of the globe who (don't) have similar interests to theirs. They can follow other students' personal bios and connect with them individually or in a group.
3. Following club pages—Whether they belong to those clubs or not, students can follow pages that spark their interest.
4. Developing their bio into a résumé—The data accumulated within the Aimee bio can easily be exported into an MS Word document résumé when students are applying to universities or looking for an internship or part-time job.
5. Sharing their thoughts and favorite moments—They call these items *Dailees*. This is a space where students can post pictures and stories of what they are doing or keep them private as memories to look back on.

Aimee also connects youth to stakeholders like schools, universities, companies, clubs, and NGOs by allowing these organizations to create their own pages, creating a two-way communication link between the youth and these organizations. Through their bios, youth get a better chance to access and present themselves to organizations that in turn get a more rounded perspective of their story.

Now that you understand what Aimee Bio is and the value proposition it offers, think about how you would storyboard this or even create a test website or app for Aimee.

NOW the story of how Aimee was prototyped.

After Tony and his team came up with the idea, they were awarded an opportunity to participate in a Business Accelerator Program that included a 6-month residency in London for business ideas that showed the most progress. The idea grew from Tony's time in London, since it gave him the opportunity to explain his concept of Aimee to experts in a variety of fields who critiqued and scrutinized the concept. They pushed the idea to its limits, tested and challenged the concept until Tony was confident that Aimee was finally ready to be designed into an actual layout as a mobile/web app.

After the experience in London, a firm specializing in in user experience (UX) and user interface design (UI) was hired to help Tony and his team turn Aimee's layout into an actual wireframe (a series of images that help explain the functional elements of a website or app). The consultancy worked closely with the Aimee team to develop the concept, the app theme, colors, fonts, and the general layout. Several rounds of discussions with customers were conducted focusing on teenagers of diverse backgrounds to get their input about the idea and whether or not they would be interested in using such an app. Additional questions were raised about the length of time these teenagers spend on their mobile devices, understanding their use of social media such as Twitter, Snapchat, Instagram, Facebook, and LinkedIn and clarifying which apps consume most of their time. This gave them a stronger understanding of the target market and helped them shape a profile or customer persona describing the type of customer who would have the strongest need for and interest in using Aimee.

The wireframes were designed based on the insight they gathered from their prospective teenage customers. With wireframes in place, the specifications for their software was developed next showing detailed screens, fields, and business functionalities. The development team used the *Agile* method of development, which focuses on quick releases or iterations rather than long-planned product releases. The following images capture the stages of development that the team experienced.

Figure 4.1 Aimee Logo

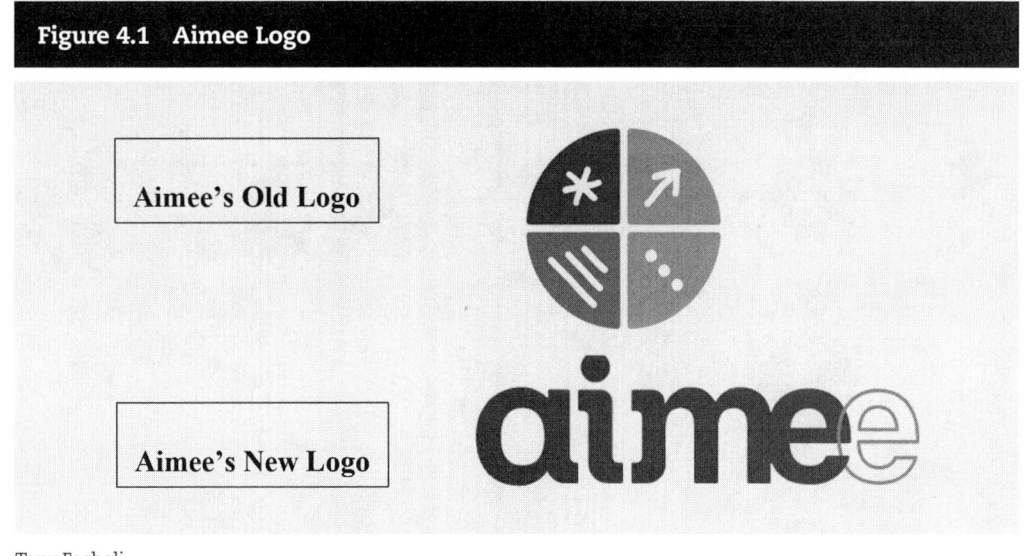

Tony Feghali

(Continued)

(Continued)

Figure 4.2 Initial Wireframes—User Interface Prototype Used for the Initial Customer Research

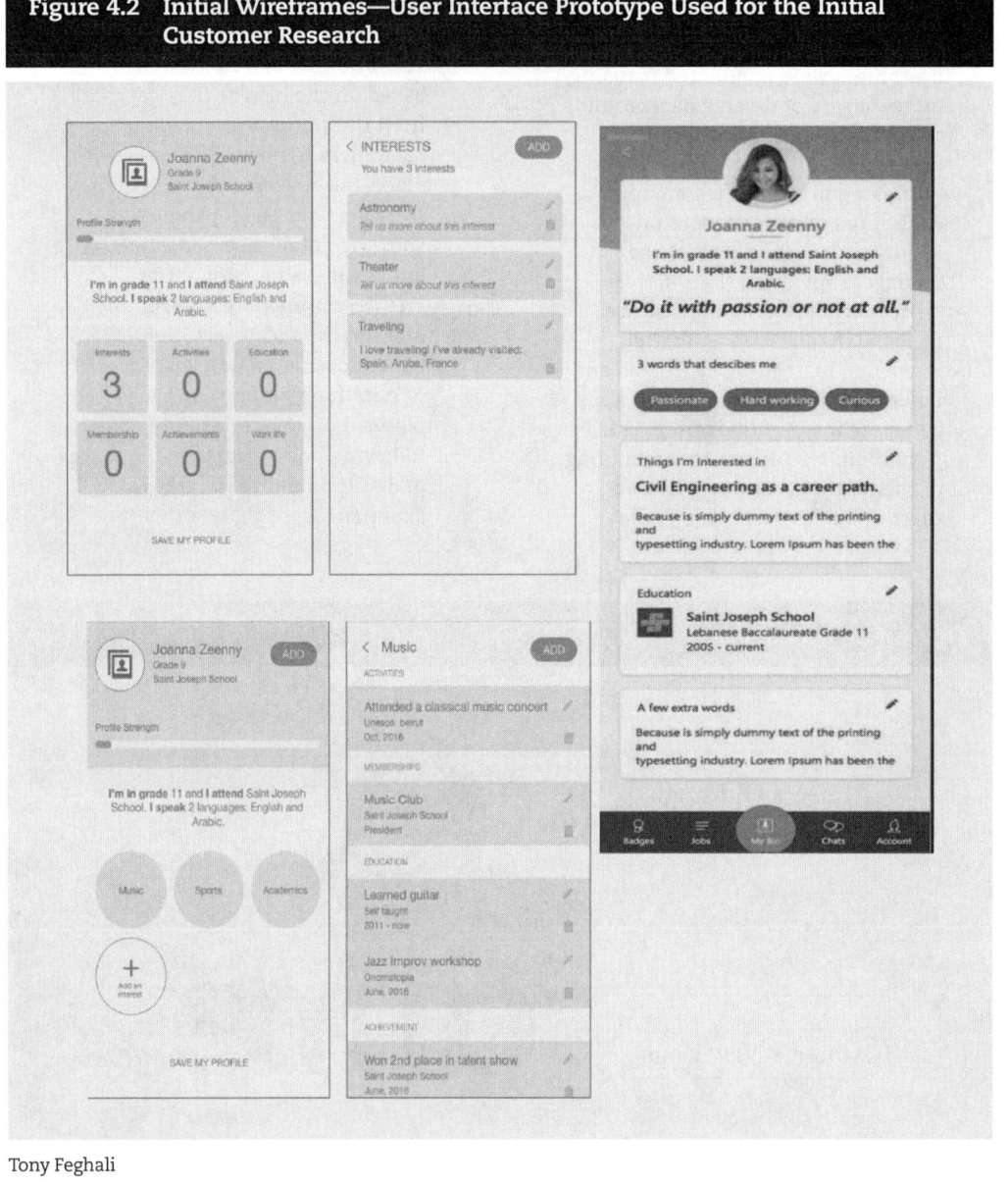

Tony Feghali

Figure 4.3 Next Stage of Development for Aimee Following the Completion of Market Research

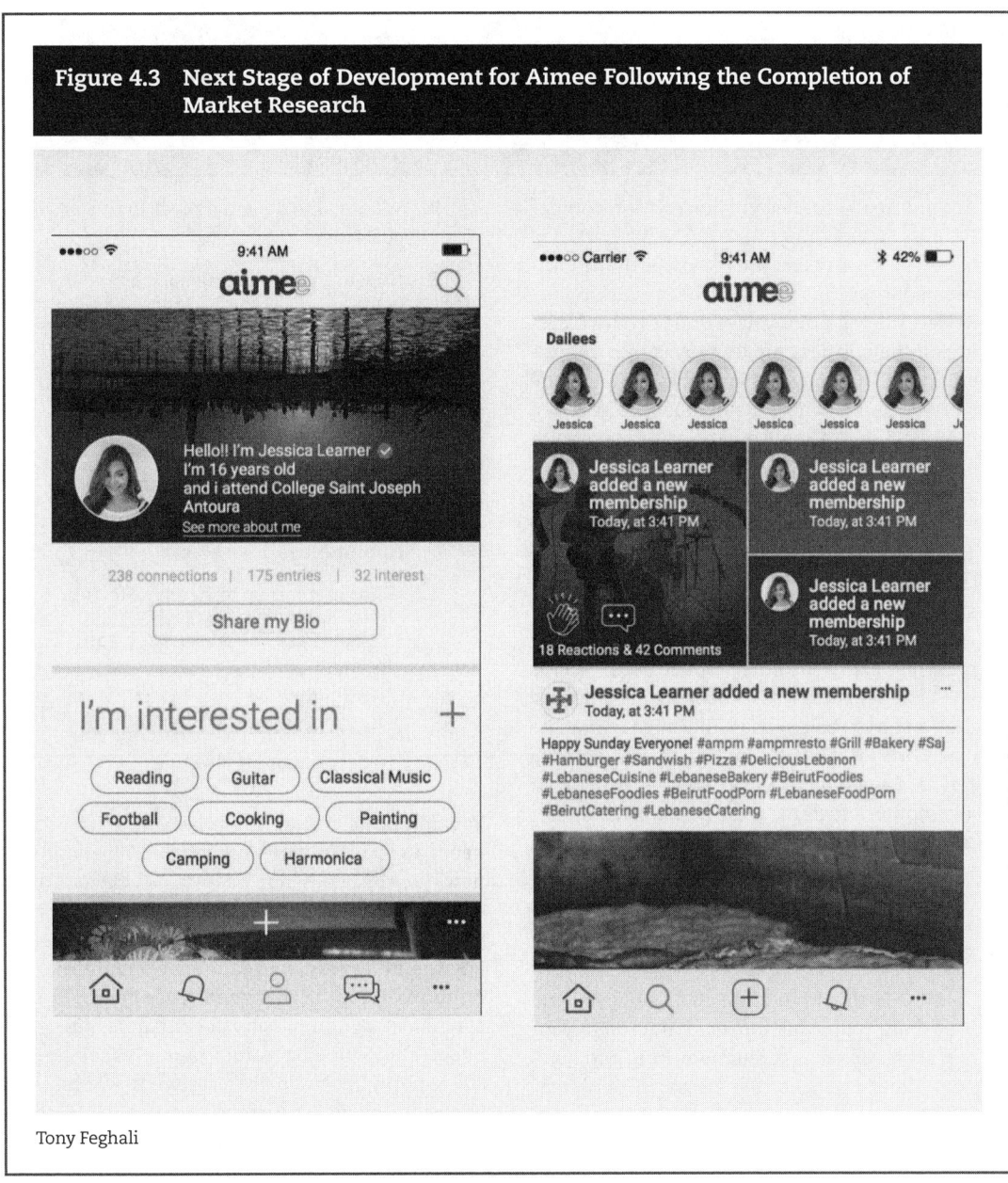

Tony Feghali

For more ideas on prototyping, visit IDEOU's blog, 6 Tips for How to Prototype a Service at www.ideou.com/blogs/inspiration/6-tips-for-how-to-prototype-a-service.

ACTION CREATES TRIUMPHS (ACT)

Now on to Your Prototype

Are you ready to design your own prototype? Here's your assignment.

Your job is to create a prototype of the business concept that you have been working on. Review the work that you've done to date focusing on the business model canvas that you are creating. Your canvas should begin to tell the story of your business. Remember the goal of a prototype is to allow you and your stakeholders (customers, investors, employees, etc.) to visualize your team's idea so they can provide feedback that helps you continue to design the end product or service. Your prototype can be three-dimensional, but it doesn't have to be. It all depends on the actual product or service that you are delivering. Your goal is to allow the other person to experience the product, see its shape and size, or experience its benefits in some way that involves their senses. You might draw the experience (storyboard it) or project it onto a screen. Even if a product is an app, website, or a computer program, using paper or computer projections that describe the steps involved with engaging with the product will save you time and money if the idea doesn't make sense to others.

Building Your Business Model

Your focus should to think about how you can best share your value proposition through your prototype. Below is a reminder from the business model canvas of the messaging and benefits that you want the customer to embrace through your prototype.

1. What is the problem you are trying to solve or the opportunity you are attempting to seize?
2. What value do you deliver to the customer?
3. How are you creating social value?
4. Which customer needs are you satisfying?
5. What bundle(s) of products and services are you offering to each segment?
6. Are you providing social value to the communities you serve?
7. What are you specifically offering?
   - What are the most important benefits to your target audience?
   - Is value sufficient to adopt your product or service?

You might be wondering what material you need to create your prototype. The good news is, this does not have to be expensive or require fancy material. You should use your creatively to design the prototype, ideally spending very limited money on material. Prototypes can be designed from cardboard, clay, construction paper, rubber bands, string, paper clips, playing cards, pipe cleaners, or straws. You get the point. Use what you have to create a visual experience for the end user. We suggest you brainstorm with your team before going out and getting material (ideally, what you already own).

Don't spend weeks designing your first prototype. The goal as a team is to quickly

> create one (perhaps give yourselves 2 hours). Then, as a team, decide if it's ready for input by others or if the team thinks you can improve it—quickly. Once you have created a prototype that you are ready to share with others, the next step is to think about whom you want to get feedback from related to its value. That's where the customer profiles come into play. However, before we create the customer profile, we want you to stay on your product or service for a little longer. Next, we will talk about the difference between a prototype and an MVP (minimum viable product).

GOING FROM PROTOTYPE TO MVP

All of these benefits will provide you with feedback you and your company need to rethink and refine your prototype, getting it closer to an MVP. You can gain even more important feedback by creating an MVP because it allows you to conduct a soft launch of your product before you begin to more seriously infiltrate the market. Minimum refers to the fact that while it delivers value to the user, it's usually still barebones in design. Viable refers to the fact that you have proven that it's feasible (you can actually create it and the user can actually engage with it in a manner similar to engaging with the end product). Therefore, you should get even more valuable feedback about its value proposition to your desired target market. Finally, the *P* for product means that it actually works. According to Madeleine Burry (2014),

> Dropbox's MVP was a video showing how to use the application. Before this near-indispensable file-sharing service was built, Dropbox cofounder and CEO Drew Houston knew there were already tons of cloud storage start-ups, and while Dropbox would offer something different and more effective, development wouldn't be easy, since a product that works across platforms and operating systems is innately tricky. If Dropbox created the application, would users sign up?
>
> To find out, Houston posted a three-minute video on Hacker News in April, 2007, showing users how to use the product on his desktop. The video played to the right audience: users had lots of helpful comments and feedback, and as well as pointing out potential problems, Houston collected 70,000 email addresses in one day. The green light was given from users—not developers, investors, or consultants—that the product was desired.

FOCUS ON APPLICATION: WAKU

The Entrepreneurial Journey

Let's talk about Waku and how the owners designed an MVP of their beverage prior to getting traction in stores and health clubs. Waku, originally named WanKu, needed to not only test their products in the U.S. market but also raise capital to pay for the production of their first production run of the beverage. They ran a campaign on PieShell (2017), a specialized crowdfunding site for food and beverage entrepreneurs.

Waku's PieShell Campaign can be found at https://www.pieshell.com/projects/wanku/. In addition to raising over $10,000 for their first-run production of the beverage, they learned about the challenges of launching an international business while being located more than 3,000 miles away from their production site. In addition, they discovered that sometimes names are misinterpreted. While running this campaign and testing their product with prospects throughout the Boston area, they learned that many people could not pronounce Wanku and confused the name with something that did not represent their company. Therefore, they found themselves changing the name to Waku—more easily pronounced and understood. Even if they had not raised all the money they desired, this benefit and feedback proved itself to be priceless, saving time and money they would have spent down the road if they had produced the product under the original name. The situation was similar to the SunChips scenario, where consumer input was critical in determining the product's success relative to the "packaging" of the product. The input was not related to the taste but to the brand they were building. Their name challenge was similar to the SunChip packaging problem, but Juan and Nico caught this

Figure 4.4 Waku Stepping-Stone

1ST STEPPING-STONE

Bring WanKu to You!

Reaching our 1st stepping-stone will provide the funds needed to make WanKu's first-ever production batch in the United States! With your support, we'll be able to bring the first shipment of medicinal herbs from Ecuador, and make our first production run of WanKu in Boston, Massachusetts.

We have developed a stable recipe that can be scaled to make bigger production runs, all while maintaining the same quality and taste as the traditional "healing water." We have established a partnership with a co-packer in Boston that can brew WanKu according to our recipe, and bottle and label it for distribution.

Thanks so much for helping us reach this stepping-stone!

Juan Giraldo, Nico Estrella

concern in time. Since they were a small start-up, they might not have been able to afford to make the change once production really got rolling.

How Did Waku Launch Its Crowdfunding Campaign?

Juan and Nico saw their crowdfunding campaign as a combined funding, marketing, and prototyping effort. They wanted to get financial support (funding), make as many people as possible aware of their product (marketing), and get their "beta" version of the product into the hands of consumers so they could receive valuable and timely feedback about its taste, look, name, and value proposition (prototyping). By talking to hundreds of consumers (both those who supported the campaigns and others who tasted it in stores and gyms), they were able to develop a customer profile of the "'ideal" consumer for Waku.

Before you craft your own customer profile, let's look at how Waku created its ideal customer, aptly named Healthy Helen.

Based on feedback from the campaign, taste tests, and a customer survey that they launched, Juan and Nico identified primary and secondary audiences to target. Their findings indicated that Waku's target customers are all genders between the ages of 25 to 35, who exercise between three to five times per week. Among this target group, most listed running, yoga, lifting, and spin classes among their key exercise activities. Some also mentioned that they participated in activities at specialty gyms, including martial arts, barre, dance, and CrossFit. Understanding how and where target customers exercise helped them recommend potential distribution channels, specifically focusing on locations where target customers exercise, such as yoga or spin studios.

They also wanted to understand what the "jobs" were that Healthy Helen needed to achieve.

Jobs

- Promote long-term wellness of her body (deeper than just "eat healthy")
- Promote sustainability through her eating habits
- Limit the amounts of chemicals going into her body (negative job to be done)
- Project conscious-consumer image to her social circle

Pains

- Healthy products are expensive.
- Healthy products aren't transparent enough.
- Consumers don't have resources to look up for the transparency of brands.
- Healthy products overpromise and under-deliver.

Gains

- Sustainable materials (other than ingredients, bottles, etc.)
- 100% natural ingredients
- Lower price (affordable)
- Functional benefits (proven)
- Attractive packaging and logo
- Low sugar (under 10 grams)
- Fewer than 100 calories
- Good taste

They combined their firsthand research with secondary research on millennials. They learned that fresh, organic ingredients combined with great taste and high quality were very important to millennials.

(Continued)

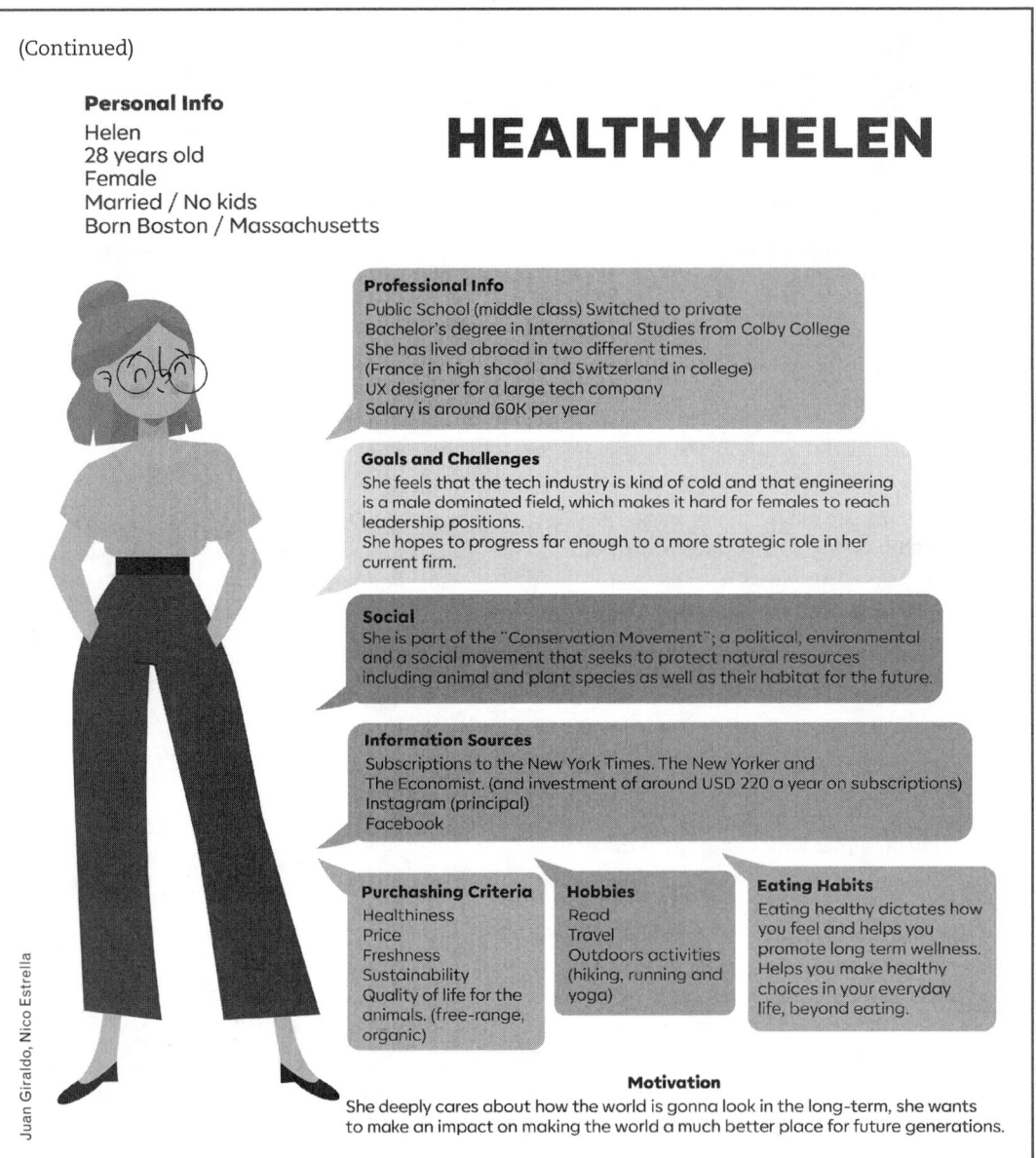

In Chapter 5, you will learn what they decided to use for their brand positioning statement, based upon their research and customer profile.

Identifying Suspects, Customers, and Prospects

We are almost ready to have you create your own customer profile. However, many of you are likely wondering how you can create this if you don't have a database of customers or prospects to contact to understand their needs. You have to get creative in your approach to ensure you have conversations with folks who fall into your target market (or who you think that market is). That's exactly what Waku did and what most start-ups will do.

Here are a few ideas that you can try to secure enough prospects to craft your Customer Profile.

1. Work with a noncompeting company that has a database of similar customers. It might be willing to share its knowledge about its customers' needs or interests or even give you the ability to communicate with its customers in exchange for your providing something valuable to those customers. For example, let's say you've started a dog-walking business and you want to find out what hours are most desired by the folks who bring their dogs to the local pet boutique (which doesn't offer these services). You can make an arrangement with the pet boutique to offer its customers a discount or a free walk in exchange for testing your appointment system and answering a few important questions about how it met their needs. If this partner company sees the value for its own customers, then it might be willing to help you. Plus, you should offer to share what you learn about the partner company's customers since that will likely support its business goals.

2. Crowdfunding Campaign. We've seen this work effectively for Waku. However, keep in mind the fact that most of these campaigns rely on your own contact list. The goal here is to try to expand your list by making the promotion so exciting that it goes viral.

3. Social Media. Friends, family and colleagues can be a powerful source of contacts, but be wary of ensuring they see the benefit of passing along your message to their contact list. Again, the win must be mutual, not just for you.

4. As a last resort, you could purchase a mailing list of prospective customers. It is usually quite easy to buy a list of prospects that fit into your customer or prospect profile, but you must keep in mind that your response rates will likely be quite low and that you will need to vet the list carefully to ensure you are not spamming participants (they didn't sign up to receive e-mails from third parties). This is only a last resort and not highly recommended.

B2B VERSUS B2C PROFILING

Is there a difference between B2B (business-to-business) and B2C (business-to-consumer) marketing as it relates to designing customer profiles? If you are asking the right questions to understand customers' motives, needs, and concerns, then the work you need to do to create profiles and then position your product to each group should not change. However, your questions will most likely need to be altered. For example, if you are trying to understand the needs of somebody purchasing a cup of coffee at a local café (B2C), you may have only one decision maker and a relatively simple customer discovery process. However, if you are selling coffee to a large corporation with multiple locations around the world, your B2B sale could be quite complicated, with multiple decision makers (the buyers and consumers in the Indonesian and Indian locations may have very different taste preferences compared to the American or European locations). This applies to many types of products. For example, if you're selling cloud-based software, then your sale might be complicated because you have users, purchasers, and other individuals whose influence on the final purchasing decision must be understood. If you are selling to the government, then the complications and levels of decision-making expand dramatically.

Therefore, it's important to keep this in mind when defining your customers. Just because you have a B2C strategy doesn't mean that the strategy is going to be simple. There can be just as many decision makers in a B2C situation as there are in a B2B one. For example, you might have a great line of toys designed for 5- to 8-year-old girls. While the girls are the users, the decision makers might range from parents and grandparents to friends and other adults who have the disposable income to make the purchase but must be confident that the product itself will be desired by the girl they intend to buy the toy for. Therefore, understanding how and which individuals make purchasing decisions is more important than the type of business model that you create. We saw this with the Aimee Bio story—the customers ranged from students to parents to educators and administrators within educational and other institutions that work with youth. Therefore, creating a customer profile for **each** of these groups will have great value.

ACTION CREATES TRIUMPHS (ACT)

Designing Customer Profiles

Finally, we are ready to focus on having you create your first customer profile, keeping in mind the fact that it will need to be refined several times (and sometimes completely thrown away and started anew) as you begin to test your product in the market and begin to narrow down WHICH qualities of your product or service are most desired by WHICH customers. It's an iterative process, so you will likely begin with Prototype #1 and test it with a few different target markets. If you discover that "Target Market A" shows the strongest interest in your product or service but cares about only 3 out of 5 of the features, then you would want to make changes to your next Prototype—let's call that Prototype #2 and test it with even more individuals in what appears to be your ideal target market. As you narrow the scope more and more, you will get closer to understanding WHICH customers desire WHICH features, and you will then be ready to create a customer profile.

By now you have accumulated a solid list of attributes about your potential customers, including demographic, behavioral, and life-cycle data revealed from your research. This is where you begin to design your customer profile or persona. Let's keep it simple. Looking at all the data you have, determine the needs this person has that you solve by describing the following, based on Strategyzer's Value Proposition Canvas. If you are interested in learning more about this framework, watch the video, Strategyzer's Value Proposition Canvas Explained (2017) (https://www.youtube.com/watch?v=ReM1uqmVfP0) or you can read more on Strategyzer's Blog (2017) (https://blog.strategyzer.com/posts/2017/3/9/value-proposition-canvas-a-tool-to-understand-what-customers-really-want). Here are the areas you will want to understand:

a. The jobs that customers need to get done
b. Pains from their current solutions
c. Gains they will achieve if the jobs are done

Once you have completed this, think about everything else you have learned about your potential customers and begin to complete the worksheet below.

Ideal Customer Profile (Persona) Description

1. Name (make this up):_____
2. Description (what the person does. Make this CLEAR and understandable.)
3. Needs this person has that you solve (list the top two or three needs).
   a. jobs that need to be done
   b. pains
   c. gains
4. What would a positioning statement look like that would encourage this person to be interested in your product or service?
   a. What do you want them to *know*—beyond what they already may know about you, your product, your business?
   b. What do you want them to *feel*—about the relevant problem or opportunity being discussed, the relative importance or urgency of the issue?
   c. What do you want them to *do*—in the form of possible next steps, such as place an order at a certain price and quantity, attend a product demo, or test the product?

AHAs

Lessons and Takeaways

Let's recap highlights of this fourth chapter focused on listening to the voice of your customer:

- Studying and responding to customers' needs early on in the development phase is easier than trying to redesign products or services at some point in the future when you are already rolling out your new products.

(Continued)

(Continued)

- Prototyping allows your potential customers and other stakeholders to interact with the product or service that helps validate need and interest and provides feedback about your product or service.

- Prototyping is equally important if you are considering launching a service business or creating a mobile app. Some methods of prototyping for these types of deliverables include storyboards, role-playing and website and social media test sites

- You can gain even more important feedback by creating an MVP (minimum viable product), which allows you to conduct a soft launch of your product before you begin to more seriously infiltrate the market.

- If you don't have a database of customers or prospects, you have to get creative to ensure you have conversations with folks who fall into your target market, including working with noncompeting companies, securing names through crowdfunding campaigns, and social media efforts.

TOOLKIT

Worksheet 4.1: Ideal Customer Profile (Persona) Description

1. Name (make this up): _____
2. Description (what the person does. Make this CLEAR and understandable.)
3. Needs this person has that you solve (list the top two or three needs)
4. Why this person is an important prospect for YOU!
5. What do next steps look like?
    a. What do you want them to _know_—beyond what they already may know about you, your product, your business?
    b. What do you want them to _feel_—about the relevant problem or opportunity being discussed, the relative importance or urgency of the issue?
    c. What do you want them to _do_—in the form of possible next steps, such as place an order at a certain price and quantity, attend a product demo, or test the product?

CHAPTER FIVE

MANAGING COMPETITION AND INERTIA

COMPETITORS DON'T ALWAYS LOOK LIKE YOU

A common myth among too many entrepreneurs is the belief that they do not have competitors because they don't see "others" who look like them. While believing you have no competition might be considered a rookie mistake, it's not uncommon to hear seasoned business owners claim that they simply don't have competitors because they haven't identified anybody in the market that produces the same product (or service) that they do. But this is a major fallacy and typically occurs because either the business hasn't done a good job researching similar products or, most likely, it has not properly defined competition. All businesses have competition, and it becomes obvious when you apply the proper definition of competitors as those companies that *satisfy the need that the consumer has*, regardless of the product or service they deliver.

CLEARLY DEFINING COMPETITION

Think about your definition of *competition* before you began to read this chapter. Did it sound something like "a company that has a product or service that is the same or a very similar to mine?" As we mentioned earlier, competition is not limited to companies that have a product or service exactly like yours. If that was true then the business environment would be a friendlier place, and few companies would compete. However, companies do not compete based on product features alone. Companies compete

Learning Objectives

In this chapter, you will learn to

- define competition and substitute products.
- conduct a thorough competitive analysis.
- use a positioning map to understand where your product stands in the market.
- create strategies that overcome the competitive power of inertia.

based on the solutions and the value they offer customers. Therefore, competition is always about fulfilling a "need"—not about offering an identical product or service. For example, if a company, like Waku, develops a new infused tea product from South America and it's unlike any other in the market, it would need to look at its competitors as other companies that satisfy thirst or those that provide health benefits. This includes numerous companies that provide options ranging from coffee and tea to vitamins and health bars.

HOW SUBSTITUTE PRODUCTS IMPACT REVENUE POTENTIAL

Let's say you have a company that has just developed the most extraordinary orange juice. It tastes great and has lots of extra vitamins and calcium, and nobody in the local area produces this exact blend of ingredients. If you think of competition merely in terms of "similar products," then you might easily, but unwisely, conclude that you do not have any competition. However, if you think of your product and competition in a broader light, you can readily see that yours is not the only company offering a product whose solutions include the following:

1. It satisfies thirst.

2. It promotes and supports a healthy lifestyle.

3. It helps maintain and develop healthy bones and teeth.

It sounds a lot like Waku's products, right? If you think of your product benefits in any of the ways listed above then you realize your competition is vast, ranging from any beverage that satisfies thirst to all health products that promote a healthy lifestyle. This is what we call substitute products, and they can significantly impact your revenue potential because they satisfy a need similar to what you offer.

Let's talk about Waku again, which on the surface doesn't seem to have anything in common with orange juice. But since it's a healthy beverage, it could be a substitute for orange juice, meaning somebody might realize he or she is thirsty, look for a healthy option (as opposed to soda) and have to decide between Waku and the freshly squeezed orange juice being offered at a favorite health food market. This would also include milk, calcium supplements, vitamins, and other products focused on obtaining and maintaining healthy bones and teeth. By thinking about your product in terms of its benefits, not simply its features, you have a much more meaningful and realistic perspective on your potential competition (including substitute products).

ACTION CREATES TRIUMPHS (ACT)

Friend or Foe?

When you think about brands like McDonald's and Starbucks®, do you think of them as fierce competitors (foes) or are their value propositions so different that they might be closer to being friends in the fast-casual dining space? What benefits does each company provide to its customers? Some of you might think of hamburgers and Happy Meals when you think of McDonald's, while Starbucks® makes you think of coffee, relaxing music and perhaps some upscale pastries. These are relatively accurate descriptions of some of the products that they feature, but remember that even in their own unique way they are offer a solution to the following problems: hunger, thirst, meeting location, and access to WiFi. Each offers its customers a clean, usually centrally located place to meet their friends or business colleagues. McDonald's sells premium coffee, and Starbucks'® food selection has expanded significantly over the years. In many ways, they offer very similar solutions and benefits to their customers, although they position themselves in very different ways.

There are many businesses that provide a solution to the varied challenges we discussed. Take a minute to write down as many companies as you can think of that offer the following benefits:

1. Clean, centrally located places to meet with friends or colleagues
2. Place to quietly get work done
3. Place to relax after a busy day
4. Access to free WiFi
5. Place with good beverages and meals

How many companies were you able to identify? The list can easily get into the double digits and serve as options and alternatives to Starbucks® and McDonald's, including your local library (except, perhaps for the beverages and meals).

THE RIGHT PERSPECTIVE

Defining your competition often is a matter of perspective. Finding the proper perspective—your potential customer's perspective—may take time and considerable work. Let's look at a marketing consulting firm company, MarketingCo, as an example. MarketingCo provides strategic sales and marketing services, including market research, marketing plan development, Web design, direct mail and brochure and sales tool development. Those are the tangible services that it offers, but at the end of the day, all its customers ultimately care about is whether these services help them grow their business. None of its customers begin their day thinking, "I really want to spend money on developing an e-mail campaign to send to thousands of potential customers." But they do wake up in the middle of the night pondering the best way to grow their business. Since the solutions this firm offers can help them achieve their business goal, its competition is not limited to other marketing consulting businesses. It potentially includes all sorts of "experts"—from Web designers to sales training coaches to management consultants. In addition, it also competes with the individuals in the firm who are running their marketing program. Therefore, in order to justify its value to prospective clients, MarketingCo needs to address these bottom line concerns to effectively compete for client business. They must create a sense of confidence and a belief that MarketingCo can help get them to market faster, more efficiently and in a more cost-effective manner, regardless of the tactical actions taken (such as e-mail campaigns and advertising) to achieve these goals. When you understand your value to customers, can clearly articulate it, and can understand your competitive position in the market, you are in a stronger position to compete for business with the multitude of companies that are also interested in engaging with your prospects.

ACTION CREATES TRIUMPHS (ACT)

Whom Do You Really Compete With?

To figure out who your competition really is, start by writing down your responses to these questions about your business:

1. What are the needs that my products or services fulfill?
2. How else can my current and potential customers have their needs met?
3. What companies fulfill this exact need?
4. What companies fulfill a similar need?
5. What do customers like about their current options?
6. Are there gaps in the solutions that other companies offer?
7. Are customers open to the concept of switching?
8. How loyal are customers to their current options?
9. If switching is a challenge, are there "improved" benefits that my company offers that will help battle inertia (more on inertia later in this chapter)?

Let's talk about your competitors. Do they appear to be able to enter new markets before you recognize the opportunity? Do you know what they're up to and how they are evolving over time? Remember, your ability to outpace competitors relies on knowing as much about their next steps as possible and focusing on how your value proposition can provide even stronger benefits to your customers and prospects. There's a lot of information posted on the Web. How much do you know and how much do you trust? What are you doing to stay on top of this data? Where do you turn for important knowledge? These are all important questions to consider as you launch your business. Next, we will talk about sources of competitive data.

SOURCES OF COMPETITIVE DATA

The following sources of competitive data can be quite valuable for you in answering the questions we proposed:

- customers and prospects
- industry conferences and trade shows
- social media and online presence

Customers and Prospects can be an excellent source of knowledge about your competitors. They very likely know exactly what your competitors are offering and how they are positioning their company (and sometimes your company) because your customers and prospects are likely being approached by them. You might be able to find out what competitors are doing by having open dialogues with customers and prospects. Many people are fearful of asking their customers or prospects how competitors compare to you in terms of value, price, customer service, and so forth. However, this is valuable data that you need to secure, and the answers will allow you to understand the value your customers place on your solution, including customer service, product features, price, and how you rank relative to others in the industry. If your industry uses independent distributors or manufacturers' reps, these people are an excellent source of information about both customers and competitors. You might consider interviewing your competitors' representatives, who can be an amazing source of information about competitors in the market. However, we can't emphasize enough the importance of ethical business practices being deployed. Make sure that you don't present yourself in a manner that isn't honest and transparent and the information that you secure does not provide you with information that you should not be privy to, like company trade secrets. It's not likely that these individuals will have this knowledge, let alone share it with you, but we caution you that establishing ethical business practices is critical to your ultimate success.

Industry Conferences and Trade Shows are a rich source of competitive data. As you already know, you need to conduct primary as well as secondary research to determine what is going on in the market. You need to uncover important clues about industry practices, norms, and trends to understand how your idea might fit into the market. One of the best sources for securing this data is attending an industry conference or tradeshow. Many smart business owners will spend days walking trade show floors talking to their competitors, potential partners, and industry experts. Some companies hire outside firms or individuals to do a complete competitive analysis while at a trade show, ensuring they secure data they might not have otherwise had access to. In the early stages of launching a business, this is not likely an option, so keep an open mind when you approach companies and try to secure as much knowledge as realistically possible.

We want to be clear—we are not suggesting you dig around for competitor trade secrets while at a trade show. Besides the fact that this is data that will not likely be available, it also crosses an ethical line. But understanding how competitors position their business (i.e., their elevator pitch, their marketing material), what they refer to as benefits their company offers, and perhaps how they compare their products to others will provide you with a wealth of knowledge that you can use to make business decisions. These can all be obtained in a professional and ethical manner. Many salespeople at conferences love talking about new projects the company is working on (i.e., new product releases). Asking the right questions can make the investment of your time and money attending the conference a worthwhile expense.

Wondering what questions need to be addressed? First, think about the those that you are trying to answer on your own about the industry and your competitors. Are there hypotheses that you have about the market and the direction it's taking that you want to validate? Think about these questions before you get to the conference; then plan which companies' booths you want to visit, which talks you want to listen to and who else attending the conference would be a good source of overall industry knowledge for you. This list includes direct and indirect competitors as well as suppliers in the industry who work with and engage with your competitors and customers.

Social Media and Online Presence provide a rich source of data. In addition to trade shows, you can clearly secure some of the same information online at company websites and through their social networks like Facebook, Instagram, and LinkedIn. Other sources of online research include the websites and social networks of trade and consumer associations, government entities, newspapers, and magazines. You simply have to be creative (within legal and ethical boundaries, of course) to get access to information that you need to stay competitive and innovative.

THE MYTH OF FIRST MOVER ADVANTAGE

Many times, business owners believe that they have to be "first to market" in order to seize and control the market. Are there real advantages to being first to market? How important is being first in terms of your competitive position? Clearly the answers to these questions depend upon many factors, including the industry you are in, the products or services that you offer, and the number of other companies in the industry trying to gain market share. However, there are certain ideas, and myths, that are typically associated with being first to market:

- Glory. Yes, if you are first to offer a cutting-edge technology or service, you can sometimes find yourself in the public eye and can take advantage of press coverage, assuming, of course, that it's positive. However, this glory can quickly turn in the opposite direction if you moved too quickly. Imagine you've developed a great new product but it was not quite ready (it's software and it still has bugs). If you release it too early to ensure you beat possible competitors, the glory could fade rapidly, as customers will be turned off and could be tweeting about the poor quality of your product, the press will grow negative, and your reputation will be tarnished. Given the pace at which social media can create and destroy a company's reputation, the glory can rapidly fade into an ugly mess of condemnation.

- <u>Profits</u>. There is no guarantee that being first to market will secure funding for your business. Nor will it assure you will have customers since being a trendsetter oftentimes means the general population may not be aware of or understand the value you offer. This can be a major stumbling block for some first movers. If your first-to-market product or service is complex or a very early entrant into the market, then it will likely take time to be accepted. Typically, first-to-market movers spend a lot of time and money educating the market about the value and benefits of their offer. This may lead to an overly cumbersome and expensive sales process which will impact your profit margin.

- <u>Access to Distribution Channels</u>. By capturing market share and developing partnerships early on, you can gain a strong lead on the distribution channels in your market. Clearly, being the first to work with customers, distributors, and partners can be an enormous advantage. If you're ready and able to demonstrate a unique value proposition, you might capture distribution channels and create your own form of inertia (where your customers or distributors might not want to make a change to one of your competitors). If you manage to capture a large share of customers first, you might be able to leave your competitors to deal with inertia. If your products are viable and you are satisfying the needs of your customers, then you should be able to keep them. Truly that's the key ingredient to success: winning over your customers and keeping them for life. Being first to market alone is not a strong value proposition. **Being best to market is powerful**.

SECOND MOVER ADVANTAGE

Now that we've talked about some of the benefits of being first to market, it's important to discuss the advantages of being second, third, or even 20th. Some of these include the following:

- <u>Ability to watch and learn</u> from your predecessors' mistakes. If you carefully watch a competitor make mistakes as they launch, then you can take advantage of the gaffes they've made. For example, if your competitors' customers are unhappy because the product is too expensive or lacks certain features, you might be able to lure customers away if your product addresses these problems.

- Offer a more complete product. If you're moving in behind the innovator, they've ideally established a customer base that can be defined and is hopefully accessible. This might give you the opportunity to communicate with these customers to understand the gaps in current product offers and address these by providing a more robust product.

- The road has been paved. If the innovators have done a good job, they've created awareness and established product need. Therefore, it's not just the trendsetters who are buying your product but ideally a larger set of customers. This larger target audience should help you get up to speed more rapidly.

- Improved benefit knowledge. With new products, customers or prospects might not truly understand all of the benefits or the value is too early for the market. For example, when the Internet was first developed, it was used for educational and government purposes. There weren't any companies conducting business online. However, as the enormous potential and power of the Internet became apparent, the business community jumped in to take advantage of the opportunity for commercial success.

- Funding options. This might be better if the industry's pioneers have established a clear set of needs. On the other hand, if there are lots of pioneers ahead of you, it might be too late, and venture capitalists or angel investors might see you as less innovative and too late to the market. In that case, you will be challenged to prove to them that you have a better product or service or value to offer and are not just another "me too" player. In addition, crowdfunding might be a solid source of funding to pursue since more people will be aware of the benefits that your "type" of product or service offers. The larger the market, the better the opportunity to seize your slice of it.

- Learning curve advantages. Ideally, the innovators in the market established the need and helped educate your prospects about the benefits of your products or services. Therefore, your learning curve should be shorter, allowing you to focus on changes and current shifts in the market.

WHAT IS INERTIA?

The renowned science fiction writer Isaac Asimov wrote in *Understanding Physics (1988)*,

> This tendency for motion (or for rest) to maintain itself steadily unless made to do otherwise by some interfering force can be viewed as a kind of "laziness, a kind of unwillingness to make a change." (p. 24)

Indeed, [Newton's] first law of motion is referred to as the principle of inertia, from a Latin word meaning *idleness* or *laziness*. Inertia is about the tendency of a body at rest to remain at rest or of a body in motion to stay in motion unless acted on by an outside force. What's the implication for your business as an outside force? If the body at rest comprises your potential customer base and they're not willing to switch to your solution, then you will have to creatively figure out how you will motivate that body, en masse, to move.

Inertia can be deadly for established companies with great products and even harder for new companies trying to persuade stakeholders to "try them." Why? If customers are already having their needs addressed, they may simply find it too much trouble to switch—even if their current product or service is just "good enough." We call this a switching cost. These costs can be financial, but they can also be psychological if the benefits are not significant enough to go through the "pain" of making a change. Therefore, if there are products on the market that are simply acceptable for your prospects, then you have to aggressively sell your added value, your wow effect that wins their hearts, or they won't make the effort to switch. It's easy to confuse customer loyalty with customer inertia. Loyal customers are those who choose to stay with your company, even if there's an appealing alternative (perhaps it's less expensive or offers different features). Customers who are experiencing inertia aren't necessarily staying with your company because they value your product or service more than an alternative. They simply have not YET found a compelling reason to leave. Therefore, if another company is able to position its product in a strong light with a compelling message, you might experience a significant exodus from your business.

An example of this is the coffee machine/pod market. Consumers buy products like a Keurig or Nespresso brand with the understanding that the consumable coffee pods that they purchase are unique to each brand. Let's say you bought a Keurig machine 2 years ago and enjoy the coffee (or the generic pods that are available) but don't love it. You've been in coffee inertia. You suspect there might be something better, but you are happy enough or simply too lazy to make a change so you stay with what you're using. It might take a major force to change your mind. Perhaps you are visiting a friend's house and try her Nespresso coffee and realize that it is superior to what your coffee options have been. Now, you have a decision to make with affiliated switching costs that you need to overcome. If you decide you'd rather drink Nespresso every day (versus the Keurig coffee) then you have to weigh the benefit of drinking this brand versus the cost of buying a new machine, new coffee pods, and potentially "lose" the money you spent on your Keurig pods. If the benefits outweigh the costs, then you will switch. But if they don't outweigh the costs of switching, then the pull of inertia is too strong to make you change.

LEAPFROG YOUR COMPETITION

Once you have a better understanding of your competition, it's critical to know how to leapfrog them to survive in the industry and remain a player. These are some survival strategies:

- Differentiate yourself. Make sure that whatever product or service you provide, it's better than or different from the product or service offered by your competitors. Remember you need to provide prospects with a compelling reason to switch from what they are currently doing (which may be nothing) in order to grow your business. How do you differentiate yourself or better serve the needs of your customers? Only you can answer that question. If you've done your homework and have a solid customer profile and competitive market research, you should know what unique role your product and or service plays in the life of your customer.

- Better serve the needs of your customers. How do you accomplish this? Clearly, you have to know what your customers' needs are before you can "better serve them." Therefore, ensuring you understand the real value you provide to your customers can give you an edge over the competitors who may not have done their homework or are missing some piece of the value chain with their offering.

- Learn from the innovators in the industry. What value do or did the first movers in the field provide to customers? You need to ask yourself how you can provide at least comparable positive value and even improve upon that value.

- Form strategic alliances. Consider aligning your company with other organizations that provide services targeting the same clients. For many small companies, a strategic alliance is the key to success. Once you have a solid understanding of how you "compete" with other companies, then you can develop a stronger sense of how to position your company to succeed in the market. What are your overall strengths and weaknesses, and how do these impact the opportunities and threats you will face? We will turn our attention to these issues in Chapter 7, Designing Marketing Partnerships that Empower Growth.

FOCUS ON APPLICATION: WAKU

The Entrepreneurial Journey

You will recall our discussion in Chapter 2 about positioning maps. A positioning map (also referred to as a perceptual map) is a visual aid to show how you will be positioned in the market relative to two factors that are important to stakeholders. It could be factors like price, quality, innovation, performance, customer service, or something else that is valued by your potential customers. This is a good way to not only view your potential competitors but to identify your brand distinction as well. Before Waku's founders created their positioning map they decided that they needed to clearly define their competition since they faced significant competition from beverages to alternatives (substitutes) that supported achieving a healthy lifestyle, including foods, snacks, and even yoga studios. They didn't want to position their map based on hundreds of competitors. They needed to focus on key advantages their beverage offered.

Therefore, they decided to assess their competitors in the narrow space of plant-based, herb-based drinks. This consisted of three major brands: Rebbl, Goldthread, and Teaonic. They also decided to compare six to seven competitive advantages or features of the different brands. They selected the following:

1. Organic
2. Fair trade
3. Sweetness
4. Leaves directly brewed
5. Ancestral tradition
6. Price
7. Natural
8. Herb based

Based on conversations with prospects about these competitive advantages, they compared them to Waku's ability to deliver these advantages (you may recall that they were called Wanku early on in the launch of their business). Below we have shared a graph that shows how customers

Figure 5.1 Waku's Competitive Advantages

COMPETITIVE ADVANTAGES
Our story and the traditional recipe is our main differentiator – which means that we have to highlight our story and traditional recipe. Our brand will differentiate our product in a crowded market.

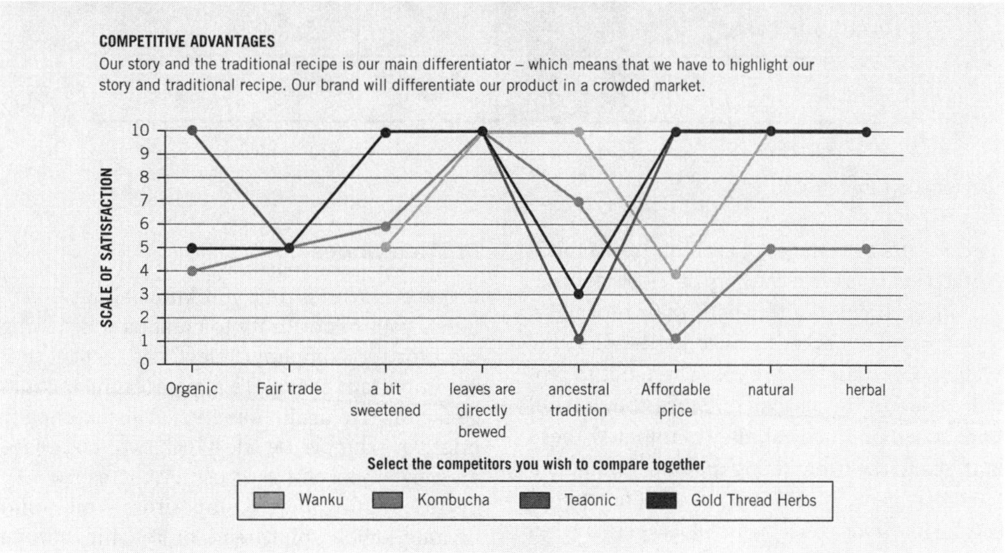

Juan Giraldo; Nico Estrella

(Continued)

(Continued)

Figure 5.2 Waku's Competitive Landscape

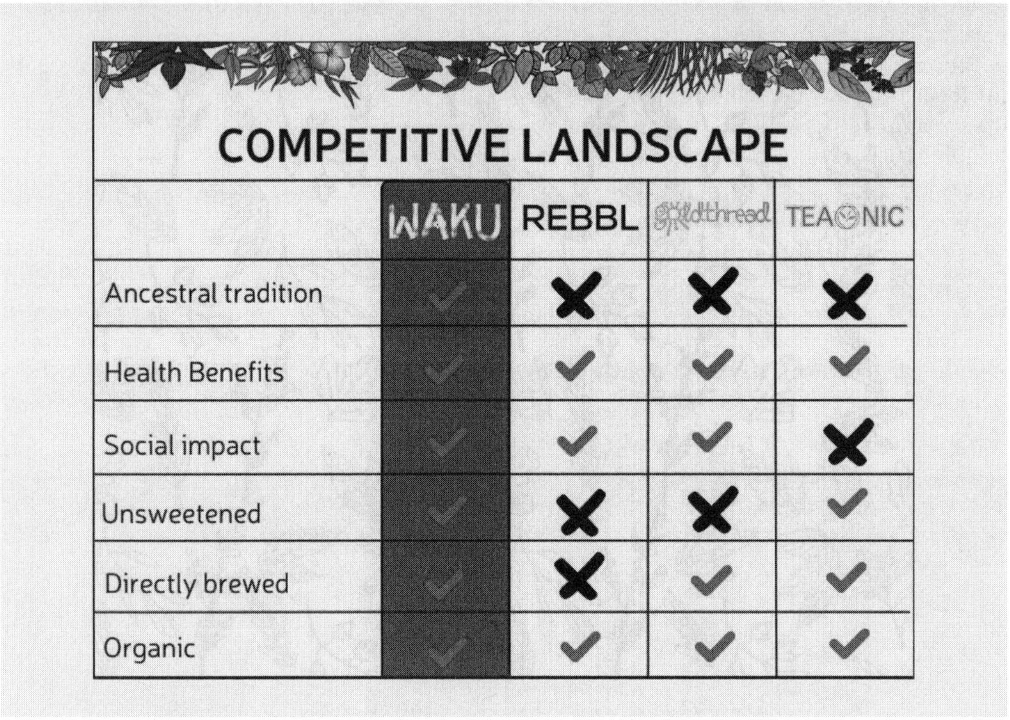

COMPETITIVE LANDSCAPE

	WAKU	REBBL	goldthread	TEAONIC
Ancestral tradition	✓	✗	✗	✗
Health Benefits	✓	✓	✓	✓
Social impact	✓	✓	✓	✗
Unsweetened	✓	✗	✗	✓
Directly brewed	✓	✗	✓	✓
Organic	✓	✓	✓	✓

Juan Giraldo, Nico Estrella

perceive the advantages of each of these brands (Kombucha refers to a category of tea products).

After discussing this with their prospects, they created a marketing table to describe how Waku offers these unique characteristics to provide value to its customers. Since they are all herb based and natural, they eliminated these features in their marketing material and added "Health benefits" and "Social Impact" (incorporating the fair-trade concept) as displayed in the key Competitive Landscape chart below. They used the knowledge they gathered about competitors to not only help them understand the market but to position their value clearly to customers.

In Their Shoes

Given everything that you know about Waku, here's your opportunity to create a positioning map for the company. Select two factors that are important to Waku's stakeholders. It could be factors like health benefits, or social impact, price, for example. Decide which two you believe are most important and position them on a map by researching their competitors. You could include Rebbl, Goldthread, or Teaonic, but we suggest you add two to three additional health beverages to show where they would fall based on customer perceptions of options available in the market today.

VIEW FROM THE TRENCHES

Go Nuts for Gonuts Donuts and Coffee

We met with Abdulrahman Al Rabah a couple of times during the first 2 years of launching his donut business, Gonuts Donuts and Coffee, in Kuwait City, Kuwait. We were intrigued by his commitment to launch a donut company in the Middle East when there was such a strong presence of competitors including Dunkin' Donuts (there are over a dozen in Kuwait), Starbucks (over 80 locations), and many local donut and bakery shops. Even more intriguing was the fact that he graduated college in 2013 with a degree in mechanical engineering. Abdulrahman actually began his successful career in the oil and gas sector and wasn't particularly passionate about donuts. As a matter of fact, he had only ever eaten donuts a few times in his life, while he was studying in the United States. So, why open a donut shop in a seemingly crowded sector in a country with a population of a little more than 4 million people?

Abdulrahman was not loving his job as an engineer. He was under constant pressure in the oil and gas industry, yet he didn't really see himself working in this sector for his entire life. He wanted to do something he was passionate about, something where he could make his mark on the world. He went into the oil and gas sector because in Kuwait, this industry dominated and drove the economy. But things were changing throughout the Middle East, and, while he was well paid in his engineering role, he believed that being an entrepreneur would give him greater long-term financial freedom. Having determined it was time to make a change, he needed to pick a growth sector that excited him.

He watched as a desire for "sweet dishes" became a trend in the market in Kuwait (and throughout all of the Middle East). With high purchasing power and an affinity for chocolate, the Kuwaiti news reported that in 2016, nearly $1 million was spent on chocolates in Kuwait every day. In 2015, more than 47 million Kuwaiti dinar (KD) (over $155 million USD) of chocolate was imported with sales adding up to over KD $100 million (over $330 Million USD). (Al-Fuzai, 2016).

(Continued)

(Continued)

Abdulrahman further researched the market and found a GCC Food Industry report published in April 2015 by Alpen Capital Investment Banking. What he learned further reinforced his understanding about the growth opportunities in Kuwait for donuts and sweets:

> In terms of GDP per capita, Kuwait is the second-wealthiest nation in the GCC region. The country's population and per capita income grew at a CAGR of 2.9% and 4.3%, respectively, between 2006 and 2014. Kuwait has undertaken measures to diversify its economy by focusing on the growth of non-oil sectors. Consequently, factors such as urbanization, growing expatriate workforce, rising population of the young and affluent as well as growth in the tourism and hospitality sectors have increased the need for food. Such factors coupled with a developing taste for international foods has attracted several international as well as regional food and beverage retailers and restaurant chains to the Kuwaiti food market. (pp. 19–20)

Gonuts Donuts and Coffee

Abdulrahman decided to pursue a sector of the food industry where he saw the greatest opportunity gap: a premium, local brand that offered exceptional quality in the donut market. He also wanted to create a brand that people would talk about and want to be affiliated with. Beyond simply offering a sweet desert, he wanted to create a brand that was purely Kuwaiti in nature. He started with the concept of offering the sweetness of cupcakes merged with the finest chocolates. While still working as an engineer, he began tinkering in his kitchen, late into the night, to create an MVP (minimum viable product) that his friends and family could test (taste) and provide him with much needed feedback and advice. It took him 6 months to create a product that he was proud of. Feeling confident that he had indeed created a unique product, Gonuts Donuts and Coffee was born.

With donuts in hand, he went to four exhibitions to showcase his new products. He began accepting orders while continuing to work as an engineer, sometimes even delivering the product himself when his new team wasn't able to deliver orders to customers in a timely manner. All the while, he kept focused on developing a unique brand, one that would allow him to go beyond simply providing donuts. He wanted to create a company with multiple products that was known as a premium brand uniquely representative of Kuwaiti values. He wanted Gonuts to be a cool lifestyle brand that represented the values and aspirations of his generation of customers (20- and 30-year-olds). As a lifestyle brand, he wanted to inspire and motivate Kuwaitis to care about his Gonuts brand, see it as a local brand that cared about its local market and roots, and talk about it with their friends, colleagues, and family. As opposed to a brand that catered to the masses, he wanted Gonuts to be exclusive in its competitive position.

In order to achieve this brand position, Abdulrahman carefully studied what his key competitors were doing to promote their brands. When he launched, his competition was coming from two primary businesses: Dunkin' Donuts, and Krispy Kreme. These two major, global brands were mass marketed in the Middle East with many stores employing ex-pats. While both have multiple locations throughout Kuwait, they were not unique in their product offer (according to Abdulrahman), and they were clearly not Kuwaiti-owned and operated businesses. He originally believed that location would be critical but, by completing an analysis of his orders over the first year, he learned that 60% of his orders were received as deliver as opposed to purchasing onsite at a storefront location. Therefore, ensuring fast delivery with a reliable platform to order and deliver his donuts was identified as a strong differentiator and a key factor for his success.

Abdulrahman tested a few platforms and settled on Carriage (www.trycarriage.com/), a service that provided delivery services throughout the Middle East, including Kuwait, Saudi Arabia, Qatar, Bahrain, and the UAE. They positioned their value in the following way:

> Carriage is a platform that aims to provide the best food delivery service in Kuwait. We want your food to arrive as fast as possible, and in the best condition possible. We have no minimum charge and you can even live-track your orders with us!

Abdulrahman was worried about customer inertia. Therefore, another critical differentiator to help him compete with the two major brands that were serving the market was to create a product unique to the Kuwaiti market—cronuts. Cronut is a croissant-doughnut pastry invented in 2013 by Dominique Ansel (https://www.dominiqueansel.com/). The pastry looks like a donut but is made from croissant-like dough that is filled with flavored cream. Abdulrahman took his inspiration from Dominique and created his own unique cronut, offering in flavors ranging from cheesecake and Nutella custard to vanilla cereal and rose. This selection was added to his flavored donuts that included Snickers, rocky road, Oreo, cappuccino, pistachio, and Reese's flavors.

His business began to really take off in November 2016, almost a full year after it was officially launched. He found supporters to help him grow, including financial and human capital sources. He applied for and received money from the Kuwait National Fund For Small And Medium Enterprise Development (the SME Fund). The fund was created to support youth, combat unemployment, and enable the private sector to drive economic growth. As an independent public corporation with a total capital of 2 billion KD, the SME Fund has the ability to finance up to 80% of capital for feasible small and medium projects submitted by Kuwaiti citizens. The SME Fund focuses on building an inclusive, collaborative, and innovative ecosystem for entrepreneurs to lay the foundation for economic opportunities in the State of Kuwait (The National Fund, n.d.). In addition, Abdulrahman found a partner whom he gave a 30% equity share in the business. He remained focused on achieving his long-term goal of not only expanding his donut business but also creating a brand with multiple innovative products.

Abdulrahman was beginning to gain traction in Kuwait. He was having a lot of success creating awareness through his Instagram site at www.instagram.com/gonutskw. He redesigned his logo to feature his donuts along with a coffee theme and was pleased with the progress he was making.

Then in March of 2017, a significant local competitor entered the market, DOH! DOH! launched using a unique strategy—they sold their artisanal donuts exclusively through pop-up locations and via delivery, also using Carriage (n.d.). They were very local and created a fun brand that caught people's attention

(Continued)

(Continued)

Figure 5.3 Gonuts Logo

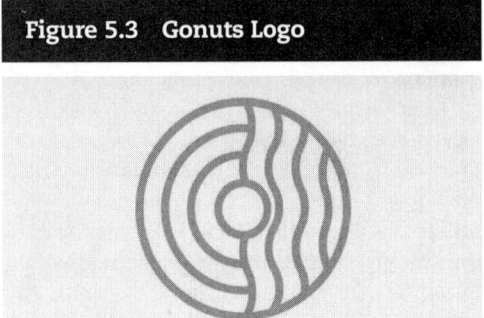

Gonuts Donuts and Coffee

with their branding, including their food truck which is bright pink. They were entertaining, and while their donuts were good, Abdulrahman explained, "It wasn't the same quality as ours, but it definitely impacted our revenue given how much attention they drew because of their exceptional marketing tactic."

In Their Shoes

Abdulrahman is successful, but the competition is a challenge. He has three locations and is about to launch his fourth in Kuwait. Think about the competitive position he has created in the market. Draw a positioning map (Chapter 2) considering two critical areas that he needs to focus on in terms of how he should grow Gonuts Donuts and Coffee in Kuwait. Remember that the goal of a positioning map is to serve as a visual aid to show how you will be positioned in the market relative to two factors that are important to stakeholders. It could be factors like price, quality, innovation, performance, customer service, or something else that is valued by your customers. This is a good way to not only view potential competitors but also identify brand distinction. Select two factors and plot where you believe Gonuts fits and what you think its marketing strategy should be going forward.

BUILDING YOUR BUSINESS MODEL

Let's return to your business model to understand how questions about competition fit into the model design. Clearly, competition impacts your value proposition since the problem you are solving or the opportunity that you are attempting to seize relates directly to what is available in the market today. Your position in the market is impacted by customer needs and the competitive forces that impact their ability to find solutions. This also impacts your channels since it's important to understand how customers are solving the problem now from similar companies as well as through alternative solutions. Please revisit your model and add information that you have learned in this chapter to create a solid picture of what your opportunity looks like with the goal of addressing its feasibility a for future launch.

1. Value Proposition

    - What is the problem you are trying to solve or the opportunity you are attempting to seize?
    - What value do you deliver to the customer?

- How are you creating social value?
- Which customer needs are you satisfying?
- What bundle(s) of products and services are you offering to each segment?
- Are you providing social value to the communities you serve?
- What are you specifically offering?
    - What are the most important benefits to your target audience?
    - Is value sufficient to adopt your product or service?

2. Channels
    - How is your target audience currently addressing the problem or need?
        - What alternatives (substitute solutions) do they have? Who's your competition?
    - Through which channels do your customer segments want to be reached?
    - How will you reach them?
    - Are your channels integrated?
        - Do some work better than others?
    - Which channels are most cost-efficient?
    - Will you integrate your channels with customer routines and behaviors?

AHAs
Lessons and Takeaways

In this chapter, we talked about the importance of understanding who your competition is and why it is critical to properly define them based on the needs your customers have, regardless of the product or service you both deliver. There are some important actions you should take in analyzing your competition and developing a competitive strategy:

- Define your competition from the proper perspective—your potential customer's perspective.
- Understand the needs your products or services fulfill and then research where or how else your customers can have those needs fulfilled.

(Continued)

(Continued)

- Ensure your competitive research includes various sources of data ranging from customers and prospects to industry conferences, trade shows, and social media.
- Understand the benefits of first versus second mover advantage and how it applies to your business.
- Define the potential for inertia and high switching costs that might impact your prospects' decisions to engage with you.
- Complete a competitive analysis to determine how to leapfrog your competitors and ideally anticipate their future moves.

TOOLKIT

Worksheet 5.1: Competitive Assessment

What needs do my products or services fulfill?

Am I a first mover? If yes, what are the

Pros

Cons

If I'm not a first mover, what are the

Pros

Cons

How else can my current and potential customers have their needs met?

What companies currently fulfill these exact need(s)?

Which respected companies fulfill a similar need(s)?

What do customers like about their current options?

Are there gaps in the solutions that other companies offer?

Are customers open to the concept of switching?

How loyal are customers to their current options?

If switching is a challenge, are their "improved" benefits that your company can or does offer help overcome customer inertia?

Worksheet 5.2: Competitive Differentiator Analysis

Identify two companies that offer directly competitive or substitute products. Visit their websites and answer the questions below.

	Your Company	Competitor 1	Competitor 2
What is the stated value proposition or customer benefits?			
Target audiences			
Existing partnerships and benefits to each company			
PR and social media messaging			

Based on this assessment, name three strategies that you will use to position yourself more effectively against these two competitors.

1.

2.

3.

Identify three market segments that you can enter and that your competitors are not dominating.

    1.

    2.

    3.

CHAPTER SIX

CREATING BRAND ENGAGEMENT

Learning Objectives

In this chapter, you will learn to

- define branding as it applies to your company or to yourself.
- differentiate between attributes of a brand (i.e., logo, taglines) versus a well-branded organization.
- consistently communicate your brand.
- describe why stakeholders value different aspects of a brand's benefits.
- create a powerful elevator pitch that describes your brand value to key stakeholders.

BUILDING A STRONG BRAND

Now that you've carefully listened to the voice of your customers, you should have a solid understanding of their needs. Next, it is critical to learn how to effectively communicate how your business meets or exceeds those needs. This chapter emphasizes the importance of creating a winning pitch that succinctly describes your company's value proposition and creates brand engagement. We will talk about what it takes to build a strong brand and consistently communicate its value to customers, prospects, and all stakeholders. The concept of branding has been popular for a long time. With all the buzz, it's important to understand exactly what branding means to you, your team, and everybody your company "touches."

DON'T LET YOUR BRAND BE A LIZARD

Many people associate a brand with a logo, tagline, colors, and Web design. While that's part of your brand image, it's clearly not the whole story. A brand represents the impression that you leave with customers, prospects, and business partners. It infiltrates every contact point and requires every employee who influences stakeholders' perceptions to be fully engaged and committed to delivering on your brand promise.

My favorite story about sending the wrong brand message is not a business story but a very personal one. It's a simple example of how easy it is to say something and have it completely misinterpreted, which is what brand messaging is all about—confidently getting your message heard and properly understood.

Many years ago, when my children where much younger (they're now in their 20s), we completed a major house renovation that lasted well into the winter. This renovation required a large blue tarp to be placed over our house to protect it from the outside elements (winter renovations in New England are not a good idea, but that's another story entirely). From inside the house, our view of the world was basically "big blue ocean." Our son Ben was three at the time and rather perplexed by this oddity. One morning he asked, "Are we living under the sea, like fish and mermaids?" he pondered. I explained that our contractor, Bob, was worried about a big blizzard that was heading our way, so he covered the house with a blue tarp, for protection. Well, this answer seemed to work until it was time to go to bed and Ben refused to sleep alone. After several nights of sleeping in bed with mom and dad, I sat Ben down to try to understand what was bothering him. He informed me that he was afraid of being eaten by the "big lizard" that Bob was protecting us from.

The moral of the story is this: **No matter how great a job you think you have done explaining something, the person on the receiving end may have a totally different perception of what you've said.** You might be talking to a 3-year-old who doesn't know what a "blizzard" is and thinks that lizards are going to attack him, or, even worse, it might be your customer who perceives your value and benefit differently the way you have attempted to deliver it. As the saying goes, "Perception is reality!" In order to have a strong brand, you need to make sure that your message and value are clear and understandable, at every customer touch point. This requires constant reinforcement along with feedback loops (such as prototypes, surveys, or a sales team) that tell you how customers and prospects perceive and experience your brand.

Are you confident that you're going to be able to communicate your value and therefore, your brand, effectively to your customers and prospects? Much of business failure can be traced to the way companies communicate—or **fail to communicate**—effectively with their stakeholders, including customers, prospects, partners, employees, and anybody else who has an interest in your business. While you are planning to launch your business, it's critical to avoid the most common pitfalls companies make communicating their value, brand, and solution. That being said, we want to acknowledge the fact that things go wrong and consumers do not expect their brands to be perfect. However, how a brand responds during a time of crisis is critical. There are so many examples of poorly handled branding crises that instead of sharing a "what not to do" moment, we want to share with you a "what to do" example from the United Kingdom. In February 2018, KFC (aka Kentucky Fried Chicken) UK ran out of chicken. Yes, we know that this is hard to believe, but some things you simply can't make up. They changed delivery partners who found the delivery of birds to be more complicated than anticipated, leading to hundreds of restaurants closing because they were missing the essential ingredient in their restaurants, chicken. This was beyond embarrassing for KFC, but their response was priceless and won them scores of accolades for its bravery, honesty, and transparency. They admitted the problem and took out a full-page ad in the *Sun* and *Metro* newspapers featuring an empty bucket of chicken with only crumbs visible and replaced their KFC logo with the letters switched around to read "FCK." The copy read, "A chicken restaurant without any chicken. It's not ideal. Huge apologies to our customers, especially those who travelled out of their way to find we were closed." They also thanked their team members and franchise partners for their efforts to resolve the situation.

This cheeky apology that showed they were human and struggling to resolve the issue won favor with their fans, and even individuals who didn't frequent their restaurants (BBC News, 2018). While appearing in just two newspapers, it was shared over 219 million times, and estimates are it reached almost 800 million people through the media coverage that followed. The campaign went on to win two Gold and a Silver Cannes Lions (Campaign, 2018), a great example of how important transparency is in building a brand. In this chapter, we will discuss branding as a tool and provide tips for you on building your brand.

ACTION CREATES TRIUMPHS (ACT)

Your Favorite Brands

Before we talk about the key elements of branding a business, spend a few minutes writing down the names of your favorite brands. Once you have written down your five most valued brands, write one or two words next to them that describes WHY you value these brands. It could be something like *trust, value, cool, innovative,* or other words that describe why these brands are important to you. Once you've completed the exercise, we'll begin to discuss why brands are important to others and the importance of building your own brand.

Most Valued Brands and why they are valued by you:

1. Brand:_____
   Why:_____

2. Brand:_____
   Why:_____

3. Brand:_____
   Why:_____

4. Brand:_____
   Why:_____

5. Brand:_____
   Why:_____

CONSISTENTLY COMMUNICATE YOUR BRAND POSITION

Every company and individual has a brand position (this isn't just for the 800 pound gorillas of the business world). Do you know what your company's brand position is now or will be in the future? Let's start by thinking about your own personal brand.

What is it? Your brand is the message that you are communicating on a regular basis to friends, professors, future employers, and others. It's the impression you leave with each of them, even if it's not the statement that you want to make. Your brand is communicated through every touch point, from phone to the Internet and via e-mail, social media, and in-person meetings. Basically, you create and reinforce your brand with every opportunity you have as you connect with various target audiences. If you are launching or running a business, your brand is communicated by every employee from the CEO and sales team right down to your department directors and shop floor managers. Your brand is what sets you apart from others in your industry and makes you unique. This is the same with your personal brand. If you've never thought of your personal brand and can't describe it, make sure you set some time aside and consider the message you are sharing with others about your value to them.

A brand (business or personal) can succeed and achieve its goal of supporting growth only if it satisfies three key criteria. If any of these factors fail, you risk major malfunctions to yourself and your business. Positive brands must

- leave a positive impression,
- be aligned with your customers' needs, and
- be delivered consistently, as promised.

WHY DO PEOPLE BUY A BRAND?

There are many reasons for buying a brand including the fact that the brand identity:

- fulfills a short- or long-term need,
- has an emotional connection,
- is trusted,
- has a positive price/quality relationship (it's worth spending the money on),
- is "hot"—meaning the brand is in vogue, and
- represents who the buyer is or with whom they want to be affiliated.

Do any of these reasons align with the reason why you selected the brands in the earlier exercise? Let's look at some examples of how brands have succeeded in achieving these goals. FedEx is a world leader in package delivery. The brand and philosophy are simple—when it absolutely has to be there overnight, FedEx has built a brand that promises it will achieve this goal. It has built tools and apps to support this brand that go well beyond the logo, messaging, and customer service. Employees are trained to understand the importance of supporting this brand value. But beyond understanding this, they believe in the brand mission and understand their role in making this happen. Every employee, regardless of position, knows the brand's philosophy and works to deliver on its promise. This is the only way a company can live its brand.

The fashion world has many examples that we can learn from in terms of emotional or in vogue connections to brands. Some women will buy only designer pocketbooks such as Chanel or Hermès (because it represents who they are or want to be). It sets them apart and makes a statement that they want to be affiliated with. This also allows the brand to command a premium price for products and services. There are also other types of emotional connections to a brand. For example, Volvo is world renowned as a "safe" automobile. The emotion of safety and security has inspired many individuals to purchase a Volvo (including the author of this book).

We spoke with Dale Bornstein, CEO of M Booth, an award-winning Global digital communications agency based in New York City, about her impression about developing powerful brands.

EXPERT INSIGHT

Developing Powerful Brands: Dale Bornstein, CEO at M Booth

As CEO at M Booth, Dale Bornstein engages with customers every day to help them build their brands. She shared her insight about creating powerful brands so your customers have a clear sense of who the brand is and what it stands for. Dale explained,

> Successful companies understand how to translate that insight into a compelling brand story that allows them to connect emotionally with their target audience(s). Successful brands are authentic and consistent in the way they tell their story and they seek to engage their audience everywhere they live online and offline. Smart brands understand the power of "surround sound"—reaching their customers with consistent messages through a 360-degree multi-channel approach.

Dale continued,

> In today's customer-driven marketplace, your brand is not yours to build or manage alone. The relationship is one that is earned. The customer is your co-brand manager and savvy marketers understand how to actively listen to the conversation and then engage customers in the brand building dialogue. There is an inherent mutuality that exists today in building strong brands and that mutuality is grounded in respect and authenticity. At every touch point, it is critical that your brand delivers on its promise—whether that's at retail, online, or through an interaction with a customer service representative or employee.

> *The brand experience must be consistent and meaningful and be part of the overall brand story. Brands that win in the marketplace understand the importance of choosing communication and marketing tactics that are authentic for the brand and that further the brand's relationship with its audiences. Branding today is about earning (and sustaining) the right to engage in a relationship with a customer or target audience.*

YOU DON'T CONTROL YOUR BRAND REPUTATION

Branding, as a part of the marketing program of a company, is highly dependent upon your customers. As Dale points out, you cannot brand yourself without your customers' supporting and reinforcing your message. If you cannot deliver on the message, then the brand that you are trying to create will be lost. Given all the social media tools available within easy reach like Instagram, Twitter, Yelp and other interactive two-way dialogue options, it's really easy for unhappy customers to share negative impressions with the world about your brand.

ACTION CREATES TRIUMPHS (ACT)

What's Your Brand Value?

Now, let's consider how to achieve a better understanding of the message you are sending to customers and prospects. There are several questions you need to answer to ensure you deliver a brand value that will generate social and economic profit:

1. What is the message that we want to convey to customers about our brand value?
2. How will we know that this is the message that is heard and experienced?
3. How will we ensure our message is consistent?
4. How will we know customers understand our points of differentiation from "like" organizations?
5. How will we measure and track their experience with our brand?
6. Finally, how will we confirm that our brand is desired and valued by customers, now and in the future?

How challenging was the process of answering these questions? This exercise was likely harder than you imagined it would be since branding is not simply about communicating your message but also relies on your ability to measure how customers experience your brand.

Components of a Successful Brand

Being a successful business owner is predicated on your ability to define or redefine how your message and value are experienced in a way that makes you unique and relevant in today's competitive marketplace. In the past, companies would develop a product and then promote it, controlling the brand message entirely. In a global economy, businesses continue to evolve and become more dynamic and competitive. Organizations must continuously define and, when needed, redefine their brand value and sometimes their business model in order to succeed. This redefining leads to the creation or reinvention of their brand.

How Do You Create a Unique Brand?

This must begin with the development of a baseline to understand your strengths and weaknesses as well as opportunities and challenges in the marketplace. It requires an open mindset, whether you're branding your company or yourself. Ask the following questions:

- What is the unique value I or my company offers?
- How do others perceive this, now?
- Does this perception need to change?
- If I were a potential customer, why would I purchase my brand (company or self)?

Next, you must evaluate your company's brand to ensure the following components exist:

- Vision: Where do I see my company going? What is its ultimate direction?
- Positioning Statement: How will my company be positioned in the marketplace?
- Value Proposition: What makes or will make my company brand unique? What service or need does my company fulfill?
- Competitive Advantage: What makes or will make my company unique? Are we just as good as or better than the competition? What facts am I basing this on?
- Leveraged Strengths: Based on an internal assessment, do I really understand our strengths and weaknesses? If so, how can I leverage these strengths with respect to our brand?
- Communication Plan: How do I communicate our company road map to others? What is our communication strategy?

As a side note, this exercise can also be done to build your own personal brand. Think about individuals who engage with your personal brand—educators, employers, friends, family, college administrators, and the list goes on. How do they perceive your personal brand? What do you need to do to create a strong brand for yourself?

ACTION CREATES TRIUMPHS (ACT)

Creating a Strong Brand: 8 Key Actions to Take

Next are eight key actions you can take to create a strong brand.

1. **Focus on the Needs of Your Target Market and Your Unique Value Proposition.** Understanding your target market will allow you to develop a brand position. How confident are you that you truly know what your customers need, want, or expect from your company? Many business decisions are based on a gut instinct about what you believe customers want, not necessarily information that you directly asked them for. You must ask existing customers as well as former and potential customers to ensure their concerns and expectations align with the value you provide. This will translate into your brand position.

2. **Recognize and Act When Outside Factors Impact Your Brand Perception.** Customers do not reside in an isolated world. Recognize how external factors (i.e., sharing economy) might impact their decisions and their ability and interest in conducting business with you. Recognizing and addressing these will strengthen customer loyalty. For example, if you run a small bed-and-breakfast and realize that formerly loyal customers are now using the peer-to-peer platform, AirBnb, to reserve other apartments, then you must act quickly to shut off the revenue drop you are experiencing before you go out of business.

3. **Carefully Review All Communication.** Is your message consistent in all of your communication? This includes everything from written documents, advertising, your website, social media, apps, brochures and direct mail to e-mail, sales presentations, phone calls, for example. Every member of your team must communicate the same brand message. It only takes one employee who isn't consistently delivering your value to wreak havoc on your image and your bottom line.

4. **Develop a Solid Elevator Pitch.** Given that an adult's attention span is quite short, do you have a pitch that highlights your brand in that short window? What are the key points you need to convey about the VALUE you provide (not necessarily the features of your products and services)? It's critical that your

(Continued)

(Continued)

   pitch be concise and compelling. The pitch objective is simple, to develop a message that ensures the other person wants to continue the dialogue. We will discuss elevator pitches later in this chapter.

5. **Present Your Company Passionately.** This is your business, your baby, in many ways. It's personal. You must be able to step outside of the company and honestly ask yourself, "Why would I do business with me?" It's a simple question, but the answer may not be so easy to express. Once you've identified the answer, make sure you convey this in words as well as in your body language. A sincere passion for the value that you provide will go a long way in business.

6. **Don't Assume Others Know Your Value.** This is often referred to as the "SWF: So What Factor" or "WIFM: What's In It For Me?" Always remember that what appears "obvious" to you may not be understood by others who interact with you. You must continually educate customers about the value you provide. Even if you believe your value is obvious, don't assume your prospective customers "get it." One of the most important aspects of selling is educating your customers about the benefits they'll receive if they make a purchase from you. We will discuss sales techniques in Chapter 9.

7. **Manage Critical First Impressions.** You only get one chance to make a first impression. Make sure it's the one you want to make. If your first touch point is through a phone call, your Facebook page, or a visit to your website, make sure it's memorable. Your brand message must provide visitors with a strong sense of who you are and why they should want to continue a dialogue and develop a business relationship with you.

8. **Branding Is Not Just the Marketing Manager's Job.** It involves all of your employees, from operations, sales, product development, research, and anyone else in the company who interacts with customers. Consistency among your employees is essential.

Everything you do has to incorporate that branded message, because if you dilute or vary the message in any way, you won't be sending a clear definition of what your company is and what value you provide to and for your customers. Therefore, branding is wrapped up not only in everything that you do but also in how you are perceived. Remember the story of the lizard—you don't want your brand message to ever become somebody's lizard.

Building Your Business Model

In connecting your brand to the business model that you are designing, it is important to review three areas: (1) your value proposition, (2) the channels through which you reach customers and they access your products and services, and (3) the relationships you build with your customers. Remind yourself of the questions that you will need to address via the business model design as you create a winning brand that is sustainable and one that customers care about.

1. **Value Proposition**
   - What is the problem you are trying to solve or the opportunity you are attempting to seize?
   - What value do you deliver to the customer?
   - How are you creating social value?
   - Which customer needs are you satisfying?
   - What bundle(s) of products and services are you offering to each segment?
   - Are you providing social value to the communities you serve?
   - What are you specifically offering?
   - What are the most important benefits to your target audience?
   - Is value sufficient to adopt your product or service?

2. **Channels**
   - How is your target audience currently addressing the problem or need?
     - What alternatives (substitute solutions) do they have? Who's your competition?
   - Through which channels do your customer segments want to be reached?
   - How will you reach them?
   - Are your channels integrated?
     - Do some work better than others?
   - Which channels are most cost-efficient?
   - Will you integrate your channels with customer routines and behaviors?

3. **Customer Relationships**
   - What type of relationship does each customer segment expect you to establish and maintain with them?
   - How expensive is ethically acquiring, maintaining, and retaining this relationship?
     - What is your customer lifetime value?
   - How is this relationship integrated with the rest of your business model?

VIEW FROM THE TRENCHES

Bali Banana

We want to introduce you to Bali Banana, a student-led start-up based in Indonesia. To learn more about this brand, we spoke with Dr. Wisnu Dewobroto, the director of the Podomoro University Centre of Entrepreneurial Leadership (PUCEL). Podomoro University, located in Jakarta, Indonesia, was founded in 2014 by Agung Podomoro Education Group (part of the Agung Podomoro Group) to offer entrepreneurship education to its students. It collaborated with Babson Global, Inc., to help design material for its entrepreneurship curriculum. Dr. Dewobroto explained that tourism is a driving force for economic development in Bali, Indonesia. Bali is an Indonesian island world renowned for its beautiful beaches, coral reefs, and volcanic mountains as well as its yoga and meditation retreats. In 2017, almost 5.7 million tourists visited Bali (Central Statistics Agency, 2018).

Dr. Dewobroto told us that

> Travel to Bali is not complete without buying some type of souvenir or gift as a memory of one's trip. Therefore, gift shops have been growing rapidly on the island. There is a great selection of items to buy, ranging from traditional products such as leather bags, wood carvings, or barong masks to popular snacks like semisweet fried peanuts, Bali cashews, and, of course, Bali's famous coffee.

He continued, "In recent years, there has been a growing interest in more modern Balinese snacks, especially amongst local tourists. Companies like Pia Legong (www.pialegong.com/i) created very successful businesses by offering a modern twist to homemade traditional Balinese pie." Dr. Dewobroto told us about the success one of his students at Podomoro University, Jessica Syella, achieved upon doing research on the tourism market in Bali. She identified an opportunity to introduce a unique snack to the growing Balinese tourism industry. In 2017, while studying entrepreneurship at Podomoro University, she decided to launch Bali Banana, with the support of her family.

Bali Banana is a banana cake wrapped with puff pastry. Banana cake itself has a very soft texture and is often served with flavored fillings. Jessica decided to launch Bali Banana with four different flavors: plain/original, chocolate banana,

Bali Banana

Bali Banana

cheese, and blueberry. Because it's made without preservatives, it only lasts a maximum of 4 days.

Jessica studied the market and learned that in Indonesia the market is changing rapidly, and she decided to target the younger generation of tourists (under 35) who travel frequently to Bali for short trips. She knew that it would be important to get them engaged with the Bali Banana brand and spent a lot of time focusing on the fine details of her product, including the packaging, the colors she used, as well as the flavors and taste. Based on her research, these aspects are very important to young travelers, and she wanted to give a modern feel to her brand.

Jessica then proceeded to research a market entry strategy that would help launch her brand. She completed a competitive analysis to understand how she could differentiate the Bali Banana brand and stand out from the crowd. The table that follows shows the strengths, weaknesses, and price points for three potential competitors that she identified.

Now, let's pause here and think about the market as it exists at this point in the case. If you were entering this market, what would you advise Jessica to do as it relates to branding her product

Table 6.1 Bali Banana Competitive Analysis

Name	Average Prices in Rupiah	Strength	Weakness
Competitor 1: Pia Legong	100,000–120,000	Well known in Bali Unique taste Location is strategic for tourist area Pioneer in Bali	The price is more expensive than the other brands.
Competitor 2: Pie Susu Asli Enaaak	30,000–60,000	Well known in Bali Pioneer in the pie market Can be easily found in souvenir and gift shops	Easy to replicate
Competitor 3: Pia & Pie Susu	20,000–55,000	Less expensive compared to better known brands	Brand is not well known Not a leader in the market Substitute product

* 100,000 Rupiah = $7.25 (approximately, at the time of the business launch)

(Continued)

(Continued)

to help differentiate Bali Banana? How would you price the product? Where would you try to place the product (distribute it) so it stood out from the crowd? In addition to price and placement, what else needs to happen to promote the product through strategic marketing channels?

Let's now learn how Jessica launched her business. She decided that it was important to keep her message and product delivery methods simple. Therefore, she used a bundling strategy to promote the cake. She priced the product bundle in packages of three Bali Banana cakes for 100,000 rupiah (approximately $7.25 at the time of the launch). In addition, her marketing strategy was also quite simple and focused on ONE social media channel: Instagram (www.instagram.com/bali.banana/?hl=en). She decided against creating a website since she believed her target market wouldn't engage with it, but that meant there was no easy way for people to "find" her since she wasn't using SEO (search engine optimization).

This put a lot of pressure on her to ensure word of mouth and Instagram would support her launch. The result was impressive. Bali Banana went viral, and awareness of the Bali Banana brand rose rapidly. Reviewing the sales growth chart below, you can see that it almost achieved its targeted annual sales goal within the first 5 months of launching the business. For a new business, this was a remarkable achievement and served as proof of concept, allowing the company to begin thinking about opening a second store.

There were long lines of customers who came to the opening, curious to learn more and to buy the product. Now, they needed to figure out how to make this growth sustainable. Their long-term strategy involved finding a location that attracted tourists. They decided that it was critical to find a location at the Ngurah Rai International Airport in Bali. By the end of 2017, Bali Banana opened in the Domestic Departure Lounge, targeting local (Indonesian) travelers who were looking to return home with gifts for friends and family.

Bali Banana achieved early success due to a combination of identifying a need in the market, creating a high-quality, unique brand that

Figure 6.1 Bali Banana Sales Growth

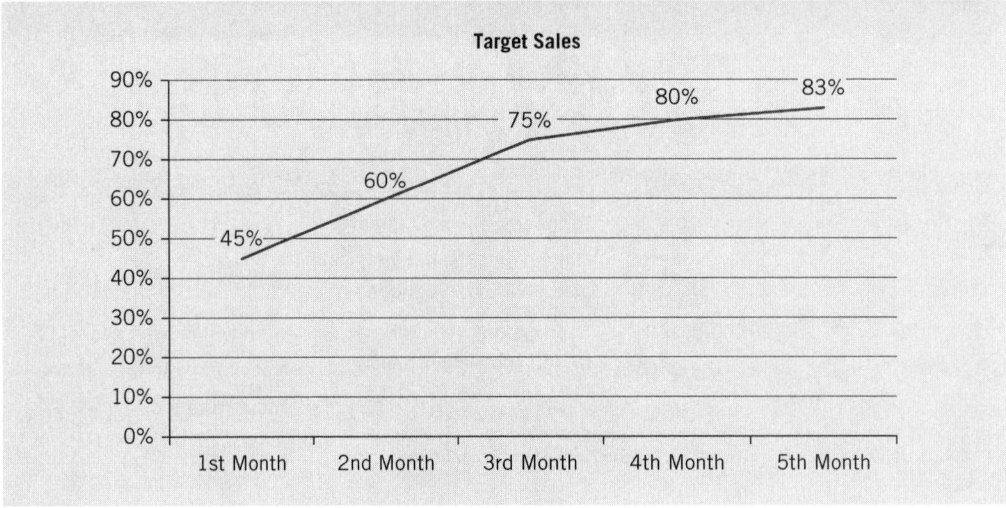

Target Sales

Month	Sales
1st Month	45%
2nd Month	60%
3rd Month	75%
4th Month	80%
5th Month	83%

> consumers could engage with and enhancing brand awareness through the use of social media. However, in order to achieve long-term success, the company now needs to keep current customers engaged, identify distribution channels that will get it access to new customers, and ensure that quality and uniqueness keep customers returning.
>
> **Bali Banana: In Their Shoes**
>
> What recommendations do you have for Jessica and her team to ensure that her brand is valued by customers in the future? List five steps you would take to ensure continued growth for Bali Banana that ensured its brand engagement remained high.

MASTER YOUR BRAND DELIVERY SKILLS

Now that we've talked extensively about the importance of building your brand, let's move on to an art form that, in this time of rampant mobile engagement, is not yet regarded as primitive: personal interactions. While many fear we have become weak in this form of engagement, since we have evolved to spending more time talking with our thumbs as opposed to our mouths, it's still critical that we engage in real, in-person dialogues. Digital natives, this is important to understand. If you want to increase your ability to recognize opportunities and be able to seize them, then mastering interpersonal relationships is essential to your success.

Studies conducted by Professor Albert Mehrabian at UCLA show that we subconsciously form impressions of or "like" others based on three different types of impressions:

1. Body language
2. Tone of voice
3. Actual words

His research (Mehrabian, 1981) showed that "actual words" represents only 7% of our impression. The study found that "body language" and "tone of voice" are essential elements in forming impressions—something we cannot interpret in e-mails, texts, social media apps, or tweets. Think of how many times you've misinterpreted an e-mail or text sent to you by a friend, teammate, or perhaps even one of your parents. You read the message with "your perspective" and react, yet the tone intended by the author of the e-mail or text might have been something completely different from the impression you've gotten and your reaction reflects this disconnect. For example, you interpret something said "in jest" as an insult. I'm confident that you know what I mean, regardless of which end of the message you were on.

We can't think of a better way to test this idea than to sit through a 9-hour meeting without understanding a word of what is spoken. A few years ago, I spoke at a conference (representing Boston University) in Beijing, China, sponsored by the Chinese Medical Device Association. As the penultimate speaker at this daylong event, I sat through about 10 other speakers who came before me who ALL presented in Chinese. While I had business associates with me who were able to translate some of the content, I honestly only understood a sliver of the concepts being discussed.

Interestingly enough, while I had very little understanding of what was actually said during those long hours, I was still able to evaluate each presenter's knowledge and power and authority without understanding the actual meaning of the words. There were speakers who were quite articulate and animated and showed their passion and knowledge for their topic. I felt confident about what they shared (even though I honestly had no idea what they were saying) and even found myself liking them and wanting to learn more about them. I equally gained distrust for others who appeared ill at ease with the topic or were clearly nervous about presenting. Several of them spoke in very flat tones and seemed to be droning on. While the audience was polite, it was their body language that told the truth. These less confident speakers had also lost the audience's attention.

WHAT ARE THE LESSONS LEARNED?

- Regardless of what you say, *how* you say it is paramount to achieving the ultimate goal of your presentation. If you want people to have confidence in what you share or want to persuade them to act on something, then you must be able to express your vision in more than words. Your body language, tone of voice, facial expressions, and inflections are critical to success.

- PowerPoint without visual support such as images, charts, and graphics, in any language, is boring and ineffective in communicating a message. If people can read your slides and know your message without having to listen to you, you've done a poor job of supporting your presentation's goals. Only use PowerPoint if it reinforces and enhances your spoken presentation. If your entire slide show comprises sentences and paragraphs that repeat what you're saying, then just SAY it and don't rely on a visual medium that will interfere with the relationship you are building with the audience. You want them to listen to you and pay attention to you, NOT your slides. That's how they'll develop a high level of confidence in you and you will achieve the goal of your talk.

Most of the in-person communication that you have will occur either one-on-one or in small-group settings versus presenting in front of large groups. Nonetheless, it's important to keep in mind the power of body language in supporting your business goals, in large-group settings as well as one-on-one. We discuss this in Chapter 9 when we discuss solution selling. Now, let's proceed to discuss how to create a winning elevator pitch.

Make Your Elevator Pitch Soar Out of the Park

Mark Twain said, "It usually takes me more than three weeks to prepare a good impromptu speech." Have you ever had the experience of walking into a business luncheon or getting on *that* proverbial elevator and realizing that Mr. or Mrs. VIP was standing in front of you? Did you think to yourself, "Here's the lucky break I need"? Perhaps it was a potential customer or investor. It could also have been a coach, a professor, or the dean. Did you find yourself unprepared and tongue-tied? Or, worse, you were so nervous that you blathered on and on about your business or yourself, never quite finding the right words to accurately or concisely describe what you do or to give this person any hint as to why she should be interested in continuing a dialogue. Did you send her running out the door once an escape was in view? Did you promise yourself that you wouldn't let this happen again?

Even if this scenario hasn't happened to you, chances are that you'll be thrown into a similar situation at some point if you aren't fully prepared. Not being prepared means possibly losing out on uncovering opportunities because others don't know what benefit you can offer them. We definitely want to avoid that mistake. Everybody needs practice creating a strong, knock-their-socks-off "elevator pitch." An elevator pitch is a prepared, concise "mini-speech" that highlights your business's or your personal benefits to somebody in the proverbial elevator.

An effective, appealing introduction is the first and usually the most lasting impression that you leave with somebody. If the person or group listening to your pitch can help you succeed, you want this time in front of that audience to count. (Elevator pitches also help in a variety of social situations, but that's another book entirely.)

Stimulate Interest

Elevator pitches have a few goals. The most immediate is to stimulate enough interest to give you the opportunity to explain and "sell" your business (or self) in more detail *at another time*. You're looking for an invitation to follow up with this person. The long-term goal can vary from developing a partnership to turning prospects into customers or even landing a job or internship. As a result, many individuals develop several targeted pitches, one for each objective. Let's start with one pitch for now, but as you improve, you'll probably develop an arsenal of ways to present yourself and your business. Keep in mind the fact that the *elevator* part of the term should not be taken literally. These opportunities occur everyplace, from the soccer field to a networking event or even a birthday party at your best friend's house.

The "So What" Factor

Whenever students or business owners create their first elevator pitch, many stumble through their presentation. We urge you to answer the questions below before putting together your first pitch or trying to improve an existing one. It might seem really simple and obvious, but it's harder than it seems.

Having a fully polished pitch, one that will lead to an invitation for a longer meeting, requires you to ask yourself these questions:

1. What might intrigue this person about my business?
2. What is important to him or her?
3. How does this person make buying decisions relevant to my company's product or service?
4. Why would this person want to buy from my company or work with me?
5. What impression do I want to leave with this individual?
6. What will this mean to the person I am speaking with?

These questions are very similar to the ones you use to profile your customers. You should now be quite proficient at answering questions about individuals who affect your business's growth.

Begin your pitch by clearly defining who the target audience is (i.e., who's standing in the *elevator* with you). Remember, you need to deliver this message in ideally less than 1 minute, so choose your words carefully. Once you have answered the questions described earlier about the person, you can begin to script your pitch. There are no perfect elevator pitches. You must deliver one that feels natural to you. It should incorporate your own expressions and phrasings. Otherwise it will sound fake and rehearsed.

Most important, once you've developed your pitch, there are three important steps to take: (1) practice, (2) practice, and (3) practice. Some people like to practice in front of the mirror, while others prefer to rehearse in front of friends and family or on video. I personally like to practice in front of one of my dogs. Our dogs, Chewbacca and Twizzler, are quite restless so if I can get them to sit for a minute while I deliver the pitch, I know my tone and inflections are working (although I'm sure all they hear is *Blah, blah, blah—Want a biscuit?*)

EXPERT INSIGHT

Art of the Pitch, Paul Horn

Below are some guidelines and tips developed by Paul Horn, an adjunct lecturer at Babson College and communication skills coach. Appropriate, well-organized content is obviously important to any presentation, speech or conversation. But your elevator pitch will also be judged—consciously or unconsciously—on how well you deliver it. Paul always reminds his students of an old saying, "The audience doesn't separate the dancer from the dance." In other words, human beings respond not only to what is being said ("the dance") but also to how it is being said (via "the dancer"), so your mannerisms, your tone of voice, and your body language are an integral part of the pitch.

Along with the vocabulary you use, the level of detail you provide, and your message, all geared toward your audience's interest and background, Paul emphasizes the importance of your

- voice (pace, inflection, and articulation),
- eye contact,
- facial expressions, and
- body language.

These all influence how effective your words are and the kind of impression you make.

1. Your voice: Be conscious of the following points related to your voice:
   - You need to pace yourself. Don't rush through the speech, or it will sound rehearsed or garbled.
   - Your inflection of certain words to provide meaning or emphasis is important.
   - Make sure you're speaking at an appropriate volume. If you're in a quiet space, your volume will be different from what it will be if you're in the bleachers watching a hockey game.
   - Speaking at a tone that keeps others' attention is of critical importance, or they'll be fidgeting, wondering when they can make their exit.
2. Eye contact: Your ability to maintain eye contact has a strong impact on your perceived credibility.
   - We are not suggesting a staring contest, but looking someone in the eye will convey confidence.
   - If you're staring at the ceiling, or if your eyes are darting around, you'll make the other person feel uncomfortable, and you might lose your shot at getting a second meeting.
   - While eye contact is important for Western business exchanges, remember that sustained eye contact may not be as appropriate in other cultures and societies.
3. Facial expressions: People will be watching you so do the following:
   - Make sure you show your excitement and sincerity.
   - Don't be stone faced and unapproachable.
   - The best way to judge your facial expressions is to videotape yourself presenting your pitch. You don't need fancy equipment. A basic smartphone will work. If that's not an option, then ask a trusted friend or colleague to critique you or simply watch yourself in the mirror.
4. Body language: Even if you have the space, you don't necessarily have to strut across the stage (and if you're really in an elevator, this won't be an option).
   - Appropriate gestures can help you explain an idea, demonstrate your passion, and channel nervous energy.
   - Guard against defensive body language, such as arms folded across the chest, or distracting habits like hands playing with change in your pocket.
   - Stand with confidence, good body posture, and ease. This alone helps establish credibility and is your opportunity to tell your story.

Think of your elevator pitch as a brief introduction of your company to somebody with whom you want to conduct business. It is designed to get the person to develop an interest in learning more about you and your company. Therefore, your challenge is to entice them to want to continue the dialogue. Don't make the mistake of trying to tell them everything about your company. You need to tell them just enough to persuade them to set up a future meeting. Your pitch should last less than a minute (approximately the time it takes to ride a typical elevator).

ACTION CREATES TRIUMPHS (ACT)
Creating Your OWN Pitch

Next, it's critical to create your own elevator pitch. Use the worksheet to develop a pitch for at least one target prospect. Remember, the key to success is to make this something that is natural for you to say. If it appears rehearsed or "fake" in any way, then it won't have the impact that you are looking for. Use this as a guide to design the pitch, but you must put this into your own words. Below is simply a suggested format to help you begin to develop a winning pitch.

Remember to Start at the End

Before you create your pitch, consider what final impression you want to leave with this individual. Then use the six criteria below to develop your pitch:

1. What might intrigue this person about my business?
2. What is important to him or her?
3. How does this person make buying decisions relevant to my company's product or service?
4. Why would this person want to buy from my company or work with me?
5. What impression do I want to leave with this individual?
6. What will this mean to the person I am speaking with?

Remember, you will need a unique elevator pitch for different types of business relationships. A prospect doesn't care about the same benefits that a potential investor does.

Your Pitch

Your pitch should include the following:

1. Compelling statement or question that captures the audience's attention and begins the dialogue (i.e., Are you struggling with . . .?)
2. Your name, your company's name, and your role in the organization
3. A brief but compelling statement about your product or service's value or benefit as it relates to the other person's needs or interests
4. A concise description of your product or service
5. A statement that reinforces your credibility or demonstrates what sets you apart
6. Your energy and passion for making this business succeed and interest in satisfying the customer's needs
7. A closing statement that leads to a "next step" (i.e., Can we have coffee to further discuss this?)

FOCUS ON APPLICATION: WAKU

The Entrepreneurial Journey

Personal Info
Helen
28 years old
Female
Married / No kids
Born Boston / Massachusetts

HEALTHY HELEN

Professional Info
Public School (middle class) Switched to private
Bachelor's degree in International Studies from Colby College
She has lived abroad in two different times.
(France in high shcool and Switzerland in college)
UX designer for a large tech company
Salary is around 60K per year

Goals and Challenges
She feels that the tech industry is kind of cold and that engineering is a male dominated field, which makes it hard for females to reach leadership positions.
She hopes to progress far enough to a more strategic role in her current firm.

Social
She is part of the "Conservation Movement"; a political, environmental and a social movement that seeks to protect natural resources including animal and plant species as well as their habitat for the future.

Information Sources
Subscriptions to the New York Times, The New Yorker and
The Economist. (and investment of around USD 220 a year on subscriptions)
Instagram (principal)
Facebook

Purchashing Criteria
Healthiness
Price
Freshness
Sustainability
Quality of life for the animals. (free-range, organic)

Hobbies
Read
Travel
Outdoors activities (hiking, running and yoga)

Eating Habits
Eating healthy dictates how you feel and helps you promote long term wellness. Helps you make healthy choices in your everyday life, beyond eating.

Motivation
She deeply cares about how the world is gonna look in the long-term, she wants to make an impact on making the world a much better place for future generations.

(Continued)

Juan Giraldo, Nico Estrella

(Continued)

The Waku brand positioning statement evolved over time. Juan and Nico continued to develop their value proposition keeping their "ideal customer" in mind. Before we share with you what they decided to use for their pitch, let's take a look back at Healthy Helen. Write down what you would say as an opening pitch to Helen.

What did you come up with? What were the key benefits that you used to create a brief but compelling statement about Waku's value or benefit as it relates to Healthy Helen's needs and interests?

Are you ready to learn what they created? Based on their market research, the Waku team created the following brand statement: *Made with 20 herbs and flowers, Waku is the world's most refreshing and invigorating infusion drink. It will naturally sooth your body and aid digestion empowered by the healing water from the Andes.*

This message, which clearly takes no more than a few seconds to share, is designed to entice the audience to ask more about Waku. Therefore, assuming somebody asks for more information, Juan is prepared to add,

Waku has a fruity and aromatic taste with a hint of lemon. Waku was developed based on a delicious herbal infusion locally known as the "Healing Water" that has been consumed for centuries in the Andes Mountains of Ecuador. People in my country have been drinking it because it naturally soothes the body and helps the digestive system. We decided to start Waku to share "the healing water" with the world while concurrently helping farmers improve their livelihoods by eliminating the middleman and buying our ingredients directly from them at fair-trade prices. Our dream is to create a brand that customers really LOVE by sharing traditions from our country, Ecuador, and make a bigger impact on more farmers in Ecuador.

As we continue to grow, our goal is to have more resources to help farmers in Ecuador, in an even more significant way, improve their livelihoods.

This is a very strong example of a brand position that evolved over time based on direct market research and the creation of prototypes that allowed people to taste the product before they began producing it in mass quantity.

AHAs

Lessons and Takeaways

Let's recap highlights of this chapter focused on creating brand engagement:

- A solid brand represents the impression that you leave with customers, prospects, and business partners.
- It is critical to create and reinforce your brand with every opportunity you have as you connect with various target audiences.
- Being a successful business owner is predicated of your ability to define or redefine how your message and value are experienced in a way that makes you unique and relevant in today's competitive marketplace.
- You must learn how to create an elevator pitch that stimulates enough interest to give you the opportunity to explain and "sell" your business (or self) in more detail *at another time*.

TOOLKIT

Worksheet 6.1: Creating a Winning Elevator Pitch

Start at the End. Before you create your pitch, consider what final impression you want to leave with this individual. Then use the worksheet to develop your pitch. Remember, you will need a unique pitch for different types of relationships.

Your Pitch

Your pitch should include the following:

1. A compelling statement or question that captures the audience's attention and begins the dialogue (i.e., Are you struggling with . . . ?)

2. Your name, your company's name, and your role in the organization

3. A brief but compelling statement about your product or service's value or benefit as it relates to the other person's needs or interests

4. A concise description of your product or service

5. A statement that reinforces your credibility or demonstrates what sets you apart

6. Your energy and passion for making this business succeed and interest in satisfying the customer's needs

7. A closing statement that leads to a "next step" (i.e., Can we have coffee to further discuss this?)

CHAPTER SEVEN

DESIGNING MARKETING PARTNERSHIPS THAT EMPOWER GROWTH

FINDING PARTNERS THAT FIT

A marketing alliance with the right company can help you achieve your business, marketing, and sales goals. In this chapter, we explore the questions that you need to answer about your company as well as your potential business partners to determine if there's a good match that can help both companies grow. We will review the pros and cons of partnerships and alliances to help you identify which might be the right fit. Then, we examine the steps to take to develop a positive working partnership.

THE RIGHT PARTNERSHIP

Partnerships are very valuable and important relationships for businesses, both large and small. A strong partnership can lead to greater effectiveness and stronger results for both parties. However, good partnerships take time to develop and require significant effort to sustain. A true partnership is a serious relationship between two parties that share common goals and have mutually agreed to join forces to achieve something that they individually might not have been able to realize.

However, partnerships are a double-edged sword. They require significant effort, a great deal of mutual trust, and a champion on each side to manage the relationship in order to work effectively. Therefore, having the right partner—and the right partnership arrangement—can provide a very powerful boost for your business and can lead to mutually beneficial opportunities being uncovered by you and your partner organization. However, partnerships are not something that you should

Learning Objectives

In this chapter you will learn to

- identify the right organizations that can support your marketing and business goals.

- use your SWOT analysis to identify partnerships that strengthen your company's ability to grow.

- assess which companies target similar markets with related products so you can develop synergistic sales growth opportunities.

- develop a balanced partnership structure to ensure the risk–reward ratio is relatively equal for each organization.

enter into casually because the wrong partnership can defeat moral and in worst-case scenarios, destroy a business.

The true challenge in establishing a winning partnership is figuring out which company or type of organization complements yours. To begin this process, you must first identify what you expect from a partner and how it will contribute to your company's growth and development. In Chapter 2, you completed a SWOT analysis of your business. Let's go back and review what you stated were your strengths and weaknesses as well as the opportunities and threats in the market place. Have any of those changed as you have completed a more thorough research-driven analysis of your customers' journey? If this has changed, please update your SWOT analysis since it is an important tool to use in determining the types of partnerships that you need to launch and grow your business.

USING YOUR SWOT AND PESTLE ANALYSES TO IDENTIFY THE RIGHT PARTNER

Ready to use your updated SWOT and PESTLE analyses? While selecting a partner, you will want to identify a few companies that are strong in areas where your company is weak, and vice versa, so that you will both be able to grow and complement each other's ability to scale. However, we are assuming that these identified potential business partners have customers that are valuable to you and you are able to develop a good working relationship with the company. A simple example of this type of win–win partnership is the alliance between a creative design firm and a public relations firm. Graphic designers typically don't provide any type of written marketing services, while most PR agents can't create visuals more sophisticated than a stick figure. However, their clients often seek out both services so this alliance makes sense if the two firms offer complementary services, focus on similar types of organizations or clients, do not compete with each other, and work well together.

ACTION CREATES TRIUMPHS (ACT)
Step-by-Step Process to Creating Winning Marketing Partnerships

Winning marketing partnerships begin with a clear understanding of your strengths and weaknesses as an organization followed by external opportunities and challenges that confront you. To do this, we need to revisit your SWOT and PESTLE assessments from Chapter 2. Think about your internal strengths and weaknesses. Review the opportunities and threats in the market and external challenges such as regulations and the political environment that requires you look beyond your internal resources to partner with an organization to support the goals of you both. Consider the following questions and then write down your responses to these:

1. How do your strengths and weaknesses help or hinder your business goals?
2. How can you minimize your weaknesses through the establishment of a partnership?
3. What types of companies can help you grow, keeping in mind the external threats and opportunities impacting your business?
4. What characteristics should these companies possess?
5. How many strong potential partners do you really have, and how many options are you truly likely to have?

Your next step is to define your key business priorities to help you determine the types of companies that could be your best allies. Ask yourself these questions:

1. What are your top three business goals for the next 1 to 3 years?
2. What types of companies can help you establish those goals?
3. Do you want to have exclusive relationships, and, if yes, are you prepared to offer this as well as receive it? What are the pros and cons of exclusivity for your company?
4. Will the partnerships be formal (contractual) or informal? How will you decide?
5. Are you interested in expanding in a certain geographic location or within a key demographic market?

Next, spend a few minutes jotting down brands and companies that you can think of that match these for your company: The four criteria noted below are critical in developing a partnership that has strong sustaining value for both organizations:

1. Offer complementary services
2. Focus on similar types of organizations or clients
3. Do not compete with you for clients
4. You can work well together

Finally, you will need to gather information from a variety of sources about potential partners. This is not as complicated as you might think. Below are suggestions to get your started:

- Google—Use the power of search to identify companies and brands that meet your criteria.
- Company websites—Check out brands that you are interested in working with. These don't have to be Fortune 500 companies. Think of small, local businesses that appear to meet the criteria that you established.
- Social Media Pages including Facebook, Instagram, Blogs, and Twitter feeds for the same companies whose websites you looked at—Sign up for their newsletters and other news feeds so you can learn more about the messages they are sending to their customer and prospect base.

(Continued)

(Continued)

- LinkedIn—Begin with your own connections. Perhaps your LinkedIn Profile is still undeveloped. Perform a search on individuals or businesses that interest you and see who you know with a connection to that person. Don't be shy about reaching out to friends, peers, your family, and even your professors for an introduction.

- Associations websites—Learn about companies in the sector that interests you and visit their sites to learn more.

- Ask—Don't be afraid to ask your peers, family, and professors for suggestions about companies. They might know somebody in the organization who is open to a discussion with you.

MARKETING ALLIANCE BENEFITS

Did you come up with a few companies meet your criteria? If you struggled, continue to think about a company that would be able to support your growth and vice versa. A strong marketing alliance offers many benefits including reducing risk, sharing costs, and improving time to market. Let's look at how these can be achieved:

- Reducing risk: Risks arise in many ways for start-ups. This includes monetary risks, as well as risks associated with a lack of manpower or people with the right expertise to do the work required to be successful. By partnering with a company offering services that support yours, such risks can be reduced because you might not need to spend as much money on securing clients, for example, because your partner has people who are able to offer that solution.

- Sharing costs: By supporting each other as you grow, you can share many costs, including those associated with marketing, sales, and lead-generating activities. Perhaps your business has better contacts in a certain geographic location, while your partner has industry connections that you are interested in developing. By working together, you can develop comarketing opportunities to offer both of your services as a package to prospective customers. This is not only a win for both of your organizations but should be a desirable benefit for your customers.

- Improving time to market: With access to your partner's prospects and customers, your growth curve and time to market *might* be significantly reduced. If you are carrying high fixed costs, like salaries or equipment, and you can gain customers faster, this can have a tremendously positive impact upon your ability to grow, or simply stay in business. However, this is not always the case so it's important to identify how your partner can help you get to market faster or stay in the market longer.

RISK–REWARD BALANCE

The key to any good partnership is ensuring that the risk–reward balance should be relatively equal for each organization. The long-term benefits must be greater than the effort required to develop the partnership. Otherwise the time and money spent on the developing partnerships may not be worthy of the final result. Developing the right partnership can be quite time consuming. However, you should think of your strategy in the same way you would think of developing a relationship with a customer who might generate a significant portion, perhaps over 50% of your business revenue. This is a key relationship that can ideally support your company's growth goals for a long time. If you develop a strong, mutually beneficial relationship, then it will be similar to creating 10 or 20 sales relationships. How much time would you spend developing 10 or 20 customer accounts? Presumably 10 to 20 times longer than you would on developing a single account, right? Therefore, you should anticipate that this might be the amount of time you need to develop each key strategic partnership so you should select those organizations that will have the strongest impact on your bottom line, basically the largest return on your investment of time.

How do you choose the right partner? By determining partnership criteria early on, even before you begin your research, which will reduce the risk of choosing the wrong partner. Clearly, you will want to develop relationships with companies that meet your standards, but you have to know what those standards are first. Many companies haven't considered the value of developing a "wish list" that outlines the traits and values that a partner would ideally possess. You don't want to establish a partnership with a company or companies that simply don't meet your standards because YOU failed to identify what those are.

ACTION CREATES TRIUMPHS (ACT)

Canine Connections: Partners in Action

Let's say you run a dog walking business in New York City and your major strength is your winning personality and ability to interact with current customers (the paying ones, not the barking customers). However, your major weakness is that you are not comfortable with the sales process so establishing new customers is a constant challenge. A partnership with a pet shop, Callie's Canine Club, in your local neighborhood might create the right balance. Assuming the shop has a steady flow of customers and is willing to introduce them to you, this partnership could eliminate the "cold calling" that you dread. In turn, you would need to provide value to Callie's Canine Club. Perhaps you could give a referral fee for each new client

(Continued)

(Continued)

you gain, or you might have a reciprocal referral system in which you recommend Callie's Canine Club to your own clients.

However, developing an alliance with a company that has the same core competencies (or weaknesses) as your business won't help either of you grow faster and could harm both businesses. Let's look at an example of a poorly designed partnership. Return to the dog walking business scenario, and you are still strong at nurturing current customer relationships but struggle to bring in new business. Therefore, if you establish an alliance with a dog groomer who is also good at nurturing relationships but very poor at developing new ones, then your partnership won't help either of your businesses grow. In addition, you might assume that the groomer is going to help you generate new customers and rely on this, thereby forgoing some of your own sales efforts. It might be a few months before you realize that you aren't getting referrals from the groomer and you haven't done a very good job generating your own leads.

Finally, you must consider the threats and opportunities in the marketplace. If competition in the dog walking business in New York City is growing fiercely, then a partnership with successful groomers and pet shops is even more critical since you wouldn't want your competitors establishing these relationships first, locking you out of important referral sources that would help you grow your business.

VIEW FROM THE TRENCHES

The Lasse Paakkonen Olympic Story

Dr. Anita Juho, a senior research fellow in international business at Oulu Business School, at the University of Oulu in Finland, connected with Olympic athlete Lasse Paakkonen to discuss his career as a Finnish cross-country skier (n.d.). When Lasse was a child, he was inspired by the cross-country skiing track that ran alongside his house in Finland. An active boy, he enjoyed a variety of sports activities and, with support from his parents, began competing at the age of 7.

"I was not a prodigy nor a teen star," Lasse explained, but he worked hard and trained extensively to compete from one season to the next. In 2008, he hired a manager to help him develop a partnership network, with the goal of achieving a medal at a national competition and to get into the World Championships by 2011. Lasse understood that after reaching these goals, he would need to find a new manager who could dedicate the time required for him to reach his ultimate goal, entering the Winter Olympics. In 2010, Lasse had achieved a lot of success and proudly represented Finland at the Winter Olympics in Vancouver, British Columbia, Canada, finishing tenth in the team sprint event.

While his success appears simple and straightforward on paper, the reality was far more complex. At 22, Lasse acknowledged that his best years in cross-country skiing were ahead of him. He needed to give "his all" to achieve his maximum capacity as an athlete, but he unfortunately lacked the financial resources to achieve this. Getting an athletic scholarship was extremely competitive and his success to date simply hadn't been enough to receive the kind of scholarships that would provide full financial freedom. Lasse realized that he needed to take charge of his own financial situation.

Lasse had studied marketing at the university and decided that he could use what he learned in his academic career to impact his athletic career. "Marketing, especially in business-to-business environments, is heavily focused on relationship building, developing strong partnerships, and networking. This is exactly the role that sports managers typically played," Lasse shared. He decided that since this was a personal strength of his, he would become his own manager. He knew he was good at building relationships, identifying important contacts, closing deals, and managing existing relationships. Plus, he was a highly disciplined and goal-oriented athlete; these dual roles were a natural fit.

Lasse's ultimate goal was to achieve financial freedom so he could comfortably pursue his goal of being an athlete full time. He decided that his most strategic approach was to create a business plan, including a pro forma budget that would outline all of his expenses for the upcoming season. Once he had a specific amount that he could see in black and white, he knew his next step was to design a marketing approach that would allow him to achieve this goal. He had one major challenge: time. He was full-time athlete in a demanding sport and a full-time university student. Time was his enemy. He had to prioritize his activities to ensure he was efficient and effective in securing the partners that would support his dream.

He mapped out existing as well as potential partners and divided them into categories:

1. Low Hanging Fruit: He began with companies he felt most comfortable contacting personally. These were companies and potential sponsors in his hometown.

2. Reach Goals: He knew that he needed to broaden his reach so decided to seek support partners and collaborators in the cross-country skiing:

    a. sports sector
    b. equipment sector

After identifying his priorities, Lasse created a sales strategy to convince these prospects to consider sponsoring him in a partnership that provided benefits for their organization and brought his dream closer to reality. He prepared a pitch that explained why they should partner with him, and he also prepared for objections. After all, he wasn't a gold medalist in the Olympics so his visibility was limited relative to the number of sports news interviews he would be asked to participate in. He recognized that he had to create value through his firsthand knowledge of the industry. Lasse decided to offer different packages to potential partners.

- Basic Partnership. This sponsorship level would give the company the opportunity to become a member of his inner circle. He created a monthly newsletter where he detailed his progress, shared insider perspectives related to professional training, and reported analyses and news of the competitions directly from the field.

- Premium Partnership. This level included all of the features of the basic sponsorship package plus visibility for the sponsors themselves. In addition, he provided lectures and training for the sponsor's employees.

With this tiered and entrepreneurial approach, Lasse was confident that he would be able to offer companies a significant "win" for partnering with him. He began the process of pitching,

(Continued)

(Continued)

recalling from his marketing class that it was important to ask for referrals. He did this whenever it was appropriate. Lasse shared his dream of being an Olympian athlete as the cornerstone of his sales pitch, even creating the tagline, "Join the Dream of an Olympic Athlete." During the sales process, he experimented with a variety of new offers, including social media campaigns. However, he discovered that the companies were not interested in this since his prospective partners or sponsors were mainly B2B (business-to-business) companies, and, at that time, social media was not appealing to them.

Lasse felt good about his pitch, but he quickly learned that the two different packages were simply not appealing to his original group of business prospects. He continued looking for the right partnership where the win–win was clear and obvious. Eventually he landed a long-term partnership with a large company in a traditional industry. It wanted its collaboration to be visible to the world and insisted that as part of the partnership agreement, Lasse would compete wearing only its colors and branding its logo on his gear. It also created very visible advertising campaigns featuring the collaboration. The company wanted to use Lasse's name in its own B2B marketing since this added value to it. This partnership was a strong and positive one for Lasse and didn't require much additional effort for him to fulfill the terms.

Lasse's "Join the Dream" campaign was a major success. Throughout his career, he was able to fully cover his training expenses through developing strong relationships with partner organizations. He spent nearly a decade funding his own sports career through his developed sales and marketing skills. There was a learning process, but he didn't allow his fear of failure to overcome him, even though it was clearly frustrating at times. The lessons learned in sports at an elite level of training are transferrable to the lessons learned in business about success, growth, and channeling one's own passion. He explained, "You just need to be prepared for the negative outcome and even a hostile approach at times. It is hard, but you need to think that you have nothing to lose even if the negative outcome hurts." He emphasized that his motivation to be an athlete was so strong that going through this uncertainty was not as bad as he thought it would be. "As an athlete in endurance sports you need to be able to challenge yourself and face the uncomfortable zone again and again." He also learned that winning is not a "solo sport." You need partners to help you throughout the process where each side wins. In 2018, he decided to end his sports career and move on to other challenges, but he took the lessons learned from his career to continue to seek new opportunities, reminding us that, "Victory is always a victory—in and outside of sports!"

A WORD ABOUT BUSINESS VALUES

Partnerships work only if the parties share similar business values and principles. Make sure your philosophy around business and customer relationships is aligned. You can have partners who seem ideal on paper, but if they don't treat their customers the same way you treat yours, the partnership simply won't work. Perhaps being socially responsible is an important part of your business's mission and you donate time and money to charitable causes on a regular basis. You would want to ensure that the partners you choose also share similar values. They don't have to donate their time to the same charities as you but there should not be a conflict in your core values. A good example of a misalignment in business values would be if you are very focused on ensuring fair trade practices with your supply chain. You might find a partner who seems ideal, but if you learn that it doesn't share these beliefs and is perhaps following practices that are not up to your standards, this could clearly be a problem for your future brand position.

Let the search begin. Now that you have established standards, you're ready to begin your search. In the same way you would prospect for potential customers, develop a similar list of the key companies that match your standards and develop a plan to introduce yourself and begin a dialogue. Let's take time now to create a short list of prospects; then we will explore further criteria to ensure a win–win scenario is achieved.

CREATING A WIN–WIN SCENARIO

One important question that you need to address that is not centered on your company and is all about your partner's organization: Will your partner benefit from this alliance? Partnership that only benefit one partner where the win–win scenario is unevenly balanced are doomed. As we have said before, partnerships take a lot of work to create, nurture, and grow. Therefore, if your partner doesn't achieve relatively equal benefits, then there's little reason for their company to spend time ensuring the partnership continues. Therefore, while asking yourself what qualities you want a partner to have, make sure to ask those same questions of the other party. If you can't determine how they'll benefit from working *with you* and they can't express their gain, then you both have an obligation to step back and carefully consider if working together is realistic. Since the level of work to create a partnership is significant, you don't want to continue this process only to have it all fall apart in a few months. You see this oftentimes when friends become partners. They might see the fact that they work well together as a major plus (which it is), but if one party believes that he or she is not getting a strong enough "win" from the relationship, then resentment can follow quickly, damaging both the business and the personal relationship.

Once you have identified a few strong partnership matches (yes, you will want at least two or three potentials), then you need to carefully review how each might work. Questions you need to address include these:

- How do each of these potential partners' strengths and weaknesses fit with my company's core competencies?
- What is the potential market opportunity if we work together?
    - What would the market potential be if I did not partner with this company?
- What advantages will I gain by working with this company?

- What advantages will the company gain if it partners with me?
- What are the risks on both sides if this partnership fails?
- What happens when market conditions or customer demand changes? How will we manage the relationship if one party believes that the partnership is no longer valuable?
- What are the opportunity costs involved with developing this partnership (i.e., what opportunities might you lose by getting involved in this partnership or alliance)?

Looking at the criteria you have established, let's begin to narrow down your list. You will want to select one (or two) leading candidates to be interviewed as potential business partners. You can do this by spending time with the key decision makers within the organization to ensure this is a good match. You may be thinking that you do not have the time required to do this; after all you are a busy entrepreneur running a business. However, by investing this time up front, you will determine if your organizations have compatible values and thus will be able to succeed long term.

GREEN LIGHT AHEAD

Assuming all signs are go, you should move forward with your selected partnership. Keep in mind the fact that a successful alliance requires a clear outline of the structure, duration, and management of the relationship, with focused goals that are measured frequently. Carefully outline in writing what each of you is required to contribute. Keep the lines of communication open and work on the relationship to maximize your success rate.

What factors will help make your partnerships more successful?

- Experience always helps. The more experience you have creating and managing partnerships (like any major account), the better the chances of success because you will understand up front how much work it takes to grow and nurture this relationship.
- Internal champions are key. There must be somebody at each organization who is responsible for the success of the program and acts like a champion to promote its growth.
- Feedback system. An efficient feedback system must be in place to deal with issues and opportunities as they arise.

The bottom line is that these relationships must be treated with as much care as you would give your largest customer account, perhaps even more if this partnership can generate enough business for you. The investment in energy and time may be significant, but the payoff can also be enormous.

WHAT COULD GO WRONG?

In establishing your partnerships, of what other challenges do you need to be aware?

- Can't meet demands. Both companies entering into a partnership will have demands and expect certain needs to be met. Even if you're focused on making this work, if your company is growing and you are not able to meet these needs, then the implications for the success of the relationship can be severely hampered. Likewise, your partner may not be able to meet your demands or needs, so you need to carefully investigate each other's ability to meet goals before entering a partnership.

- Time constraints: You may not have the time to manage, nurture, and grow the partnership since you are still growing, managing, and nurturing your own company.

- Management: You may not have the right people, or enough people, to manage the relationship. The reverse can also happen if your partner is not able to dedicate enough people to work with your company. This can lead to a great deal of resentment if you're working diligently to provide business leads for your partner company but your efforts are not reciprocated.

- Excess reliance on partner: You take a risk in relying on your partners to perform their role, especially if you are relying on them to help fuel growth. If it doesn't happen and you have no control over their actions, then the impact to your bottom line can be severe. You should never rely too heavily on any one relationship to grow your business. This rings true not only for partnerships but also for customers and major business accounts.

- Scale and growth: You don't know if they'll be able to scale or grow with you or vice versa. What if you grow so rapidly the partnership doesn't make sense or if their growth leapfrogs your company's contribution to their bottom line? As with all of the other pitfalls, the best way to try to avoid this is to do your homework beforehand and find out as much about the organization as possible to ensure the greatest opportunity for success.

Below are some ideas to keep in mind in establishing your partnerships:

- Identify your strengths and weaknesses from the outset.
- Make sure the goals of the partnership are clearly outlined.

- Map out a clear process of working together.
- Measure and review the progress and problems on an ongoing basis.
- Ensure that your brand and reputation match those of your partners.
- Dedicate a champion at each organization, someone who will support the growth and development of the partnership.
- Communicate openly in both directions.
- Make sure that the projected outcome is a win–win for both organizations.

Most business owners will tell you that they've experienced both good and bad partnerships. The ones that worked well were partnerships that were entered into slowly, ensuring both parties understood the other company's goals, vision, and business ethics. In establishing partnerships, it is critical to approach them slowly and with caution before you enter into any serious commitment and try to quickly end a partnership that is having a negative impact on your company's growth and brand reputation.

BUILDING YOUR BUSINESS MODEL

Now is the time to make sure you update your Business Model Canvas. Look at the questions under Key Partnerships and fill in the information that addresses the following:

- Who are your key partners?
- Who are your key suppliers?
- Which key resources or expertise or experience do we need from partners—optimization, economy of scale, reduction of risk, access to customers or markets?

VIEW FROM THE TRENCHES

Artistia—Connecting Customers With Artisans

Lulwa AlSoudairy was getting her MBA at Babson College, outside of Boston, Massachusetts, when she came up with an idea for a new business back home in the Kingdom of Saudi Arabia. The idea came to her when she was discussing a business challenge that her mother was facing with her business, based in Saudi Arabia. Her mother produced original handicrafts spun from palm tree fronds. Her products were quite desirable, but marketing them to the right customers (especially outside of the Kingdom) was difficult. Lulwa realized that if she could create a connection between

customers and local artisans, she could solve part of the challenge her mother, and artisans like her, faced. Lulwa recognized that Instagram was very popular and was the default platform used by artists to share their products with the world. However, this platform simply didn't work well for most local small business owners. As she explained, "Instagram was not built to be an e-commerce platform. It is quite complicated to use as a platform to sell local brands online. However, people use it because they did not have many other alternatives."

Lulwa realized that she would also to provide a variety of support tools to enable the artists to get their products into customers' hands. The challenge the artists, like her mom, were dealing with went beyond simply identifying potential customers. They struggled to access methods that would easily facilitate shipping purchases to customers' homes. Since they were small (micro) businesses, they also had to recruit new talent as demand grew for their wares. Lulwa worried that she would create a system whereby customers would learn about the products and begin buying them only to create havoc for the artists because they simply could not get the products to their customers quickly and efficiently, creating a bottle neck and negative customer experiences. Therefore, before she knew that, she needed to create a holistic platform that would not only allow them to sell their products but would also support their business's ability to fulfill the orders. She was committed to ensuring she addressed the challenges that go along with successfully growing an artisan's customer base, which included shipping and access to new talent. Basically, she wanted to create a platform that supported partnerships amongst artists, their infrastructure partners and customers around the world. This platform would need to satisfy the criteria discussed previously in the chapter, including businesses that offer complementary services, focus on similar types of organizations and clients, do not compete for clients, and come together in a simple-to-use platform where they can work well together.

As Lulwa and one of her cofounders, Leena Al Aufi, considered options to address the challenges the artists were facing, they knew they also wanted to create a platform whose mission focused on the value of buying local. The Saudi economy is heavily dependent on one export product, oil. Therefore, by creating a platform for local brands to grow they would

(Continued)

(Continued)

help diversify the Saudi product mix, which would not only support the economy but also keep more Saudi riyals in the country by allowing citizens of the Kingdom to buy their locally designed products from artisans (versus buying abroad, which was common). In addition, non-Saudi citizens would concurrently be exposed to the impressive craftsmanship of talented Saudi artists. The team saw these benefits as major goals in the design of their new business model. They wanted to design a partnership with the artists and the vendors supplying the artists, impacting the Saudi economy in a very positive manner.

Lulwa and her two other cofounders brainstormed ways to achieve their vision, and in September 2015, they registered Artistia in the United States, Dubai, and the Kingdom of Saudi Arabia. Since they were all based in the United States at the time of the launch, they tried to take advantage of the tools that existed in the U.S. market to support start-ups, including online tools and expert advice. Artistia (https://artistia.com/) focused on offering the following solutions to enable their artisans to thrive and positioned their company's benefits in the following way:

1. Offers an online community that enables users to learn about the MENA (Middle East and North Africa region) artists and directly purchase crafts from them
2. Helps artists identify, recruit, and train less-skilled practitioners to help them in their work
3. Creates a community where the artists can get support from their peers
4. Helps local artists develop their e-commerce business by supporting their sales efforts and helps them promote their products to customers across the region and the globe

Lulwa AlSoudairy

5. Helps the artists develop partnerships with local and international shipping companies to streamline the process of getting their products to customers

When asked how they would compete with the popular Instagram platform, Lulwa's cofounder Leena explained, "Instagram has the advantage of being free, but Artistia, which is a paid platform, offers higher value for users. We enable artists to focus on what they are good at doing, while we take care of the marketing and sales." Lulwa added,

> In light of the dependency of the Gulf countries' economy on oil, we're helping diversify it. We are heavily focused on selling customers on the idea of 'buying local products,' helping to create more self-sufficient and sustainable future generations. In this way, we are partnering with the artists to support their business and personal goals.

The team wanted to ensure the integrity and quality of the products offered on the Artistia site because they are committed to building the company as a global brand. Therefore, artists who are interested in joining the platform are evaluated by the Artistia team for the quality of their products before being approved to list them. The revenue model that they designed to support the business provided Artistia with a commission of 15% to 35% for every product that was sold. The commission depended on the type of service the vendor required, such as storage, fulfillment, or account management.

The site has been growing and, in 2016, it was Selected by *Forbes Middle East* as one of the Top 50 Emerging Companies in Saudi Arabia. In addition to the two cofounders, Artistia has four team members as of 2018, with more than 400 artists using the platform, most of them from Saudi Arabia, the United Arab Emirates, and Bahrain. The platform currently has over 3,000 weekly visitors.

As they are growing, they decided to launch a complementary platform called Rishatee (artistia.com/blogs/artful-articles), which features a series of interviews with local artists sharing advice and experiences. They have also launched additional social features on the platform, enabling artists to collaborate on crafting their products. "The artistic scene is growing rapidly in Saudi," shared Lulwa, "and we are committed to helping these talented individuals, who are based at home, be productive and generate an income from their talents."

In Their Shoes

After reading about the success of Artistia, what recommendations do you have for Lulwa and her team to continue to grow their business?

- Are there additional tools or services that they should provide for their artists?
- What do they need to do to become a global brand?
- What additional partnerships should they consider to support their growth as well as the growth of their artists?
- What do they need to be aware of to ensure their artists don't leave their platform?

FOCUS ON APPLICATION: WAKU

The Entrepreneurial Journey

You've read about a few partnerships that worked for organizations in the United States as well as in Saudi Arabia. Let's revisit our friends Juan and Nico as they work on identifying the best partners for Waku.

With a focus on health food stores, Juan and Nico recognized that getting into the Whole Foods Market chain was an important goal for them. Whole Foods is an American supermarket chain that specializes in selling organic foods products, aligning with Waku's mission and values. Having been acquired by Amazon in August 2017, this chain, Juan and Nico believed, could help them have a national presence in the United States. However, Whole Foods's quality standards for accepting new suppliers of products to their stores is quite steep (Whole Foods, n.d.). As outlined on their website, suppliers must:

(Continued)

(Continued)

- carefully evaluate each and every product they sell.
- feature foods that are free of artificial preservatives, colors, flavors, sweeteners, and hydrogenated fats.
- are passionate about great tasting food and the pleasure of sharing it with others.
- are committed to foods that are fresh, wholesome, and safe to eat.
- seek out and promote organically grown foods.
- provide food and nutritional products that support health and well-being.

They knew Whole Foods was an ideal match for Waku but also acknowledged that their tea (and future products) needed to be certified organic to be seriously considered as a supplier to the chain. This was a challenge for Juan and Nico since they found themselves reliant upon small farmers to produce the right quantity of herbs they required to produce their tea. While sourcing locally from a variety of Ecuadorian farmers was critical to their value proposition, this put them in a position where they lacked control over production. As demand in the United States began to increase and their brand was growing, Juan and Nico found themselves struggling because they didn't have enough of the right mixture of herbs to produce their next batch of tea. Nico, based in Ecuador during their start-up, found himself going to local markets in Ecuador to locate the plants that the farmers had not been able to produce enough of. They knew they could not scale Waku without the right supply chain from their partner farmers.

Their challenge was clear. In order to become certified as a vendor of organically grown products, they would need to certify each farmer's products and ensure that enough product was on hand during the various production stages. This was much more challenging than they had anticipated when they launched the business. They recognized that organic certification was critical for growth and paramount to their brand's reputation, but without control of production, they would need to work with a partner. This partner would have to share their values, be able to source enough herbs throughout the year from local farmers, and have a vested interest in working with Juan and Nico (see a win for them). While Ecuador is a small country with a population of about 17,000,000 (Worldometers, 2019), they needed to identify a business that not only possessed all these qualities desired of a partner but could also be relied upon to supply them with the organically certified herbs they required.

After a deep search, they were fortunate to identify a large company based in Ecuador, Ile (ile.com.ec) that not only had a line of organically certified herbs, spices, condiments, and other products but was also quite interested in getting deeper traction in the U.S. market (here was the identified win for Ile). Ile's vision also

Juan Giraldo, Nico Estrella

Juan Giraldo, Nico Estrella

tightly aligned with Waku's—they focused on fair trade and worked directly with many farmers around Ecuador, thereby allowing them to get the organic certification they needed and also provide enough raw material on demand. This was a win for Waku. However, on the downside, Waku represented a tiny portion of Ile's business, and Nico found himself struggling to get their attention when it came time to getting quotes on products they needed to manufacture the next batch of tea to export to the United States. This was an obstacle that led them to look at other suppliers. However, in the Ecuadorian market, no other vendor had access to as many farmers as Ile and also shared Waku's values. Ile was clearly the best option. In addition, while Ile only used 8 of the 20 herbs that Waku required in their own products, they were willing to work with their farmers to plant and grow the 12 other key ingredients that Waku used. This was a major selling point for Waku and convinced them that they would continue the relationship with Ile, even though there were obstacles.

The key to this partnership clearly relied on Waku being able to offer Ile greater access to the U.S. market, making Waku a valued partner for them. While this did not make the partnership 100% equal in terms of value, it helped to ease Waku's fear that their reliance on the partnership was not completely lopsided. Nonetheless, if they could not help Ile grow, they recognized that the partnership would not be sustainable for long term success.

In Their Shoes

As we have discussed, partnerships need to be as close to equal as possible in order for them to succeed. Thinking about the benefits we discussed earlier in the chapter, reducing risks, sharing costs, and improving time to market, what suggestions do you have for Juan and Nico as they struggle to ensure this partnership works, since it is paramount to their ability to scale Waku. List three actions below that they should take to further develop this partnership strategy.

1.

2.

3.

AHAs

Lessons and Takeaways

Chapter 7 focused on the importance of creating strategic partnerships that can help you grow your business. We also discussed the importance of identifying the right partnerships where the investment required to nurture the partnership provides a solid return on your time as well as your bottom line. Highlights of the chapter include the following:

(Continued)

(Continued)

- Ensure you identify partners who offer complementary services, focus on similar types of organizations and clients, do not compete with you for clients, and are companies and individuals with whom you can work well together.
- Confirm your understanding of the importance of a balanced risk–reward ratio that should be relatively equal for each organization.
- Understand how to develop partnership standards by using your SWOT analysis.
- Define your key business priorities to help you determine the types of companies that could be your best allies.
- Understand that partnerships that benefit only one partner or are unevenly balanced in terms of value to each company are doomed to fail.
- Be cognizant of things that could go awry when establishing partnerships such as an inability to meet demands, time constraints, and an excess reliance on your partner to grow your business.

In the next chapter, we focus on the sales process and ensuring you align your marketing goals with your sales tactics. We will also discuss the difference between B2B (business to business) and B2C (business to consumer sales) approaches and how to select what will work best for your organization.

TOOLKIT

Worksheet 7.1: Getting Partnerships Right

Please use the worksheet to answer the questions below before committing to a new partnership:

1. Have you clearly defined your most important goals and made sure that your prospective partner shares those same goals?

2. Have you assessed what specific gaps—in skills, in relationships, or in any other assets—that this partner needs to fill in order to help you succeed?

3. Have you determined how you will help him or her succeed based on the skills or assets you bring to the relationship?

4. Is it clear that both parties stand to benefit more from being partners in this arrangement than working separately? Is this a win–win arrangement where 1 + 1 clearly equals more than 2?

5. Have you spent the time working with this prospective partner to be sure that the fit is right before structuring the specifics of your partnership deal?

6. Do you share mutual business beliefs and ethical practices about how you treat customers and clients?

Worksheet 7.2: Partner/Alliance Analysis and Strategy

List the strengths and abilities below that are critical to succeed in your industry.

Then, place a plus (+) in the column where your company is strong and a minus (–) where you are weak. To the best of your knowledge, complete the form for two different potential partners.

Business Strengths	Your Company	Partner A _____	Partner B _____
1.			
2.			
3.			
4.			
5.			
6.			
7.			
8.			
9.			

Worksheet 7.3: Individual Partnership Assessment

Think about several companies with whom you'd like to develop a partnership. For each company, complete the worksheet. You might not be able to answer all, or most, of the questions immediately, but you should know the answers before you launch into any type of formal agreement.

Possible Partner _____

Partner strengths:

Partner weaknesses:

How will their strengths be leveraged to further grow your business?

How will you handle their weaknesses?

What are the pros of the partnership strategy?

What are the cons of the partnership strategy?

What does your company offer theirs in terms of growth?

How can they help you grow your business?

What costs can you share?

Do you share geographic territories or have other areas in common, such as contacts or industry relationships?

What values are important to you that your partners must share?

What is the potential market opportunity if you work together? If your partnership does not work, how will this impact your market opportunity?

Will the partnership include a formal contract or be informal?

What are the risks on both sides if this fails?

Can this partner meet the demands of your agreement and vice versa?

Do you each have enough time to fulfill the demands of the partnership?

Who will manage the partnership and be an internal champion?

What's the risk of relying too heavily on this partnership?

Can they scale their business as you grow and vice versa?

Will the partnership be exclusive, and, if yes, are you prepared to offer this as well as receive it? What are the pros and cons of exclusivity for your company?

Worksheet 7.4: Partnership Checklist

Checklist of critical factors influencing partnerships

- ☐ Clearly understand each other's strengths and weaknesses from the outset
- ☐ Make sure the goals of the partnership are clearly outlined
- ☐ The process of working together is clear
- ☐ Progress and problems are measured and reviewed on an ongoing basis
- ☐ Your brand and reputation match those of your partners
- ☐ There's a champion at each organization who is dedicated to supporting the growth and development of the partnership
- ☐ Communication is flowing openly in both directions
- ☐ The projected outcome is a win–win for both organizations in a relatively even manner

CHAPTER EIGHT

CREATING SALES PROCESSES AND SYSTEMS

Learning Objectives

In this chapter, you will learn to

- define the differences and similarities between sales and marketing goals.
- design sales tracking processes and systems that align with business and marketing goals.
- identify the processes that need to be created so sales, marketing, and product development collaborate to address customer needs.
- differentiate between B2B (business to business), B2C (business to consumer), and C2C (customer to customer) sales and marketing strategies to identify which path is right for your company.
- analyze the data you have to project sales targets, goals, and other information required to make informed business decisions.

SALES IS ALL ABOUT BUILDING RELATIONSHIPS

The sales process is critical in building relationships. Unfortunately, sales and marketing departments, even in small companies, do not always spend the time required to ensure they understand each other's goals to successfully align their activities. In this chapter, we will show you how to develop sales processes and systems to analyze your current data and track future data so sales tactics are aligned with marketing goals. Your goal is to ensure these two critical areas of your business work hand in hand to deliver the right message to the right profit-generating markets—those identified in the customer discovery process. Each has a role in securing and retaining customers for the benefit of achieving overall business goals, and it's critical that these areas collaborate on ensuring they both have their eyes focused on the same proverbial ball.

In the next chapter, we'll do a deep dive into sales skills that you personally need to develop to be successful. We will also discuss the various sales stages that many individuals go through to be successful, such as phone call preparation, in person appointments, and follow-up and servicing accounts.

SALES AND MARKETING DATA FLOW

When sales and marketing teams don't communicate or understand each other's unique perspectives, the business suffers and is put in a position where success is harder to achieve. This applies to small companies as well as larger, established organizations in a range of industries. There are numerous companies that have spiraled downward and failed. We are sure that you can name a few. Perhaps

Blockbuster, Toys "R" Us, or Sears comes to mind. They are among many that might come to mind. If you study these companies, you will see that they were clearly not tuned into the changes taking place in their market space as customer needs evolved. They were enormously successful at one point in their business but failed to maintain a clear understanding of customers' needs.

Let's take the sales challenge to the small business level. Sales people often complain that the marketing people simply don't "get it" and often ask "Why don't they spend some time in the field with us so they can see what it's really like to work with customers and then produce material that helps us sell?" Likewise, the marketing team can oftentimes be heard grumbling about how the salespeople are never satisfied with the material and messaging that they produce and ask "Why can't they just go out there and sell? They have all the tools they need!"

Who's right in this situation? Possibly both, but we would obviously need more information to really be able to answer that question. You may be wondering, how does the disconnect happen? Think of your typical salesperson, out on the road, meeting with customers, and motivated to achieve and exceed sales goals. This person is usually gregarious, a good public speaker and active listener, and in touch with customers and prospects on a daily basis. On the other hand, the marketing gurus are in their offices, especially those who focus on business analytics, spending time crunching numbers and reviewing the data from the field. If they communicate with customers, it tends to be one step removed, in the form of a survey or other response vehicle. Therefore, while both roles are critical, if they don't respect the other group's expertise and understanding of customer needs and how each plays an important role in meeting customer demands, the animosity and resentment will continue. Remember, both groups play critical roles in identifying new and evolving customer needs and helping to address them.

DIFFERENT WORLDVIEWS

Sales and marketing see the business world from different perspectives. Let's briefly discuss this so we can talk about how they can create a harmonious working relationship that is critical for business growth. Marketing's role is to understand customers' needs to support internal product development, deliver the brand message to the customer via the right channels, and support the sales effort to connect with customers. The salesperson's role is to work closely with the customer to close the sale. Salespeople also need to understand customers' needs, deliver the brand message, and communicate those needs to marketing and other internal divisions in a company. These two areas are so closely intertwined that sometimes turf wars occur and one group thinks the other is not doing its job, which in turn impacts their ability to be successful. Now we introduce the world of social engagement, and the line between sales and marketing becomes even fuzzier. As we have discussed in previous chapters, customers now have a strong say in your brand message, impacting both the sales and marketing teams' ability to do their jobs. The easiest way to differentiate these two areas is to think of marketing as the method of communicating a company's brand value to *many*, via a variety of channels and methods as we have discussed throughout the book. Sales, on the other hand, is more intimate. It is about communicating brand value to an *individual* or a small group, with the goal of closing the deal. Sales is the last few feet in the step of getting products and services into the hands of the customer. While these responsibilities oftentimes overlap, if you think of marketing's role as focusing on *many* and sales' role focusing on *individuals*, it should help clarify in your mind the jobs they each have to get done.

How do we get these two tightly intertwined groups to work together, given that their ultimate mission is the same: growing a business by driving sales? Well, it isn't rocket science, but it does require hard work, effort, and incentives. Goals should be aligned, and each group should have the opportunity to experience life on the other side, so they grasp firsthand the value that each plays in growing the business. Once they see how the other group contributes to improving the customer experience and addressing needs, they will better appreciate each other's role and also be better at performing their own job.

Many books have been written about the disconnect between sales and marketing. If your new business has two separate areas responsible for these functions, then it's critical to have each group think of the other as their internal customer. With this goal in mind, they can learn to better understand the needs and values of their *internal customers* and the entire organization will benefit.

SALES AND MARKETING COLLABORATION

What is the best way for sales and marketing to collaborate to identify customer needs? Let's look at a simplified **Sales and Marketing Collaboration Model**, where information flows from the customer to the business and back to the customer.

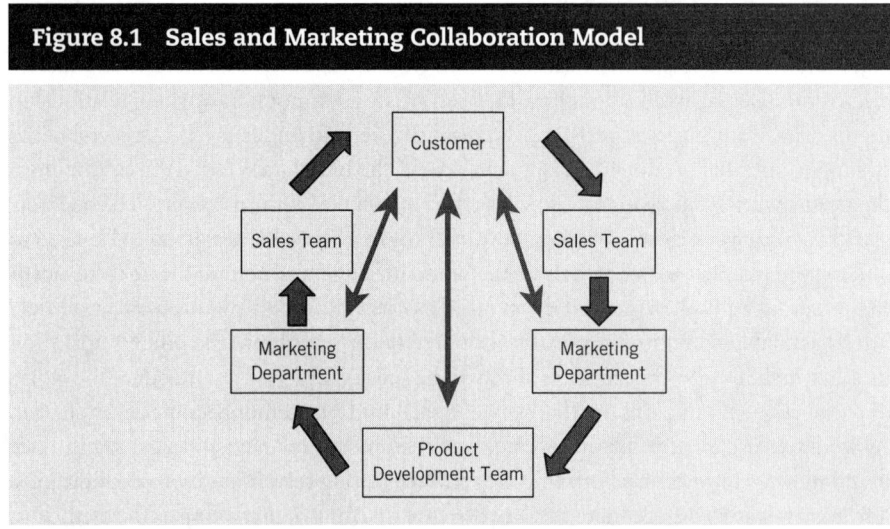

Figure 8.1 Sales and Marketing Collaboration Model

SALES AND MARKETING COLLABORATION MODEL

In this ideal collaborative scenario, data moves in the following flow:

1. Product need identification begins with customers sharing their needs with the sales team or perhaps the marketing team during a market research activity.

2. If the sales team learns about this need first (usually they are hearing the same need identified by a number of prospects or customers), they will then share this knowledge with the marketing department.

3. The marketing department will then conduct research to determine if there's sufficient need in the marketplace for a new product or service (not usually a need voiced by only a small percentage of their customers or prospects).

4. If there is a significant and valid need, then the marketing department will work closely with both the product development group and select current and future customers to ensure the new product or service that is creates satisfies the needs of the target market. This critical task is completed during the product development stage through prototyping and MVP (minimum viable products) development and design.

5. Once the product development team determines that the product is ready for market, the marketing department will then create messaging and identify the appropriate value proposition statements along with marketing material, website messaging, and social media campaigns to support the sales effort.

6. Finally, the sales group will begin to sell the product to customers. They will also provide updates to the marketing department related to what customers are telling them about the new product or service.

This is clearly a best-case-scenario model of how new products are brought to market. As you can tell, continuous communication is critical in order to be successful. Marketing teams should work closely with the sales team to continually gather information required to develop new products and improve current deliverables to ensure they meet customers' needs as they evolve over time. This free flow of information from customers to sales to marketing to product development and then back to customers will allow you to grow your business for the long term.

Whether you are starting a beauty care product line or a cloud-based software business, every type of organization will benefit from using this flow of information. This is guaranteed to be a much more effective approach than creating products without customer research to support their need. Even the most experienced and sophisticated organizations don't always grasp the value of developing products based upon customer requirements FIRST. Ironically, analyzing and reacting to your customers' needs before and during the development of products and services is easier than developing products based on engineers' or CEO's interests. So, why do so many companies get it backward? Because many companies begin by thinking about what they offer instead of to WHOM they offer the product. One of the goals of this book is to turn that notion upside down, and we hope we have begun to show you how even small student-run businesses can develop an intimate understanding of their customers and, by doing so, better address their needs, without spending a fortune on research, consultants, or even technology.

ACTION CREATES TRIUMPHS (ACT)

Sales and Marketing Collaboration Model

Thinking about your business, create a Sales and Marketing Collaboration Model that will work. Write the names of the individuals who will be responsible to ensure the communication flow from customer to sales, marketing, and product development so that all can work together. Think about the processes that need to occur to ensure these lines of communication are open and flow back and forth. Sketch this out with the key players in the sales, marketing, and product development groups. Think about the type of communication required and how often you will communicate both internally and externally.

B2B OR B2C OR SOME COMBINATION OF THE TWO?

Now that we've talked about the importance of sales and marketing working together to develop products, let's talk about the sales distribution strategy that will help your business get your products into the hands of customers as rapidly as possible, securing feedback along the way. Many small businesses grapple with the decision to focus their efforts on either B2B (business-to-business) or B2C (business-to-consumer) sales. If you are asking yourself the right questions to understand customers' motives, needs, and concerns, then you should be able to determine which of these approaches will work best for you. However, keep in mind the fact that they are not mutually exclusive and you may decide to deploy your sales effort by targeting both types of distribution channels, depending on the target markets you have identified are most interested in your products or services and the way your industry is structured. For example, a florist might determine that the best way to get the product into customer hands is direct to the consumer (B2C) through her website or a store. On the other hand, if you manufacture razor blades then the typical model of distribution is through major retail stores like Target, Walmart, and supermarket chains (B2B). On the other hand, if you want to create disruption in your sector by changing these, then you need to consider how you will be able to do that. Some studies have found that the majority of consumers would rather buy directly from a brand if they had the option (Sterling, 2017).

Therefore, you need to carefully select your strategy. Two good examples of mixing up the distribution model include (1) a florist who decides that selling directly to businesses is a better model for her or (2) manufacturers who sell directly to consumers (bypassing the retail distribution model). Examples include The Dollar Shave Club (manufacture and sell razors and other grooming products by mail) and, for a while, Dell computer company, which sold computers only directly to consumers.

We will begin by quickly defining the difference between B2B and B2C sales. B2B sales, aka business-to-business, refers to scenarios when you are selling to a business. Typically, these products are used for the purpose of growth of your customer's business such as enterprise software or public relations services. On the other hand, B2C, aka business-to-consumer, refers to products that are sold to the consumers, typically for personal use but not exclusively. Examples of these products might be buying a Mac from the Apple store for your own personal use or coffee from Starbucks on your way to work. In general, B2C purchases tend to be simpler in terms of the number of decision makers, although, once again, this isn't always the case. Not to confuse the discussion, but if you were selling health care services for a child with a broken leg (B2C), you might have multiple decision makers involved in the purchase, ranging from his parents to his medical practitioners to his insurance companies. However, we will try to simplify the discussion here to ensure you fully comprehend the differences and similarities in these approaches so you can identify which will work best for your company.

In addition to B2B and B2C, you might want to develop your business model as a C2C (consumer-to-consumer). This is a model that has become easier to develop with the advent of companies that can facilitate this and take a small share to enable individuals to communicate. For example, if you are an artist and have a side business where you draw pictures of your friends' dogs but are not ready to launch this full time, you might open a store on Etsy. This platform allows you to sell directly to other consumers without the full-time investment of creating your own website or opening a store. Amazon.com, eBay, and Souq.com (an Amazon company) are other examples of how consumers can sell to other consumers with minimal expense through a platform designed exactly for that purpose. If you prefer to sell in person, you might pay to get a booth or stand at a flea market or antique fair that attracts consumers interested in the type of product you offer. This minimizes your cost and investment and provides you access to many consumers through a group that offers these types of shows.

FOCUS ON APPLICATION: WAKU

The Entrepreneurial Journey

Waku is a great example of how a company can use both B2C and B2B sales and marketing efforts to grow their business. Waku sells its beverages online directly to consumers (B2C) and to businesses and stores (B2B) that then sell to consumers. Waku's B2C marketing efforts mainly focus on social media campaigns and the use of e-mail marketing to encourage individuals to order products available through the website. However, the company is also using its B2B successes and connecting consumers with local stores and encouraging them to go to these stores to buy their products.

Let's talk about Waku's B2B sales efforts. Waku is investing a great deal of time to get its products into small and larger grocery stores. For local grocery stores, the challenge is gaining access to the owners and convincing them to stock their shelves with Waku. There's typically only one individual at these small, mom-and-pop stores who is responsible for determining which products to stock, so while it requires a solid sales effort, the time to complete this sale for each store might be 2 to 3 weeks. The challenge here is that these small stores will not deliver the volume of sales that Waku needs, so Juan and Nico have to go to many stores to achieve the same level of sales that they might realize if they were able to convince the decision maker at a large supermarket chain, like Whole Foods Market (an American supermarket chain that specializes in selling organic foods), to sell their products. However, these larger sales are obviously significantly more complicated to secure, involving many levels of decision makers and could take them months, sometimes years, to win the sale and have their product appear in a select region of Whole Foods.

Nico explained,

Opening new doors is simple but getting volume is the challenge in our business. Our sales approach is to offer "Sampling Events" in each store where we are introducing Waku. We have discovered that usually 25% of the people who test our product during the sample event will buy a few to take home. After we have conducted three samples in each store, then the product really begins to sell effectively and creates loyal customers. Seeing the products sell early on encourages the store to continue to reorder our product, which is critical to our success. However, a sampling event lasts about 3 hours and after we have done our round of three initial sample events (usually within the first month of introducing the product into each store), we need to remain in contact with the store. We are beginning to discover that it's important to continue to offer samplings on a monthly basis until our brand is better known in the market. While this is effective, it is incredibly time consuming and not extremely efficient. Nonetheless, if we are in a store with significant store traffic, we can sell a few cases each day.

Nico and Juan learned that their sales approach is more complicated than they originally believed it would be. They can't simply go into a store, pitch the idea of offering the product to the store manager, and then move on to the next store. They have to dedicate 9 hours in the first month to offer samples (three events lasting 3 hours each) and then return each month for another 3-hour event. They plan on doing this for all major B2B accounts where volume justifies the cost of their time (they are planning on hiring trained interns to do this for them). Therefore, they need to understand and calculate the cost of their sales efforts to business customers and compare this to their cost of securing individual consumers via their social media and other online campaigns to identify which is most cost effective. They also need to understand how long it takes to land a major food chain like Whole Foods.

They have clearly discovered that it can be time consuming to secure businesses to buy products. However, if the cost to obtain a consumer is lower via the B2B model than the cost for marketing to individuals online (B2C), it will be worthwhile for them. What costs do Juan and Nico have to understand? What would you do next to better identify which approach works best for their company?

A basic understanding of next steps for Juan and Nico, the data they need to secure includes the following:

1. All costs affiliated with securing one customer. For the B2B model, this includes the time for the person to set up and offer free samples of Waku during sampling events, the cost of the product given away, and any other costs such as marketing material, or banners to entice potential customers to try their product. They would compare this for a variety of businesses, including Whole Foods, small grocery chains, health food stores, and even yoga or exercise businesses where they are starting to experience an interest in their products.

2. B2C costs that they would need to understand include the time required to develop social media campaigns and other online marketing efforts, any giveaways or promotions that they might have used to appeal to new customers, plus any other online costs such as purchasing Facebook ads or giving products away to thought leaders or influencers.

Finally, they need to compare these costs across all distribution channels.

While the Waku example provides a simple view of customer retention costs, we will further explore this concept in Chapter 13. Next, let's talk about the sales processes and systems required to develop your sales program.

DESIGNING SALES PROCESSES AND SYSTEMS

In developing sales processes and systems, you have to first identify the critical areas that impact your company's success. These will be unique to each company; however, understanding your customers' and prospects' current and future behavior is essential to your success. There is a long list of metrics and numbers to crunch that you will want to review for your company, but the most valuable lesson in this chapter is for you to determine which sales and marketing numbers are most critical for you to evaluate and watch on a regular basis to navigate your path to success. As mentioned previously, in Chapter 13, we will do a deep dive into the numbers and ratios that are critical for you to understand as they relate to overall business growth. Our approach in that chapter will be more holistic in nature. For now, let's explore the numbers and metrics that give you the most critical data about your business's current and future growth as they relate directly to your customers and prospects.

ACTION CREATES TRIUMPHS (ACT)
Sales Goals

Let's look at your company's top sales goals required to successfully launch your business. As you identify these goals, we will step back and think about how you capture this information. What are the processes that are critical for you to be successful in your sales goals? Review the information below, outlining the information that you need to capture. Using the "Sales Analysis Projection Worksheet" included in the Toolkit at the end of the chapter and understanding the information that follows, begin to project your sales information for your business. Keep in mind the fact that you might not have all of the data required at this point. However, it's important to understand the type of data that you will need to capture before you launch and as you grow your business.

SALES ANALYSIS AND PROJECTIONS

A good sales analysis system begins with looking at past sales activity. If you don't have any numbers to review, make sure you study the numbers that you do need so you can ensure you are capturing this data as your company launches and grows. The data review begins with the number of active customers (those you've transacted business with in the past 12 months), total revenue, profit, and revenue per customer. You should measure these numbers comparing this year's results relative to your prior year results (if you have any) plus projections for the future. Are there surprising changes (either good or bad) that you recognized but didn't truly acknowledge until you saw it in black and white on paper? If so, what's impacting this change and how will it affect you in the future?

Prospect/Sales Cycle

Next, let's look at your sales cycle. Again, you might not know all of these numbers but make sure you have a system designed to capture this information since it will be critical in decision making. Below are numbers that you should be projecting on a regular basis once your business is operational. These numbers include the number of new prospects required and anticipated repeat customers, and you will want to compare that to the number of prospects in your system. Even if you are a start-up, you should try to develop these projections, setting them as milestones to track over time to understand how close you are to your estimates. This will help you understand if the sales and marketing activities that you are deploying are actually generating business that supports growth. You will start by looking at your sales goals, and be careful to track what is happening to understand which marketing and sales activities are effective and which are not helping you achieve your goals.

- Number of new prospects required for next year's projections _____
- Number of repeat customers (if appropriate) required for next year's projections _____
- Number of prospects in your system to date _____
- Percentage of prospects anticipated to convert to sales _____%
- Sales cycle (time to close a sale) _____ days

Customer Revenue and Profit Analysis

These numbers measure the percentage of revenue generated by your top three customers, top 20% of customers, and those customers with you more than a year. You might not have data yet for this, but in reviewing this list, think about how you will secure this data so in a year, you will have numbers to review, analyze, and use for future business decision-making activities. Calculating these will help you understand if a few customers are driving revenue to your business and how that dependence on a limited number of customers impacts your business practices and marketing and sales tactics. Perhaps you have heard of the 80:20 rule: 80% of your business comes from 20% of customers. This isn't always true, although it happens more often than not. What do your numbers say about your business, and do you depend too highly upon a few select customers to generate the majority of revenue for your business? Can you change this since the more you depend on a limited customer base, the greater your risk if this base goes away. What can you do to further service this group, if this is the case, or to expand your outreach?

Marketing Tactics

Next, you should break down the various marketing tactics that you have deployed and study what you have achieved from each in terms of actual sales. Realistically, not every tactic will produce DIRECT results, but it's important to review each to ensure they are making a contribution (even if indirect) to your revenue stream and to the number of clients you generate. Many entrepreneurs find this activity to be quite enlightening since they might not have realized how some of these tactics had very powerful impacts on their revenue, while others, which they had spent a lot of money on, had almost no impact. Once again, you may not have this data yet, but in setting up your system, make sure you have a way to capture this. Otherwise, you might find yourself spending money on activities that simply don't generate enough money to justify their cost.

Data Capture Plan

You will need to understand and review the specific data required to secure to make informed sales and marketing decisions. Please use the worksheet included in this chapter so you don't find yourself looking back at the business in a year and realizing that you can't complete key pieces of sales analysis because you didn't capture all the data that you needed. Please being sure to include

- what the specific measures are,
- how you will obtain the data,
- who is responsible for collecting the data, and
- how frequently you need to update and review the data.

Managing Customer Relationships

Most business owners say that their customers are their number one priority. So why do so many stumble when it comes to customer relationships? It's simple: Treating your customers as your top priority requires significant effort and, most important, the right tools to help you do that. Many companies have not invested in these tools to support their growth. Managing five customers is quite different from managing 50 or 500, and you need to ensure you have the tools to support your growth BEFORE you need them or you may find yourself going from five customers to 500 and right back to five (or less).

One tool that can be highly effective is a CRM (customer relationship management) system. Don't panic. This system need not cost a lot of money. It does, however, involve a more sophisticated system than an Excel spreadsheet since these are flat file databases. A flat-file database is a database that stores data in a plain text format. Each line of the text file holds one record, with fields separated by delimiters, such as commas or tabs. While it uses a simple structure, a flat-file database (think of text files) cannot contain multiple tables the way a relational database can. Building systems where there are "relationships" among the data allows you to see trends and understand paths, helping you make important business decisions. There are a variety of systems designed to support small businesses that are affordable and relatively easy to use. We aren't going to recommend any specifically in this book, but we advocate that you do your research to identify what will work best to meet your needs. However, we want you to understand the benefits of implementing a CRM System, which can include

- improvements in customer retention and loyalty because you're better able to serve their needs;

- increased market share through the use of cross-selling and upselling;

- ability to provide more customized levels of customer service;

- increased efficiency and effectiveness for you and your team because the system helps you manage your time and activities; and

- increased competitive advantages because you have solid access to data about your customers, which you can use to strengthen relationships.

KNOWLEDGE IS POWER

Having the ability to use the data stored in a CRM system will enable you to turn raw material (numbers and facts) into knowledge, which in turn will allow you to better serve your customers' needs and see trends that will help you build your business and your brand.

How do you figure out which is the best system to use for your business? Some important benefits to look for include the following:

- Easy-to-use interface that encourages customer communication. If you're running a small business, you should not need an IT department to help you run the system.

- Customizable and easy to integrate with your current programs

- Customer data available on demand, in real time. This means the data is not buried and you are able to "pull up" or access customer details easily.

- Able to capture and integrate customer demographics data that you either purchase or have in another program. By being able to use all the data you have about customers and prospects, you can better customize and target your markets. This allows your marketing team to run campaigns that are targeted to specific audiences (i.e., women over 65 within 15 miles of your office).

- System should be able to help with your time management challenges by offering to-do lists, action items, callback times, alerts, and schedule overviews

- Ability to create and track the results of mailings (e-mail, social media, and good old-fashioned snail mail attempts) to individuals and target groups

- Ability to create e-mail of even phone calling lists to individuals and target groups based on specific demographics or their status/ID
- Able to share information across internal groups and departments so that marketing and sales can work with operations, production, and anybody else who needs access to the data
- Reporting and analytical capabilities that simplify the process of reviewing your pipeline, assessing your leads, and help you forecast future sales. This is a great tool that also will enable sales managers to track how their team is doing so they can better support their efforts.

From a business perspective, some of the benefits that can be achieved through the deployment of a CRM system include

- increased conversion of prospects to customers
- increased customers' knowledge about your products and services
- increased opportunities to customize and develop new and improved products and solutions because your awareness level of customers' and prospects' needs has increased and is more focused
- ability to more efficiently gather data about customer needs
- decreases lost customers and brings back lost ones
- increased personalized service

CRM helps you manage and create knowledge. The CRM system that you use should be viewed as a knowledge center. Therefore, from a management perspective, you should be able to generate reports that

- show your pipeline of prospects, which will help you predict future sales and determine if new campaigns or outreach strategies are needed.
- show how many and what type of calls have resulted into sales (increasing ROI).
- identify which lists work best if you are segmenting your list of prospects or customers.
- help you determine which target groups (based on status, demographics, or industry type) bring the greatest return to your marketing investment.
- calculate how much time and money you spend converting each separate account into customers.

- determine the most—and least—effective salespeople, allowing you to support and guide those who need more assistance.

- break down the revenue per call, in addition to the number of calls or contacts reached.

- simplify the follow-up and fulfillment of sales and marketing requests.

MANAGING YOUR TEAM'S SALES CYCLE

Now that we've reviewed the overall benefits of deploying a CRM system in a company, let's review the benefits of using the data to help manage your team's sales cycle. This is data that can not only be used to manage and improve your sales team's performance but can be valuable data for your marketing team to understand so they can identify strategies to support your sales team. Remember, whether you are running a small business or getting ready to launch one, everybody in your organization needs to support sales and understand the patterns and needs that emerge. You will start securing a lot of data and will want to be efficient in how you capture and use the information to make informed business decisions. The better your company is at managing your sales cycle, the more efficient and cost-effective the efforts will be.

Your sales cycle refers to the period of time it takes to identify a lead, bring it from cold lead to hot prospect and then to a sale (ideally). To be more specific, turning a cold lead into a purchase may involve moving the person to a warm lead (an expression of interest), to a hot lead (an expression of strong interest), to a commitment to sign a contract, and finally, to a sale. That process may take a few minutes for inexpensive sales (a household product selling for less than $50) or more than a year for larger engagements, such as the purchase of a new integrated technology system priced at over a million dollars.

CHEWIE'S COLOSSAL COOKIE COMPANY: LETTING THE DATA INFORM YOUR NEXT STEPS

Let's revisit Chewie's Colossal Cookie Company from Chapter 3. After completing their market research, the team decided that selling homemade dog food was more complicated than they anticipated. They decided that their B2B strategy would include selling to small boutique pet shops and supermarkets, including specialty markets and mainstream supermarkets with a natural foods section. Ideally, they wanted to land a major account like Whole Foods, which has hundreds of stores in North America specializing in natural and organic food. However, they realized that this was an ambitious goal and, even if they were successful, it would likely take a long time to land that

account (same problem as Waku). Therefore, they decided to diversify their sales approach and target a variety of pet stores and small retail boutiques.

Let's say that you're the new sales director for Chewie's Colossal Cookie Company. You don't have a lot of data on sales, but you know that your team needs to land 15 new accounts for the upcoming month. You've heard that sales conversions in your industry run around 6%. How many prospects does your team need to achieve your sales goals, and how much time will it take them? Below, we will walk you through the process so you can replicate this for your own company.

We will start by calculating how many prospects your team needs to meet their sales goal. We're going to estimate some of the information, as you might need to, because we simply don't have all of the data that we need right now:

A. Number of new business customers required in the next month: A: 15

B. What percentage of phone calls result in a conversation?
You estimate 20%.   B: 20%

C. What percentage of conversations result in an in-person appointment?
You estimate 50%.

    C: 50%

D. What percentage of in-person appointments result in a sale?
You estimate 50%.

    D: 50%

Now, we perform the following calculation to figure out how many prospects you need to achieve your goal:

E. Number of prospects in pipeline required for success

$$\frac{(A) = 15}{(B) \times (C) \times (D)} \qquad E = 300$$

$(20\% \times 50\% \times 50\%) = 5\%$

You now know that your team needs to identify 300 prospects to secure 15 customers and meet their goals. That's assuming, of course, that your conversion assumptions are accurate. If your team can convert phone calls to actual conversations at a higher rate or turn more in-person appointments into sales, then they won't need 300 prospects. But it's better to err on the conservative side because, worst case scenario, your team will exceed its goals.

Next, you need to figure out how much time the team needs to spend to achieve this goal. Begin by multiplying the number of prospects needed times the percentage of phone calls that result in a conversation.

F. The number of complete calls your will have
(F) = (E) × (B) = 300 × 20% = calls   F = 60 calls

Then calculate the number of in-person appointments they need to complete by multiplying the number of phone calls times the percentage of calls that result in an in-person meeting:

G. Number of in-person appointments (G) = (F) × (C) 60 × 50%   G = 30 appts

Based on your past experience as a sales director, you know the following:

- Each phone attempt takes 1 minute on average
- Each live phone conversation with a prospect lasts 10 minutes
- Each in-person appointment lasts 30 minutes
- Each salesperson has to meet with a prospect only one time to close a sale

Now you are ready to figure out how much time it will take to meet your team's sales goal:

H. Minutes spent on incomplete calls: 1 minute per phone call   H = 1 minute

I. Minutes spent on complete conversations 10 minutes per live call   I = 10 minutes

J. Minutes spent meeting with prospects in-person 30 minute meetings   J = 30 minutes

K. Time spent on incomplete calls = (H) × (E – F) 1 min × (300 – 60)   K = 240 minutes

L. Time spent on complete calls = (I) × (F) 10 min × 60 calls   L = 600 minutes

M. Time spent on in-person appts. = (J) × (G) 30 min × 30 appts   M = 900 minutes

N. Total minutes spent acquiring customers = K + L + M

N = 240 + 600 + 900 = 1740 minutes   N = 1740 minutes or 29 hours

O. Total minutes spent per customer acquisition = N divided by A

O = 1740/15   O = 116 minutes

P. Hours spent per customer acquisition (O) divided by 60 min

P = 116/60   P = 1.9 hours

Now you know that in the next month your team needs to spend <u>29 hours</u> prospecting to land <u>15 new client accounts</u> and meet their goal.

Finally, consider how long the sales cycle takes. If it takes 3 months to close a sale and your company does not have enough prospects in your pipeline to achieve your goals, you realize that you will need to make changes to your sales and marketing strategy to develop more prospects to achieve your team's sales objective. In this case, you need 300 prospects to meet the goal, but based on the original information, you only had 60 in your entire database. This is a perfect example of how sales and marketing need to work together to ensure goals are met. If you realize that you need more prospects, now is the time to discuss with marketing how you're going to get more prospects put through your system. Does marketing need to develop a specific marketing campaign or focus on more outreach to online sources?

BUILDING YOUR BUSINESS MODEL

Let's revisit your business model. With a focus on #3 Channels, #4 Customer Relationships, #7 Key Activities, and #8 Cost Structure, look at how the sales planning process impacts your model. When you plan sales activities, the channels that customers use to learn about products and services will impact how you approach sales, how much your sales strategies will cost, and how long your sales cycle is. It's important to look at all of your sales channels and customer relationships to ensure they align with the key sales activities that you deploy to be successful. Spend a few minutes reviewing the questions in these four sections of the business model canvas to ensure your plan aligns with target customers' needs and fits into your budget.

VIEW FROM THE TRENCHES

DetraPel—Repelling Stains One Customer at a Time

David Zamarin's business started like most entrepreneurs, from a problem he was personally facing that he was determined to solve. However, most entrepreneurs don't start their first business at the age of 15. Nonetheless, David's business vision began when he received his first pair of Nike Jordan sneakers. He was quite excited about his purchase, but his happiness quickly dissolved into a level of dismay when he realized how dirty his new sneakers looked after only a few weeks. He turned his frustration into a business, a shoe-cleaning business specifically, which he sold shortly after growing it to $25,000 in monthly revenues. Then, like any dedicated entrepreneur, he moved on to his next idea, creating a liquid repellent spray for shoes.

While in his sophomore year in high school, David secured access to a local laboratory where he could run a series of tests to find the right product mix to repel liquid from a variety of materials. After many rounds of trial and error, he created a new product, which he called DetraPel. David had his first product on the market by the middle of his sophomore year.

Let's step back a minute and discuss the problem David identified in the market. He explained, "It's hard to keep valuables, things like clothes, carpets, and vehicles, clean and stain-free. Today's stain repellents last under a month, are not always unsafe, and offer little versatility in terms of being able to use them on a variety of products." This was the focus of David's business—to create a line of hydrophobic sprays that repel liquids from porous and nonporous objects. DetraPel was formulated to be a nonflammable, water-based product that is 100% ecofriendly and EPA compliant. David clarified, "One application lasts approximately one year so you don't have to continuously spray your valuables. Plus, it utilizes superhydrophobic nanotechnology to protect a wide range of materials including wool, cotton, suede, velvet, leather, vehicles, and even building materials."

As a rising junior at Babson College, David's company is now run by a team of four students. They were featured on the TV show *Shark Tank* (ABC, 2018) in January 2018, where they landed a $200,000 deal from investors Mark Cuban and Lori Greiner for 25% of his company. *Shark Tank* is a popular American TV show that features

(Continued)

(Continued)

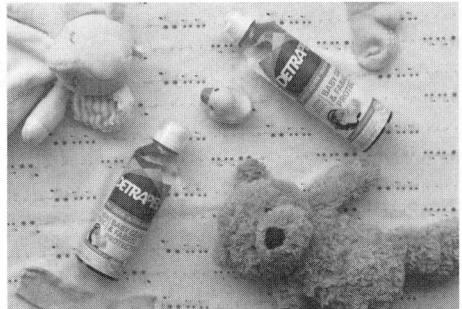
DetraPel

entrepreneurs who present their business ideas to a group of five investors with the hope of landing an investment deal from at least one of the experts.

While the deal remains under negotiation, the experience of being on *Shark Tank* at the age of 19 taught David, and his team, a lot about negotiating a deal. Plus, the publicity opened many doors for them, taking them from earning around $300 a day in revenue to $1,000 a day, literally overnight. They were able to leverage this immediate success and the attraction it garnered for their company to project revenue close to $6 million in 2018. That's not bad considering they earned around $300,000 in 2017. This led them to consider what the next stage of their business would look like. They concluded that being more consumer focused would support their current B2B model.

Nonetheless, David was committed to ensuring he didn't lose sight of the importance his large industrial business customers played in his business's growth and didn't want his sales to suffer if he took his eye off the ball and focused solely on the consumer market. David shared, "During the past two years, we'd been focusing on B2B, but now we want DetraPel to also become a household name. In 2018, we have decided to focus our marketing dollars on B2C, a new segment for us, in order to raise brand awareness. We believe this approach will allow us to get our foot in the door of more businesses, mainly large, industrial companies, and sell them more product, since they will have heard of our brand. We are already working on some very big deals, including one with a car manufacturer, and another with a large movie theatre chain. It's all very exciting, but clearly requires a different sales approach than we've had before."

Hear David's story directly from him—watch his interview on NewTV (2018) in Boston.

In Their Shoes: Achieving DetraPel's Sales Goals

Think about the opportunity as well as the challenges David and his team face. What specific next steps would you recommend to him to grow his business? Please describe five actions you believe he should take to secure more consumers (B2C) customers while concurrently continuing to market and service his very important business (B2B) customers.

Five actions that you believe David and his team should take to grow his B2C customer base:

1.

2.

3.

4.

5.

FOCUS ON APPLICATION: WAKU

The Entrepreneurial Journey

It's time to revisit Waku. While Waku is a consumer product, Juan and Nico recognized early on how difficult it would be to sell their products online to consumers. They understood that their product needed to be distributed by businesses whose values and mission aligned with theirs.

Therefore, they recognized that they needed to work with small, local food markets that catered to individuals who cared about all-natural beverages and whose customers were willing to spend a premium to purchase these types of products, since Waku was priced at the high end of the market relative to other premium drinks. Their first step was to create a database of stores within a 50-mile radius of Boston, their home base, and once they established this database, they agreed to create categories that represented each store's value to them. They didn't own a database program so decided to add the following categories to an Excel file to track their progress with prospects. They came up almost 200 prospects in the area.

1. Store Name
2. Address
3. Website
4. Buyer—Decision Maker
5. Phone/E-mail
6. Type of Store (natural, specialty, restaurant, etc.)
7. Waku Account Manager
8. Purchase Date(s): first, second, third, etc.
9. Demo Date(s): first, second, third, etc.
10. Monthly Volume
11. Pricing of Competitive Products
12. Number of Rows of Shelf Space
13. Store Social Media Sites
14. Number of Visits
15. Dates of Visits and Outcome
16. Next Steps With Customer

They actually had more categories but as they began to use this system, linked to a Google Sheet so they could exchange information, they realize that this wasn't going to be effective. There were too many fields, and given the "flat" nature of an Excel file (or Google Sheet), they couldn't easily crunch any numbers and analyze the data. They were very focused on getting out to begin selling but also wanted to be efficient and effective in how they managed

(Continued)

(Continued)

prospects so they could analyze their sales data and all activities.

In Their Shoes: Creating a Customer Sales Database

Think about Waku's challenge.

- What do you recommend they do going forward?
- Should they maintain an Excel file/Google Sheet to track information or should they purchase a simple database?
- What should they include in the database?
- What categories do you recommend they create to better manage customers?
- Is anything missing that you think is important for them to understand about their business customers?

AHAs
Lessons and Takeaways

In this chapter, we focused on the critical steps that you need to take to align sales and marketing goals. It should be clear after reading the chapter that creating a harmonious working relationship between sales and marketing requires hard work, effort, and incentives. Key highlights of the chapter include the following:

- Understand that sales and marketing goals must be aligned, and each group should have the opportunity to experience life on the other side, so they grasp firsthand the value that each plays in growing the business.
- Analyze and react to your customers' needs before and during the development of products and services is easier than developing products based on engineers' or programmers' interests.
- In developing sales processes and systems, you begin by first identifying the critical areas that impact your company's success. These will be unique to each company; however, understanding your customers' and prospects' current and future behavior is essential to your success. You will need to understand and review the specific data required before you launch your business to help you make informed sales and marketing decisions.
- Having the ability to use the data stored in a customer relationship management (CRM) system will enable you to turn raw material (numbers and facts) into knowledge, which in turn will allow you to better serve your customers' needs and see

trends that will help you build your business and your brand.

- Whether you are running a small business or getting ready to launch one, everybody in your organization needs to learn how to sell. Once you have spent a few months wearing your "sales" shoes, you will begin to see patterns and cycles emerge as you better understand what your customers need and want from you.

TOOLKIT

Worksheet 8.1: Sales Conversion

Begin the sales calculation by answering the following questions about your business to the best of your ability. If you don't know, take an educated guess. You will need these numbers for the next worksheets, so be careful in completing your calculations.

A. Number of new business customers required A _____%

B. What % of phone calls result in a conversation? B _____%

C. What % of conversations result in an in-person appointment? C _____%

D. What % of in-person appointments result in a sale? D _____%

Now perform the following calculation to figure out how many prospects you need to achieve your goal:

E. Number of prospects in pipeline for success: $\frac{(A)}{(B) \times (C) \times (D)}$ E _____%

Now you need to figure out how much time you need to spend to achieve these goals. You begin by multiplying the number of prospects you need times the percentage of phone calls that result in a conversation.

F. The number of complete calls you will have (F) = (E) × (B) F _____%

Then calculate the number of in-person appointments by multiplying the number of phone calls times the percentage of calls that result in an in-person meeting:

G. Number of in-person appointments (G) = (C) × (F) G _____%

Worksheet 8.2: Sales Time Analysis

Now complete a time analysis to understand how much time you will spend prospecting. Please make sure you use the numbers you calculated in the previous worksheet to complete your time analysis.

Insert the numbers calculated in the previous **Sales Conversion Worksheet**.

A _____ E _____ F _____ G _____

Sales Time Analysis

- H. Minutes spent on an incomplete call — H _____
- I. Minutes spent on a complete conversation — I _____
- J. Minutes spent meeting with a prospect in person — J _____
- K. Time spent on incomplete calls = (H) × (E − F) — K _____
- L. Time spent on complete calls = (I) × (F) — L _____
- M. Time spent on in-person appts. = (J) × (G) — M _____
- N. Total minutes spent acquiring customers = K + L + M — N _____
- O. Total minutes spent per customer acquisition = N divided by A — O _____
- P. Hours spent per customer acquisition (O) divided by 60 minutes — P _____
- Q. Sales cycle (how long it takes to close a sale) in days — Q _____

If your sales cycle is 90 days from cold-calling a prospect to closing the deal, and you don't have any prospects in your pipeline or not enough to achieve your goals, you need to take action immediately to increase the number of prospects you have.

Worksheet 8.3: Sales Prospect Calculator

Use the formula below to determine how many prospects you need based on your ability to convert prospects into new customers.

- A. Number of new business customers required — A. _____%
- B. What percentage of prospects become qualified leads? — B. _____%
- C. What percentage of qualified leads become hot leads? — C. _____%
- D. What percentage of hot leads become sales? — D. _____%

Number of prospects required in your pipeline is

   E. Prospects _____ = New Clients Required _____
   (B) _____ × (C) _____ × (D) _____

Q. Sales cycle (use formula from Sales Time Analysis Worksheet) _____ days

If you don't have any prospects in your system now and it takes 3 months to convert a prospect into a sale, you will need more prospects to meet your goals.

Compare E to Q and develop a plan that increases your opportunity to meet your goals.

   E. _____ (number of prospects in pipeline required for success)
   Q. _____ (sales cycle in days)

Worksheet 8.4: Sales Analysis Projection

Sales	# Active* Customers	Total Revenue	Total Profit	Revenue/ Customer
Year _____				
Year _____				
Year _____				

*Active = purchase in the last 12 months

Prospect Data

- Number of **new prospects** required for current year projections _____
- Number of **repeat customers** required for current year projections _____
- Number of **prospects** in your system _____
- Closure Rate: Percentage of prospects that **convert to sales** _____%
- Sales cycle _____ days

Customer Revenue and Profit Analysis

Customer	$ of Total Revenue	% of Total Revenue	% of Total Profit
1.			
2.			

Customer	$ of Total Revenue	% of Total Revenue	% of Total Profit
3.			
4.			
5.			
6.			
7.			
8.			

Top 3 Product or Service Sales	Year ___		Year ___		Year ___	
	Revenue	Profit	Revenue	Profit	Revenue	Profit
1.						
2.						
3.						

Worksheet 8.5: Customer Profit and Time Analysis

1. Write down the top 10 profit-generating customers or distributors or businesses for your company (this can be a combination of B2B and B2C customers).

2. Note the percentage of total profit (or revenue if you do not know the profit) next to each.

3. Then write down the percentage of YOUR time spent growing and supporting each customer

Distributor/Customer	% of Total Profit (or Revenue)	% of YOUR Time Spent Growing/Supporting
1.		
2.		

Distributor/Customer	% of Total Profit (or Revenue)	% of YOUR Time Spent Growing/Supporting
3.		
4.		
5.		
6.		
7.		
8.		
9.		
10.		
Future:		
Future:		

4. How large is the GAP between % of profit and % of your time supporting this person/company?

5. Is there anybody or company on this list who has great potential if you spend more time with them? Highlight their name on the chart.

6. Create five actions that you will commit to taking to align the amount of time you spend with your top revenue generators. When you're done, add these actions to your plan:

   a.

   b.

c.

d.

e.

Worksheet 8.6: Data Capture Plan/Dashboard

Data You Need to Make Sales and Business Decisions	Process to Obtain Data	Frequency of Updating and Reviewing Data	Person(s) Responsible

CHAPTER NINE

SOLUTION SELLING

SALES IS ABOUT LISTENING

In this chapter, we will explore the importance of sales skills for every entrepreneur, regardless of your interest in pursuing a career in sales. Many entrepreneurs are comfortable and familiar with the sales process. However, for those who dread networking or see sales as self-promotion, this chapter of the book is a must-read. Selling is not about forcing a service or solution upon somebody who doesn't want or need it. It's about actively listening to your prospective customers, identifying their key needs, and determining how you can meet their needs. It's an essential part of marketing your business. Owners, entrepreneurs, and visionaries for a company or concept must be great salespeople in order to grow their organization and learn how to convince others to join them on the journey. They won't simply be selling their vision to customers but to investors, potential employees, business partners, and many other stakeholders. In this chapter, we will cover the sales process from networking and planning sales calls to cultivating business relationships.

SALES FOR THOSE WHO HATE SELLING

Unless you are trained in sales, the word itself tends to conjure up an impression of doing something malevolent or evil. Think *used car salesman* and you'll know exactly what we are referring to (even if you aren't from the United States where the term was coined). Let's explore an example of an organization built around a salesforce but never used the word *sales* to describe the professionals who worked for the company who were, yes, selling the health care company's services. New Medico was a firm operating in the 80s

Learning Objectives

In this chapter, you will learn to

- learn and practice the various techniques for improving and gaining comfort with your ability to sell.
- discover important tactics your sales efforts.
- understand how to prepare for the various stages of the sales process.
- embrace the importance of networking as a way to grow your business.

throughout the United States. They offered neurologic rehabilitation services to individuals who had suffered a traumatic brain injury. The company understood that hiring medical professionals such as nurses, physical therapists, and speech therapists to tell their brand story (e.g., sell) would be a strategic part of building their business. These health care professionals were called "marketing associates" but they spent time in their territory providing information to individuals who needed the neurologic services the firm offered. In other words, they were salespeople. But the concern New Medico had was, if they called their sales team "salespeople," few people would be willing to speak to them. As a sales-focused organization, the company truly mastered the ability to uncover opportunities in the market through the creation of a very large (250 person) sales team dedicated to understanding and then satisfying the needs of the market. They achieved a lot of success and were able to bring much needed health care rehabilitative services to patients who needed them.

In the 1980s, when New Medico was at its pinnacle, *sales* plus *health care* did not go together and were rarely spoken in the same sentence. Some of that has changed and it's more commonplace nowadays to see medical practices sell and promote their health care services, but the stigma associated with selling was prohibitive to success in that time period. How much has changed about perceptions about sales? Well, the stigma still lingers in many people's minds when they think about selling. Why does sales make so many people think of unethical, perhaps even dodgy practices? Have all of those "used car salesmen" ruined it for the rest of the salespeople who are proud to sell their services because they know that it doesn't mean pushing unwanted products or services on people who don't want them? Perhaps we need to begin with a definition of *sales* that will increase your comfort level with the process.

Sales is about creating a dialogue with potential customers to educate them about the benefits your products or services can offer them. It's truly an educational process and all good sales conversations are two way and engaging. The more you learn about your prospects, the better you will be able to explain to them how you can meet their needs (if there is an alignment of needs with what you offer). Plus, the more prospects learn about your company, the better they will be at making an informed purchasing decision. Think of it like dating. Do you want to continue exploring mutual connections, or is a second date out of the question?

Many business owners have stated that "they really don't sell anything; their approach is more professional." Let's translate that to mean that they don't think sales is a professional endeavor. But they couldn't be further from the truth. When these "non-salespeople" describe what they do to win customers, it sounds a lot like selling. They meet with potential customers to better define and understand their needs and then help them explore solutions that will address those needs. If they can offer a solution, terrific. If not, then hopefully they will point these potential customers in the direction of somebody who can solve their problems. If you don't call that sales, then what would you call it?

There's nothing wrong with that, right? Well, from their perspective, this is not selling but exploring opportunities. But trust us, it's sales, and regardless of the word they use to describe the process, it's important for them and their businesses. Many of them are actually quite good at it as long as they don't view themselves as salespeople.

OK, let's drop titles and discuss skills that make selling a pleasure (or at least not a chore). Before you begin the sales process, you must first make sure you know all of the benefits that your products or services provide so you can then align the most critical benefits with your various prospective customers. This needs to be done in advance of your sales planning activities. Review your customer profiles and determine which customers need which benefits and think about this before EACH communication with a prospective new customer. Before you begin, let's create a clear definition of your customer because you will be selling to more than just the individuals who use your products. Remember, the end user is not always your customer. In addition to end users, your customers include the following:

- Decision makers—This includes individuals such as parents who make purchases for their children or managers who buy products for members of their team. They may not use the product, but they make the yes or no determination about purchasing it.

- Influencers—This category includes people who may recommend your product or service to others. In social media, an influencer is somebody who has secured a reputation as an expert in specific topics and shares his or her recommendations with others. These individuals don't only exist in the virtual world. They can be respected thought leaders on a topic or a respected businessperson or mom whom others look to for guidance in decision making.

- Partners—These individuals are critical for success. Most small businesses need to develop partnerships with organizations and individuals who can help them succeed. Their needs will be different than those of your end users, so it will be important to understand what they care about and what is important for them to be successful so they can support you.

Now, let's answer the following questions will allow you to service prospects better and show them how your product helps solve their problems. They may sound a lot like your market research question. They should, since understanding your customers' needs at this stage is just as vital as it was during the customer discovery phase.

- What are their needs?
- What are their habits and behaviors that influence their decision-making processes?
- Why do they value my products or services?

- What questions do I need to ask to uncover their needs?
- Based on what I already know about the customer, what benefits are likely the most important?

READY TO START SELLING?

What skills do you need to have meaningful discussions with potential customers to better define and understand their needs and then help them explore solutions that will address those needs? Here's a list of critical skills that will help you be a proficient salesperson, and—oh yeah—a better business person.

1. Communication and listening skills
2. Analytical skills
3. Organizational skills
4. Time management and discipline
5. Keen interest in learning
6. Passion

Communication and Listening Skills

Number one on the list is communication skills. What does it mean to have good communication skills? Does it mean that you must be able to talk for 20 minutes nonstop about all the features of your product or service? No, although being able to express yourself well is an important part of being a strong communicator. The key to being a good communicator is knowing when to speak and when to listen. A good salesperson is one who knows how to ask key questions, who then sits back and actively listens to her prospective customer, and then asks a few more questions and listens again for the customer's response. If the salesperson is doing all the talking, then it's impossible for her to understand her prospect's needs. As a rule of thumb, try to speak no more than 20% of the time; instead, spend your time actively listening to what your prospect is telling you. That person is giving you clues about how you can solve his needs; if you don't listen, you'll miss the clues and lose the opportunity to present information and solutions that could help you develop a new customer relationship.

Analytical Skills

What does it mean to be analytical when it comes to selling? Do you have to have an engineering degree to be able to succeed in this category? Of course not. Having strong analytical skills means being able to see, hear, and understand the information that your prospective customer gives you; analyze the clues; and turn those data into a discussion of how you can provide a solution for the customer. For example, if customers share information about the various products they have purchased in the past that did not meet their needs, plus you are able to secure data about their buying habits, attitudes, and other areas of interest, you should be able to take this information and analyze it. How? You would want to first identify how you can differentiate your offer so it addresses their needs that the other products they tried did not. Second, you should begin to look for trends. Are individuals with similar buying habits and attitudes sharing the same challenges with you? If you see a trend, begin to go through your database of prospects and try to discover individuals who have similar characters who might be good candidates for your next sales meeting. Basically, take the information that you learn and turn it into knowledge through analysis of the facts shared.

Organizational Skills

Why is being organized important in selling? Sales can be a very complicated process. You must have some type of system to help you keep track of your customers and prospects, and their identified needs. Otherwise, the chances are that after your first or second meeting, you'll have a hard time remembering the specifics of each customer's needs and thus will be unable to meet those needs. You also need to be able to organize your process so that you work effectively and efficiently and don't waste customers' time. Fortunately, there are many good and reasonably priced customer relationship management systems on the market to make the process easier for you. Review Chapter 8's discussion on CRM systems. These systems can also help with your analysis of the data and provide easier methods for you to see correlations among the data gathered about customers.

Time Management and Discipline

Time management goes hand in hand with being organized. Great salespeople don't simply have a system for managing their time; they manage their time to their best advantage. What does that mean? It means setting priorities. They understand which prospects have the greatest propensity to buy so that they can determine how much time they will spend with each category of prospects. Prospects who fall into the A category—perhaps defined as those who are likely to buy within the next 30 days—should get more attention than those in the C category, who might be viewed as being unlikely to buy in the next year. Great salespeople don't have more time on their hands than the average person; they just know how to use their time to their advantage. Recall from the last chapter how Waku was categorizing its prospects. This is an important activity for you to complete for your business.

Why do salespeople need to be disciplined? With the ease of a click on a website, mobile app, or social media site, it's quite simple for anybody to show an interest in learning more about a product or service. This is a double-edged sword. On the positive side, you might secure more leads than ever before. However, on the downside, identifying those that are genuinely good leads (likely buyers) is quite a tedious task. Therefore, being disciplined is required to make numerous calls and accept rejection along the way. These are all part of the sales process. Discipline is also required to follow up and follow through with everything that you promise to your prospective customers. Nothing leaves a worse impression than committing to share something (perhaps a sample or demo) and not delivering on your promise. Part of your time management process should involve defining and categorizing your most important leads. Do you spend the majority of your time working the leads that will generate the greatest revenue or business for your company, or do you work all your leads at the same pace?

Keen Interest in Learning

Even before you begin working with your customers, understanding and defining their needs, you have to know your product inside and out. While this might begin with the features of the product that you are selling, it expands well beyond that into translating those features into benefits that your products or services provide to your customers. These benefits will vary greatly depending on the customers, but you have to know all of them so that when you are listening to your customers, you can explain the specific benefits that will hold the greatest appeal for each target customer.

Passion

How many times have you purchased a product or service from somebody who was wishy-washy or lackluster about its value? Probably not very often, right? Even if you were really excited about the product, if the salesperson didn't seem to care, that could easily deflate your interest level. On the other hand, when people have been passionate about what they were selling and convinced you that they really believed in the value of the product, this could easily sway you from your own wishy-washy position and be enough to get you over the proverbial fence to make the purchase. That's why business owners are typically the best salespeople for their companies; it's rare that they don't feel passionately about what they're selling. If you're hiring individuals to sell for you, keep this idea in mind, because you want your salespeople to have the same enthusiasm and zeal that you have for your products or services.

DO YOUR HOMEWORK

Have you ever been in a store and asked the salesperson a question about the product, only to spend the next 20 minutes listening to them talk endlessly about all the product features, even ones you could not care less about? This type of sales approach tends to overwhelm most prospects and may even turn you off from doing business with them. It's critical that you customize your presentation to address the customer's needs and concerns. Talking about product features and benefits that are irrelevant is simply a waste of the customer's time—and yours.

In order to be effective at selling, you must perfect the art of "active listening." This means that while prospects are answering your questions about their needs and interests, you are formulating smart responses that show how your products offer the benefits and value they seek. Before you meet with any prospect, you must know the benefits of the products that you offer and know which of those benefits match their needs based on your current knowledge. There are many ways to learn this. Begin by searching their company's website and social media sites. What are they talking about? What matters to this company? In addition, what do you personally know about the prospect? Can you read about their background on the website or check out their LinkedIn profile? What mutually shared values and interests do you have that are relevant to your product or service? Now, we are not implying that you should stalk the person but a certain level of research should be completed so the person understands that you truly care about understanding their needs, even before you have a one-on-one dialogue with them.

In addition to researching their company, you need to have a very good grasp of the industry and environmental issues that impact them. Why? If your customer is part of an industry that's changing in some way, either in decline or growing, you have to understand how that affects their goals and decisions. For example, if you sell products that have a negative environmental impact (perhaps they can't be recycled or contain hazardous materials), then understanding the implications of this is critical in your sales technique. Your product may have benefits that offset the negative features, providing value for your customers, but you need to understand how to positively position the benefits while downplaying (not ignoring) the negative features. That doesn't mean lying or hiding information, but you need to address the concerns up front and understand how they will affect your sales. The better prepared you are, the better the chances that you can respond to customer concerns with information demonstrating other strong features and benefits or by making comparisons with similar products.

Finally, understanding your competition is critical in every sales activity and is important in navigating a path to success. You need to have a solid knowledge of how your product or service compares to that of your competitors or substitutes. As with industry knowledge, the better the data you have about all the forces that affect your solution, the better prepared you will be to combat any questions prospects have and to be able to focus on the value you offer relative to your competitors. This is critical in your role of opening doors. Remember, your competition is not only those companies providing identical or similar services, but also those companies providing a substitute *solution* that rivals yours.

FIVE STAGES OF THE SALES PROCESS

Are you ready to think about specific strategies that you can use during various stages of the sales cycle? This information should be seen as a guide for you to determine how you can sell your products or solutions using a customer-focused model. However, it's important for every entrepreneur and business owner to develop strong sales skills and your own style to grow your business. If you're not comfortable with selling, then we strongly advocate that you attend a sales training program to improve your skills and confidence to enhance your relationships with prospects and customers.

There are five key stages to the sales process:

1. Preparation
2. The Introduction
3. Preparing for the In-Person Appointment
4. The Meeting
5. Follow-Up and Servicing the Account's Needs

Stage One: Preparation

Cold calling/e-mailing is an activity that almost every person—even highly skilled salespeople—loathe. Ideally, you will have warm leads (where you have met the person, they have indicated an interest via your website, or somebody has suggested you call) so you don't need to make a lot of completely cold calls (no introduction, no knowledge of the person). Your goal should be to secure some type of introduction to the person before you call or e-mail them (through a mutual acquaintance or some other connection). It helps to use tools like LinkedIn to see who in your network might know the prospect you are contacting.

What should your approach be when preparing to call a prospect? Many salespeople begin this activity by reviewing their prospect database and choosing which prospects to contact. Important strategies for success include

- Organized contact list: Making sure the names of your prospects are in one central location such as a customer relationship database or even an excel spreadsheet. An important note is that spreadsheets are not ideal for tracking customer information, as we mentioned earlier, because once you begin to track meeting dates and important details about their business, it will be more difficult to access this information quickly and use it.

- Prospect status/ID: Once you have all of the names in your system, review your list carefully and try to determine the status of each person. Status/ID refers to the person's role as it relates to your company. Some general categories include these:
    - Customer
    - Key account: very important customer generating a lot of business for your company
    - Partner: for marketing purposes, usually refers to a company or individual with access to multiple prospects
    - Prospect (rank this—see below)
    - Competitor
    - Former customer
- Prospect rank: Once you have determined the status, it's important to now rank the potential of each prospect (A = hot, B = lukewarm, C = cold lead). Your criteria will be strictly related to your business. Some ideas to begin the ranking process are noted below:
    - present or past relationship with your company (might not be ready to buy but are not cold leads)
    - potential business revenue or volume they can generate
    - expressed interest in a specific product
    - completed an inquiry online
    - known purchaser of similar products sold by your competition
    - other factors that impact sales potential
- Prioritize list by rank: Prioritize A/B/C prospects in your database so you can easily begin making calls to A prospects, then B, and maybe C. You might want to use your B list to practice calls. The hardest folks to call are your C list of cold leads. However, make sure you have a polished presentation before speaking with your A list.
- Set a phone or e-mail schedule: It's important to create a schedule for phone calls, e-mails and meeting times. This is critical because if you don't set aside certain times of the day and specific days to complete this outreach activity, then the calls very likely won't happen (something else will always get in the way).
- Set a call or e-mail target: Schedule a minimum number of hours that you will make calls or send out e-mails. If this is going to be 10% to 15% of your time then you may dedicate 5 hours a week to this activity. Pick a schedule that

works best for you AND one that you will stick to. Many people have found that making calls or sending e-mails out on Monday morning and Friday afternoons are not very effective because prospects are simply not available during those times or are cleaning out their inboxes from the weekend. But this criterion varies depending on your customers and your business. You might need to try various times before you make your own determination. Below are a few different schedules to consider:

- Tuesday–Friday: 9:00 a.m.–10:15 a.m.
- Tuesday and Friday: 9:15 a.m.–10:30 a.m.; Wednesday & Thursday: 1:15 p.m.–2:30 p.m.
- Tuesday and Thursday: 8:30 a.m.–11:00 a.m.

- Predetermine potential meeting schedule: Schedule a minimum number of hours a week to go on in-person appointments but allow for flexibility based on prospects needs. You may decide that you are going to spend the same number of hours going on in-person calls as making calls and sending out e-mails until business picks up and then you will spend more time in person with prospects. Perhaps include one morning and one afternoon each week. For example, you decide that Wednesday mornings and Thursday afternoons are the times you would ideally like to go out to meet with prospects but hold Friday mornings as a possibility. This will help when you schedule appointments because you can state "Are you available on Thursday at 1 p.m. since I'll be in your area visiting other customers?"

Stage Two: The Introduction

It sounds obvious, but it's worth emphasizing: The introduction—whether it's an actual phone call or a well-written e-mail, is critical to your success, so plan it carefully. Below is a sample script that you can use as a guideline for developing your own. The important aspect of a script is to have ownership of it. What does that mean? It should reflect your own ideas, be in your own words and in your own conversational style. If it appears that you are reading a script or have memorized something that you're saying to your prospects, you'll sound insincere and probably won't land an in-person appointment.

Script Template

Introduction: Good morning {their name}. I am the {title} for {your company name}. My name is {your name}.

Reason for the call: The reason I am calling is to because you completed an online inquiry form about our new service OR we have a new business services designed for owners like you to BENEFIT, BENEFIT.

Seek more information/Actively listen: {their name}, I'm wondering what you or {their company name} is currently doing in terms of xxx services? {THEIR RESPONSE} Are you satisfied with the services you are receiving?

Request for the appointment: {their name}, from what you've told me, I really think we'd both have something to gain by sitting down for 15 minutes. I'm going to be visiting (ANOTHER BUSINESS) next Wednesday morning. I'd like to stop by to briefly discuss our services with you. Does 11 a.m. work for you or would after lunch be better?

Close: Thank you! I look forward to seeing you next week. If you need to reach me beforehand, please e-mail or call me at xxxx@xxx.xxx or xxx-xxx-xxxx.

There are many factors that increase your success with phone calls:

- Know your value proposition or benefits as they relate to each prospect.

- Listen carefully.

- Practice and tape record your pitch to see how you sound. If your prospect is OK with this, you can tape your phone conversations so you can listen to how you sound and critique and improve yourself. However, keep in mind the fact that you have to inform the person with whom you're speaking that you are recording the conversation. If you think that might make the other person uncomfortable, don't do it. Another option is to role-play with colleagues, friends, and family and then have them critique you. Remember, the more you practice, the better and more confident you will be.

- Have a rehearsed script that you are comfortable following but be prepared to improvise as you uncover more information about your prospect.

- Be professional.

- Be confident.

Stage Three: Preparing for the In-Person Appointment

Assuming you were successful and have landed an in-person appointment, how should you prepare for that meeting? Below are some steps and guidelines to follow.

1. Preplanning Session
    - Update your database with information about the prospect that you learned from the phone call or e-mail response you received.
    - Determine your meeting goals based on your phone conversation. Did you learn anything new about the prospect and his or her needs? If so,

make sure you address these needs and prepare your presentation based on this knowledge.
- What do you expect or want to occur as a result of this appointment?
- Do you want to close the deal or ideally get a presentation with other key decision makers at the organization?
- Be realistic in determining your goals as you prepare for success.

- Research the organization or company and person online or through contacts and use this information to demonstrate to the prospect that you have taken the time to learn about their business and about them and are seriously interested in working with them.
- Imagine your meeting or conversation. This may sound very "new age," but imagining a conversation can be very empowering, forcing you to think through the opening, closing, and goals of the meeting.
- Practicing what you're going to say in front of the mirror will help prepare you and develop confidence in what you're going to say and how you're going to say it.

Stage Four: The Meeting

Now you're ready for your meeting. Below is a sample outline of how the conversation might unfold. This is just a guide. The key is to be prepared and actively listen so you don't need a prepared speech. However, you should have questions that will help you better identify their needs. This will allow you to have a focused meeting where you can discuss those benefits that you think will be of highest value to the prospect.

1. Small Talk/Introduction: Many meetings begin with small talk, which should be limited to a few minutes to allow you to get to know the person better and understand their personal and business goals. Some topics for small talk include recent events, sports, weather, and kids (if you notice pictures of their children on their desk). However, don't get too personal and avoid politics completely. This is simply a warm-up for the real dialogue to follow. This is not a personal visit, and you really want to get down to business. If you spend too much time on personal information such as talking about kids or community activities, then you might not get to your real goals (especially if time is a factor).

    - If small talk allows you to uncover critical information as it relates to your product, then it's OK to explore it further.
    - Remember, this prospect agreed to meet with you for a specific amount of time. It's critical to respect that limit.

2. Acknowledge the reason for your visit.
   - Demonstrate your knowledge of their business.
   - Confirm the amount of time allotted for the meeting. You can state something like "I mentioned in our phone call that this wouldn't take more than 15 minutes of your time. I want to be sure that still works with your schedule."
   - Conversation/Exchange stage—Ask probing questions to discover more about her business or personal needs as it relates to your product or service
   - Please note the following: Prospects should speak approximately 80% of the time. This is only a guideline, and there's no scientifically "correct" amount of time, but if you use 80% as a benchmark, then you can target this to help you think about the amount of listening time you should allocate.
   - Determine in your mind the solutions that will best meet the customer's needs. Now you have entered into the Solution Selling Stage of the conversation.

3. Solution Selling Stage: Now that you understand their needs and have thought about a solution for this prospect, you should do the following:
   - Confirm her needs and present your solutions.
   - Check for understanding or acceptance. You should make a statement that ensures you're both in sync about the customer's needs, such as, "It appears that texture and taste are critical factors in deciding which new pies to purchase for your restaurant. Based on all the taste test we just completed, do the pies you've tested meet your needs? Is this what you expected?"

4. Closing Stage: Finally, you should close the conversation by
   - asking for the next step, which should be your meeting goal. This does not necessarily need to be "asking for the sale" if it's not appropriate at this stage.
   - suggesting that the next meeting be with her business partner (so you can close the deal), or perhaps suggesting there should be a meeting next Wednesday at 9 a.m. to review specific customized products or to sign paperwork. The following is *not* a request for a next step: "I'd love to get together again to discuss your needs. Give me a call when you're ready." It does not necessarily lead to any activity related to the purchase of your product and takes you out of the driver's seat. You want to be in control and move forward.

Stage Five: Follow-Up and Servicing the Account's Needs

Initial follow-up to a meeting is just as critical as the actual meeting. You've come all this way with a prospect; don't "blow the opportunity" because you simply didn't bother to follow up. When you return to your office remember to

- update your database with
    - notes of your conversation and important info about the prospect.
    - ranking of account (if it's changed from a B to an A—we all hope not vice versa).
    - next steps and dates.
- Send a thank-you to the prospect. This can be e-mail or a letter (a letter being more impressive and memorable these days). You should include
    - a thank-you for their time,
    - restatement of prospect needs,
    - restatement of benefits discussed, and
    - list of promised action items.
    - Include additional ideas or research that you conducted after the meeting related to the topics discussed or questions raised. For example, "I want to send you an article I was reading that, based on our conversation, I think you will find valuable." That makes you an even more important asset.

Once you're updated your system, make sure you set aside the time to complete the follow-up steps, which may include other action items agreed to during the meeting or perhaps more research required.

The sale doesn't stop once the customer has paid his bill. When you are selling a solution to a customer, you are part of the team that is responsible for the experience he or she has with your company. This is especially important when selling a service to a customer. The level of support that you and your company provide customers pre-purchase through post-purchase impacts the customer experience. Remember, customers have the power to share their vision of your brand with others, many others, making them an unofficial member of your marketing and sales team. Therefore, if their experience with you after you have sold the product to them is negative, they will share this story over and over again. This will impact your ability to sell if the experience is negative and will empower you if the experience is positive. You want to ensure that the customer experience is a positive one throughout the life cycle of their engagement with your company. While many salespeople do not see this as part of their job, it will clearly impact their ability to convince others that their products and services are reliable and that the company cares about its customers based on how they treat them after they have paid their final invoice.

DEALING WITH OBJECTIONS

Dealing with objections is a concern every salesperson faces. What if your customers don't like what you are saying or disagree with you? How will you respond? The best way to deal with objection is to prepare for it by anticipating what the objections will be. Basically, facing your fear head on and realizing that, worse-case scenario, the prospect will end the call or the meeting. Let's face it, if that's the worst thing that can happen to you, then your risk isn't very great. Nonetheless, many people are so overwhelmed by this notion that they sometimes don't even try to meet with a prospect who they believe will basically reject them. However, mastering and conquering this fear will greatly increase your chances of success. Preparation is your friend. The best way to prepare for uncertain sales situations is to do your homework. Follow the next three steps to prepare for these tough calls:

1. Write down the person and company's name and describe very clearly what they do as it relates to your company.
2. Next, in detail, describe the needs this person and company has that you are confident you can solve or address. Remember, they quite likely don't know that you do this.
3. Review your competitors and understand how they solve or address these same needs. Make sure you understand how you compare to them.
4. Finally, anticipate their three biggest objections. Write these down and then note specifically what you will say or ask to overcome their objections.

Now you're ready. Use the worksheets in the toolkit at the end of the chapter to prepare for your next tough sales call.

SALES TIPS FOR BUILDING RELATIONSHIPS

Below are some additional ideas and tips to keep in mind throughout the relationship building process.

Contact Times

To increase your chances of speaking directly with the decision maker (and avoid the secretary or administrative assistant who screens calls), try calling or even e-mailing them at these "off" hours:

- 7 a.m. to 9 a.m.
- Lunchtime
- 5 p.m. to 7 p.m.

Typically, the higher up in the company a prospect is, the better this strategy works, since C-level individuals (CEO, CFO, CIO) tend to get in early or stay late. However, keep in mind the fact that in larger organizations C-level individuals are very difficult to reach and it may require additional creative thinking on your part to locate them and speak to them. You might want to pursue connecting to them via LinkedIn or via a contact who knows them.

Hot Buttons

All decision makers have a series of "hot buttons," issues that can keep them up at night. If you discuss one of their hot buttons and show how your product or service will address this issue, you will be able to connect with the prospects. Below are the typical big picture ones that may help you connect with prospects:

- quality
- service
- price
- competition
- industry changes
- regulations or tax implications

Open Versus Close-Ended Questioning Techniques

You should use a variety of open- and closed-ended questions or probes to learn more about prospects' needs. An open-ended question is one in which you give the person the opportunity to speak on a topic at length:

- During our phone call, we talked about xxx; how is this impacting your business?
- Given today's economy, what business issues keep you up at night?
- Where do you see your business 2 years from now?

A closed-ended question is one that seeks a short "yes" or "no" response. Examples of closed-ended questions include

- Have I given you enough information to allow you to set up our next meeting with your boss (identified critical decision maker)?
- Can you meet next Wednesday at 3 p.m. to discuss this further?
- Based on the information that we have discussed, can I e-mail you an invoice to begin the ordering process?

FOCUS ON APPLICATION: WAKU

The Entrepreneurial Journey

Clearly being able to present their value proposition was a critical goal for Juan and Nico. As founders of the company, they were quite confident that they could sell their brand and convey their benefits to the stores they were approaching. However, as they were growing, they realized that they were each wearing too many hats and needed to bring on a sales team to support them. Given the fact that they were very early stage in the development of the business, they were worried about spending money on hiring experienced salespeople. Nonetheless, they knew this is the type of person that they needed so, they decided to identify students with the right skill set and train them to sell their products for them. They agreed that would free up their time to work on the "key accounts" that the business had or was pursuing while their sales team could focus on smaller accounts, gain the skills they needed, and help them further gain traction in the market. They were also hoping that a superstar would appear from their crowd of newly trained salespeople who could be trusted with working larger, more critical accounts for them. To achieve their goal, they created a Sales Guide and did extensive one-on-one training with three new employees. Below is the guide that they used during the training program:

Waku Sales Process and Product Pitch

Below are critical steps to help you prepare for your sales calls.

1. Select a geographic territory where you will focus your time during a given day.

2. Plan your sales route the day before and work closely with us (Juan and Nico) to confirm that this is the right geographic territory and there are sufficient stores, cafes, and fitness centers in the area.

3. Pack your cooler with enough samples for the prospects you will be visiting. Make sure they are always cold when you offer them to the managers and owners.

4. When you arrive at a prospect, go inside and approach the cashier. Have a Waku bottle in your hands to be prepared to explain our story and benefit to the store in less than 15 seconds.

5. **Each time you walk into a prospect's store, remind yourself:**

   - I love this product.
   - I am a great salesperson.
   - I am amazing.
   - I will close this deal.
   - And smile a lot—this will boost your confidence and likeability.

Pitch Template for the Store

Hello, my name is _____. I am a sales representative of Waku food and beverage company. Have you heard about our product?

We are a local Boston-based food and beverage start-up looking to expand into _____.

(Continued)

(Continued)

Hopefully they will respond by saying something like "Great, what do you have to show me today?"

"Our product is a refreshing wellness tea called Waku—It is made with more than 20 herbs and flowers from the Andes Mountains of Ecuador. I am out today sharing our story and brand with a few new businesses in the area. Can I give you a sample of our product so you can see for yourself how refreshing it is? I also have a flyer to share with you."

Show them the flyer.

From here the conversation will progress naturally. Use your common sense and try to evaluate who you are talking to. First, determine if this person are the decision maker. If that's the case and the person seems to be somebody who cares about products that are ethically sourced or care about social impact and organic ingredients, focus on those benefits.

Juan Giraldo, Nico Estrella

However, if he or she seems more business-oriented, talk about the revenue and profit the company can gain from selling Waku.

Ideally, the conversation will flow and depending on how the direction it takes, below are a few key items that you should mention:

- We are a local brand started by Babson students.
- All of our ingredients are ethically sourced from small farms in the southern part of Ecuador.
- This is one of the most popular drinks in Ecuador. It is consumed either hot or cold with food and after working out.
- Our distribution is made through a local company in the greater Boston area. They also offer a variety of dairy products.

Make sure you show interest in their business. Ask about their needs and customers.

After the prospect understands what Waku offers, then ask the prospect to try the product. Questions you can ask tasting after include these:

- *What are the first three things that come into your mind after trying Waku?*
- *What do you think of the flavor?*
- *What do you think about the packaging?*
- *Do you think that your customers would be interested in buying Waku?*
- *How do RTD (ready-to-drink) beverages sell in your store?*
- *Which brand is your best seller?*

After giving you feedback, the prospect is more likely to be invested in Waku, and it will be easier to begin to close the deal. Questions you can ask to begin to close the deal include the following:

- *Would you like to offer our product to your customers? We will support brand sales in your store by offering free tasting demos and will also send social media messages to our audience to go to your store.*
- *We can start with a case deal. If you buy four cases, you will get one free or, even better, if you buy eight cases, you will get three free. Which would you prefer?*

Before you complete any follow-up, make sure you complete Waku's Sales Tracking document:

- Fill out your visits tracking tab with the highlights of your sales conversations. This tab serves as a journal to remind you about key highlights of your prospect interactions.
- Fill out the store database tab if you found new stores that Waku currently does not have in the system.
- Add stores where you "closed sales (closed sales refers to deals that have been won)" in the weekly check-ins tab (organized by territory). This tab helps you keep track of your visits ensuring you can easily remember to visit each account at least once every 2 weeks. The difference about the Waku brand and other brand is "We SHOW UP and take care of our customers."
- Add stores that you believe you will close a deal with in the near future (30–60 days) in the pipeline tab. This tab helps you and the company see the potential business that is likely in the next few months.

Always make sure you leave the store with the contact information of the decision maker so you can follow up. Depending on the outcome of the visit, one of the e-mails that follow will be appropriate to send. Feel free to make slight modifications in the wording based on your personal style. We don't want this to sound like a script, but we also want to ensure we consistently deliver a similar message about our brand through all customer touch points.

Scenario 1. Buyer was not that interested in the product

Dear xyz,

It was a pleasure to meet you yesterday! Again, my name is Juan Giraldo, cofounder of Waku—Healthy Tradition—a natural food and beverage company bringing ancestral traditions from the Andes Mountains of Ecuador. Our first product is a

(Continued)

(Continued)

herbal infusion locally known as "the Healing Water" that has been consumed for centuries in the Andes Mountains of Ecuador for its health properties.

We are a local brand born at Babson College, and we have a pipeline of products based on aromatic herbs from the Andes Mountains that are really tasty, healthy, and refreshing that I think can be a great fit for your brand and customers. Did your team like the product? I hope they did!

I know you know more than anyone else that consumers' preferences regarding beverages are drastically changing and they are demanding healthier and different options in restaurants. Our goal is to complement your menu with a healthier option that definitely has a space in the market.

We are in a learning stage and feedback is really important to us so, even if you are not interested in carrying our product, I would really appreciate your feedback. I am sure we can learn a lot from your experience.

Thank you so much and I wish you a great day!

PS: Here is our website and social media information in case you want to learn more.

Scenario 2. You left a sample with the decision maker

Dear xyz,

It's a pleasure to e-meet you. My name is Juan Giraldo, cofounder of Waku—Healthy Tradition. We are a natural food and beverage company bringing ancestral traditions from the Andes Mountains of Ecuador. Our first product is a herbal infusion locally known as "the Healing Water" that has been consumed for centuries in the Andes Mountains of Ecuador for its health properties.

I visited your Cambridge restaurant today and received your contact information from Steve. I wanted to share a sample of our product with you and get your feedback about it. Did you like the product?

We are a local brand born at Babson College, and we have a pipeline of products based on aromatic herbs and superfoods from the Andes Mountains that I think can be a great fit for your brand and customers.

Are you in the restaurant on Friday morning so I can visit with you? Please let me know and have a great week!

In the meantime, please check out our website and social media channels to learn a bit more of what we are doing.

Scenario 3. Follow up after meeting with buyer

Hello xyz,

This is Juan Giraldo with Waku—Healthy Tradition. It was a pleasure meeting you today and thank you for your time.

Please find attached to this e-mail our sales sheet, which outlines our prices and our communications plan to make Waku sell off the shelf with high turnover.

Once again, thank you, and I look forward to building a win–win business relationship with you!

In the meantime, please check out our website and social media channels to learn a bit more of what we are doing.

Scenario 4. Follow up after they bought their first case

Hello xyz,

This is Juan Giraldo with Waku—Healthy Tradition. It was a pleasure meeting you today and thank you for helping to share Waku with your customers at XYZ!

Please find our sales sheet attached to this e-mail, which outlines our prices and a few key features of our product.

Once again, thank you and I look forward to building a win–win business relationship with you!

In the meantime, please check out our website and social media channels to learn a bit more of what we are doing.

In Their Shoes

What do you think about the sales process that Juan and Nico have established? Do you think this is the right approach to training their salespeople? What would you recommend to them if you were hired as a sales consultant to help them with their sales strategy? List three to five recommendations that you have for them to secure more customers. Please make sure these recommendations are SMART (specific, measurable, actionable, realistic and time based).

AUTHOR'S NOTE

Trust and Building Relationships as Seen Through the Eyes of a Car Buyer

When I was in my mid-20s, I had my heart set on buying a 2-door Saab 900s. I knew what amenities I wanted and went to a dealership recommended by a friend. As I was test driving the car (and falling madly in love with it), I told the salesman (whose name I still remember almost 30 years later) that I always wanted to drive a manual, stick shift but had never learned. He asked me, "If you knew how to drive one, would you prefer that to an automatic?" and I responded, "Absolutely." "Great," he stated, "then I will teach you how to drive one and ensure that you are safe and comfortable before you leave the dealership." Not only did he get me a great price on the car, but he also kept his promise and taught me how to drive it. He did such a great job teaching me that on my ride home through downtown Boston, I didn't stall once, even after getting caught in baseball traffic driving through Kenmore Square (the heart of Red Sox nation).

I was so thrilled with that buying experience that when I was ready to buy my next car, I went back to the dealership and asked for the same salesman. He had left, but the salesperson I worked with was just as responsive to my needs as my Saab salesman had been many years ago, and I purchased my next car from the same dealership. That's the type of salesperson you want to be. You want people to want to work with you and to remember your name 5, 10, and 30 years later. You want them to trust that their interests are your interests (and this should be the truth), and your goal is to provide them with a solution to their problem or challenge.

I hate to beat a dead horse by discussing my car buying experiences again, but my purchase of a Volvo SUV (XC90) serves as an ideal example of understanding why understanding benefits and customer needs is critical to the sales process. I like to shop around before I purchase a car. After deciding the Volvo XC90 was the car I wanted, I decided to visit three car dealerships before making a buying decision. You already know which dealership I chose (the same one

(Continued)

(Continued)

where I bought my Saab), but you don't know the experiences I had in the two prior dealerships. The first dealership I went to was in the suburbs where I visited them on a Saturday afternoon with my two rambunctious kids (my son was 9 and my daughter 11 at the time). I wanted them to be involved in the purchasing decision. Well, the truth is I didn't want them heavily involved but I did want them to support my decision since I believed that if they liked the car they would be more vested in helping maintain its cleanliness. Well, that was a misnomer . . . nonetheless, I took them with me and allowed them to check out the cars in the dealership.

Their definition of checking out a car meant testing every funky feature from how easily the back seats can disappear and enlarge the trunk space to hearing how loud the horns are on various models. After 10 minutes in the dealership, I had a strong desire to sneak out the back door, leaving them on their own. Unfortunately, the manager didn't allow me to get away with that and came to my side to show me the features on the SUV. He pointed out every safety feature known to man or to future Volvo owners. Volvo is clearly known for safety, but the hoard of information that I heard about safety, children, and Volvos was unbelievable. Clearly, this manager honed in on features and benefits that he believed (accurately, I will state) are important to a mother of two children.

A week later, I entered my second Volvo dealership in a rather classy suburb west of Boston. Accompanied by nobody under the age of 12, I had a business suit on and was on my way to a client meeting. The benefits that were pointed out to me included the sleeker, sexier options available on the car such as the interior design, color options, and music system.

What's the point of the story? Basically, each well-trained salesperson was able to learn enough about me to decide what he believed were the most important features and benefits to share with me. But each missed the key factor that was going to pull me over the fence and make the purchase: price. If the first dealer had spent the entire time telling me about the cool options available and never mentioned the safety features, so important to parents, then his ability to close the deal would have been minimized dramatically. But if he had determined that price was the bottom line for me, he might have closed the deal. Likewise, the second dealer did not believe that safety was an important issue to me since I told him this car was for my business. Each salesperson had a menu of benefits in his head that he could offer me. But first he had to learn about my needs to decide which benefits to present from the list. He had to **actively** listen and assess my needs as either a mother or businesswoman, since discussing every single benefit (as so many of us are tempted to do) would not have been the best way to win my business. In the end, they each tried to sell the car to me but failed to fully understand the one critical factor to close the deal . . . giving me the best price option.

BUILDING YOUR BUSINESS MODEL

Let's revisit your business model. Your sales plan will impact a number of the areas covered in the canvas. The ones that you should focus on the most include: #1 Customer Segments, #2 Value Proposition, #3 Channels, #4 Customer Relationships, and #8 Key Partnerships. Revisit the questions from these components of the canvas and confirm that your sales plan aligns with those areas that you will need to be successful.

NETWORKING TO JUMP-START AND GROW YOUR BUSINESS

Networking is one of the most useful and cost-effective methods of jump-starting and growing a business. What do we mean by *networking*? More than collecting business cards, it's creating "give-and-take relationships." Think of networking as formal socializing *with a twist*. Your goal in business networking is not to establish friendships but to meet as many individuals as possible who have the ability to help you grow your business and vice versa. That can mean seeking out people who will refer business to you or even someone who knows someone who can send customers your way.

IT'S NOT ABOUT MAKING FRIENDS

If in the process of networking you develop new friendships, terrific. But that is not your objective! If you are currently attending networking events and found some great new buddies, but they are not giving you referrals or introductions to individuals who can help you grow your business, you're not performing the networking task correctly. You have to set clear objectives about the results you hope to achieve through networking; and make sure you are asking for leads and also reciprocating.

Networking is a two-way street. You have to help others establish or grow their businesses, just as they help yours. Therefore, a critical part of networking is giving and receiving. It's important to know how to comfortably ask for advice, input, and, of utmost importance, referrals. The key is being specific about what the type of contacts that you need. If you're looking for an introduction, don't ask, "Do you know any marketing directors?" Instead be very precise and ask "Can you introduce me to the marketing director at XYZ Corporation?" If they know the person, make sure you get as much information as possible about that individual. In addition, the best lead is an actual introduction, so ask if they would be willing to call or send the person an e-mail formally introducing you and explaining why the two of you should connect. But make sure you reciprocate or leads won't keep coming back to you.

EXPERT INSIGHT

Paul Horn: Golden Rules of Networking

Paul Horn, whom you may recall from Chapter 6, is an adjunct lecturer at Babson College and communication skills coach. He generously shared advice that he has found to quite effective when it comes to networking. Paul suggested that we follow the four strategies below:

(Continued)

(Continued)

1. Meet with people face-to-face. To grow a business, you have to be out there meeting with customers and with new prospects. You can't rely on banner ads, letters, word of mouth, or having an attractive building and convenient evening hours.
2. Use a personal touch. Many businesses offer services and products that are not that different from those provided by competitors. In such cases, consumers often decide <u>whom</u> to conduct business with based on <u>personal relationships</u>. Therefore, entrepreneurs can gain a competitive edge by taking the time to really understand what is important to the person with whom they are trying to establish a relationship. As the old saying goes, "People don't care what we know until they know that we care."
3. Smooth out your rough edges. How we talk with our customers and prospects is as important—sometimes even more important—than what we say to them. You may need to develop or polish your public speaking or presentation skills.
4. Keep practicing your networking skills. For some people, networking comes easily, but for many others, it doesn't. If you're in the latter category, don't worry; like other skills, these can be honed with practice and coaching.

Paul follows two golden rules when it comes to networking:

Rule # 1: Networking Is Reciprocal.

Networking is effective only when it's a give-and-take process. You should be looking for ways to help others even as you ask them for help. That, of course, is more than a "business strategy." That's a philosophy or approach to life! "What goes around, comes around," as they say. That Golden Rule applies here. How do you want to be treated? With just a sales pitch? No, of course not. You want to believe that someone is listening to you and wants to understand your needs and goals.

Networking is many times used in a job search context. For example, you want a job in banking, but you don't know any bankers so you might ask the people you know if they can make some referrals to the bankers they know, and schedule some "informational interviews." There is nothing wrong with that. That's part of what is meant by networking. If you've developed good relationships with friends or acquaintances, they're usually happy to do you a favor, especially if they know you well and sense that you would be willing to reciprocate at the appropriate time. It's critical to think of networking as a give-and-take process of building relationships with people to develop win–win situations.

Warning: No stalkers, please. You shouldn't feel that you have to "work the room" as though you were some sort of hungry predator. You can be purposeful in your approach without pouncing on or cornering people. If you're focused on learning about other people—their goals, their challenges, their interests and how you might help them, not just yourself—you will not come off as selfish and will probably feel more comfortable with networking, too.

Rule # 2: Opportunities Are Unlimited

If we define *networking* in a broad sense—a give-and-take process for building relationships—then it's obvious that the opportunities for networking are everywhere. Virtually any encounter we have, whether at work or during leisure time, can offer us a chance to create or strengthen a relationship. So networking can take place not just at formal networking events, but in the supermarket aisle, at your kids' soccer games, or while conversing with a fellow passenger on a plane.

In fact, it's often in these chance encounters where the most effective networking takes place—because no one feels there's an ulterior motive at work. There's simply room to develop a degree of familiarity and trust that may open the door to a business conversation later on. If you've had a nice chat with a fellow passenger about the book you noticed he was reading and the conversation rolls around to what you each do for work, you might offer your card, ask for his and send him a note later on. If the conversation has been mutually enjoyable, then he or she is likely to respond to that later outreach—or maybe even refer someone else to you.

While networking with individuals, there are some things to keep in mind:

- Make sure your approach is friendly and open—put yourself and the other person at ease with a smile and handshake.
- Ask for and use the other person's name.
- Show interest in the other person's business or industry—ask questions and listen for ways that you might help them and, if appropriate, extend an offer or invitation (e.g., for an appointment or perhaps to share some new information sources that might interest them).

Paul also points out that networking can take many forms, in addition to being actual conversations. These include:

- e-mailing articles of interest to people you've just met, especially if the topic came up during your exchange with them.
- inviting them to appropriate business events as your guest.
- developing and practicing your elevator pitch so that it sounds casual and natural.
- Looking for opportunities to introduce other people at events.

CONFERENCES AS A GREAT OPPORTUNITY TO BUILD YOUR NETWORKING SKILLS

Attending or exhibiting at conferences gives you an opportunity to network by exposing you to as many people as possible in a short period of time. It can also give you the chance to

- check out the competition,
- learn the latest trends in the industry,
- identify new customers, and
- identify new partners.

However, conferences can be overwhelming, similar to drinking water from a fire hose. You're thirsty and want a drink, but it's too much at once so you end up dry and parched. This won't happen if you have a game plan. In advance of attending a conference do the following:

- Find out who's going to be there and who could be potential
    - prospects,
    - partners,
    - competitors, and
    - important networkers or relationship builders (people who know people you want to get to know)
- Decide whom you'd like to meet with and learn more about them (research their business online).
- Prioritize this list and make sure you approach the most important ones first (in case you run out of time).
- Develop a plan to meet them.
    - Will you introduce yourself right away or try to network at various events?
    - What will you say to introduce yourself?
- Prepare a list of opening statements that will make you more comfortable approaching them.
- Prepare a list of frequently asked questions (and responses) about your products so you're not caught off guard without a response.
- Prepare a list of general small talk topics that you might ask somebody to begin a conversation.
- Prepare a list of key benefits and perhaps "new" information that you can share about your company.

In order to network efficiently, make sure that you have your business cards on hand at all times and that you get business cards from those individuals you meet there. On the back of each card, write information about the person, what you talked about, any follow-up items your promised and rank how important they are to your business. (Don't make this complicated. A simple ABC method of ranking them is more than sufficient.) This will help you tremendously when you get home and enter all the names into your database. This information will also help you prioritize your follow-up strategy and personalize your message to each person when you contact them (i.e., when we met last week, I recall you were interested in . . .)

HOLDING YOUR OWN SEMINARS AND WEBINARS

In addition to attending conferences, you can hold your own seminar or webinar. This allows you to feature your business and even yourself as the expert on a topic. You can invite individuals whom you are interested in getting to know better to hear your presentation or the presentation by your colleagues or partners. You should definitely sell this as a learning opportunity since it's rare that somebody will want to attend an event just to hear about you and your company. If you choose a topic that is important and valuable for them to learn about, your attendance rates will increase. If you hold a live seminar, then it's best to conduct it during hours that are convenient to your audience (before or after work) or during an event where they are already going to be listening to presentations. For example, if you are selling Chewie's Colossal Cookie Company's homemade cookies and learn that there's a conference for dog walkers in your local city and you see from their agenda that there are gaps when the audience won't be attending any prescheduled meetings, then you might want to contact the conference planner and see if you can offer a free mini-seminar on a topic that would provide additional educational value.

Some ideas that will increase the odds that your own seminar will be successful include

- making sure it's educational and valuable for attendees;
- having plenty of literature on hand, both about your company and the topic;
- holding breakfast events or cocktail parties;
- Following up with all attendees, even those who did not sign up for your event but were on your mailing list;
- Following up with no-shows since sometimes these busy folks may very well be your best prospects.

STILL NOT CONVINCED

As a business owner and the face of your company, you will very likely be required to sell, regardless of your comfort level with the activity. Therefore, learning the skills and techniques outlined in the chapter is critical for the success of your business. If you have the luxury of hiring somebody to perform this critical task, focus on hiring for the skills that we have outlined so you can bring the right person onboard. If your business grows rapidly and you elect to hire a sales manager to work with your salespeople, it's important to understand that the best salespeople do not necessarily make the best sales managers. There are numerous books written about sales management, but for now remember that the skills required to be great at selling are not exactly the same skills required to manage a team. Because selling is so challenging, it requires a level of tenacity and relationship building that is different from the coaching and mentoring support required to be a successful manager and lead a team. When and if you are ready to build a sales force, make sure you get the advice you need to hire the right team to grow your business.

AHAs

Lessons and Takeaways

In this chapter, we are talking about the importance of being comfortable with your own sales skills. Selling is not about forcing a service or solution upon somebody who doesn't want or need it. It's about actively listening to your prospective customers, identifying their key needs, and determining how you can meet their needs. It's an essential part of a marketing program. Highlights of the chapter include the following:

- Make sure you know all of the benefits of the products that your products or services provide so you can then align the most critical benefits with your various prospective customers.

- Understand the skills required to sell, including communication and listening, analytical, organizational, time management, and discipline, possess a keen interest in learning and passion for your product.

- Sales can be a very complicated process. You must have some type of system to help you keep track of your customers and prospects and their identified needs. Otherwise, the chances are that after your first or second meeting, you'll have a hard time remembering the specifics of each customer's needs and thus will be unable to meet those needs.

- Having passion for your products is important. With that in mind, if you're hiring individuals to sell for your company, make sure your salespeople have the same enthusiasm and zeal that you have for your products or services.

- In order to be effective at selling, you must perfect the art of active listening. This means that while they are answering your prepared questions about their needs and interests, you are formulating smart responses that show how your products offer the benefits and value they seek.

- Understanding your competition is critical in every sales activity and is important in navigating a path to success. You need to have a solid knowledge of how your product or service compares to that of your competitors or substitutes.

- There are multiple stages to the sales process: Preparation, the Introduction, Preparing for The In-Person Appointment, the Meeting, and Follow-Up and Servicing the Account's Needs. You need to ensure you are ready for these stages to ensure a higher chance of closing the deals you need to make to grow your business.

- The best way to deal with objection is to prepare for it by anticipating what the objections will be. Basically, facing your fear head on and realizing that, worse-case scenario, the prospect will end the call or the meeting.

- Networking is critical to your success. Remember you must meet with prospects and customers face-to-face to grow a business. You can't rely on banner ads, letters, word of mouth, or having an attractive building and convenient evening hours. In addition, networking is reciprocal. You should be looking for ways to help others even as you ask them for help or support to grow your business.

TOOLKIT

Worksheet 9.1: Sales Stages Checklist

1. Preparing for the Call
   - ☐ Make sure your contacts are in a central, easily accessible location.
   - ☐ Review status/ID of various prospect groups.
   - ☐ Rank the potential of your prospect groups by potential to purchase.
   - ☐ Prioritize list for calling.
   - ☐ Set a phone schedule.
   - ☐ Set a call standard for minimum number of hours.
   - ☐ Predetermine potential meeting times.

2. The Actual Phone Call
   - ☐ Develop a script, including the following stages:
     - Introduction
     - Reason for call
     - Seek more information/active listening
     - Request for appointment
     - Close
   - ☐ Speak with confidence.
   - ☐ Know your value to the prospect.

- ☐ Listen carefully.
- ☐ Ask relevant questions.
- ☐ Update database with information learned during the call.

3. Preparing for the In-Person Appointment
   - ☐ Review database/CRM system with contact information.
   - ☐ Determine meeting goals.
   - ☐ Research company information if needed.
   - ☐ Imagine the conversation.
   - ☐ Practice, practice, practice.

4. During the Meeting
   - ☐ Remember to actively listen.
   - ☐ Meeting flow might follow this pattern but make it natural:
     1. Small talk/introduction
     2. Acknowledge reason for visit
     3. Confirm amount of time available
     4. Begin asking probing, open-ended questions
     5. Confirm need
     6. Check for acceptance/agreement
     7. Present solutions
     8. Close to get to meeting goal
     9. Agree upon next step

5. Follow-Up and Servicing
   - ☐ Update database with notes, ranking, and next steps.
   - ☐ Send you thank-you including
     - appreciation for meeting,
     - restating needs,
     - restating benefits discussed,
     - listing promised action items, and
     - additional ideas or research that you conducted after the meeting related to the topics discussed or questions raised.
   - ☐ Complete all follow-up activities.

Worksheet 9.2: Selling to Difficult Customers

1. Write down the person and company's name and describe very clearly what they do as it relates to your company.

2. In detail, describe the needs this person or company has that you are confident you can solve or address. Remember, they may not be aware of how you solve their problem or challenge.

3. Review your competitors and understand how they solve or address these same needs. Make sure you understand how you compare to them.

4. Finally, anticipate their three biggest objections. Write these down and then note specifically what you will say or ask to overcome their objections.

Objection	Response

CHAPTER TEN

DOING WELL WHILE DOING GOOD

Learning Objectives

In this chapter you will learn to

- define the characteristics of business models that are designed to create social value.
- understand the importance of creating economic value along with social value to sustain a business or organization.
- define the similarities and differences between socially driven businesses and economically driven businesses.
- understand the importance of being authentic to engage customers.

ALIGNING YOUR MESSAGING TO UNDERSCORE YOUR SOCIAL VALUE

In this chapter, we will explore businesses with a social mission including for-profit and nonprofit businesses and organizations. We focus on organizations that create social value as their primary mission as well organizations whose primary mission is to create economic value but are also committed to fulfilling a social mission, typically related to their product or service. Our goal is to show you how similar their marketing and customer outreach efforts are. Plus, we will talk about the differences that you need to understand related to their journey to create social value. We will also discuss how "doing good" can provide a marketing advantage but only when the value proposition is genuinely aligned with a social cause and not perceived as some type of deceptive "spin" to promote the company's brand or product.

ARE YOU A SOCIAL ENTREPRENEUR?

Do you consider yourself to be a social entrepreneur? How do you define this term? According to the book *Creating Social Value: A Guide for Leaders and Change Makers* by Cheryl Kiser and Deborah Leipziger (2014), a social entrepreneur is

> an individual who adopts a mission to create and sustain social value, recognizes and pursues new opportunities to serve that mission, engages in a process of continuous innovation, adaptation, and learning, acts boldly without

being limited by resources currently at hand and is highly accountable to the constituencies they serve, dedicated to the outcomes they create. (p. 9)

As you're reading this you might be thinking, wow, that sounds a lot like me. It also, perhaps, sounds a lot like a *typical* entrepreneur except for the focused drive toward "creating and sustaining social value." Bingo, you're very much on target with the theme of this chapter (and this book). Being a social entrepreneur is quite similar to being a traditional or typical entrepreneur. So, what is the difference? Most people believe that it's the structure under which the company operates, for-profit versus nonprofit. However, there are many for-profits that focus on creating social good, in addition to economic value. Being a for-profit business does not mean that you cannot have a mission that creates social value. However, by its very nature, a for-profit organization is structured to create economic (think profit driven) value first, and herein lies the differentiator. Social enterprises and the social entrepreneurs who run them are focused on the social value creation aspect of their business. What is social value? Basically, this refers to changes that are not simply about making money but that impact lives. Examples might be companies focused on helping women, solving poverty in a region, or working with marginalized communities to improve their lives. You can make money running these types of businesses, obviously, but driving profit to your company's bottom line is not the main driver of the business. Therefore, providing equity to shareholders or economic value to their stakeholders is not a key part of the mission of a social business. On the other hand, for-profit companies can be driven to create and drive both social and economic value but, in their design, economic value is the primary component that drives their company.

WARBY PARKER

Revolutionizing an Industry

If that sounds confusing, let's look at one example of for-profit organization on a mission to create social value. You can also ready about other for-profit organizations that are doing good at the Classy website (Gauss, n.d.).

Beginning with their mission statement, Warby Parker (WP) aims to differentiate its business. "Warby Parker was founded with a rebellious spirit and a lofty objective: to offer designer eyewear at a revolutionary price, while leading the way for socially conscious businesses" (Warby Parker, n.d.). If you're not familiar with the brand, WP sells eyeglasses online and has a variety of retail stores around the United States and in Canada. However, they recognized early on in the process that there are obstacles to buying eyeglasses online; people can't see how they look in the glasses before they purchase them. Therefore, WP addressed customer concerns by creating a business model where customers can select five frames to try on at home, for free. Upon arrival, customers have 5 days to try them on and once they find a favorite, they can upload their prescription. Sounds like a great solution, right? Plus, their prices are relatively low for the U.S. market, starting at $95 (including the lenses). Their website explains their mission.

> We believe that buying glasses should be easy and fun. It should leave you happy and good-looking, with money in your pocket. We also believe that everyone has the right to see. Almost one billion people worldwide lack access to glasses, which means that 15% of the world's population cannot effectively learn or work. To help address this problem, Warby Parker partners with non-profits like VisionSpring to ensure that for every pair of glasses sold, a pair is distributed to someone in need.

They further describe how they have distributed more than four million pairs of glasses since they launched their business in 2010. Here's how they explain their process:

> 2.5 billion people around the world need glasses but don't have access to them; of these, 624 million cannot effectively learn or work due to the severity of their visual impairment. To help address this problem, we work with a handful of partners worldwide to ensure that for every pair of glasses sold, a pair is distributed to someone in need. There are two models we employ:
>
> 1) Empowering adult men and women with training opportunities to administer basic eye exams and sell glasses for ultra-affordable prices. (This accounts for the majority of our distribution.)
>
> 2) Directly giving vision care and glasses to school-age children in their classrooms, where teachers are often the first to spot issues . . . Alleviating the problem of impaired vision is at the heart of what we do, and with your help, our impact continues to expand.

Warby Parker also created a program called Pupils Project, where they work with local government agencies like the Department of Health in Baltimore, that provide free vision screenings, eye exams, and glasses to schoolchildren, many for whom this is their first pair.

> Eliminating barriers to access—by donating glasses and meeting children in their classrooms, where vision issues often first come to light—is the top concern as the American Optometric Association estimates that 80% of childhood learning occurs visually. As part of our work in Baltimore, Johns Hopkins University is conducting a longitudinal study to better understand the correlation between the intervention of vision treatment and reading scores as well as the benefits of ensuring access to glasses for children in urban settings.

EDITING OTHERS INTO THE CONVERSATION ABOUT YOUR MISSION

Clearly, you don't have to be a nonprofit business structure to create social value and give back to society. Cheryl Kiser, executive director at The Lewis Institute & Babson Social Innovation Lab, emphasized this point and explained,

> It's critical to understand the problem that you are solving. If I want to work on problems related to poverty or clean water, for example, don't simply be an advocate of the cause. You must first become educated about the issues and then educate others. It's important to enroll people and allow them to edit themselves into the conversation to create the strongest impact. Let them understand the important aspects of the issue so they can see how they can become involved. (personal communication, July 2, 2018)

Is there a difference between marketing for a social venture versus a business whose primary mission is to create economic value? In marketing a social cause, *it's critical that others also believe in the cause.* However, for-profit organizations need their customers to first and foremost believe and trust their products and services. Customers do not necessarily have to be as committed to your mission or social cause to engage with your brand and buy from you. However, as Cheryl pointed out, with social ventures, you want to engage others while concurrently educating them about the mission so it becomes a part of "their story" and their mission and vision. It's critical to ensure customers know how you are addressing the problem and making a difference. The business structure (for profit or nonprofit) does not matter when it comes to engaging customers. As you tell your story, Cheryl points out, "you should only share 80% of the story. Don't tell the whole story because you want to leave that 20% open for the 'customer' to figure it out themselves. That's where they edit themselves into the story and become engaged with your brand." The key is in the story that you share. You need to build a relationship with customers who range from sponsors and donors to recipients of your services. Think about the important aspects of your cause that you want them to be aware of so they can comfortably edit themselves into the story. Think about how you want them to feel about your company and your mission. You want them to not only believe in your cause but to also feel an emotional connection that allows them to be a part of the story and the solution.

THE AD COUNCIL: INSPIRING CHANGE, IMPROVING LIVES

A good example of getting others edited into your campaign is a well-known campaign designed by the Ad Council (2019a). The Ad Council focuses on public service advertising and their motto is "Inspiring Change, Improving Lives." In 1983, they launched a campaign titled "Friends Don't Let Friends Drive Drunk." Some of the campaign taglines included "Drinking & Driving Can Kill A Friendship" and "Friends Don't Let Friends Drive Drunk" (Ad Council, 2019b). This enormously successful campaign engaged many Americans. Since the campaign's launch, nearly 70% of Americans have reported that they had tried to prevent someone from driving after drinking. Five years later, in 1998, America experienced its lowest number of alcohol-related fatalities since the U.S. Department of Transportation began keeping records. The campaign may not be able to take credit for the entire drop, but its ability to capture awareness and engage viewers to act is quite impressive. This is the same level of action that you want to create with your marketing campaigns.

How do you go about creating this level of engagement? Clearly, it's not easy, but there are many resources available to support you. YouTube has even created an "Impact Lab" (2019b) where it shares best practices and tips on creating engaging videos that help bring others along on your social mission. Below is some important advice it shares. Check more out on the YouTube site (2019a).

FIVE FUNDAMENTALS FOR MAKING SOCIAL IMPACT ON YOUTUBE

1. **Shareability:** Make sure people will pass along your videos to a network of supporters. Be relatable by telling your story in the most accessible way possible. Be topical by including something everyone is currently talking about in your story. And be valuable by providing practical value in your story.

2. **Discoverability:** Make sure your video rises to the top of search results. Craft your story in a way that references trending topics and "evergreen" content like how-tos and tutorials. That way, when popular topics create increased traffic to the site, your video can be found as a "related video."

3. **Consistency:** Posting your videos frequently and on a regular schedule helps viewers who love your content continue to engage with your cause. Using a consistent format, topic, or personality for your videos also helps build a loyal subscriber base and continuing engagement.

4. **Community:** Start a dialogue with a community of viewers. In your videos, speak directly to your audience and prompt them with questions. For example, ask them to respond in the comments section with their ideas or experiences and use those responses as elements in future videos.

5. **Sustainability:** Maintain the attention of your audience by creating an easily repeatable series. "Big-splash" videos can drive a lot of traffic to your channel, but it's a good idea to support your high-profile projects with other, easier-to-make videos that can hold your audience's attention between the bigger efforts.

CORPORATE SOCIAL RESPONSIBILITY

Clearly, a firm can do well (create economic value) and do good (create social value) at the same time. The two values are not diametrically opposed. A business does not have to sacrifice an opportunity to drive profit by deciding that it also wants to focus on creating social value. A classic example is American Express's campaign in the 1980s that focused on a specific cause: preserving the Statue of Liberty. Here's how it succeeded. American Express (2019a), a U.S.-based multinational financial services firm headquartered in New York City, decided to create a partnership with the nonprofit organization, The National Trust for Historic Preservation. The goal was to help raise funds to restore the Statue of Liberty. The website's Corporate Responsibility page explains the mission:

> As early as 1983, American Express launched a cause-related marketing effort that raised $1.7 million for the preservation of the Statue of Liberty and Ellis Island. Since that time, American Express has been committed to supporting two major initiatives in partnership with the World Monuments Fund and the National Trust for Historic Preservation. These initiatives aim to increase public awareness of the importance of historic and environmental conservation, preserve global historic and cultural landmarks, educate visitors on sustainable tourism and strengthen local communities through preservation efforts. (American Express, 2019b)

Here's how it achieved the goal. It donated a portion of every purchase customers made using their American Express credit card directly to the Statue of Liberty cause. In addition, they made a donation for every new customer who applied for their credit card. "The results are legendary: The Restoration Fund raised over $1.7 million, and American Express card use rose 27 percent. New card applications increased 45 percent over the previous year. All this was accomplished with a three-month campaign" (The BalanceSmallBusiness, 2019). This is an excellent example of a for-profit company partnering with a nonprofit organization to "do well" (use of the American Express card increased by 27%) and to "do good" (They raised over $1.7 million dollars to help restore the Statue of Liberty).

Corporations around the world are interested in trying to achieve a mix of economic and social value. Their customers are hopeful that they will succeed and believe that it's an important role for businesses to play. Let's look at research conducted by Cone Communications, a Boston, Massachusetts–based public relations firm that is focused on "helping organizations make a difference on critical social and environmental issues." (2019). They conduct a Corporate Social Responsibility (CSR) Study on a regular basis. Their 2017 report found

- 63% of Americans are hopeful businesses will take the lead to drive social and environmental change moving forward, in the absence of government regulation;
- 78% want companies to address important social justice issues;
- 87% will purchase a product because a company advocated for an issue they cared about; and
- 76% will refuse to purchase a company's products or services upon learning it supported an issue contrary to their beliefs.

TAKING THE NEXT STEP IN CORPORATE SOCIAL RESPONSIBILITY

What do constituents expect from companies they engage with when it comes to being socially responsible? Based on the data we have already shared, it's becoming clear that customers and other stakeholders want and expect brands that they engage with to transform into innovative companies driving social change. In *Creating Social Value*, Cheryl Kiser defines Corporate Social Innovation as

> a strategy that combines a unique set of corporate assets (innovation capacities, marketing skills, managerial acumen, employee engagement, scale, etc.) in collaboration with the assets of other sectors and firms to co-create breakthrough solutions to complex economic, social, and environmental issues that impact the sustainability of both business and society. (2014, p. 8).

What exactly does this mean? Below we have included a chart from Jason Saul's (2010) book, *Social Innovation, Inc.: Five Strategies for Driving Business Value through Social Change*. The chart highlights the primary differences between what is known as traditional corporate social responsibility (CSR) versus corporate social innovation (CSI). As you can tell, the innovative drivers in the areas of CSI focus on strategically and holistically impacting an organization's long-term focus. Instead of a short-term perspective of creating areas or sectors of philanthropy, the organization that innovates does so with the intent that the social value they create will be part of the DNA of the organization.

Table 10.1 What Makes CSI Different?

Traditional CSR	Corporate Social Innovation
Philanthropic Intent	Strategic Intent
Money, Manpower	R&D, Corporate Assets
Employee Volunteerism	Employee Development
Contracted Service Providers	NGO/Government Partners
Social and Eco-Services	Social and Eco-Innovations
Social Good	Sustainable Social Change

Source: Kiser, 2014, p. 8

This concept of corporate social innovation (versus responsibility) aligns with the findings in the 2018 Deloitte Millennial Survey (2019). This survey includes more than 10,000 millennials questioned across 36 countries and more than 1,800 Gen Z respondents from 6 countries.

They discovered the following:

- Millennials want leaders to more aggressively commit to making a tangible impact on the world while preparing their organizations and employees for the changes that Industry 4.0 is impacting.

- 48% (a minority) believe that corporations behave ethically (down from 65% in 2017).

- 47% believe business leaders are committed to helping improve society (down from 62% in 2017).

- Three quarters see businesses around the world focusing on their own agendas rather than considering the wider society (59% in 2017).

- Nearly two thirds say companies have no ambition beyond wanting to make money (50% in 2017).

Clearly, businesses have come under fire for not doing enough to protect the world around them. Therefore, building social value into their core mission, in addition to economic value, is critical for the future success of many companies around the world. Their customers and key stakeholders are demanding it and are clear that they will emphasize their demands with their wallets.

THINK LIKE A DONOR

Throughout the book, we have talked about the importance of thinking like your customer. Below we share some important statistics about how donors think, based on research conducted by Non-Profit Source (2019). Clearly different generations think differently and act differently when it comes to how they donate and how much they give. Understanding these differences is important, especially if your donors are from different generations. Take this into consideration if you are working on a business model that requires support via contributions from individuals outside of your business scope.

- 11% of total U.S. giving comes from millennials.
- 84% of millennials give to charity, donating an annual average of $481 across 3.3 organizations.
- E-mail prompted 31% of online donations made by Gen Xers.
- 59% of Gen Zs are inspired to donate to charity by a message or image they saw on social media.
- 24% of boomers say they were inspired to give an online donation because of direct mail they received.
- 72% of boomers give to charity, donating an annual average of $1,212 across 4.5 organizations.

Table 10.2 Millennials/GenY, Gen X, and Baby Boomers

	Millennials/Gen Y	Gen X	Baby Boomers
Percentage of U.S. population	25.9%	20.4%	23.6%
Enrolled in a monthly giving program	40%	49%	49%
Gave tribute gifts	26%	31%	41%
Donate to crowdfunding campaigns	46%	45%	35%
Donated on #GivingTuesday 2017	15%	14%	15%
Donate through Facebook fundraising tools	16%	19%	21%
Volunteer locally vs. internationally	64%/9%	64%/8%	71%/9%
Attend fundraising events	55%	56%	58%

Source: Adapted from NPSource (2019). Retrieved from https://nonprofitssource.com/online-giving-statistics/

ACTION CREATES TRIUMPHS (ACT)
Finding Passion Around a Mission

At this point, you might be wondering how this discussion about social ventures relates to you and your goals. Let's hit pause for a minute to think about what motivates your interest in social entrepreneurship. Is there a problem or an opportunity that you see in your own community that needs to be addressed? For example, are you worried about poverty or unemployment locally or perhaps in another part of your state, region, or country? Write down three to five social problems that you are aware of and that concern you. You can also research this if you're struggling to identify social problems that you are or could become passionate about. You might want to check out the UN Sustainable Development Goals to learn more by visiting their website (www.un.org/sustainabledevelopment/sustainable-development-goals/).

The UN Sustainable Development goals are targets for 2030 and address challenges that the world faces such as poverty, inequality, climate and environmental issues, peace, justice, and many more. You will likely find a cause here that you can believe in and can connect with. Next, pick one that you feel most passionately about. Once you've selected one cause, it's time to identify a number of solution(s) where you can edit yourself into the picture to help address the problem. This will require some reflection about what motivates you. You should find a group of classmates or peers and brainstorm solutions.

Think about the following:

- Do you see opportunities to address these challenges locally, in your own backyard?
- What about in another region or country?
- What solutions do you bring to the table that can be enacted by you and perhaps your peers?
- What challenges are too difficult for you to address on your own but you care enough about to want to help make a difference?
- How can you edit yourself into the picture?

Now, let's return to your own business. Can you build corporate responsibility about your newly(?) discovered passion to your mission? What would be required to adopt a mission where you can create and sustain social value and pursue opportunities to serve that mission? Can you create bold acts without being limited by resources that you currently have at hand?

PASSIONATE ENTREPRENEURS CAN MAKE A DIFFERENCE

The next two businesses that you will read about feature two women who not only found a way to edit themselves into causes that they cared about but were also able to create companies around the causes to ensure they would create an impact with their solutions. The two women entrepreneurs you about to meet are both passionate about helping other women in the countries where they were raised. They each have a unique approach to solving an environmental problem while concurrently employing women who otherwise would not have an opportunity to prosper. We begin with Diana Rayyan, a Palestinian living in Saudi Arabia and then introduce you to Angela Sanchez, a native of Colombia, now living in the United States.

VIEW FROM THE TRENCHES

Kees Chic—Saving the Planet . . . One Plastic Bag at a Time

Diana Rayyan is a Palestinian citizen who grew up in Jeddah, Saudi Arabia, never having lived in Gaza where her family is from. After graduating from Al-Ahliyya Amman University with a degree in pharmacy, she spent the first few years of her career as a pharmacist. Unfortunately, the career did not suit her personal passion for helping others. Therefore, she decided to work for the British Council in Jeddah, Saudi Arabia, as an environmental framework tool advisor. In this position, she attended a variety of conferences, and one in particular, Earth Day 2009, changed the course of her career . . . forever. If you're not familiar with the origin of Earth Day, let's review its goals and achievements. Earth Day began on April 22, 1970, when as many as 20 million Americans are estimated to have demonstrated to bring attention to environmental challenges that faced the United States as well as other countries around the world (Earth Day Network, 2019a). The U.S. Congress and the president of the United States, Richard Nixon, created the Environmental Protection Agency (EPA), and laws such as the Clean Water Act and the Endangered Species Act were designed to address these growing concerns. Earth Day has become an annual event, recognized around the globe with estimates of as many as 1 billion people in 192 countries participating each year in what has become known as "the largest civic-focused day of action in the world" (Earth Day Network, 2019b).

Diana was impressed with the 2009 Earth Day event in which she participated. While she was aware of the danger plastic bags posed to the environment, such as harming sea and wild life, she didn't realize the enormity of the problem until one of the speakers at the conference shared statistics that Diana found shocking. In further researching the problems, she learned the following from the U.S. Environmental Protection Agency's (n.d.) website on Toxicological Threats of Plastic:

> It is estimated that about 80% of marine debris originates as land-based trash and the remaining 20% is attributed to at-sea intentional or accidental disposal or loss of goods and waste. . . .There is a growing concern about the hazards plastic pollution in the marine environment. Plastics pose both physical (e.g., entanglement, gastrointestinal blockage, reef destruction) and chemical threats (e.g., bioaccumulation of the chemical ingredients of

plastic or toxic chemicals sorbed to plastics) to wildlife and the marine ecosystem. . . . Plastic trash and particles are now found in most marine and terrestrial habitats, including the deep sea, Great Lakes, coral reefs, beaches, rivers, and estuaries. Persistent, bioaccumulative and toxic (PBTs) chemicals or substances pose a risk to the marine environment because they resist degradation, persisting for years or even decades. PBTs are toxic to humans and marine organisms and have been shown to accumulate at various trophic levels through the food chain.

Diana continued researching this problem, looking for a way to contribute to a solution for this growing crisis. She knew that upcycling (taking discarded products and converting them into something unique that typically has greater value than its origin form) was a growing trend among socially and environmentally conscious communities. She began to wonder how she could upcycle discarded plastic and what those products would look like.

She came up with an idea to create beautifully designed items like bags and purses using plastic bags that would otherwise have ended up in the streets, water, or landfills. But she wasn't confident that she could create a business from her simple idea, especially since she was an expat in Saudi Arabia (short for expatriate, meaning she is a foreigner living in another country). At the time, it was very difficult for non-Saudi citizens to run a business. (Note: As of 2018, foreigners residing in the Kingdom are eligible to apply for a foreign license to conduct business in Saudi). She kept thinking about the idea and finally, in 2011, when entrepreneurship was becoming quite fashionable in the Kingdom, she decided to give it a go. She met with a number of Saudi women and offered to pay them to create a sample, not with the cotton they were used to working with, but with discarded plastic. After approaching a dozen women, all who turned her down, she finally found one woman who agreed to crochet a few bags for her. It took her a week but she produced five different samples of products. Diana loved the samples and knew that she was onto something. She became very focused on trying to build a business around beautiful products created from plastic.

Next, she reached out to over 20 friends and shared the samples and asked for input on ideas for other products that could be made out of plastic. She networked and was introduced to a woman who shared her passion and gave her the funds she needed to produce her first 20 items. She then identified a gallery where she held an event to show her MVPs and get feedback. Through her own guerrilla marketing techniques, she sent 200 invitations to the event, hoping that maybe a dozen women would attend. To her surprise, over 150 showed up, and many were disappointed that they were not able to buy the MVPs at the show. The show was clearly an enormous success. Diana had all attendees complete a survey before they left, giving her feedback about the products, and this gave her enough data to select the top six items that she would create to launch her business.

By 2013, she was in business and began to actively promote her company as a social enterprise. She participated in Harvard Arab Weekend's Pitch Competition, an event held annually on the Harvard University campus celebrating innovation and entrepreneurship. She won first place and received a prize of $30,000 to help move her concept from idea to market. At the time, her business was named Trochet and she was running it with a friend

(Continued)

(Continued)

who was a Saudi citizen. Unfortunately, the partnership did not work out as she had hoped, and in 2014, she split with her partner. Diana grew concerned that this business was not going to make it off the ground. She thought about her network and recalled a friend from Jordan, with whom she had gone to college and asked her for advice. She suggested that Diana participate in the King Abdullah II Award for Youth Innovation & Achievement (KAAYIA) in Jordan. Diana didn't hesitate and was thrilled to win the prize of $50,000 for her newly named business, Kees Chic. *Kees* is the Arabic word for plastic bag (King Abdullah II Award for Youth Innovation & Achievement, 2016).

In 2016, with the money available to grow the business, she created an aggressive marketing campaign to make women aware of her products. She collaborated with the Amman Design Week event in September 2016 and created canopies to create shade for visitors to the event. By hand, she and her design team used 25,000 plastic bags and turned them into 800 triangles and 10 diamonds in only 10 days (Kees Chic, 2016).

Since her early successes, Diana has been working diligently to figure out the best distribution and marketing channels for her items. Diana explained,

> I don't want people to buy our products just because it's a charity. We want them to also see that while the product is simple, it's quite innovative. Everything is created entirely by hand. We are proud of the fact that we are creating environmental awareness, preventing plastic bags from suffocating birds or being eaten by turtles and camels causing major health problems or death and at the same time employing and empowering women.

What's next for Diana? She's struggling to identify the right marketing channels for selling her products. She had tried to promote her items online but discovered that people want to see and feel it in person before they buy. Online sales channels have not worked for her. She has begun to sell her items at a concept store called Homegrown located in Jeddah, Saudi Arabia. Homegrown features products from artisans in Saudi (Homegrown Market, n.d.) and she has found that sales are flourishing there. Should she find more boutiques to sell her products in?

Diana has also begun to sell "corporate gifts" such as stress balls. Her approach has been to go directly to companies in Saudi Arabia (and beyond) that have CSR (corporate social responsibility) departments. She explains her dual mission of caring for the environment and empowering women. She gives the CSR manager a sample and they love it. She's had a lot of luck, including a major order of stress balls from the United Nations.

In Their Shoes

Now that Kees Chic has finally achieved a level where Diana can begin to focus on more aggressive marketing campaigns and identify the right channels, she's considering which types of tactics will best meet her goal of scaling the business. What do you suggest Diana do next? Should she continue selling to boutiques in Saudi or expand outside of the Kingdom? Should she focus on online marketing or is corporate (B2B) the best way to grow Kees Chic? Keep in mind the fact that Diana contracts the women who create the items for her, so she's operating on her own with limited time and financial resources.

VIEW FROM THE TRENCHES

Artyfactos—Helping Women—One Orange Peel at a Time

Angela began her career in a technical field that was quite different from where her entrepreneurial spirit led her. She was a civil engineer by background, having received an undergraduate degree from Pontificia Universidad Javeriana in Bogotá, Colombia. However, Angela was very entrepreneurial and launched a few different businesses after graduating with an MBA from Babson College in Wellesley, Massachusetts. Having relocated to Boston from her home in Colombia, she found herself making frequent trips back home to visit family. During these trips, she oftentimes found herself buying beautiful and very colorful jewelry from women (many of them poor, single moms) who were selling their handmade items out in the street. When Angela returned to the States from these trips, her friends and colleagues would marvel at the uniqueness of the necklaces or earrings that she was wearing, asking her to buy some for them on her next trip.

At first it didn't occur to her to turn this "demand" into a business. Afterall, she was an engineer working in construction. What did she know about the jewelry business? Angela explained,

> I've always been very passionate about caring for our planet. The jewelry that these artisans design are 100% recycled, made with natural materials such as orange peel, cantaloupe seeds, coffee beans and vegetal ivory (tagua). They also have amazing natural aromas that enhances the experience of wearing them. Plus, the fact that these women use free, recycled materials means that they won't end up in landfills. Every year, tons of orange peel and unused seeds are dumped into landfills and are burned, generating greenhouse gases.

With the idea that she could be a part of a solution to help care for the planet and also create sustainable economic opportunities for these single moms, Angela decided to launch Artyfactos (https://artyfactos.com) in the fall of 2014. Her vision was to create an eco-exotic, statement jewelry business that features handwoven designs by entrepreneurial moms in Latin America. She wanted to combine the concept of creating beautiful products from discarded objects that harmed the environment while helping to support and empower women artisans.

Business took off immediately with a strong interest from her friends and family (and the author). Oftentimes, the jewelry sold

Angela Sanchez

(Continued)

(Continued)

itself because friends would wear a necklace or bracelet and the unique design and beautiful colors attracted other women to inquire about its origin. Angela explained that the product and her brand have evolved as she learned more about being in the fashion world, quite different from the world of civil engineering. When she launched, she would always ask her customers and prospects for feedback about the product design. Since Angela worked with poor women artisans in Colombia, they were not aware of trends in the market. It became her responsibility to develop an expertise in jewelry and fashion, and she found herself paying close attention to what women wear in the United States. For example, she might see a new or interesting necklace made out of pearls or even plastic and she would send pictures back to the artists in Colombia to see if they could create a similar item using acai berries or perhaps orange peels. They worked collaboratively to create beautiful jewelry pieces.

Angela Sanchez

Earthy Yet Innovative

In addition, her branding has changed over time. Angela explained, "We began with a logo that we made ourselves in a very simple format. But we heard that the logo didn't properly express how artistic the brand is. We played around with it and using a new, trendy font created an image that was earthy yet innovative. We changed the color to a warm purple and even designed the o in Artyfactos to look like an orange peel.

In addition, Angela spent a lot of time thinking about the pricing of her products. In the industry, jewelry prices range from very inexpensive (under $10) to thousands. While she clearly didn't see Artyfactos jewelry being priced so high that it was out of reach of the everyday customer, she also didn't want her jewelry to be cheap. For example, Artyfactos necklaces range from $35 to $110, depending on the natural products used and the time required to craft each unique piece of jewelry.

Now, starting her fifth year of business, Angela is working on her brand identity. Like Waku's founders, she doesn't want people to simply buy her products because of the story behind them. She wants to ensure they also LOVE the design and will keep coming back to buy more products and share with their friends. She wants them to edit themselves into her brand story and be as passionate about it as she is. She wants them to also wear the jewelry as a social statement ensuring they share the importance of protecting our planet and upcycling products that might have ended up in landfills. With this goal in mind to brand her company as a business that is eco-friendly and exotic, she is working on a variety of social media marketing campaigns.

Understanding Your Customer Base

Currently over 80% of Artyfactos customers are women 40 to 60 years of age with strong, disposable income. However, she believes that she needs to appeal to a younger audience, a market that is known to not only care greatly about the environment but also spends its more limited money supporting businesses that share its values. She launched an Instagram campaign featuring two women in their 20s: one blond and blue-eyed and the other dark haired and more Latina-looking. Even though this target market typically has less disposable income than her older audience, she believes it can support the growth she needs to take her business to the next level. She is working with a marketing firm to design an Instagram account featuring a new piece of jewelry for each day of the week. Her messaging blends a love of jewelry with a respect for the planet, including the following statements:

- At #artyfactos we have a deep respect for nature and we know you do too! We create organic pieces of jewelry that will make you look stylish without harming the planet!
- Our designs are inspired from our core values—love and social responsibility.
- Accessories are made with love and conscious obsession.
- Surround yourself with things that inspire you!! Environmental responsibility inspires us!!

Overall, Angela is trying to better understand her customers, build her company's brand awareness and increase her sales revenue. She has created a viable marketplace for the women in Colombia who are beginning to develop their own microbusinesses. In order to help them, Angela has begun offering workshops to teach them how to further develop their businesses and build capacity. She is engaged in creating a win–win situation where Artyfactos prospers and her artisans also benefit, at the same time. This mindset is quite similar to the Artistia business model that you read about in Chapter 7.

As Angela is analyzing her business, she knows that online sales have enormous potential but are only a small percentage of her current revenue, contributing around 10%. Events, basically exhibiting at jewelry, fashion, and craft fairs, account for 40% of her revenue. Finally, the wholesale market has started to really impact her business model. Business has grown over 500% in the wholesale space in the past year. She explained,

Angela Sanchez

(Continued)

(Continued)

I tried to sell to boutique stores on my own but didn't have the right connections. Then I began using specialized jewelry sales reps, and my business exploded, in a very positive way. This wholesale side of my business now accounts for approximately 50% of my total revenue due to the fact that these reps have the right relationships with the right boutiques and have been able to get her into many stores that I wasn't able to get into on my own.

What's next on the horizon for Angela? She is struggling to understand what her customers want from her and how they experience her brand. She realizes how important it is to talk with them directly and let them share what they want. "In fashion, you have to learn how your product makes the customer feel. They should always feel great about what they are wearing. At the end of the day, I am selling an experience rather than just a necklace. I know that is the key to good branding."

To learn more about the beautiful products designed by Angela's artisans and to get an inside look at how they are created, check out the following videos:

- *Artyfactos*: https://www.youtube.com/watch?time_continue=29&v=QruNAp5FLSU
- *Make A Statement With Artyfactos*: https://www.youtube.com/watch?time_continue=1&v=TROBuHhiiMM
- *Artyfactos—The New You*: https://www.youtube.com/watch?time_continue=1&v=y0F1lXydvKs
- *Behind Artyfactos: A Look at The Orange Peel Jewelry*: https://www.youtube.com/watch?v=9pxX2NHGkn0&t=218s
- *Behind Artyfactos: A Look Behind Tagwa Manufacturing*: https://www.youtube.com/watch?v=tV_dTKhQgO8&t=186s

In Their Shoes

Based on what you've read and the videos that you have watched about Artyfactos, what do you recommend Angela focus on to further build her brand? She's considering a variety of tactics that will best meet her goal of scaling the business. Who is her target market and how should she message her value proposition to attract more customers to buy from her? Should she sell direct to consumers or focus more on the wholesale aspect of the market, giving her access to stores and customers that she could not reach on her own?

FOCUS ON APPLICATION: WAKU

The Entrepreneurial Journey

Are you ready to return to Juan and Nico whose social business model was inspired by their goal of helping small farmers continue to produce the herbal infusion "healing waters" and maintain a livelihood while at the same time bringing a delicious and healthy drink to the world? Before

Made with 20 herbs and flowers, Waku is the world's most refreshing and invigorating infusion drink. It will naturally soothe your body and aid digestion empowered by the healing water from the Andes.

they conducted extensive market research, their brand positioning statement focused heavily on the fact that they were helping farmers improve their livelihoods by eliminating the middleman and buying their ingredients directly from them at fair-trade prices.

However, they learned that their dream of sharing traditions from their country, Ecuador, and making a big impact on the lives of farmers in Ecuador, was not enough of a strong brand statement and would not create enough of a call to action for their customers to buy from them. Customers cared first about the product's health benefits and taste and were then interested in contributing to a cause. Juan and Nico recognized that they could not go to market by simply sharing the cause. All of their research said that they needed to focus on the benefits of the drink itself, not on their mission. They were passionate about creating social value but also recognized that they could not do so without also creating economic value (generating revenue). You may recall their brand positioning statement:

Their philosophy about succeeding and growing is aligned with what Angela shared about ensuring that people FIRST loved their products and then became engaged around the social value the company created. In crowded market spaces like jewelry, women's fashion accessories and healthy beverages, it's a great differentiator to have a social mission but the mission itself will not carry the brand if the product is not desirable. This is a critical lesson learned by all of the business owners who were not blinded by their mission but recognized that the mission was a part of the brand, not the whole brand story.

ACTION CREATES TRIUMPHS (ACT)

Mission-Focused Brands

Think about brands that you love that have social missions. Why do you engage with them? Do you buy their products simply because their mission aligns with what is important to you or do you also love their products? List your top five brands with social missions. Describe their value to you and their value to their supporting cause. How are these related? How do they make you feel and why do you engage with them?

1.
2.
3.
4.
5.

AHAs

Lessons and Takeaways

In this chapter, we discussed a variety of companies that are focused on creating social value, along with economic value. Highlights of the chapter include the following:

- Being a social entrepreneur is quite similar to being a traditional or typical entrepreneur. Likewise, being a for-profit business does not mean that you cannot have a mission that creates social value.

- For-profit companies can be driven to create and drive both social and economic value but, in their design, economic value is the primary component that drives their company.

- In marketing a social cause, it's critical that others also believe in the cause. Therefore, it's critical to enroll people and allow them to edit themselves into the conversation to create the strongest impact. Let them understand the important aspects of the issue so they can see how they can become involved.

- A business does not have to sacrifice an opportunity to drive profit by deciding that it also wants to focus on creating social value.

- Businesses have come under fire for not doing enough to protect the world around them. Therefore, building social value into their core mission, in addition to economic value, is critical for the future success of many companies around the world. Eighty-seven percent of consumers will purchase a product because a company acted as advocate for an issue they cared about. At the same time, 76% will refuse to purchase a company's products or services upon learning it supported an issue contrary to their beliefs.

CHAPTER ELEVEN

DEPLOYING OMNICHANNEL MARKETING TO CREATE CUSTOMER ENGAGEMENT

LET THE GAMES BEGIN—TIME TO FOCUS ON YOUR MARKETING CAMPAIGN DESIGN

This is likely the chapter you have been waiting for—how to create engagement with your customers to start driving revenue to your top line. This is the first chapter of two where we cover how to select the right marketing channels to connect with your customers, prospects, and other business stakeholders (e.g., potential partners, future employees, investors). If you're like most entrepreneurs, you've been thinking about getting your message out since the first day you came up with your product or service. However, this chapter is located toward the end of the book, perhaps further than you hoped, because the process of identifying the best way to get your message out to your market requires that you first have a solid understanding of your customers' needs and their decision-making processes before you can begin to consider how to approach them.

You should be wary of identifying the customer touchpoints too early in the process because you risk wasting time and money on channels that your customers don't engage with. You first need to properly assess the market, identify customer needs and determine the value proposition that is most appealing to your customers, then identify how they find solutions. In addition, we will discuss the importance of creating an omnichannel, versus multichannel, approach and define what the difference is. This includes traditional, old school methods of communicating with customers as well as mobile, social and other technology-driven methods. We will explain how to deploy these channels so online aligns with offline strategy, thereby creating a seamless experience—hence the term *omnichannel*. Finally, this chapter could alternatively be titled

Learning Objectives

In this chapter, you will learn to

- use your customer profiles to develop an integrated online and offline marketing program.
- define what an omnichannel versus multichannel marketing approach is and how to deploy this strategy.
- identify the aligned online and offline channels that will target the right customers and build brand engagement.
- develop content that resonates with your customers' needs.

"Content is King" because attracting customers online and off is all about delivering the right message, the one that your customers care about.

GETTING YOUR CUSTOMERS ENGAGED THROUGH AN OMNICHANNEL MARKETING APPROACH

In a time when we have continuous, oftentimes overwhelming, access, 24/7 to information about more products and services than we care or need to know about, how do you ensure your brand's message gets heard and is validated? This is a daunting feat to accomplish, especially when you have a limited budget. Identifying and engaging with your customers, the ones who want to do business with your brand, is not as easy as you might have believed before you began reading this book. We have seen this with the numerous entrepreneurs featured in the book as they struggle to achieve customer traction.

Let's begin by defining the difference between *omnichannel* and *multichannel* marketing since this is the underlying premise of how to successfully grow a company. The Merriam-Webster Dictionary (2019) defines *omni* as "All, universally" while *multi* is defined as "many, more than one." Using these definitions as a starting point, the difference between omnichannel marketing and multichannel marketing is that omnichannel marketing creates a unifying (universal) message across many platforms, thereby creating a seamless experience for the user. With a multichannel marketing approach, one

Figure 11.1 Multichannel Marketing

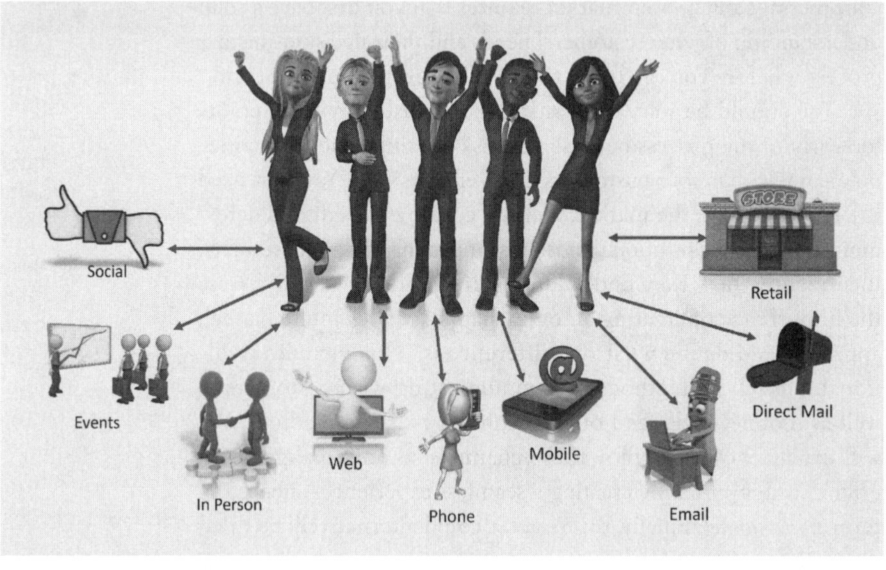

might be able to learn about a company using different platforms, but the experience isn't always seamless; you can't go from one platform to the next with ease, and sometimes your leap from channel to channel feels as if you're visiting a "different planet." From the customer perspective, multichannel is less than ideal and doesn't support a level of brand engagement that is important for a growing company. Omnichannel marketing requires that you apply a strategic and holistic approach to your marketing that includes all customer touchpoints. If you have multiple individuals or departments working on your messaging, you might be aiming for a consistent brand engagement, but the outcome feels more like a mixed-up patchwork. This inhibits the delivery of your brand message. Still confused? A picture is worth a thousand words. With that in mind, look at the difference between the two images and this might help you to better understand the differences between multichannel versus omnichannel marketing approaches.

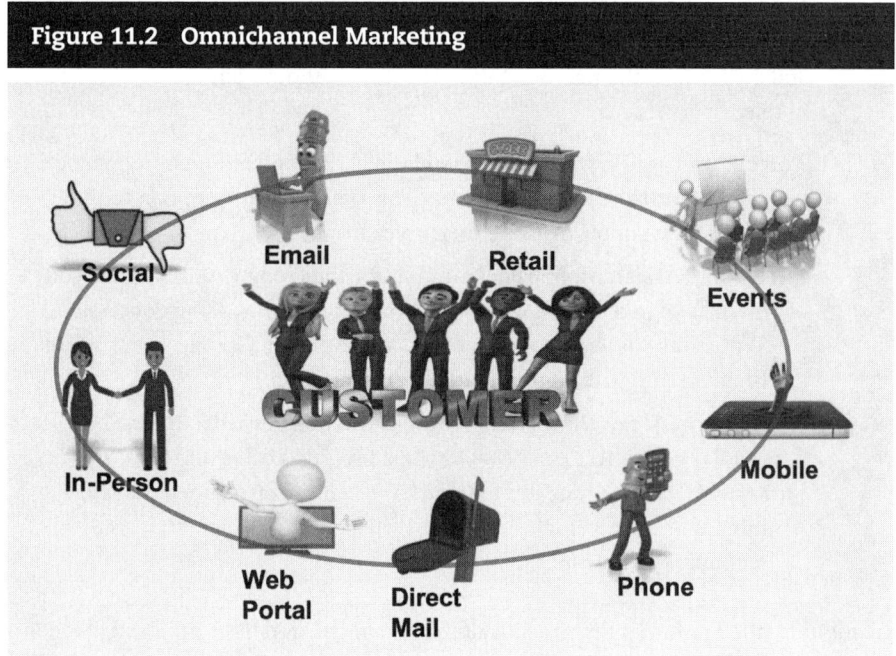

Figure 11.2 Omnichannel Marketing

THINK LIKE STARBUCKS

Let's look at an example of strong, holistically designed, omnichannel engagement. Starbucks, the international coffee retailer, is a great example of a strategically deployed customer marketing approach. As of July 2018, Starbucks operated 28,720 stores in over 75 countries around the world. While it is clearly a well-established brand with a budget much larger than your start-up, it exemplifies what an ideal customer experience can be and how a company can provide a seamless experience for its customers. For example, if you are ordering any type of drink, perhaps a grande latte, from any of its stores, whether in Saudi Arabia, Mexico, Boston, or London, your experience will be the same. Starbucks strives to ensure customers will experience its brand in the same way through a selection of tools and channels that it has deployed. As the factsheet at the company website explains:

> No matter how you prefer to order from Starbucks, our goal is to deliver a seamless experience. By providing a variety of ordering options, Starbucks allows customers to choose the method most convenient and relevant to them. Options include:
>
> - **In Person**: Whether at the register or in the drive-thru, customers can order in person in more than 26,000 stores around the world.
> - **Starbucks Mobile Order & Pay**: Starbucks Mobile Order & Pay feature on the Starbucks mobile app lets customers place and pay for an order in advance and pick it up at their chosen Starbucks store without waiting in line. Available in select markets.
> - **Voice Ordering**: As we further extend the barista and customer interaction within the Starbucks digital ecosystem, customers have the option to order from Starbucks simply by using their voice from:
>   - **Google Assistant**: Starbucks Action for the Google Assistant lets you order food and beverages from the Starbucks menu using your voice. With your phone or smart speaker, just say "Hey Google, order a Grande Blonde Latte with Almond milk from Starbucks."
>   - **Amazon Alexa Platform**: Through the Starbucks Reorder Skill, regular customers can reorder their favorite coffee and food by saying, "Alexa, order my Starbucks" to an Alexa-enabled device, including Ford vehicles equipped with SYNC3 voice-activated technology. (Starbucks, 2018a)

In addition, the Starbucks Rewards loyalty program has over 15.1 million U.S. members, representing 40% of U.S. company-operated sales with Mobile Order and Pay representing 13% of U.S. company-operated transactions (Starbucks, 2018b).

The app, which is part of the user experience, allows customers to find the store closest to them, order and pay, even if they are not physically in the store, plus easily track their rewards. Customers can also view and reload their rewards card via their app, the Starbucks website, by phone, or in the store and their account is updated immediately. If their approach was multichannel, versus omnichannel, this seamless integration would not exist and your experience, while it might be a positive one, would not likely keep you as engaged with the brand.

Obviously creating an omnichannel experience is not an easy task but is something that all businesses, small and large, should strive to achieve ... even if it's not at the level that Starbucks has attained. Your role is to create brand engagement and "buzz" about your business, strengthening your customers' experience with your company (brand) and spurring loyalty.

ACTION CREATES TRIUMPHS (ACT)

Creating Seamless Experiences

Before we continue, we want you to practice creating a seamless experience for your customers. Let's say you have been running a popular coffee shop in your neighborhood. It features locally baked breakfast items like muffins and bagels and you're really proud of the coffee that you serve. Your customers are loyal and you have become friends with many of them. However, you know that Starbucks is about to open a new shop just two blocks away. You're concerned about the customers' loyalty being tested. What can you do? Write down three tactics that you can deploy to ensure you create a seamless experience for your customers so they don't abandon your business. How can you be like Starbucks, deploying some of its best practices while still effectively competing? What needs to happen to your customer touchpoints so current customers and hopefully new prospects will want to continue engaging with your business?

CREATING BRAND ENGAGEMENT AND BUZZ

To gain another perspective on how to create brand engagement, we spoke with marketing consultant and industry thought leader Katie Martell (n.d.). She shares,

> In my point of view, public relations has evolved to a more ambiguous discipline of buzz-building, which involves a highly orchestrated combination of tactics (like anything else, any tactic that exists in a silo doesn't work). You could consider buzz-building as the new intersection of thought leadership, content marketing, social media, awards, speaking, influencer and media engagement, and events. But, to be honest, every company features a different application of these tactics depending on their industry, staffing, budget, experience, and expertise. Great buzz commands attention, changes narratives, and creates a platform upon which to build relationships, drive sales, secure funding, or hire great talent. Buyers don't do business with companies they've never heard of, and with those they do not trust. Creating the right kind of buzz impacts both.

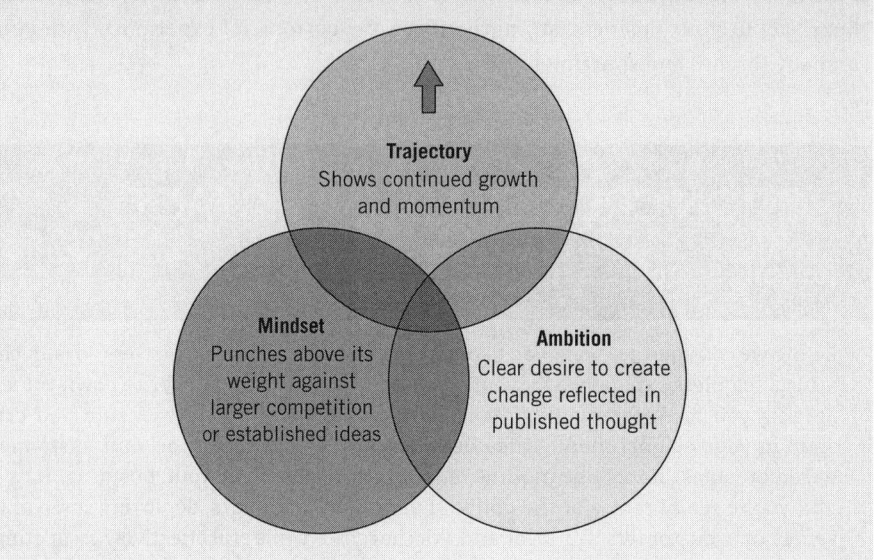

Figure 11.3 Key Traits of an Ascending B2B Brand

Katie Martell

Katie continued, "You're an ascending B2B brand if you demonstrate continued growth and momentum, punch above your weight against often larger competition or bigger ideas, and operate with a sense of ambition that is reflected in the thoughts you put into the world."

Ascending brands are those that earn buzz. Merit alone does not a market leader make. However, some still believe that a remarkable product alone is enough to earn customers and grow over time. That's simply not the case. If you're not a name brand, your best chance at breaking through, earning attention, and convincing buyers to trust you is to become really, really good at creating the right kind of buzz. Get people talking about your ideas, start to change how others see their own world. **Act like an ascending brand**. The late poet Leonard Cohen said, "Act the way you'd like to be and soon you'll be the way you act. If you want to be a market leader, *act like a market leader*. If you want to disrupt the market, *act like a disruptive brand*."

Finally, Katie concluded with her thoughts on market leaders.

Market leaders and disruptive brands set the agenda for their space—not only in what features they build, but how the market thinks and talks about their category. These brands have the ability to influence the overall narrative because they are *confident* in their point of view, and highly strategic in how they make that POV (Point of View) heard.

DISRUPTIVE BRAND MARKETING CAMPAIGNS

You may be thinking, "I'd love to be an ascending brand and create brand excitement, but I'm a start-up with very limited funds. How can I launch a marketing campaign that creates sufficient buzz and brand engagement that will grow my business?" Clearly, this might seem like the million-dollar question, but there are some clear methods that you can follow that improve your chances of success. Let's think of your marketing campaign as a series of conversations that you will have with your customers. Each conversation should be strategic and focused on building your brand message, allowing potential customers to experience your brand and empowering them to not only become advocates in communicating your brand to others but allowing them to become brand ambassadors themselves, helping you to spread the word. It's important to understand your unique value proposition because this will always be a key differentiator that supports your brand position. You want your customers to be advocates in spreading the word about your unique value proposition. Finally, remember Cheryl Kiser's comments from Chapter 10 about the importance of customers editing themselves into your narrative and your mission. This applies to all types of companies, and this "editing" also helps you build your brand engagement and creates loyal customers.

CEDING CONTROL OF YOUR BRAND

Wait—Does that mean that you need to give up control of your brand message? Are you comfortable putting control in the hands of people who buy your brand but don't work for your company? Welcome to marketing in the age of social media. You have already ceded control . . . now you simply need to acknowledge this and work within the new boundaries of marketing. With access to information on a continuous basis and multiple ways to not only learn about a brand but to learn about others' experiences with it, control already lies in the hands of the consumer. You have to first recognize that you don't have complete control over your brand message. Once you've done that and have managed to not completely panic, it's important to focus on the fact as long as your brand delivers on its promise and you do a solid job of sharing your message to your prospects, your chances of success are strong.

Let's return to our million-dollar question—How do you create a marketing campaign that creates sufficient buzz and brand engagement to grow your business? It all begins with a solid understanding of your customers and the value you create for them. You've already done that homework, right? Therefore, you need to revisit your research findings AND look carefully at your customer profiles, using these findings (not your gut instinct) to identify the marketing channels that you will deploy along with the value proposition and message that you will share with customers. What does your research tell you about your potential and current customers?

RETURN TO YOUR RESEARCH FINDINGS TO GET CUSTOMER TOUCH POINTS RIGHT

Can you answer the following questions with confidence based on your research findings?

- Where do our customers find out about our products or services now, and is that evolving?
- When are they looking for the products and services that we provide?
- Why do they buy from us now, and do they also consider purchases from our competitors?
- How do we deliver our products and services to them, and does it align with how we communicate with them?
- Can we measure results from our efforts? At the end of the day it's always about ROI (return on investment).

Have you asked the right questions to ensure you understand their unique needs and how they discover new products and services that meet those needs? Without being able to answer those questions directly, you'll be throwing money into marketing campaigns in the same way you would be throwing money into a lottery or raffle. It's a gamble and not the strategic, omnichannel approach that we have been discussing throughout the book.

VIEW FROM THE TRENCHES

Clothing Consignment: Research First—Channels Second

Let's consider the case of a clothing consignment retailer that we'll call "Second Is Best" (SIB). This was a clothing consignment business with 20+ stores around the United States. SIB wanted to develop a more proactive marketing strategy since it was relying too heavily on customers finding them when they walked past their retail shops, which strategically located in high-traffic areas in major cities. Before they began their research efforts to identify customer needs, they were focusing on two social media tools, Facebook and Twitter, to let their customers know about upcoming sales and events at their stores, encouraging them to share what was happening with friends. They even hired a highly paid social media expert whose job was to help the individual store managers send out "tweets" and "messages" on a daily basis. But the result was not positive—this wasn't working, and they were spending money with no increase in business. They pondered what they were doing wrong. After all, everybody was on Facebook and Twitter, right?

Their marketing campaigns continued while they concurrently ran a survey with thousands of their customers. One of the survey questions was, "How do you prefer to communicate with us and learn about sales and store events?" This question may sound familiar (Chapter 3: Identifying Your Customers' Journey). They discovered that an overwhelming majority (83% of their customers) preferred e-mail communication, while only 9% expressed any interest in communication through social media. This outcome surprised them because they believed their market was women in their 20s, based on foot traffic at two of their most popular stores located in a major metropolitan city. However, upon further research, they discovered that the majority of their customers were over 35 years of age, not the younger audience. How did this misunderstanding about their customers occur? They based their customer knowledge on gut instinct, because they saw lots of women in their 20s in their main store. But until they sent the survey out, they had never done any real research, inquiring about the ages and backgrounds of their customers. Interestingly enough, they also learned through the survey that even their 20- to 30-year-old customers had a strong preference for e-mail and limited interest in social media for learning about SIB's sales and other related news. With this new knowledge, the store owner pulled the plug on the Twitter and Facebook campaigns, refocused the social media expert's efforts and time and began to focus marketing on methods that his customers wanted him to use for communication: e-mail. He could immediately sense a direct correlation between e-mail campaigns and revenue and foot traffic in the stores.

The lesson learned with Second Is Best is not about the use of social media as a tool to connect with customers. On the contrary, for many businesses this method can be quite beneficial. However, the key learning is that your tactics and communication channels must align with the defined needs of your unique target market. If they want to engage via Facebook and you use this tool, great. However, if they don't and you are wasting precious marketing dollars on this tool, then you're throwing money down the drain.

OMNICHANNEL: COMBINING THE BEST OF OLD SCHOOL MARKETING WITH NEW SCHOOL CHANNELS

As we said earlier, gone are the days when businesses had total control over their marketing and communication with their customers. Old school marketing—which we will define next—still exists, but the rules of marketing engagement must align with new expectations that our customers have for communicating with us. Let's begin with a discussion of old school marketing practices before we dive into its synergistic relationship to new media channels such as Facebook, Twitter, Instagram, YouTube, and other forms of mobile and digital engagement.

In very simple terms, when we say "old school," we are referring to the use of traditional marketing channels that are typically viewed as "one-way communication" from the business to the potential consumer. The control over the message lies entirely in the hands of the company. Think of marketing campaigns that are paper based such as newspaper and magazine advertising, brochures, fact sheets, and direct mail—basically, things that you can actually touch but can't engage with or comment on as a customer. The business controls and distributes the message, and the customer is passive in the communication. These old school methods are NOT social and don't typically include the voice of the customer (other than some testimonials that the business captured and controlled). Included in the old school category is TV advertising as well as radio. You obviously can't touch them but they are not fully interactive experiences that you can readily engage with (shouting at your TV doesn't count). In terms of TV and radio, engagement is changing because many advertisements will try to push you to a computer or mobile device (or even landline phone) to connect with the business. However, as a stand-alone tool, you are not yet able to engage immediately.

On the "new school" side of the marketing spectrum, we have more social tools. These allow you to engage with the business and provide more interactive marketing experiences, immediately. These include a varied list of outreach methods with a common denominator: They allow you (the consumer) to engage with the medium and the brand. In addition, they usually allow you to hear what other customers have experienced as consumers of the brand, making the engagement more experiential and ideally more credible (if the customer feedback is not edited by the company). Hence, the term *social media*, since it's not simply the business saying "We are the best" but users sharing why they think the company's brand is the best, or, on the downside, not liked at all. With social engagement, control lies in the hands of the consumer, and the business's role is to

- ensure their brand delivers on their stated value promise,
- encourage and support the discussions that customers have about their brand, and
- defend or explain the brand when consumer feedback isn't representative of the value they portray.

As an entrepreneur, you likely have a limited budget, right? So, how do you ensure you spend money on the marketing channels that align best with your customers' needs? You can't do this in a vacuum. Some companies will try techniques like creating a blog or a YouTube series simply because they don't want to seem out of touch or risk losing an opportunity to communicate their value or because their competitors are already using these tools. However, when these tools are deployed to reach an audience that doesn't use them, it is potentially an expensive (time and money) recipe for disaster for a firm with a limited marketing budget. Finally, remember that investments in marketing tools should not simply be thought of in monetary terms, but also need to be measured in time invested by your team, especially given how scarce a resource time and human capital is for almost all start-ups. If you cannot justify your time and effort, then don't do it (even if your competitors are).

LET'S TALK SOCIAL

When the Web went from a scientific platform to a commercial one, individuals and companies flocked to it as if it were the Holy Grail. The Internet became the message and was not seen as another distribution or communication channel to support your marketing effort. But now that the Web is part of our everyday lives, the excitement has settled down and our comfort level with social tools as a way of communicating with prospects, customers, and stakeholders of all kinds is commonplace. Smartphones allow us to engage in real time with prospects. According to Statista (2019), as of 2018 there are over 2.5 billion smartphone users around the world, with those numbers projected to continue increasing each year. In the United States alone, Pew Research Center states that 95% of Americans own a cell phone, with 77% owning smartphones (2019a).

What are the implications for your start-up? Clearly your current marketing tactics will vary depending on the product or service that you offer and who your audience is, but if you plan on marketing in the United States, then having a mobile strategy will be important for your business. How important depends on what your research shows in terms of how customers want to engage with companies that offer solutions similar to yours. Remember, the relevance of each channel is based on your customers' needs, decision-making options, and preferred communications tools, now and in the future. For some organizations, mobile tools may not rank as critical today, but that doesn't mean that a year from now, customers won't want to engage with you using a mobile device. If your customers are online and are using mobile tools to learn about products and services similar to yours, then you need to be there. If they aren't, then you need to figure out where they will want to engage in the short and long term and how much of your marketing budget and time needs to be devoted to each channel and communication tool.

CONTENT IS KING

There are so many channels for social and offline communication that it's impossible to cover all of them here. Plus, the proliferation of marketing channels will continue evolving well beyond the publication date of this book. Before we discuss some popular tools and options, it's critical to embrace the importance of selecting the right channel for connecting to your customer. But you must also have the right message. The message that you convey is critical, must reflect what your customers care about, and exemplify your brand as a leader is engaged in sharing factual content through your selected omnichannels. It's important and quite powerful to be a "thought leader" or "influencer" in the industry that you are in. However, you must remember the importance of sharing facts and not spreading misinformation. You don't want to become a company that is known for creating false or misleading urban legends that can be debunked because this will cause harm to your brand. We strongly advocate that you take great care of your brand reputation and don't use the opportunity, when communicating with customers, to speak negatively about your competitors. Your brand should be powerful enough to allow you to share valuable information about your business and avoid disparaging others. That type of communication strategy will always backfire.

PUBLIC RELATIONS AND CREATING THOUGHT LEADERS AND INFLUENCERS

Public relations (PR) activities vary widely, from managing media or analyst relationships to helping companies with trade show support, running focus groups, and the one type of service you hope you never need to use, crisis communications. Sometimes you need a great PR agency to protect and defend your reputation so that you can build and maintain your company's image.

As with all marketing activities, the more focused you are on your goals, the more successful your PR strategy will be. While most small businesses don't need to hire a PR agent immediately, a PR expert who is fluent in your industry will have connections that you may have no chance of reaching. Plus, remember that while you may want to be in *The Wall Street Journal*, in reality an industry trade journal will likely be more effective and a better way to get you in front of the decision makers and customers that you care about. As with all marketing efforts, it is important to identify appropriate channels to target and weigh the cost of accessing an expert versus the benefit to your business. There are many small PR firms that will charge you a lower retainer fee to help you get started, and once you are established, you can then determine if the ROI (return on your investment) is evident.

Let's hear from an expert on marketing communication, Lisa M. Murray, principal at Trevi Communications, Inc. Lisa is a communications and media relations strategist who specializes in creating sustainable brands for executives, experts, and entrepreneurs. She generously shares her insight on what it takes to become a thought leader and Influencer in your field.

EXPERT INSIGHT

Becoming a Thought Leader and Influencer—Lisa Murray

The terms *thought leader*, *influencer*, or even *guru* may be overused, but the underlying premise remains invaluable. Public relations, and in particular thought leadership activities, such as being quoted in the media and writing articles that appear in trade and professional journals, are viewed as important "credentialing activities." Some reports state that a mere three quotes in respected publications can serve as a third-party endorsement equal to that of an actual customer referral. An earned media (or free media) strategy is a powerful educational tool in helping to establish and build credibility within target audience circles.

Entrepreneurs should take every opportunity to educate prospective and existing clients, referral sources, and colleagues. They should serve as media sources (even if only on background to educate the journalist), article and book authors, and public speakers. Newsletters are an additional tool for educating your audience. However, if you create a newsletter and have no one to send it to, the effort will net little in return. Approach topics from a variety of angles, including business, industry trends, legislative, public opinion, or funding perspectives.

Fortunately, content can be repurposed quite often, extending the life of nearly any topic and reaching a wider audience. When writing a newsletter or blog, consider how the topic and content can be reused for media pitching or as the basis for a speaking proposal. The library of ensuing published quotes, articles, and presentations will serve as credentials that will unequivocally position you as a subject matter guru.

To cut through the clutter of messages in today's global market, your public relations efforts need to be genuine, consistent, and frequent. Genuineness is important because sophisticated customers will rebuff a sales pitch disguised as valuable information. To be a consistent and frequent promoter, try scheduling PR activities at regular intervals during the month. It is all too easy to procrastinate on a "soft" marketing action item, so you will need to approach PR as if it were an appointment. Eventually, personal PR will become habitual. And, once you experience positive results, the business benefits will encourage you to remain on track.

In the New Information Age, it is easier than ever to achieve an air of omnipresence. There are nearly infinite choices for clients and prospects to receive content. The multitude of communication channels today includes, among others, traditional broadcast and print media (newspapers, trade journals, etc.), Web-based and mobile media (blogs, podcasts, Facebook, Linked-In, Twitter, etc.), and event-based media (conferences, associations, webinars, etc.). Your quote in Tuesday's print edition of *The Wall Street Journal* can exist in perpetuity on the Web, can be shared with your contacts through social media, and can be found by anyone through a simple Google search. But choose your distribution outlets wisely. Let the topic and objective dictate the medium and the distribution and build a strategy that will maximize your effort. For instance, it may not be appropriate to arbitrarily "friend" the CEO of a Fortune 100 company on Facebook, but it may be suitable to get an introduction to an executive at that company through a shared LinkedIn contact.

Don't dismiss or take a scattershot approach to social media, such as LinkedIn, Facebook, Twitter, and Instagram, as well as blogs and podcasts, as a way to educate and build a reputation as a thought leader. A well-planned social media strategy that reaches your target audience via the appropriate social channel (remember your research) can be highly beneficial for building your company's brand (and even your personal brand). Ultimately, an integrated PR approach that includes both earned and social media will help attract qualified prospects to your business. Bylined articles, speaking engagements, social media, and press coverage can work together to strengthen your reputation as an authority in your field.

Find a Voice

One of the most effective ways to be heard and remembered over competing messages is to define and exploit your unique differentiators. If you are fortunate to be able to claim a "first" in a particular niche, then you have a ready-made opportunity to distinguish yourself. Most, however, will need to craft a personal brand statement, which can be based on experience, personal attributes, and market knowledge, for example. If you are a woman in a male-dominated industry such as the construction industry, you may be able to leverage that distinction to your advantage. Even a personal hobby, philanthropy, or commitment to a cause can serve to provide you with a unique voice.

Find a different angle or a new wrinkle on a current issue. Identify a new trend. Take a crystal ball view of the future of your target market. Each of these techniques will help set you apart from your competition, and will garner the interest of the media, trade groups, clients, and your peers.

(Continued)

(Continued)

If blogging is part of your marketing strategy, infuse your personality into the blog posts. Use the opportunity to both inform and entertain your target audience. If the overall subject matter isn't exciting, make sure your delivery is lively, which will afford you a unique voice and set you apart.

Course Correct (if needed)

Agility is essential. Sales and marketing can be an imperfect science. Global business is in a constant state of flux, and audiences can be fickle and unpredictable. Evaluate your PR efforts each quarter to measure the return on your investment. Your PR efforts should be generating qualified business leads. If you haven't moved the needle, it may behoove you to shift your message or redirect your strategy.

The most successful business owners will be those who develop their own PR and brand strategy—a strategy that drives business goals and creates a competitive edge by building a professional profile in specific industries and with high value clients.

Lots of great insight shared by an expert who's been in the industry over 30 years and has seen it evolve. However, just as in the "old days" when your marketing and thought-leadership building tools were mostly paper driven, the right content is critical to your success. Don't create a post, blog, or even company e-mail newsletter and write about YOU and YOUR company. Use the medium to give advice and educate your customers so they want to engage with you. This is NOT the place to hit them with a sales pitch but to demonstrate that you are an expert in your field. For example, if you're a home improvement specialist, perhaps you can share tips about activities they can do to improve their home's safety. If you're a fashion designer, share advice on the latest trends or perhaps companies in the industry that are doing "good" and helping individuals in disadvantaged neighborhoods. The point is that self-promotion is NOT the way to become an influencer in a market. You must create content that creates value for your customers.

WHAT IF YOU'RE NOT AN EXPERT

As Lisa Murray points out, there's great value in becoming a thought leader or an influencer in a market. But perhaps you're not there yet. Is your opportunity lost to secure your company as a leader in the industry? Definitely not; you can always connect with thought leaders or influencers in the industry and partner with them. Allow them to be a voice that is connected to your business. This type of partnership can be quite powerful and effective. For example, let's say you have definitely an upscale fashion line featuring beautiful women's dresses. You're an expert but you're not well known. Securing a relationship with an influencer who attracts similar customers in a complimentary but not competing sector of the market can be an effective marketing strategy. Perhaps you can work with a jewelry designer who attracts the same customer base. Work with them: They can talk about your brand in their blog or in their Instagram posts. That could be quite effective. You might need to pay to have these influencers work with you or perhaps you offer them an opportunity to capture more customers or followers because you have secured individuals they don't yet connect with. Spend a few minutes thinking about a few influencers who attract similar customers to yours who don't compete with you. List them and think about ways to partner with them to create win–win solutions to build both of your brands.

CREATING AND DELIVERING CONTENT

There are a variety of ways you can create content. In this section we will discuss four methods: blogs, webinars, podcasts, and videos.

Blogs

You might create a blog, basically a Web-based journal, that provides commentary and news about a specific topic. If you link to other websites and social media related to the blog topic, then you are providing readers with content that they value. This can be a great opportunity to demonstrate your expertise. You might then link your blog to your own website and to other respected industry websites and help increase your ability to be found online via search engines. However, one word of caution: This is time consuming. The expectation is that there will be a reasonable frequency (somewhere between "every hour" like a news report and "once a month" like newsletters), so be prepared to blog a few times a week if you want to gain traction.

An interesting example about a successful blog is the story behind Kate Rumson, interior designer. In the summer of 2018, the *Wall Street Journal* ran a piece about her success (Ang, 2018). Five years before the article was published, Kate Rumson was flipping houses on a part-time basis while she worked in the banking industry. According to the article, "After she ran out of storage on her phone, she created an Instagram account to share interior design pictures. The photos went viral, and now Ms. Rumson has 1.8 million followers and a new career as an interior designer and social-media celebrity" (Ang, 2018). Obviously, this isn't going to happen to everybody who posts images on social media, but there are numerous stories to be found online about individuals whose careers have been launched as a result of their "sharing" advice online.

Perhaps writing your own blog is simply too time consuming or not something that you want to focus on now. There are still ways that you can connect with customers and influencers online. Some things to consider include the following:

1. Commenting on influencers' posts
2. Sharing their posts with customers and people who might value the advice
3. Reaching out to influencers to express your appreciation for their advice and perhaps even explore becoming a guest blogger on their site

Any of these tactics will help get you out in front of your market and build your brand as somebody who is an expert they want to engage with.

Webinars

Have you participated in a webinar (Web-based seminar)? These can be quite beneficial because they allow you to offer valuable information to customers and prospects and demonstrate, once again, your knowledge as a thought leader or influencer in the industry. This allows you to feature your business and yourself as the expert on a topic. This platform gives you the opportunity to invite prospects, customers, and other stakeholders whom you are interested in getting to know better to hear your presentation or presentations by your colleagues or partners. You should definitely sell this as a learning opportunity, since it's rare that somebody will want to attend an event just to hear about you and your company. If you choose a topic that is important and valuable for people to learn about, your attendance rates will increase. Typically, webinars are free or low priced to get individuals who are interested in a special topic (i.e., small business marketing, selling to the government) more engaged with your company.

For service providers, this can be a powerful tool. You can create a few free webinars, share your expertise and then, if appropriate, present a more complete solution to participants (that they will pay for). Many companies have found success with webinars, especially when they have prospects around the globe. Keep mind the fact that you will need to carefully select the vendor who can best support your technical needs. You need to ensure that the tool is accessible, the technology is reliable (people can hear you and see you without losing connections), the customer service is top ranked, and the price point works for you. You will also want to ensure that you can download and edit the final webinars and will have access to post them as webinars and podcasts (audio versions) on your own website. This gives prospects another reason to visit your site and provides influencers with an incentive to link to you; they love to share valuable content.

Some tools that will support the creation of a webinar, and you might already be familiar with, include Google Hangouts, Skype, Zoom, YouTube Live, Webex, ReadyTalk, Adobe Connect, Facebook Live, and AnyMeeting. Depending on where your stakeholders are located around the world and what their specific Web-based options and challenges are (i.e., poor cell or WiFi coverage), you should research the options and then test the tools before launching your webinar.

Podcasts

Podcasts are basically audio-only versions of your webinar. You can actually use a number of the previously mentioned tools for your webinar to create your podcast. However, you want to keep in mind the fact that since there without visuals, you will need to make changes to your recording. If you are interviewing somebody, your podcast might very easily need no adjustments from a visually recorded version. However, if you rely on charts, graphs or photographs to explain, then the podcast might need to be adjusted to give the listener a true understanding of what you are sharing. You can share links to your website for more information or to look at the images. Keep this in mind since you want to ensure a successful and engaging outcome. Remember, you don't want to simply be another company creating another podcast. Make this interesting so that your brand engages customers and prospects and encourages them to share with others. That means that your information should not be "about your company" but focus on listeners' needs and what you, as a thought leader in the industry, can offer them in terms of advice and support.

You will want to make sure individuals can listen to the podcast on multiple platforms including iOS(iTunes), Android (Google Play) and in a Web browser. If they need to download new software, the process should not be so cumbersome that it inhibits them from listening. We also suggest that you listen to a few of the most popular podcasts so you can understand what they do to intrigue and educate the listener to keep them coming back. According to Podtrac (2019b), an organization that tracks popularity of podcasts based on the number of listeners in a given month (http://analytics.podtrac.com), the top 10 podcasts as of March 2019 (Podtrac, 2019a) were

Videos

When you think of video, what do you think of? If you're like most people, your answer is YouTube. According to the YouTube website (2019c), there are over 1 billion

Table 11.1 Podcast Rankings

RANK	PODCAST	PUBLISHER
1	The Daily	*The New York Times*
2	The Ben Shapiro Show	*Daily Wire*
3	This American Life	This American Life/Serial
4	Stuff You Should Know	iHeartRadio
5	Up First	NPR
6	TED Radio Hour	NPR
7	The Ron Burgundy Podcast	iHeartRadio
8	RadioLab	WNYC Studios
9	Pardon My Take	Barstool Sports
10	Planet Money	NPR

people who access YouTube. That's over a billion hours of video watched every day, with more than half of that content originating on a mobile device. YouTube is global with "local versions in 88 countries... accessed in 76 languages." While Google (its parent company) owns almost 72% of the share of the market for search (Net Marketshare, 2019). YouTube is often used as a starting point for search. That means that you will want to follow the same best practices for creating engaging videos that you apply to your webinars and podcasts—and all your marketing campaigns. If you're interested in further understanding YouTube statistics, you can check out more on Social Blade (2019a), an organization that tracks user data for YouTube, Twitter and Instagram. Social Blade even offers a course titled YouTube101 (Social Blade, 2019b), showing you best practices in creating videos. They have incredible advice on their educational site. Below are some of their tips:

- Decide how often you're going to upload your videos.
- Don't sacrifice quality for quantity.
- Stick to a schedule so your viewers know when to expect new content.
- There's no need to have a fancy camera, your iPhone will do just fine!
- Ensure you're filming horizontally, NOT vertically
- Quality means nothing if your content isn't consistent.
- Personality drives viewers. Be yourself!
- Growth is exponential. It's slow at first, but will pick up!
- Keep intros to about 5 seconds maximum.
- Tease content first to get the audience invested in that piece of content, then roll the intro.
- Engage with other creators and make friends.
- Get personal!
- You can't use commercial music on your videos. Just because you bought it on iTunes does *not* mean you can use it. Use royalty-free music instead.
- Ask viewers to subscribe and like your videos at the end.
- Most people mean to like and subscribe, they just forget!
- Comment on videos that are similar to yours.
- Don't just promote yourself!

- Be clever and witty; talk about the video you're commenting on, so that other viewers will give it a thumbs up.

- Reply to other comments to make friends.

- Network with others: Search for similar channels that are about the same size and connect.

- Use social media to make friends. Friends will ultimately be your biggest motivators!

EXPLORING TOP SOCIAL TOOLS

Now, let's discuss the five social tools that are most popular in the United States as of the publication of this book (as mentioned before, these are subject and likely to change). That doesn't mean that these are the tools that you should necessarily use. You need to communicate via the channels that YOUR customers want to engage with, even if they are not the most commonly accessed ones. They might be industry specific or more relevant based on your customers' demographic or geographic composition.

According to the Pew Research Center (2019b), as of February 2019. the five most popular social media sites access in the United States are (in order):

1. YouTube (73%)
2. Facebook (69%)
3. Instagram (37%)
4. Pinterest (28%)
5. LinkedIn (27%)

These are all followed closely by Snapchat, Twitter, and WhatsApp.

Let's explore the top four channels in greater detail to understand how each might help support your ability to become an influencer in your industry and increase brand engagement. Remember that the world of social engagement is rapidly changing and evolving. Between the time we went to print with this book and the time that you are reading it, the numbers stated here will almost certainly change. That means that the responsibility for understanding and identifying the sites most desired by your customers is yours. Don't rely simply on the data in this book (or any book). Your role to explore and stay on top of current and developing trends is a critical one in the process of identifying the ideal omnichannel marketing mix to deploy.

We are confident that you likely use some or all of the following channels as a consumer. However, we want you to understand the business side of each marketing tool.

YouTube

YouTube, owned by Google, is a great way to share video with friends, colleagues, prospects, and other key stakeholders with whom you want to engage. They state on their website (YouTube, 2019a) that "Our mission is to give everyone a voice and show them the world". YouTube has created its own blog called Broadcast Yourself, which you can access at https://youtube.googleblog.com/. According to Business Insider (Gilbert, 2018) as of May 2018, YouTube had over 1.8 million users (individuals who logged in) every month. However, this doesn't mean much to you as a small business owner if you don't know how to access your potential customers. In addition to Social Blade's tutorial, there's an excellent overview of how to start your own YouTube channel for your small business published by *Business News Daily* (Kuligowski, 2019). It covers everything from setting up your account to interacting with others and partner programs.

Facebook

Facebook, a social tool used by individuals and businesses alike, claimed over 1.47 billion daily active users as of June 2018 (Facebook, 2019b) with 2.23 billion monthly users. Chances are strong that you are one of these billions of individuals who log in to use Facebook for personal reasons. However, it's not as likely that you've set up a business page there. Facebook has made this relatively simple by providing clear instructions at their website (Facebook, 2019a). They review everything from how to name your page to how to convert a Facebook profile into a page for business and start posting. Of course, it's critical to connect with your prospects and customers as well as measure the impact of your posts. Learn how to access Page Insights (Facebook Business, 2019), and you can read more about what the numbers mean to your business and understand if Facebook is the right tool for you to target audience engagement. You can learn

- how many people your posts reach and how many people engage with your posts,
- the number of people who telephoned your business from your page, and
- the number of check-ins people made to your business with their posts.

Instagram

Instagram was purchased by Facebook in 2012 for $1 billion. However, this was significantly less than they paid for WhatsApp in 2014 ($19 billion). Instagram allows you to share photos and videos with customers and prospects. Launched in 2010 with 25,000 users signing up the first day (Instagram, 2010), Instagram now claims over 1 billion active monthly users, over 500 million daily users and over 400,000 daily stories. Daily

Stores, launched in 2016, is a feature that "lets you share all the moments of your day, not just the ones you want to keep on your profile. As you share multiple photos and videos, they appear together in a slideshow format: your story . . . The photos and videos will disappear after 24 hours and won't appear on your profile grid or in feed." (Instagram, 2016). As with Facebook, you need to set up a business profile on Instagram, giving you access to analytics to understand viewer engagement. Their site explains how to set up a profile and use a variety of business tools (Instagram, n.d.).

Pinterest

Pinterest, a virtual "board" where individuals can upload, view, save, and even sort images (also known as *pins*), through pinboards. While it's not as popular as YouTube, Facebook, and Instagram, it does have a strong following, especially by individuals planning a purchase. According to Sprout Social (Carter, 2019), 29% of U.S. adults use Pinterest, with 50% of millennials using the site at least once a month. Sprout Social shared some interesting statistics about these users, data that will help you determine if this tool is appropriate for your business:

- More than 14 million articles are pinned daily.
- 40% of pinners have a household income of $100k+.
- 93% of active pinners said they use Pinterest to plan for purchases.
- 50% have made a purchase after seeing a promoted pin.
- Nearly 85% of Pinterest searches happen on mobile.
- 78% say it's useful to see content from brands on Pinterest.
- Pinterest delivers $2 in profit per $1 spent on advertising.
- Pinners spend 29% more on retail than those who don't use Pinterest.
- Pinners plan twice as early than people on other platforms.
- 70% Search, Save, or Click on a pin.

Pinterest makes it very easy to convert a personal account into a business account, or set up a new account (Pinterest Business, n.d.).

SNAPCHAT AS A MARKETING TOOL

How do you, as a small business owner, use this as a marketing tool? Melinda Emerson, also known as the SmallBiz Lady, posted a helpful article on Huffpost titled "How to

Use Snapchat to Market Your Small Business" (Emerson, 2019). Below is a summary of Melinda's suggestions. You can read the entire *Huffpost* article online (Emerson, 2016).

- **Focus on Your Followers:** It may seem counterintuitive to center your Snapchat shares on what your followers are doing online, but it's great for engagement. Who doesn't love to be the center of attention?

- **Hold a Snapchat Contest:** Snapchat users are an interactive bunch, and by holding contests or giveaways, you can get them to spread the word about your brand for you. Make sure the prizes are drool worthy, and the contest entry rules are simple. You could ask followers to snap a photo of them using your product or go with a holiday theme, like dressing in their scariest Halloween costume, and you choose a winner.

- **Provide Exclusive Content:** When followers get sneak peeks or insider views into your brand that non-followers don't get access to, they feel special. This might come in the form of unveiling a new product before it hits the shelves, going behind the scenes at a big event, or even getting your followers' opinion on which direction to take your product line.

- **Take Over Another Brand's Account** (*with their permission*)**:** Another way to get exposure on Snapchat is to take over another user's account that targets your demographic. It's a great way to build a connection with an audience who might not otherwise know about your business.

- **Try Sponsoring a Filter:** While Snapchat filters that turn you into a superhero or an animal are fun for users, they also pack a punch when it comes to marketing your brand.

Melinda explained,

> My rule of thumb is that you need to be anywhere your best target audience is spending the majority of their time online. If your audience is using Snapchat find unique ways to engage them there. Don't assume you know the culture of Snapchat. Study it! Make sure to emulate other brands who have proven success on the app as well as trying your own innovative ideas. (Emerson, 2016)

As you can tell, there are many venues for you to use to engage with customers. As we've discussed throughout the book, the decision about how to engage and what your message is relies 100% upon your customers and what they need and expect from you. That means that you need to review all methods of getting in front of them, from social media and website engagement to old school methods like direct mail, traditional advertising, and in person at events, conferences, and other networking opportunities. Before we explore some of these more traditional options, let's look at e-mail marketing, basically a hybrid of digital plus traditional direct-mail marketing.

EMAIL MARKETING

You can't forget about e-mail marketing when talking about social campaigns. While using e-mail as a method of reaching your customers and prospects is not as "social" as blogging or creating videos, its role can be quite powerful. A study by MarketingSherpa (2015) discovered that "72 percent of U.S. adults indicate a preference for companies to communicate with them via email followed by postal mail (48%), TV ads (34%), print media (e.g., newspapers, magazines) (31%), text message (19%), social media and in-person conversation/consultation (both at 17%)."

There are clear best practices that you should be aware of to increase your response rates using e-mail as a channel to connect and stay connected to customers. To learn more about best practices, you should check out Constant Contact's e-mail marketing blog (Pinkham, 2019). Here you can find an extensive list of links to great content on how to design e-mails that won't get deleted immediately. Another source of e-mail marketing advice is through MarketingSherpa's website.

According to the market research firm, The Radicati Group (2018), the total worldwide e-mail traffic, including both business and consumer e-mails, is estimated to be over 281 billion e-mails a day by year-end 2018, growing to over 333 billion e-mails a day by the end of 2022. With over 3.8 billion e-mail users worldwide, that's a significant amount of e-mail traffic heading into inboxes. How do you ensure that your e-mail is seen by prospects and doesn't end up being deleted immediately or lodged in the spam filter? Well, it's clearly not easy. Below we have provided some tips and advice to get you started. We also encourage you to check out the sources discussed previously where you will find lots of advice about getting your e-mail viewed.

Email Marketing Tips to Get You Focused

- Making sure your message is clear and to the point. Don't allow it to sound "salesy" or full of hype. It should be real and speak to your customer or prospect in an appropriate tone.

- Read and reread your e-mail before sending it, not only for clarity but to ensure you haven't introduced any typos or grammatical errors. That will leave the wrong impression with your prospect or customer

- Make sure there is a clear and easy "Call to Action" to create engagement.

- Make sure it addresses the pain points that your customers are experiencing (reference your customer profile, once again) or shares information that matters to them.

- When they click on a link, make sure it sends them to a unique landing page so you can easily track their engagement with your e-mail that led them to your site. For advice on creating landing pages, check out Hubspot's blog (Cook, 2019).The e-mail should contain valuable information for the customer to use—not just be an advertisement about your company. An example would be a fashion designer sharing tips about the hottest trends in fashion and colors for the upcoming season. There could be a link to buy that person's clothes, but the message is focused on educating the reader about fashion, not the designer herself.

- The subject line of your e-mail matters. Make sure it's intriguing enough for the reader to want to read the content . . . at the very least, the opening line should capture their attention.

TOOLS, TIPS, AND TRAINING RESOURCES

The following links provide insight that goes beyond the scope of this book. Spend time checking out a few of these as you begin to think of the channels that will work best for you company.

Website and Social Media Management

- Canva (graphic creator): https://www.canva.com/
- Trello (project management for team collaboration): https://trello.com/
- Buffer (social media management): https://buffer.com/
- Wix, Wordpress, Squarespace (build websites and blogs):
    - Wix: https://www.wix.com/
    - Wordpress: https://wordpress.com/
    - Squarespace: https://www.squarespace.com/
- Hubspot (Pull Marketing and CRM, free and paid options):
    - Home Page: https://www.hubspot.com/
    - Website Grader (Hubspot tool) (Measure your website's performance): https://website.grader.com/
    - Creating Landing Pages: https://blog.hubspot.com/marketing/landing-page-examples-list

Training and Advice to Set Up and Measure Social Media Sites

- Google and Paid Search
    - Google Analytics Academy: https://analytics.google.com/analytics/academy/
    - Think with Google: https://www.thinkwithgoogle.com
    - Google Ads Video Tutorials on YouTube: https://www.youtube.com/user/learnwithgoogle
    - Paid Search help (Q&A): https://support.google.com/google-ads/?hl=en#topic=7456157
    - Paid Search articles that discuss new SEM tactics and trends: www.searchengineland.com and www.searchenginewatch.com
- YouTube 101: https://socialblade.com/youtube/education
- Facebook Insights: https://www.facebook.com/business/learn/facebook-page-insights-basics
- Facebook for Business: https://www.facebook.com/business/learn/set-up-facebook-page
- Instagram Business Tools: https://help.instagram.com/307876842935851/
- Pinterest for Business: https://business.pinterest.com/en/creating-your-account

ACTION CREATES TRIUMPHS (ACT)

Social Media Critique and Campaign Development

An important way to understand how to develop a social media campaign is to first critique a social media piece that your competitor (or a business that provides similar products or similar solutions) has been using to promote their company or a specific product. Then, you will be in a stronger position to develop your own campaign. Ready to begin?

Part One: Social Media Critique

When completing your evaluation of a competitor's social media piece, consider the following:

- Who is the target market for this material?
    a. Does the message appropriately address the needs of this market?

(Continued)

(Continued)

Evaluate the following	Ineffective				Effective
Visually appealing	1	2	3	4	5
Easy to read or hear and understand	1	2	3	4	5
Clearly communicates the product's unique benefits (brand value)	1	2	3	4	5
Further engagement with the company or product is offered	1	2	3	4	5
Compels you to act (i.e., learn more, test, buy)	1	2	3	4	5
Rate the overall effectiveness of the piece	1	2	3	4	5
				Total Score: _____ /30	

- Is the channel of communication that was used appropriate?
- Is the unique value proposition (brand value) clear and believable?

1. Describe changes (if any) your team recommends for this social media piece that would allow the company to better communicate its value to its audience. *This could include a change to the message or to the marketing channel or something else.*

2. You MUST also include in your critique at least ONE insight learned from the assignment that you will apply to the business you are working on. Explain how your critique has impacted or will impact the social media campaign(s) that you create (what you did that was similar, what you did that was different and why).

Part Two: Social Media Campaign

Using the lessons learned from the social media critique, you will develop at least one, ideally two, social media campaigns to promote your business. This can be any type of social media, including, but not limited to, Facebook, Snapchat, Instagram, Pinterest, and YouTube. If you are creating video content, try to keep the campaign to no less than 20 seconds in length and no more than 90 seconds. This campaign should be one that you will use to attract new customers so make sure you spend time doing this right.

As you are creating your campaign, think about your "**Big Idea.**" Your message should hold an audience's interest, and your "Big Idea" should create an identity for your product and brand. It should

- position the brand in the market,
- show how it is distinct from competitors' brand value,
- explain the value of the brand, and
- create an ACTION on the part of the viewer.

You want to create a brand that creates energy and excitement and compels the viewer to ACT. Action that you will want to generate can include but not be limited to the following:

- Look for/**use** a special offer/**BUY**.
- **Praise** or **recommend** it.
- **Visit** its webpage or other channels.
- **Look up online** reviews.
- Give **advice** on the brand online and offline (WOM).
- **Post** reviews online.
- **Share** with friends and colleagues.

Present to Your Class

Think of this as a formal presentation to your board of advisors. You should prepare a **PowerPoint presentation** that is professional. Your team must share your social media campaign and be able to clearly explain its goals and justification for the strategy you designed. Make sure there's time allocated during your presentation (typically 8 to 10 minutes) to show both the competitors' campaign that you critiqued and your campaigns along with your analysis. Make sure you explain how your social media critique influenced the campaign design.

Information to Include in Your Social Marketing Campaign Presentation

A. **Marketing Goal**—Specify sales and marketing objectives for the campaign.
   a. State objectives so that they are SMART (*Specific, Measurable, Actionable, Realistic and Time based*)
   b. *Examples include the following*: Increase sales from 10 to 200 people by July 15; Secure 300 likes on Facebook and 25 shares by July 1.
   c. Explain how your critique influenced your thinking in terms of design for your social media campaign

B. **Target Audience(s)**—Identify primary target audiences based on your market research.
   a. Highlight the known demographic, geographic, psychographic, and behavioral characteristics of your target audience.
   b. Note that your target audiences (decision makers, purchasers) may be a subgroup from the actual user profile or a totally different group.

C. **Marketing Channels Justification**—Discuss the marketing channels that you selected.
   a. Which channels did you create the campaign for?
   b. Why do you believe these channels will be most effective in reaching your target audience(s) and communicating your message?
   c. Will you use other channels in addition to the selected ones demonstrated?

D. **Brand Value Proposition and Benefits**—Explain the product benefits that you emphasized in your campaign.
   a. Explain why those were selected.
   b. Highlight your product's competitive advantage (what distinguishes your product from the competition).

E. **Slogan/Tagline**—Will you have a slogan or tagline?
   a. Consider a short phrase that will help establish an image, position, or identity for the brand, and increase memorability.

AHAs

Lessons and Takeaways

In this chapter, we discussed a variety of omni-channel marketing efforts to connect with your customers, prospects, and other stakeholders. Highlights of our discussion include the following:

- Omnichannel marketing creates a unifying and universal message across many platforms, ideally creating a seamless experience for the user.
- Public relations has evolved to a more ambiguous discipline of buzz-building, which involves a highly orchestrated combination of tactics.
- Market leaders and disruptive brands set the agenda for their space—not only in what features they build, but how the market thinks and talks about their category.
- Old school marketing techniques afford the business the opportunity to control and distribute the message it wants its customers to passively receive. Digital marketing cedes control to customers to engage with the brand message. You shouldn't worry about abandoning control as long as your brand delivers on its promise and you do a solid job of sharing your message to your prospects; your chances of success are strong.
- The message that you convey is critical, must reflect what your customers care about, and exemplify your brand as a leader that is engaged in sharing factual content through your selected omnichannels.
- Securing a relationship with an influencer who attracts similar customers in a complementary but not competing sector of the market, can be an effective marketing strategy.
- The world of social engagement is rapidly changing and evolving. Therefore, the responsibility for understanding and identifying the sites most desired by your customers is yours. You must stay on top of current and developing trends in the process of identifying the ideal omnichannel marketing mix to deploy.
- All communication requires that your message address the pain points that your customer is experiencing. Make sure there is a clear and easy "Call to Action" to create customer engagement.

In the next chapter, we continue our discussion about omnichannel marketing efforts, with a greater focus on more traditional methods of reaching your customers. We'll also continue our discussion about Waku and see what that company's campaign looks like.

CHAPTER TWELVE

LEVERAGING OLD SCHOOL MARKETING TACTICS

OLD SCHOOL NEVER GOES OUT OF STYLE

In this chapter, we continue our conversation about omnichannel marketing, but begin to focus on more traditional methods of engaging with customers. We'll call them "Old School" but they clearly never go out of style and can be leveraged to deepen your customer relationships.

OLD SCHOOL METHODS OF REACHING YOUR CUSTOMERS

It's easy to convince yourself that everything you do must be digital, but the reality is, there's oftentimes a need for getting your message across using more traditional (think pre-Internet) pulp-based methods such as brochures, direct mail pieces, and advertising through magazines, newspapers, billboards, and other collateral media that you can actually touch.

Brochures

The cost of printing brochures has always been an expensive proposition, especially considering the fact that when there's a change in your product or perhaps your service, the brochure becomes obsolete, forcing you to start over and spend more money printing and distributing. However, there is still a value of providing somebody with a "takeaway" or a "leave-behind" that they can refer to.

We encourage you to think creatively about this when determining what you really need. Perhaps you're going to a conference

Learning Objectives

In this chapter, you will learn to

- differentiate between traditional and current methods of communicating with customers and prospects.

- develop an understanding of when to apply different communication strategies with customers and prospects.

- develop important networking skills to help you succeed in business.

- design a marketing campaign strategy that aligns with your customer and business goals.

and you offer interior design services to wealthy homeowners. You might be convinced that a portfolio featuring homes that you've redesigned will be a powerful sales tool. It very well might be, but before you spend a large percentage of your budget on a fancy brochure, weigh the benefit (likelihood of getting a new customer) against the cost and time required to produce and print the brochure. Perhaps printing a postcard with a few designs and a link to your website might be a better way to attract the right customers and close just as many deals. In reality, you might close more deals because you could feature an unlimited variety of your projects (more than a brochure would show) and seeing them on a screen where prospects can zoom in might provide a more optimal sales outcome. They might also be more likely to keep your postcard (or even a nice business card) than a heavy brochure. You'll have a strong impact without the cost. It might even free your budget up enough to allow you to hire a professional photographer or website designer to help ensure your site shows off your work in the best light.

Direct Mail

Does direct mail still work? Yes, it can definitely work if you align the message and the call to action with prospects who want or need your product. According to the DMA's (Data & Marketing Association) 2017 Response Rate Report (2017), the following are rates for responding to direct mail pieces by businesses they surveyed (Note: A house file is the business's own customer list—basically, people known to them who have given them permission to communicate with them):

- **Postcards**—A house file has a 5.7% response rate with an ROI of 29%, and prospect file has a 3.4% response rate with an ROI of 23%.
- **Letter Sized Envelopes**—A house file has a 4.37% response rate with an ROI of 29%, and prospect file had a 2.5% response rate with an ROI of 23%.
- **Flat Sized Envelopes**—A house file had a 6.6% response rate with an ROI of 37%, and prospect file had a 4.9% response rate with an ROI of 30%.

Clearly, postcards and flat-size envelopes stand out in the mail and have a stronger chance of being opened and responded to. Keep in mind the fact that one of the keys to success is that you need to connect with prospects and customers using a variety of channels to have the best impact. Like sales literature, direct-mail pieces come in a variety of shapes, sizes, and format, as noted above. Some businesses choose to send letters in plain envelopes with your name and address handwritten, while others may use postcards or send interesting pamphlets enclosed in fancy, colorful envelopes to try to increase their chances of getting their customers to open the mail. You will likely have to test a few different methods to identify the method that works best for you.

According to an article in *Forbes* magazine in August 2017, direct is still a contender for attention (Pulcinella, 2017). "It's no surprise then that a study conducted by the UK Royal Mail, The Private Life of Mail, concluded that the upswing in the use of direct mail and its enduring effectiveness is because, 'Giving, receiving and handling tangible objects remain deep and intuitive parts of the human experience.' This emotional effect is what's at the bottom of its effectiveness: 60% said this effect made a more lasting mental impression on them, making it easier to recall later on. 57% of respondents said that postcard marketing makes them feel more valued and creates a more authentic relationship.

The common belief that traditional old school methods of reaching customers via channels like direct mail don't work is not necessarily true. It can be part of a rich, omnichannel campaign. However, success will vary by business. You need to diligently and continually work on capturing your customers' attention as well as building your relationship with them over time.

Get Them to Act

The discussion related to the effectiveness of your campaigns is a moot one if your message is not of value nor on target. You already know that this begins with understanding your audience and relying on your customer profiles to address needs and values. If you have several different audiences and your message is different for each, don't try to send all of these audiences the same campaign. It will fail. The message has to match the audience in order to succeed in any sales and marketing effort.

One critical aspect of your direct-mail campaign is your "Call to Action." Don't simply send customers or prospects information about your business without giving them a variety of ways to respond to you. This can be a reply card for them to request more information about your product or service, but it most likely will be something that drives them to your website or social media platform for a continued dialogue. Without this, you won't be able to measure the success of your campaign, and you will be missing a major relationship building opportunity.

Traditional Advertising

Advertising can work for certain companies, but be prepared to make a heavy investment if you want it to have an impact. Therefore, managing your ROI (return on investment), as in your PR efforts, is critical. Traditional advertising takes many forms including newspapers and magazines, radio, cable, and TV as well as outdoor billboards. Given the cost of advertising, and the fact that readers often need to see an ad multiple times before they act, buying ads may not offer the best return on your investment. For example, it is believed that when somebody reads a magazine, that reader will notice each ad only one out of every three times he or she looks through the publication. Since it takes a reader approximately seven exposures, "strong notices" to act on your message, you'd need to advertise 21 times to capture the reader's attention and brand your company. This "Rule of Seven" originated with the movie industry back in the 1930s when it was determined that a viewer would need to see an ad for a movie seven times before going to see the picture. Given the competition that exists today for viewers' attention and the bombardment of ads that we see each day in every medium, you really need to ensure that you target only those channels that will provide you with a solid return on your marketing spending. Therefore, if you decide to "test" advertising in a specific publication that is read (either online or in paper form) by your prospects, be sure you can measure its impact (does it generate hot leads that convert into prospects) before you spend an excess of your budget on this tool only to learn, 6 months later, that it doesn't drive the level of traction that you need.

The most important aspect of old school marketing techniques is the fact that you are not limited to one tactic or channel. Your campaign can be rich and vibrant by using a variety of channels including traditional in-person or direct-mail efforts with social media, e-mail marketing and anything else that aligns with how your customers want to engage with you.

THE POWER OF NETWORKING: MAKING THE RIGHT CONNECTIONS AT THE RIGHT EVENTS

Networking in person is most likely on your list of marketing activities. If not, it should be since it's critical to make new connections to grow your business and nurture the creation of growth opportunities. Therefore, a list of strategically aligned conferences, trade shows, and networking events (both in person and online) should be top of mind.

It's important to begin by identifying the right events. Let's think about what factors influence your decision to attend an event. Here are a few key criteria:

- Who is speaking at the event?
- What topics are being presented?
- AND THE KEY CRITERIA: Who will attend the event as participants because the topic intrigues them? These are likely the people who you want to meet.

Every organization is built on relationships—both product and service-oriented businesses. Relationships begin by meeting the right people in the right circumstances, and these relationships, if nurtured, will ideally blossom over time through mutual goals and interests. Therefore, it's important to attend events where the attendees are most likely people that you want to meet—even if the presenters are not the most sought-after experts in the industry.

We recognize that networking can be intimidating, especially if you're not a naturally outgoing person (many people are not comfortable networking). So, how do you ensure that you maximize the value of an event? First, keep your goal in mind. You are there to meet the right people, introduce yourself and BRIEFLY explain who you are. This is where your elevator pitch is particularly useful. But most important, listen. Find out as much as you can about the other person's background, business, and interests to determine if this is somebody with whom you want to continue a dialogue. If not, politely find an excuse to move on. However, if there seems to be potential for good synergy, get permission to follow up at another time and THEN move on. Your goal is to meet as many people as possible and build a relationship going forward. If you meet one great prospect but spend your entire time with that person, you miss an opportunity to meet many more individuals who can help you build your business (as customers or perhaps partners).

What do you remember about networking from Chapter 9's Golden Rules of Networking discussion? Paul Horn reminds us that

> Introductions are simply that—introductions. This is not the place to share your life story. We've all had the experience of waiting to talk to a speaker or another person at an event, only to be stuck behind someone who is sharing an endless story with the speaker. The person who does that runs several risks, not just in annoying others waiting for him to finish, but also in making the speaker apprehensive (remember, he or she also wants to speak to as many people as possible). This person could create the impression that meeting with them again just might not be that much fun—if they talk more than listen. **Don't be this person!** Make your point, exchange business cards, agree to follow up, and then let others have a turn.

While networking with individuals, some things to keep in mind include the following:

- Begin at the end. What is your goal in attending the event? Before you even step out the door, make sure you know how you'd like the evening (or day) to end.

- Make sure your approach is friendly and open.

- Try to put the other person at ease.

- Introduce yourself with a smile and a handshake.

- Ask for and use the other person's name.

- Ask questions about the other person's business or industry.

- If appropriate, extend some kind of offer or invitation or share some articles that the other person might be interested in.

Networking can take many forms, in addition to actual conversations:

1. Sending articles of interest to people you've just met, especially if the topic came up during your exchange with them
2. Inviting people to events as your guest
3. Creating relationships with nonprofit organizations and attending and/or helping out with their events
4. Developing and practicing your elevator pitch so that it sounds casual and natural
5. Looking for opportunities to introduce other people at events

WHERE ELSE CAN YOU MEET THE RIGHT PEOPLE?

Attending or exhibiting at industry conferences (which tend to be much larger in scope than small networking events in your local area) gives you an opportunity to network by exposing you to as many people as possible in a short period of time. It can also give you the chance to do the following:

- Check out the competition
- Learn the latest trends in the industry
- Identify new customers
- Identify new partners

However, large industry conferences can be overwhelming. This won't happen if you develop a plan to meet the people that will help your business grow. Don't just show up at the conference and then figure out which companies you want to meet. Think through the process in advance. Consider not only whom you want to meet but what you will say to introduce yourself.

In advance of attending a conference, you should complete these activities:

- Before the conference begins, find out who's going to be there and who could be potential prospects, partners, competitors, or important networkers or relationship builders (people who know people you want to get to know).
- Decide upon the people you'd like to meet with and learn more about them (research their businesses online or though LinkedIn).

- Prioritize this list and make sure you approach the most important people on it first (in case you run out of time).
- Try to connect with your priority list in advance and ideally arrange to meet them at the event.

Here are some ideas to help you prepare what you will say during the event:

- Prepare a list of opening statements that will make you more comfortable approaching these people (this is your elevator pitch).
- Prepare a list of frequently asked questions (and responses) about your products so that you're not caught off guard without a response.
- Prepare a list of general small-talk topics that you might use to begin a conversation.
- Prepare a list of key benefits and perhaps new information about your company that you can share.

In order to network efficiently, make sure that you have your business cards on hand at all times and that you get business cards from the individuals you meet. On the back of each card, write information about the person and rank how important she or he is to your business. Don't make this complicated. A simple A-B-C (A = hot prospect, B = medium, and C = lukewarm or cold) method of ranking people is more than sufficient. This will help you tremendously when you get home and enter or scan all the names into your computer—yes, you need to capture this information since we all know those cards are really easy to lose.

This information will also help you develop your follow-up strategy and personalize your message to each person when you contact her (e.g., "When we met last week, I recall that you were interested in . . .").

While it's obvious that you shouldn't attend a conference without having done your homework, there are several steps that are critical to ensure you take advantage of all opportunities. Let's briefly walk through the process. Keep in mind that as you're trying to establish yourself as a thought leader and influencer, the ideal scenario for conference attendance is when you're the featured speaker. This provides access to a host of decision makers whom you might not have otherwise met by simply walking around booths in a meet-and-greet fashion.

1. First, define your specific outcome and goal for the show. This didn't mean "meet as many people as possible" or "sell something." Your goals need to be precise (remember SMART Goals). For example, meet at least 75 to 100 executives of small to mid-size (XYZ) firms and find out more about their needs and interests (problem you solve).

2. With this goal in mind, now think about how you will achieve this. If you conclude that being a featured speaker is the best opportunity to meet these individuals, contact the conference organizer and see what their criteria are for being a speaker. If you are able to create a one-paragraph overview of your "talk," this will help open the dialogue.

3. Next, conduct market research. Conferences are a great opportunity to conduct research. Therefore, consider creating a brief survey with an offer to individuals who agree to complete it. This might give you critical data about your customer market that you haven't had access to, especially as a start-up. For example, if you give a talk you can ask attendees to complete your survey at the conclusion and provide you with contact information so you could send them an invitation to an exclusive workshop providing more details on the topic.

4. The final step is to be completed when you return back to your office. You want to avoid the mistake many companies make when they return from a conference: return to their normal routines and don't complete the follow-up required to ensure these new contacts become a part of their network. Your plan should include not just pre-show preparation but post-show follow-up as well. For example, after the shows send each person who completed the survey a personal e-mail thanking them for attending, letting them know the details about the upcoming workshop, as well as explaining other larger, more comprehensive programs that you offer. They also became part of your mailing list for future events relevant to their needs as well as part of your research findings to help refine your brand offer. This completes the cycle of conference attendance.

DEVELOPING YOUR NETWORK: YOU CAN'T SUCCEED ALONE

In his best-selling book, *Winning*, former General Electric CEO Jack Welch (2005) discusses strategy as resource allocation. Welch explained that every company has finite resources and how a leader chooses to allocate those resources will influence the success of the business. Therefore, as you design your marketing plan, you must prioritize your finite resources to ensure you deploy those that will allow you to meet, and ideally exceed, your customers' expectations. Goals without the resources to support them are like responsibility without any true power, it simply doesn't produce the desired outcome. Moreover, resources within a small business are generally quite limited, so you need to allocate them carefully. You have already defined your customers' most important interests and needs, and by now should understand which of them you can satisfy, given your company's resources, capabilities, and strengths.

ACTION CREATES TRIUMPHS (ACT)

Create a Networking Plan

Over the years, meeting people at industry and other networking events has helped many small business owners and entrepreneurs not only make new business acquaintances (and sometimes friends) but also help identify resources to assist them. Many entrepreneurs build their careers and businesses by learning early on how to make the right connections with the right people. But their success has been predicated of the fact that they have pursued building a relationship with the people and have built win–win relationships that helped both of them succeed.

Be realistic about your resources and understand what and who that includes. You can have the loftiest goals, but without the resources to support them, they are just ideas, not a business. Resources take different forms: money, time, and people being the most compelling. Think about which of these you and your company are strong in and where you will need support. You will need to develop a strong network. Before you begin your plan, create a list of potential advisors who can play an important role in helping you shape your company vision and focus your passion. Note each person's area of expertise to ensure that you have a variety of experiences to rely upon. Consider your network. Write down the names of 10 individuals, their expertise and experience and keep that close to you. Build that list as a resource for those days when everything goes awry.

VIEW FROM THE TRENCHES

Stallion Deliveries

Muhammad Hassan Khan was a student studying at the Institute of Business Administration (IBA) in Karachi, Pakistan, in 2014 when he recognized a growing problem in his country. Pakistan is a cash-driven society where small business owners will sell items to customers and receive payment upon delivery of the item. Hassan, as his friends called him, recognized that there were a variety of gaps in the market, which he saw as an opportunity to address with the launch of his company. These gaps impacted both the small business owner and the customers.

The pain from the small business owner's perspective included the following:

- Unhappy Customers Due to Long Delivery Time: C.O.D (Cash on Delivery) service providers usually took around 36 to 48 hours to deliver a product to a customer.

- Delayed Payment to Business Owner: It took around 15 to 20 days, on average, for the business owner to

(Continued)

(Continued)

receive the cash after the customer paid the delivery service, tying up their working capital.

- Price and Process Constraints: There were very few single delivery pick-ups options and the parcel weight was usually rounded up (e.g., 1.1 kg is counted as 2 kg).
- Poor Customer Service: The providers focused on large businesses (businesses with more than 250 deliveries per month) and neglected the small business customer.

The challenges outlined in this system created a service where small business owners could not satisfy their customers' needs given the delays in processing and delivering their orders. They were also challenged by not having access to their working capital. Hassan decided that he didn't need to entirely reinvent the wheel when it came to addressing the needs of his customers—the small business owners. He could simply modify the already existing Cash on Delivery service and address the neglected but profitable segment of the market, the small business customers. He called his business Stallion Deliveries. He modified the services that existed by altering his to cater to the basic needs of small businesses owners with the goal of offering them

- cash payback within 24 hours
- single order pickups at no extra charge
- speedy delivery within 24 hours
- no rounding up of the weight of parcels
- no hidden charges such as cash handling fees
- prompt response to customer queries

Seizing this opportunity, Hassan's business took off from its initial launch in Karachi with the goal of serving all of Pakistan. Recognizing that 60% to 70% of the orders would reside in three large cities, Karachi, Lahore, and Islamabad, he began to target these markets exclusively. Hassan explained that "Many of the rural areas are not accessible via roads and some areas in the northwest are not safe for civilians. Moreover, expansion requires relatively expensive fixed assets such as purchasing delivery vans. We knew from the start that it would be relatively difficult to offer our service beyond these three main cities so we needed to get our model set up properly before we considered expanding outside of Karachi, Lahore, and Islamabad."

Upon the business launch, Hassan hired a coordinator to handle all of the phone calls and coordinate services with their drivers. They launched an on-campus delivery services to IBA, where he was a student, allowing him to test his model and use his resources until he was able to generate enough COD orders outside of his "friends and family" network. He calculated that Stallion Deliveries needed 264 deliveries per month to break even. His initial offer to IBA faculty, students, and staff was to provide delivery within 12 minutes of anything ordered from a campus small business to be delivered anywhere on campus. They got a positive response from the campus, with orders averaging up to 12 per day. A very nominal amount was charged for these deliveries allowing Hassan to address the operational challenges he would face and to understand his customers' needs. Hassan explained,

We started the business by creating a database of small, online businesses in the areas we wanted to target. We finalized our price list and standard operating procedures before we began calling the businesses from that database. We also sent bulk e-mails to more than 1,000,000 recipients (mass market) all over Pakistan. The primary purpose of this mass market bulk e-mail campaign was to create buzz about our company and to let potential target clients know about our services. We used other tactics to create buzz about our company in the first month, including

- creating an SMS marketing campaign reaching more than 50,000 people,
- launching an e-mail campaign to IBA students,
- launching an e-mail campaign to IBA alumni by securing access from our alumni department,
- developing a social media marketing campaign that allowed us to post in a variety of group relevant to our business.

Since the stallion horse is our brand and mascot, I decided to rent a horse for one week to create buzz about the company. This was really effective and we were able to do this without spending too much of my limited marketing resources.

Hassan explained, "Our mission was to revolutionize the supply chain and logistics industry by employing and implementing innovative ideas. The innovation was not limited to our operations. We knew that we need to innovate when it came to our marketing because that was the only way to enter the market and get the message out about our business." Hassan described a variety of creative marketing campaigns that they ran to launch the business forward.

Mother's Day Campaign

We partnered with Body Wash, Gul Ahmed, and Bombay Chocolates to launch a Mother's Day Campaign. We offered different gift packages: lowest priced package was PKR (Pakistani Rupee) 1699 (~$14 USD) and highest priced package was PKR 3599 (~$29 USD) and we featured these on our websites using our partners' products. This generated revenue of 36,000 PKR (~$290 USD) and a profit of 14,000 PKR (~$113 USD) in a period of 5 days. This service was also launched to increase the effective utilization of our existing resource while concurrently increasing revenue.

Send a Smile: Eid (Celebration) Day Campaign

During the Eid in July, we partnered with Red Riding Hood Bakery, Allure, and Al-Karam. We prepared Eid gifts packages and offered them on our website and Facebook page. Customers ordered those package(s) to be delivered to their desired addresses. We earned revenue of 18,270 (~150 USD) PKR from this campaign. This also utilized our existing resources and we earned a nice profit from this campaign.

Hassan's business took off and while he only had three COD orders during his first month, by month three, they had over 169 COD orders and 15 clients. He was experiencing a significant amount of success but realized that his business was limited. He decided that the next step for him to grow was to offer a more complete solution to small business owners. This would include warehouse options, fulfillment,

(Continued)

(Continued)

labeling, and packaging. The complete solution, similar to the Amazon model except using Cash Upon Delivery, was an important next step for Hassan.

In Their Shoes

Based on what you've read about Stallion Deliveries,

- what actions do you think Hassan needs to take to grow his business?
- do you think that he should expand his service offering or stay with delivery only? Why or why not?
- what else does Hassan need to understand about his customers' needs to make a decision about the growth of his business?
- should Hassan do further research about his customers and his competition? If yes, what does he need to learn and how should he discover it?

FOCUS ON APPLICATION: WAKU

The Entrepreneurial Journey

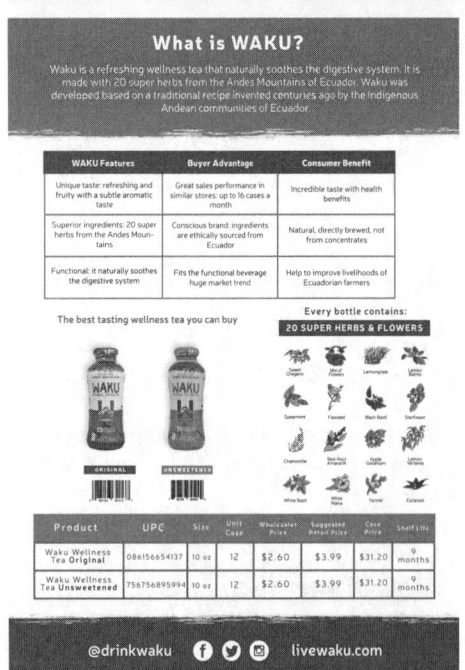

Juan Giraldo, Nico Estrella

Finally, let's revisit Juan and Nico to learn more about their omnichannel marketing approach.

Their campaign involves a variety of marketing channels: in-person sales, social and interactive media, as well as working with influencers. One of their primary objectives was to host free Waku "tastings" at pop-up locations around Boston. We learned about this in an earlier chapter. They targeted stores where Waku was available or they were hoping to secure traction in the store.

As part of Waku's efforts to extend customer engagement long after the tastings, Juan and Nico understood that they needed to leverage their in-person interactions with their social media channels. This would allow them to stay connected with customers, providing customers with updates and the opportunity to continue to engage with the brand. This would allow Juan and Nico to expand their brand awareness in and beyond the greater Boston community. Since they knew that they wanted to use a variety of messaging platforms, they agreed to use Hootsuite, an online platform designed to schedule and manage social posts across multiple platforms. Hootsuite would also allow them to analyze social media metrics, thereby tracking what was working against their goals. The campaigns Juan and Nico focused on included Facebook, Instagram, and Twitter, but they were also considering other social media platforms, depending on the outcomes they achieved. They decided to send targeted e-mails to customers who supported their crowdfunding campaign early on in the launch as well as those who opted in to giving Waku permission to contact them via e-mail.

Another important objective of Waku's marketing campaign was to partner with local influencers in the Boston area to promote Waku to the influencers' followers. This would include influencers who blog about health, fitness, and new drinks introduced into the market. Juan and Nico already knew some of them, and they used their own network to connect with others to begin a dialogue.

As part of their social media efforts they ran a "Taste Waku" campaign. The goal of this campaign was to amplify Waku's presence on social media by encouraging customers and tasters to post their best description of Waku's taste. Customers who published the most creative posts won a case of Waku and a branded shirt.

In order to encourage participants to follow Waku on social media and post their opinions during the tastings, Juan and Nico created posters with instructions including social handles, appropriate hashtags, and sample posts. They also showed the prizes consumers would win to entice the prospects tasting Waku to participate in the social media dialogue.

Content for the campaigns always had a heavy educational message along with a spirit of fun, fitness, and health. Since this was the brand message that was important for Waku to communicate, they wanted to ensure a focus that was consistent and aligned with their brand's value. This included highlighting the 20 ingredients

Juan Giraldo, Nico Estrella

that come together in Waku to make it unique. Each week they focused on one specific ingredient and posted information about this ingredient throughout the week to educate the followers on taste, health properties, and general facts about that ingredient. Each week they began with a post on Sunday and then followed up with four to seven posts throughout the week across the three identified social channels.

They also ran a secondary campaign designed to educate consumers on Waku's brand progression. Content for this campaign shared sampling locations, celebrated sales results for Waku, and aligned with influencer posts. It also allowed followers to learn about the expansion of Waku in retail locations throughout the Boston area.

Of course Juan and Nico realized that they needed to establish key performance indicators (KPIs) to evaluate their campaigns' success and understand what was working and what was not. The goal was to use projected metrics based on

(Continued)

(Continued)

their analysis and grow their social engagement numbers. They believed that they could grow their following at least 25% each quarter with a focus on social metrics like shares, likes, and impressions upon the launch of each campaign. While having followers is a great starting point, the true measure of success was going to be sales results. By June of 2018, they had a quarterly growth in the number of followers of 83% on Twitter, 134% on Instagram, and 97% on Pinterest. Facebook growth was only 5% but they already had a strong presence on this platform. They also increased website traffic by 65%, all organically. In addition, they were thrilled that their Social Media Reach (number of unique accounts viewing a post) grew from 2,886 in Quarter One 2018 to 11,278 in Quarter Two, accounting for a 291% increase.

They didn't stop at using social media. Juan shared, "The most cost efficient way to market our products is to allow consumers to experience the product themselves. That is why field marketing is our primary focus. We have taken a grass roots approach not only to create connections with the Boston community but to get feedback from our customers regarding our products and brand. By June, we were holding over 90 demonstrations each month."

You can see how they continue to create a true omnichannel marketing program by checking out their website, blog, and social media sites. It's important to note the consistency of their images and their messaging throughout all of their various channels. It is clear when you land on their website that this is "one" brand with a similar look, feel, and message that aligns with their brand value.

- Facebook: https://www.facebook.com/drinkwaku/
- Website: https://livewaku.com/
- Blog: https://medium.com/@livewaku/a-magical-place-in-the-middle-of-the-world-9f61ea014cde
- YouTube: https://www.youtube.com/channel/UCZ8pAbhfQs48NrCQwmUFQFA
- Pinterest: https://www.pinterest.com/drinkwaku/
- Instagram: https://www.instagram.com/drinkwaku/
- Twitter: https://twitter.com/drinkwaku

Figure 12.1 Waku Social Channel Reach

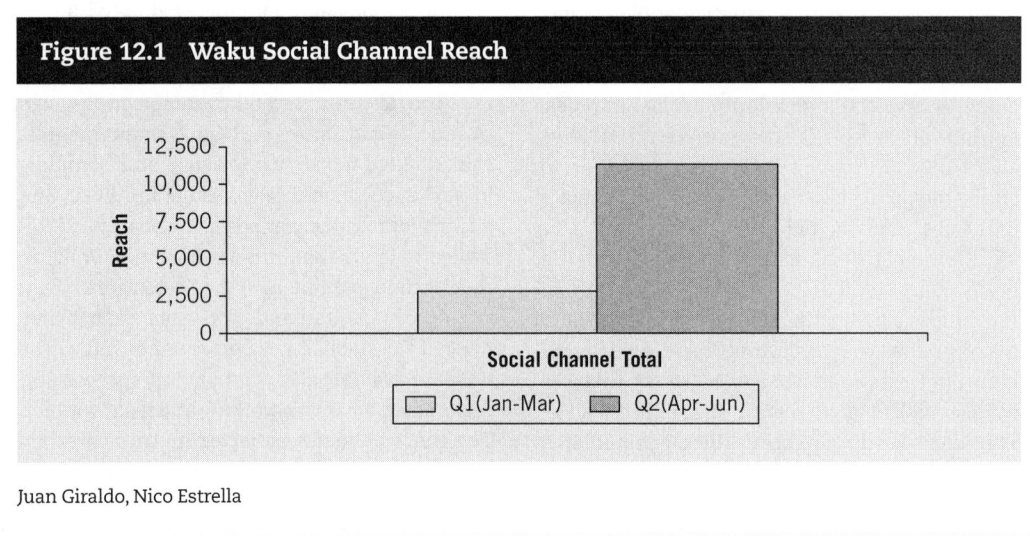

Juan Giraldo, Nico Estrella

YOUR MARKETING CAMPAIGN ROLLOUT

It's time to pull all of this information together and develop your marketing campaign strategy that will help launch and grow your business, keeping in mind the importance of creating an omnichannel approach where there's clear synergy between your old and new school tactics. Let's begin by analyzing your current marketing tactics. If you have spent any money to date on marketing, note how much you've spent in the Current Year column and then project what you anticipate the spend will be in the upcoming year. You should do this for the number of customers generated by tactic (if this is known) along with revenue. Don't worry if your current year is completely empty. The most important aspect is projecting what you will spend in the upcoming year (calendar or fiscal) and what you anticipate these actions will generate in terms of customers and revenue. Realistically, not every tactic will produce DIRECT results but it's important to review all of them to ensure they are making a contribution (even if indirect) to revenue and the number of customers generated.

Below is a list of channels and tools to consider. This list is not exhaustive by any means, and there are likely channels that are not listed here that you will want to include that are specific to your unique business' needs. Consider this a starter list to generate ideas.

Channels and Tools

- **Personal**—You, sales team, influencers, customer service, distributors, other experts

- **Traditional**—Brochures, direct mail, PR, sponsorships, TV/radio, magazines, billboards, print articles, signs, door hangers, vehicle wraps, events

- **Virtual/Social Media**—Website, SEO, videos, podcasts, QR Codes, banner/digital ads, industry-specific social networks, e-mail, blogs, articles online, review sites, influencers, directories, mobile, text and communication apps, podcasts, webinars, social media sites like Facebook, YouTube, Instagram, Pinterest, Snapchat, WhatsApp

We have included three frameworks or worksheets for you to use to develop your campaign strategy. First, use the **Marketing Channel Projections and Analysis Worksheet** to identify your budget for each channel, the goal for the number of customers you will reach, and the revenue; you should identify a plan for each channel and describe it in your marketing plan. Next, you will use the **Omnichannel Marketing Campaign Worksheet** to identify more details about each channel's strategy. Finally, use the outline for the **Marketing Campaign Strategy Outline** to develop your strategy for your new venture.

AHAs

Lessons and Takeaways

We have covered a lot of material in this chapter as it relates to rolling out your marketing campaign. Highlights of what we have discussed include the following:

- You should be wary of identifying customer touch points too early in the process because you risk wasting time and money on channels that your customers don't engage with. You first need to properly assess the market, identify customer needs, and determine the value proposition that is most appealing to your customers; then you can begin to identify how they will find your solution.
- The difference between omnichannel marketing and multichannel marketing is that omnichannel marketing creates a unifying (universal) message across many platforms, thereby creating a seamless experience for the user. With a multichannel marketing approach, one might be able to learn about a company using different platforms, but the experience isn't seamless, and often the brand creation process is broken.
- Market leaders and disruptive brands set the agenda for their space—not only in what features they build, but in how the market thinks and talks about their category.
- The rules of marketing engagement must align with new expectations that customers have for communicating with your brand.
- With social engagement, control lies in the hands of the consumers, and the business's role is to (1) ensure their brand delivers on their stated value promise, (2) encourage and support the discussions that customers have about their brand, and (3) defend or explain the brand when consumer feedback isn't representative of the value they portray.
- It's critical to embrace the importance of the message to your customer and what it means to be "the messenger." The message that you convey is critical, and your role as a brand in sharing the right content plays a critical role in your marketing communication.
- You need to communicate via the channels that YOUR customers want to engage with, even if they are not the most commonly accessed ones. They might be industry specific or more relevant based on your customers' demographic or geographic composition.
- The common belief that traditional old school methods of reaching customers via channels like direct mail don't work is not necessarily true. It can be part of a rich, omnichannel campaign. However, success will vary by business and how well your own business does in capturing customer data and communicating with them throughout the life of your business relationship.
- Networking in person is most likely on your list of marketing activities. If not, it should be since it's critical to making new connections to grow your business and nurture the creation of growth opportunities.

TOOLKIT

Worksheet 12.1: Marketing Channel Projections and Analysis

Channels	Budget		# Customers Generated		Revenue	
	Current Yr 20__	Next Yr 20__	Current Yr 20__	Next Yr 20__	Current Yr 20__	Next Yr 20__
Logo						
Website						
Mobile/App Design						
Speaking Opportunities						
Conference Exhibiting/Sponsorship						
Networking						
Event Marketing						
Partner Marketing						
Public Relations						
Direct Sales Efforts						
Sales Material						
Direct Mail Campaigns						
E-mail Campaigns						
Social Media _____						
Social Media _____						
Social Media _____						
Video _____						
Podcasts & Webinars						
Digital Advertising						
Traditional Advertising						

Channels	Budget		# Customers Generated		Revenue	
	Current Yr 20__	Next Yr 20__	Current Yr 20__	Next Yr 20__	Current Yr 20__	Next Yr 20__
Radio						
TV						
Giveaways and Promotions						
TOTAL	_____	_____	_____	_____	_____	_____

Worksheet 12.2: Omnichannel Marketing Campaign

Use the following worksheet to identify the channels that you will focus on to create awareness about your business. The sites might be online networking communities (i.e., Facebook, LinkedIn, Instagram, Twitter, YouTube) or traditional events or in-person channels. For example, if you want to target women in their 30s with children under 10 years of age, you might want to work with websites like iVillage.com plus connect with speakers at conferences and influencers on YouTube who focus on women's topics. Once you have identified each channel, determine what the measure of success will be (e.g., likes, shares, recommendations, word of mouth) and then note the actions required to achieve

Channel (Personal, Traditional, and Social)	Measure(s) of Success (Likes, Shares, Links, Purchases)	Action(s) Required to Achieve Success	Deadline/ Milestone Dates	Resource Investment (Time, People and Money)	Networking Source

Channel (Personal, Traditional, and Social)	Measure(s) of Success (Likes, Shares, Links, Purchases)	Action(s) Required to Achieve Success	Deadline/ Milestone Dates	Resource Investment (Time, People and Money)	Networking Source

these designated measures of success, deadlines and milestone dates, and finally, the resources that need to be invested: time, people and money. Finally, note if there's a networking source who influenced this initiative. This is an important step since it will help you understand the value of building the right connections and bridges.

Worksheet 12.3: Marketing Campaign Strategy Outline

The final step will be to develop a 1-year marketing campaign strategy for the new venture concept that you are about to launch. This is an important part of your learning experience involving the development of an omnichannel marketing campaign that will create traction and engagement with your customers. This assignment gives you the opportunity to explain and justify your campaign and how it will address the business goals and the customer segments you have identified as critical to your success.

One important criterion is that this plan must be **launchable**, using a realistic budget that includes key performance indicators (KPIs), metrics and milestones that you can benchmark your success against. In addition, you must demonstrate that you are able to effectively allocate limited resources and budgets across diverse marketing channels.

I. Campaign Overview

A. **Business Goals and Objectives**—Provide a brief summary of your product, the current situation you find yourself in, and your company's goals and objectives

B. **Marketing Objectives**—Specify sales and marketing objectives for the campaign. Consider sales or market share objectives. State objectives so that they are

S.M.A.R.T. (*Specific, Measurable, Actionable, Realistic and Time-Based*) (i.e., Increase sales from 5 million to 6 million; Increase market share from 15% to 20%).

C. **Target Audiences**—Identify primary and secondary target audiences based on your Customer Discovery Survey. Highlight the demographic, geographic, psychographic, and behavioral characteristics of your target audience. Note that your target audiences (decision makers/purchasers) may be a subgroup from the actual user profile or a totally different group.

D. **Positioning Strategy**—How will you position your product to your target audience(s)? Develop a *positioning statement* that highlights your product's differential competitive advantage (and distinguishes your product from the competition).

II. Marketing Channels and Media Mix

A. **Marketing Tools**—Present the marketing tools and vehicles that you will use to reach the target audience(s). What tools will be most effective in reaching your target audience(s) and communicating your message? Consider advertising, publicity (press releases), social and interactive media, direct marketing, sales promotion, and personal selling.

B. **Justification**—Justify your choice of communications vehicles for each target audience(s). Be sure to explain why the vehicles selected will be most effective and efficient in reaching the target audience(s). Describe which target audiences are being reached with each communications vehicle and the geographic reach of your recommended vehicles.

C. **Specific Vehicles**—Specify specific vehicles (e.g., specific magazines, newspapers, social media networks, etc.) that you will use to deploy the campaign. Ensure you present accurate and current pricing based on research conducted.

III. Creative Brief

A. **Message**—Describe your creative strategy and message for your campaign. What is the campaign theme you have chosen for your product or service? Describe your "Big Idea." The big idea creates an identity, positions the brand, is distinctive, holds an audience's interest, defines the look and feel of the brand, synthesizes product attributes, and relates the value of the brand. Be sure that this follows from your positioning strategy.

B. **Benefits**—Describe the product benefits that will be emphasized in your promotions.

C. **Slogan/Tagline**—Will you have a slogan or tagline? Consider a short phrase that will help establish an image, position, or identity for the brand, and increase memorability.

D. **Present** the actual marketing material—ready for launch.

IV. Marketing Budget

A. **Total Budget**—Your budget should be presented and based on a determination of what it will take to reach your marketing objectives.

B. **Allocation**—Explain specifically how you plan to allocate your budget to each communications vehicle and target audience and justify. Indicate how your budget will be spent over the course of the launch and expenditures required to obtain your level of reach, frequency.

C. **Spending by Tool**—Using a chart, show your proposed spending for each promotional tool for each period of time.

V. Timeline and KPIs Overview

A. **Timeline/Benchmarks**—Using a graph or chart, describe your timeline for implementing your marketing campaign reflecting launch dates as well as significant benchmarks and milestones over the course of the campaign.

B. **KPIs**—Explain the KPIs (key performance indicators) that you will use to measure success along the way (what interim goals that you are looking for—i.e., 200 leads or 50% conversion of referrals by week 4).

Worksheet 12.4: Networking—Making the Right Connections

Below is a summary of steps you should take for successful networking at any type of event (large or small) that will lead to business growth, the ultimate goal of conference season. Use the worksheet to answer the important goal-setting activities needed to prepare for every event you attend so you can maximize your ability to identify lucky opportunities.

1. Determine Your Specific Goals for the Show: Before you decide to attend any conference or expo, think about what you expect to come back with (i.e., contact names, research, partnership opportunities). Use this goal to determine if the outcome justifies the cost and time involved with the conference. If it doesn't, don't bother attending.

2. Preparation, Preparation, Preparation: Assuming you've outlined some concrete goals that seem achievable, now ensure you've got enough time to prepare the items that you will need for success. This includes presentations, surveys, handouts, and even a networking plan so that you don't arrive at the show unprepared.

3. Do Your Homework Well Before the Event: Make sure you know who's going to be exhibiting at the show and, if you are able to, get a list of other VIPs, media, or folks who you want to meet. Set up these meetings in advance. Don't get to

the show and simply scout out the floor, hoping somebody will be there who will make your trip worthwhile. Plan a route for networking so that you're not simply racing up and down the aisles.

4. Remain Flexible: As much as we try to prepare, there are often new opportunities that greet us along the way. Perhaps you'll learn about a new prospect or partnership opportunity. Don't book yourself so solid that you don't have the ability to seize these opportunities.

Follow-up is the key to success. Don't allow yourself to simply take the cards you collected and leave them in a drawer or just enter them into your system. If you do this, then you've wasted your time and energy going to the conference. Put these names to good use and communicate with individuals you have met. Consider the following follow-up methods: Send them an article of interest (one that you wrote or perhaps a respected colleague did), invite them to be a guest of yours at an event, send a copy of your newsletter, or perhaps introduce them to other folks who might help them.

CHAPTER THIRTEEN

USING DATA AND PASSION TO MOVE FROM IDEA TO MARKET

UNDERSTANDING THE CUSTOMER JOURNEY THROUGH THE DATA

Now that you've gone through all of the critical steps required to identify your customers' needs, understand your business value proposition, and have created your marketing campaign, you are ready to use your passion and commitment to your vision to jump into the launch of your venture. However, there is one final piece that you need to be prepared for to ensure your vision is sustainable. This final phase of turning your business vision into reality requires the measurement of the impact of the channels selected to reach customers, continuously identifying what's working and what is not. This chapter begins with an understanding of the importance of having passion about your business, even when things don't go as planned and your business stumbles or fails. Then we will focus on how to define these metrics and key performance indicators so that you can determine if you are achieving a realistic and sustainable return on your marketing investment. This includes the return on investment (ROI) on each marketing campaign as well as understanding the lifetime value of key customer groups to ensure you are attracting the right customers using the most effective and efficient marketing channels. This chapter ties all of the pieces together with a revisit of our discussion in Chapter 1 about the importance of SMART goal design to ensure you are able to create a customer-centric and omnichannel marketing plan. Your SMART goals and the dashboard you create to support them, will inform your plan and allow it to be a living document that can change as market conditions and customer needs evolve over time.

Learning Objectives

In this chapter, you will learn to

- channel your passion to ensure you achieve your business goals and projected outcomes.
- view failure as path to moving forward with your business goals.
- evaluate your commitment to launching your business.
- secure the right data to make business decisions and measure outcomes.
- measure customer lifetime value to support customer acquisition and retention.
- launch your marketing road map to navigate a path to success.

Before we dive into your plan and the importance of rolling this out properly, let's talk about two critical concepts that will support you throughout your journey: channeling your passion and learning to accept failure.

CHANNELING YOUR PASSION TO FUEL SUCCESS

Former U.S. first lady Eleanor Roosevelt said, "Do not stop thinking of life as an adventure. You have no security unless you can live bravely, excitingly, imaginatively, unless you can choose a challenge instead of a competence." Does a business need a challenge and a passion in order to thrive? Why do companies with a leader who is truly passionate about the business fail, while others with the same level of passion and a less compelling business model prosper and grow? Is there a magical formula that makes one business successful while another fails? What separates the winners from the losers, and what role does passion play?

There are several ingredients that go into a winning business, including a great idea, a great team, great passion, and great leadership. All are important, but great passion can be the fire that helps fuel the success. It can also destroy the business when it is misguided.

WATCH THE FLAMES

Like all fires, passions can spark other flames and become contagious, igniting the passion of investors, business partners, and customers, as well as employees. If left uncontrolled, passion can consume, destroy, and leave a business with an empty dream. However, when controlled, directed, and focused, it can boost a business's chance for success.

It isn't, however, the only important ingredient in the success of a business. In fact, time after time, when investors have been asked to identify the most critical factor, they've responded, "It's the team that makes the difference." A great business idea alone will not make a business profitable, but a passionate team that has the vision and the ability to execute the idea, even if the idea is only pretty good, can help a company achieve success. A winning team has a passionate leader and a team that is equally committed to achieving success. Your business idea doesn't have to be the most ingenious or creative—just a solid concept that will satisfy a need.

Is there a magical formula to creating a winning team? Is it 50% passionate team and 50% concept? No, there's something missing here. It's the team's ability to execute on the idea. This ability is fueled by passion, vision, experience, and the ability to focus on customer needs. It's the use of basic business principles that makes the difference when this is done properly. Therefore, in order to be successful in business, you don't have to come up with the most ingenious and creative business concept. You must have a solid concept that satisfies a need, and you must be able to properly funnel your passion to execute the plan. There's no magic, but these elements must exist.

Before you put all the pieces together to launch your plan, the one final ingredient that is critical to success is *you*. *You* have to be ready to devote your heart and your mind and your *passion* to making your business come alive. There will be challenges and setbacks along the way that cannot be anticipated and that can be survived only if you believe in your business and work to make it happen. Success takes hard work, commitment, and real sweat equity.

If you were training for a marathon, or the Olympics like Lasse Paakkonen from Chapter 7, you wouldn't start off by running 50 miles on day one, right? To improve your chances for success and minimize the likelihood of failure, you might begin your training by working on strength and speed exercises, then progress to endurance and aerobic capacity. Operating your business is like training for a marathon. When the whistle is blown to begin, you use everything that you've learned up to that point and start running. In a business, there are many starts, stops, and whistles going off, oftentimes at the same time. You must create a plan, determine your channels, understand your customers, and search for individuals who will support you throughout the journey. You may train slowly for some of these activities, but at the end of the day, you have to begin running in order to succeed and complete the race.

Now is the point in time when all your planning, preparation, worrying, thinking, shouting, wishing, and dreaming must be interrupted with a strong dose of reality. Virtual planning ceases, and execution, simply doing it, must begin. You must channel your passion and the knowledge you have gained and put them into action. Otherwise, you will have wasted your time and energy on the dream.

LEARNING TO ACCEPT FAILURE

Along with great success oftentimes come failure. Let's talk about that four-letter word: *fail*. Malcolm Forbes once said, "Failure is success if we learn from it." Use what you've learned from the exercises you've completed throughout this book and from all of your life experiences to move forward. Don't fret about failing. Failure is not your enemy—**inertia** is, and you should fear inertia. There are many ways to move forward and seize an opportunity to achieve a dream. But if you allow the fear of failure to prevent you from moving forward, then your chances of succeeding are significantly decreased.

Many successful and passionate business owners have failed at least once in their career. Let's look at two classic examples that show how now-famous individuals fueled their passion through downturns and when their concepts simply don't work. Most people think of Steve Jobs as the genius behind Apple, and that is accurate. However, in

1985, Jobs was fired from Apple after a power struggle with the CEO, John Sculley and Apple's board. He explained at the Stanford University commencement (Jobs, 2005) that "What had been the focus of my entire adult life was gone, and it was devastating. . . . I was a very public failure." This failure didn't stop or get in the way of his innovation. He went on to found NEXT and Pixar Animation Studios, eventually returning to Apple and making it the world-renowned company that it is today. Another example of failure that fueled greatness is the story of J. K. Rowling, the author of the Harry Potter book series. Her pitch for the book series was rejected 12 times, yet she pursued her passion. In an interview with Oprah Winfrey, Rowling explained, "Failure is so important—it doesn't get spoken about enough. We speak about success all the time, but, you know, I do not know any—I haven't met—and I've been so fortunate and met extraordinary people through Harry Potter, and not one of them didn't have their failure—more than one failure" (Hosain, 2014). The list goes on; Bill Gates's first company, Traf-O-Data, failed. Michael Jordan, the legendary basketball player missed more than 9,000 shots in his career explaining, "I've failed over and over and over again in my life. And that is why I succeed" (Lifehack, n.d.). The one thing successful people have in common is their belief that failure is a part of success. You have to keep trying and risk failing in order to achieve greatness. As the great hockey player Wayne Gretsky explained, "You miss 100 percent of the shot you never take." No words can be truer.

ACTION CREATES TRIUMPHS (ACT)

Test Your Readiness to Commit to Your Venture

You will recall the story of Olympic athlete Lasse Paakkonen, from Chapter 7. His commitment and passion to cross-country skiing kept him going, even when confronted with seemingly impenetrable obstacles. Let's see if you have the commitment of an Olympic athlete by taking the **Business Commitment Scorecard**. This is a simple self-assessment tool designed to give you an objective perspective of your readiness and willingness to spend the time it takes to launch your business. It will help you understand the influence of many critical business drivers and how they impact growth, profit, and, ultimately, your company's future success.

Scorecard Instructions

Please provide an honest evaluation of your commitment to launching your business. You don't need to share this with anybody. It's an assessment of how important the success of your business is to you. If you come across a question where you're not certain of the answer, simply respond *to the best of your ability*. When you are done, please add up your score. The maximum that you can achieve is 100 (there are questions).

Review the statements and provide a score for each. A 1 means that you strongly disagree and a 5 means that you strongly agree.

1 Strongly Disagree, 2 Disagree, 3 Neutral, 4 Agree, 5 Strongly Agree

How strongly do you agree with the statements below?	
1. I have a clear vision for how I want my company to be positioned in the next 3 to 5 years.	1 2 3 4 5
2. I have set clear goals for my business results for the next year.	1 2 3 4 5
3. I will use a dashboard on a monthly basis to track the performance of my business goals.	1 2 3 4 5
4. Our team has the right mix of experience and skills, and the right individuals are in the right positions to support the goals of the company.	1 2 3 4 5
5. I have a clear understanding of my company's key points of differentiation compared to my competition.	1 2 3 4 5
6. I will track and monitor two major competitors at least every quarter.	1 2 3 4 5
7. I will attend trade shows, industry events or webinars at least three to four times a year to keep up to date on changes, opportunities, and threats that may impact my business.	1 2 3 4 5
8. I have a plan to address the changes required to remain competitive based on industry changes.	1 2 3 4 5
9. We capture key demographic and behavioral information about our customers' needs (and update this at least once a year).	1 2 3 4 5
10. I will not be deterred by failure and have a plan to identify alternative paths to take when things don't go as planned.	1 2 3 4 5
11. We conduct secondary research (study buying trends of noncustomers) on an annual basis to incorporate into our own primary research.	1 2 3 4 5
12. We calculate the lifetime value of our customers, and eliminate those customers whose value is less than the return on our sales and marketing investment.	1 2 3 4 5
13. I am comfortable taking risks.	1 2 3 4 5
14. I am confident that our branding and value proposition addresses the key needs and concerns of our customers.	1 2 3 4 5
15. We track which marketing channels have been the most successful in terms of generating profitable customers.	1 2 3 4 5
16. All of our marketing campaigns include a "call to action" and reinforce the opportunity for prospects to communicate with us.	1 2 3 4 5

(Continued)

(Continued)

17.	I am ready to use my passion for my idea to carry me through the challenging times that I will face as I launch the business.	1 2 3 4 5
18.	I have created a solid network of experts who will guide me through the journey ahead.	1 2 3 4 5
19.	My elevator pitch provides credible proof of how we meet customer needs better or more effectively than our primary competitors.	1 2 3 4 5
20.	I am confident that I possess strong communication skills (i.e., I ask the right questions, am a good listener, and clearly present our benefits and value to prospects).	1 2 3 4 5
		Total _____

How did you score? Did you achieve an 80 or higher? Perhaps you scored below a 60. Please review your responses and circle the five most important business commitment drivers that you need to address in the next 90 days! Write these down below and come up with at least one action to address this so it doesn't get in the way of moving forward with your business.

Your next step is to ensure that you are measuring all of the data that is critical to the success of your business. Once you have completed this activity, you will be ready for your final step, to launch your Marketing Road Map, aka your marketing plan.

1.

2.

3.

4.

5.

CUT ONCE, MEASURE TWICE

Unfortunately, many companies simply don't take the measurement of their business results as seriously as they should or they are simply overwhelmed by how challenging this data is to capture. According to the Campaign Monitor and Ascend2's report, *The Eye-Opening Truth About Data-Driven Marketing* (Campaign Monitor, 2017), 81% of marketers consider implementing data-driven marketing strategies to be somewhat to extremely complicated. The good news here is that social media and other digital channels have significantly changed the ease of collecting data about your customers, making this complicated effort more worthwhile. The report found that marketers consider the following tools the most effective for collecting marketing data:

- social media—59%
- website—57%
- mobile apps—43%
- e-mail communication—34%
- organic search—29%

Twenty years ago, marketers might have simply reviewed sales revenue on a weekly or monthly basis but skipped or avoided a careful analysis of their profit margins by product or service or customer, because it was hard to get the data they needed. The famous British physicist William Thomson (1883) (aka Lord Kelvin) said,

> When you can measure what you are speaking about, and express it in numbers, you know something about it; but when you cannot measure it, when you cannot express it in numbers, your knowledge is of a meager and unsatisfactory kind. It may be the beginning of knowledge, but you have scarcely, in your thoughts, advanced to the stage of science.

Can we make business success scientifically predictable? No, there are too many variables for that to happen. But we need to face the fact that business success eventually comes down to a couple of numbers that drive your business—numbers like sales revenue and growth, profit margins, and return on marketing investment. Doing the right set of activities should ultimately lead you to achieve positive results in some if not all of these areas. There is a long list of metrics and numbers to crunch that we can recommend for your company, but clearly the most valuable lesson in this chapter is for you to determine which numbers are most critical for you to evaluate and watch on a regular basis to navigate your path to success. These numbers and metrics are the ones that give you the most information about your business's current and future state.

Once you have determined what your business display or dashboard needs to look like, then you need to determine how you will capture, measure, analyze, and benchmark your success relative to achieving these established numbers. They must, of course, align with your SMART marketing goals.

JUST THE FACTS: GETTING THE RIGHT DATA AND GETTING THE DATA RIGHT

Data is everywhere, but you must analyze it and interpret its meaning relative to your business or it will be of little value. Where does data come from? Throughout the book, we have explored ways for you to collect data about your customers and markets. Primary

Table 13.1 Business and Country Data

General business statistics	Find statistics on industries, business conditions	• NAICS: https://www.naics.com/search/ • FedStats: https://fedstats.sites.usa.gov/ • Statistical Abstract of the United States: https://www.census.gov/library/publications/2011/compendia/statab/131ed.html • U.S. Census Bureau: https://cbb.census.gov/sbe/
Consumer statistics	Gain info on potential customers, consumer markets	• Consumer Credit Data: https://www.federalreserve.gov/releases/G19/ • Consumer Product Safety: https://www.cpsc.gov/Research--Statistics
Country entrepreneurship data	Capture information about entrepreneurship in other countries	• Global Entrepreneurship Monitor (GEM) Report: https://www.gemconsortium.org/US Dept. of Commerce Country • Commercial Guides: https://www.export.gov • Euromonitor Passport: https://go.euromonitor.com/passport.html • Global Competitiveness Report (World Economic Forum): http://reports.weforum.org/global-competitiveness-report-2018/ • Emerging Markets Information Service: https://www-emis-com. • Doing Business: Measuring Business Regulations: http://www.doingbusiness.org/en/reports/global-reports/doing-business-2019
Demographics	Segment the population for targeting customers	• American FactFinder: https://factfinder.census.gov/faces/nav/jsf/pages/index.xhtml • Bureau of Labor Statistics: https://www.bls.gov/bls/demographics.htm

Economic indicators	Know unemployment rates, loans granted and more	• Consumer Price Index: https://www.bls.gov/cpi/ • Bureau of Economic Analysis: https://www.bea.gov/
Employment statistics	Dig deeper into employment trends for your market	• Employment and Unemployment Statistics: https://stats.bls.gov/bls/employment.htm
Income statistics	Pay your employees fair rates based on earnings data	• Earnings by Occupation and Education: https://www.bls.gov/cps/earnings.htm
Money and interest rates	Keep money by mastering exchange and interest rates	• Daily Interest Rates: https://www.federalreserve.gov/releases/h15/ • Money Statistics via Federal Reserve: https://www.federalreserve.gov/data.htm
Production and sales statistics	Understand demand, costs and consumer spending	• Consumer Spending: https://www.bea.gov/data/consumer-spending/main • Gross Domestic Product (GDP): https://www.bea.gov/data/gdp/gross-domestic-product
Trade statistics	Track indicators of sales and market performance	• Balance of Payments: https://www.bea.gov/data/intl-trade-investment/international-transactions • USA Trade Online: https://usatrade.census.gov/
Statistics of specific industries	Use a wealth of federal agency data on industries	• NAICS: https://www.census.gov/eos/www/naics/ • Statistics of U.S. Businesses: https://www.census.gov/programs-surveys/susb.html

data is critical. Yet you will clearly want to compare your own findings with known data and facts that are secondary sources for you, as we discussed in Chapter 2. Below you will find additional sources of data that you can integrate into your plan to help inform your understanding of the market place.

WHERE TO BEGIN YOUR ANALYSIS

Let's look at all of the data that you have compiled to support the development of your marketing plan. The following are measures that you should carefully consider capturing and analyzing on a regular basis and benchmarking over time to see how your business and marketing activities impact your bottom and top line. Let's face it—your business dashboard is similar to one on your car. If you aren't paying attention to the level of gas, oil, and other inputs on your journey, your trip will likely have an unplanned and unhappy ending.

Measuring Your Input and Outcomes

The information that follows is not an exhaustive list and you will have to decide which numbers to track in your business to help you make business and marketing decisions. Therefore, if there are other measures that you plan to use, please make sure you capture those.

Sales Analysis and Projections

A good sales analysis begins with reviewing the number of active customers (those you've transacted business with in the past 12 months), total revenue, profit, and revenue per customer. You should measure these numbers comparing this year's results relative to your prior year results and projections for the future. Are there surprising changes (either good or bad) that you recognized but didn't truly acknowledge until you saw it in black and white on paper? If so, what's impacting this change and how will it affect you in the future

Prospect and Customer Sales Cycles

Next, let's look at your sales cycle. Below are numbers that you should be projecting on a regular basis, including new prospects required, anticipated repeat customers and compare that to the number of prospects in your system. Are the activities that you are performing to generate business getting you the results you need to grow? Does this match the goals established on your road map? You might not know all of these numbers now, but as you proceed forward, think about what data you need to capture to ensure you do have these numbers for future planning.

- Number of new prospects required for next year's projections _____
- Number of repeat customers required for next year's projections _____
- Number of prospects in your system to-date _____
- Percentage of prospects anticipated to convert to sales _____%
- Sales cycle _____ days

Employee Analysis

Understanding the cost and benefit that each employee provides to your business's growth is critical to capture. You should capture any costs that you incur based on having employees in the business along with sales and profit per employee. Why is this important? Perhaps you've added a number of new members to your team because you're growing. Typically, your revenue or profit per employee will take a short-term hit and decrease. However, the goal of adding employees is to ensure you can sustain growth.

If your profit margins continue to drop, then you need to carefully look at management practices and your business model to ensure that you're able to justify new employees. However, this is not a black-and-white situation. Sometimes you have to add employees to service your customers because you simply won't be able to meet customers' expectations without skilled employees. This is simply ONE set of data in a slew of benchmarks to review and keep track of. It's also helpful if you don't have any employees now but are considering adding members to your team. It can help you justify new positions since the goal is to ensure this supports your business growth. For example, if you add 10 employees and you aren't able to increase sales and profit, then this might tell you that you need to look further into your business model to ensure it is sustainable for the long term.

Customer Revenue and Profit Analysis

These numbers measure the percentage of revenue generated by your key customers, typically those generating the most revenue. You will want to analyze your top three to five customers, top 20% of customers, and those customers with you more than a year. Calculating these numbers can help you understand if only a few customers are driving revenue into your business and how that dependence on a limited number of customers increases your risk and influences your business practices and marketing and sales tactics.

You may have heard of the 80:20 rule: 80% of your business comes from 20% of your customers. This isn't always true (although we have found quite often it is). What do your numbers say about your business and is your dependence on a limited number of customers too high? Can you change this? The more you depend on a limited customer base, the greater the risk is to your business stalling (or sometimes failing) if this base goes away. What can you do to further service this group or to expand your outreach to target more customers?

Product/Service Analysis

It's important to look at your mix of products and services to determine how revenue and profit change over time for each solution you offer to customers. Analyzing these numbers, comparing last year's results to the current year and reviewing next year's projections will help you determine if the mix is sustainable. You might want to compare these results to your target market mix. How are purchases from different target markets changing over time? What are the implications to your marketing plan?

Marketing Tactics

Next (we won't say finally since as we mentioned before, this list is NOT exhaustive by any means), you should break down the various marketing channels that you are using and study the results from each. You already worked on this in the previous data so make sure you are using this in your planning process. Realistically, not every tactic will produce

DIRECT results, but it's important to review each to ensure that they are making a contribution (even if indirect) to revenue and the number of clients generated. When we ask entrepreneurs to complete this, they usually find it enlightening since they might not have realized how some of these tactics had very powerful impacts on their revenue while others, which they had spent a lot of money on, had almost no impact to their top line sales data.

CUSTOMER LIFETIME VALUE

There's a famous quote from George Orwell's *Animal Farm* (1945) that describes a concept that is important to embrace. At the end of the book the farm animals come to live by a single commandment, *All animals are equal, but some animals are more equal than others*. The same could be said about your customers. Not that we are comparing your customers to animals, but some of them are more equal, or shall we say, more valuable to you than others. Being able to identify those who provide greater value to you is critical to your success. You will recall our discussion about understanding your customers' journey in Chapter 3. This chapter provided you with a way to segment your market. As we have discussed, you don't want to be *all things to all people* because you will fail. You have to understand which customers value the benefit you provide and target those groups. That's why assessing customer lifetime value is so important. It supports the segmentation of your market, allowing you to focus on customers who truly care about your company's value proposition.

Let's talk about this concept of trying to be ALL things to ALL customers. Here's an example of a company attempting to do this. Perhaps Bandito's T-Shirt Company has just launched and they decide that they are going to have the fastest turnaround, offer the most highly customized T-shirts, and concurrently be less expensive than their competitors. Eventually they will likely come to the harsh realization that the more they try to meet all three criteria (time, product, price), the more they damage their reputations and their profit margins, no matter how lean and efficiently they operate their business. Successful businesses almost always discover that certain customer groups are willing to pay for a select number of the features that they offer. For example, the customer groups that are willing to pay for a custom-designed product with a relatively short turnaround might also be willing to pay a premium. Or perhaps these customers would accept a longer turnaround time for the same product if the price were a bit lower (allowing the company to fit them into their production schedule better and lower its costs). They might also be willing to pay for something that you don't currently offer but could provide (or could partner with a company to provide).

Identifying which customers value what YOU uniquely offer is critical to the success of your business. The best way to identify this is to understand the lifetime value of customers, allowing you to target those who value your unique solution and value proposition. Let's start with a very simple definition of *lifetime value* (LTV) because you don't need to wow your friends with your calculus skills to figure this out. The formula basically calculates how much revenue each customer generates for you minus the cost to attract and maintain them. This number includes not only the customer's own purchases but also the purchases of individuals whom they might refer. In some businesses, this referral amount may be small. But in businesses that operate on heavy volume and rely on customers "telling friends" about their products or services, this can have a significant impact on success or failure. Some service firms can claim a referral rate as high as 90% of their new business clients simply because their current clients are prolific referrers.

Basically stated, LTV represents the amount of net cash flow and profit you generate from a customer relationship, over its lifetime, including the revenue customers drive into your business over the duration of your relationship with them, **minus** the cost to attract and maintain them as a customer. You are obviously looking for the highest number possible. If that number is close or starts to approach zero, or is negative (perhaps because the sales, service or maintenance costs are too high), it is time to figure out how to (1) raise the revenue you generate from these customers or (2) decrease the cost to attract them or maintain their business or (3) get rid of them.

Is LTV simple? Yes, it is, but most business owners don't take the time to do the math and miss seeing, in undeniable black and white, that some of their customers need to be "fired" because they're generating less revenue than they cost to bring into and maintain in the business. When customers' LTV doesn't work for you, typically you don't fit well with these customers' needs either. Ready to try the formula?

First, pick the two or three customers generating the most revenue for you. Next, select the two or three customers generating the least revenue for you. Then, run the formula for each of the customers. You might need to select a "specific customer" or a customer who "represents a typical customer" purchasing from your business.

Calculate Lifetime Revenue

A. How much does your target customer spend on each or on an average purchase from your company?   A = $ _____

B. Annually, how often does your customer make a purchase from your company?   B = _____

C. How many years does your customer stay with your company?   C = _____

D. How many new customers will he or she refer to your business?   D = _____

E. What percentage of referrals become clients?   E = _____ %

    A $ _____ × B _____ × C _____ = gross sales over customer's lifetime $ _____ (F)

    D _____ × E _____ % × F $ _____ = gross sales from new referrals $ _____ (G)

    F $ _____ + G $ _____ = total lifetime value of a satisfied customer $ _____ (I)

Now you need to figure out how much it costs you to attract and retain (don't forget that one) each customer. Go through the same process of asking what your cost of sales, service, product, maintenance, and administration (i.e., billing and collection, at a minimum) is, for each of the years you have the client. That is your customer lifetime cost.

Customer Lifetime Value = Customer Lifetime Revenue MINUS Customer Lifetime Cost

Customers whose lifetime value is zero or negative may not be the right customer for you. However, that doesn't mean that you necessarily have to fire them. This might be an opportunity to increase your price or decrease the cost to maintain their business.

SELECTING THE RIGHT CUSTOMER MIX

Not every customer will be right for your company, but there are ways to ensure that both sides are making the best decisions to create win–win business scenarios. Here are five steps to get you started on understanding what you will do with the information you learned about customer lifetime value.

1. Begin by determining the lifetime value of your customer groups. Keep it simple: Determine the revenue you achieve and the cost of attracting, servicing, and retaining various categories of customers (this might be by industry, region, or other criteria that are important to your business), and, voilà, you have your calculation.

2. Make sure you understand why your customers buy from you. Is it your service, your expertise in an area, or perhaps turnaround time? Whatever that criterion is (best determined through an objective survey), make sure you use that knowledge to create customer profiles and messaging for target markets that will gain the greatest benefit from your business's value proposition.

3. Rank your customers by LTV and target your marketing and sales outreach toward only those ideal customers and not toward the "less desirable" ones. If some customers are price sensitive and they are the ones you want to avoid, then set the price out of their comfort zone so you don't waste time with individuals who either won't buy from you or will make the buying experience a miserable and unsatisfying one.

4. Review your database and create a list of customers whose value is approaching zero (or might even be negative). Develop a strategy for eliminating them (without burning bridges). Think about gentle ways to eliminate customers. Perhaps you can reduce your service level so they decide to discontinue doing business with you on their own. This might then allow you to focus on your more desirable customers, improving your service level to them, making

the buying experience with you even better. You could also consider a price increase. Ironically, you might discover that if you increase your price and these customers with lower LTVs stay with you, their value to YOU might improve enough to make them more desirable.

5. Develop a road map that proactively targets the customer groups that are most profitable for your business and stick with the plan. In hard times, it's tempting to try to attract as much business as you can, but, in the long run, this can create more damage than the short-term infusion of cash—because now you're "stuck" with less desirable customers who are preventing you from truly focusing on the customers you want to keep who will support your future business growth.

YOUR DATA CAPTURE PLAN

Creating a data capture plan and displaying it in the form of a dashboard, like the one in your car that shows when you're low on gas or in need of a repair, is a powerful tool. This reflects the data you need to capture to make business decisions.

- Data you must capture to make business decisions
- What the specific measures are
- How you will obtain the data
- Who is responsible for getting the data
- How frequently you need to update and review the data

In summary, there are many measurements that you can make to benchmark results. This list is by no means complete but we hope is a good starting point for you to explore revenue and profit by customer, employee, product, and tactic. This is not a one-time measure but an analysis that you should do on a regular basis (i.e., quarterly or at least annually). Benchmark results and performance over time so that you can adjust your road map based on data, and not just a gut instinct about what's working.

READY, SET, LAUNCH: YOUR MARKETING ROAD MAP

Finally, you should be ready to pull together all of the material learned throughout this journey and launch your campaign by rolling out your marketing road map. Remember, as an entrepreneur, you need to see your marketing road map as a process that requires a variety of data to inform your business decisions. Data collection and data analysis are incredibly important at every stage of your company. For example, understanding your business model and what drives your costs needs to be clearly understood relative to meeting your customers' needs and values.

Below is the table that we introduced in Chapter 1. Please review this and use it as a guide to develop a strategic marketing plan and campaign for your company.

Table 13.2 Questions to Address Based on the Business Model Canvas Framework

1. **Customer Segments**
   - For whom are you creating value?
   - Who makes up the potential and target audience that you are addressing?
     - What are their key defining characteristics, that is, demographics, behaviors?
     - What is their compelling problem or need or pain?
     - Which segment(s) are most attractive? Why?
     - Do your target customers care about how you create or offer social value?
   - How large is this market?
     - How many people and/or companies and organizations?
     - What evidence do you have to support this estimate?
     - What assumptions did you make? How might you confirm them?
     - How easy is it to target the market?

2. **Value Proposition**
   - What is the problem you are trying to solve or the opportunity you are attempting to seize?
   - What value do you deliver to the customer?
   - How are you creating social value?
   - Which customer needs are you satisfying?
   - What bundle(s) of products and services are you offering to each segment?
   - Are you providing social value to the communities you serve?
   - What are you specifically offering?
     - What are the most important benefits to your target audience?
     - Is value sufficient to adopt your product or service?

3. **Channels**
   - How is your target audience currently addressing the problem or need?
     - What alternatives (substitute solutions) do they have? Who's your competition?
   - Through which channels do your customer segments want to be reached?
   - How will you reach them?
   - Are your channels integrated?
     - Do some work better than others?
   - Which channels are most cost-efficient?
   - Will you integrate your channels with customer routines and behaviors?

4. **Customer Relationships**
   - What type of relationship does each customer segment expect you to establish and maintain?
   - How expensive is ethically acquiring, maintaining, and retaining this relationship?
     - What is your customer lifetime value?
   - How is this relationship integrated with the rest of your business model?

5. **Revenue Streams**
    - What are your customers willing to pay?
    - What do they currently pay?
    - How are they currently paying?
    - How would they prefer to pay?
    - How much does each revenue stream contribute to overall company revenue?
    - How will you charge for your product or service?
6. **Key Resources**
    - What key resources does your value proposition require?
    - What are your needs in terms of physical, intellectual, and financial resources?
    - What needs do you have to ensure you can ethically distribute through identified channels?
    - What resources do you need to acquire and maintain customer relationships?
    - What resources will you need to launch and how do you plan on accessing them?
        - What resources are required by any business operating in this space?
        - What resources are unique to your solution or competitive position?
        - What do you still need to research?
    - What are the most critical skills and people resources needed to successfully launch the business?
        - What are the values that you and your team expect to exemplify and communicate in this venture? What kind of culture do you want to create?
7. **Key Activities**
    - What activities are required to deliver your value proposition?
    - How do these activities support the social value you will create or build into your business model?
    - How do these activities impact the following areas: production, problem solving, network, distribution channel, customer relationships, and revenue stream?
8. **Key Partnerships**
    - Who are your key partners?
    - Who are your key suppliers?
    - Which key resources or expertise or experience do you need from partners—optimization, economy of scale, reduction of risk, access to customers, and/or markets?
9. **Cost Structure**
    - What are your key costs? Are they primarily fixed or variable?
    - Which key resources are most expensive?
    - Which key activities are most expensive?
    - Are you focused on minimizing your cost or maximizing your value?
10. **Is the Venture Feasible?**
    Based on your answers to the questions here about your business model:
    - Does your proposed business model and strategy work?
    - Are you able to support a model that creates and/or supports social value?
    - Do you need to explore changes to any element of your business model to increase your chances of success?
        - What additional research do you need to conduct?

NAVIGATING YOUR PATH TO SUCCESS

We have designed this book to support your vision and your entrepreneurial journey. We hope that you've had the opportunity to use the exercises to help move your business vision forward. While you have done your homework, we want you to recognize that the entrepreneurial process is an iterative one. Therefore, you will likely need, and hopefully want, to revisit many of the exercises in this book as you address different markets and embrace the notion that each market is forever evolving. Growing a business is a fluid process that simply never stops. Think of this book as a toolkit that you will use throughout your business career, deploying the tools you need at various times throughout the building process.

A JOURNEY OF EXPLORATION

As with every experience in life, this book has been a journey of exploration. We leave you with these incomparable words and thoughts written by one of my favorite authors, a Massachusetts native, Theodor Seuss Geisel, aka Dr. Seuss (1960).

Oh! The Places You'll Go

Congratulations. Today is your day. You're off to Great Places! You're off and away!

You have brains in your head. You have feet in your shoes. You can steer yourself any direction you choose. You're on your own. And you know what you know. And YOU are the guy who'll decide where to go.

You'll look up and down streets. Look 'em over with care. About some you will say, "I don't choose to go there." With your head full of brains and your shoes full of feet, you're too smart to go down any not-so-good street.

And you may not find any you'll want to go down. In that case, of course, you'll head straight out of town. It's opener there in the wide open air.

Out there things can happen and frequently do to people as brainy and footsy as you.

And when things start to happen, don't worry. Don't stew. Just go right along. You'll start happening too.

Oh! The Places You'll Go!

Now you simply need to get out there and make it happen. Think of this book as a toolkit that you can keep by your side as a steadfast resource to help you plan and develop your business and marketing strategy. Remember, action is the only way to turn your business vision into reality. Let's see how far you can go and all the places you will see.

TOOLKIT

Worksheet 13.1: Data Capture Plan

Data You Must Capture to Make Business Decisions	Metrics or Key Performance Indicators Required	Process to Obtain Data	Frequency of Updating and Reviewing Data	Person(s) Responsible

Worksheet 13.2: Measuring Your Input and Outcome

Sales Analysis and Projections

Sales	# Active* Customers	Total Revenue	Total Profit	Revenue/ Customer
Prior Year _____ (yr)				
Current Year _____ (yr)				
Next Year _____ (yr)				

*Active = purchase in the last 12 months

Prospect/Sales Cycle

- Number of **new prospects** required for next year's projections _____
- Number of **repeat customers** required for next year's projections _____

- Number of **prospects** in your system to-date _____
- Percentage of prospects anticipated to **convert to sales** _____ %
- Sales cycle _____ days

Employee Analysis

Employees	# FT or FTE Employees	Total Cost	Cost/ Employee	Profit/ Employee
Prior Year _____ (yr)				
Current Year _____ (yr)				
Next Year _____ (yr)				

Customer Revenue and Profit Analysis

Customers	% of Revenue From Top 3 Customers	% of Revenue From Top 20%	% of Revenue From Customers w/You > 1 year	Net Promoter Score
Prior Year _____ (yr)				
Current Year _____ (yr)				
Next Year _____ (yr)				

Product/Service Analysis

Top 5 Products/ Services	Prior Year		Current Year		Next Year Projection	
	Revenue	Profit	Revenue	Profit	Revenue	Profit

Worksheet 13.3: Customer Lifetime Value

A. How much does your target customer spend on each purchase from your company?
$_____

B. Annually, how often does your customer make a purchase from your company?
_____

C. How many years does your customer stay with your company? _____

D. How many new customers will he or she refer to your business? _____

E. What percentage of referrals become clients? _____%

    A $_____ × B _____ × C _____ = gross sales over customer's lifetime $_____ (F)

    D _____ × E _____% × F $_____ = gross sales from new referrals $_____ (G)

    F $_____ + G $_____ = total lifetime value of a satisfied customer $_____ (H)

    How much it costs you to attract and retain these customers _____ (I)

If I (your investment) in attracting and retaining customers is greater than H (their lifetime value to you), list three actions that you will take to ensure H is significantly greater than I.

    1.

    2.

    3.

REFERENCES

ABC. (2018, January 7). *Shark tank*. Retrieved from http://abc.go.com/shows/shark-tank

Ad Council. (2019a). *About us*. Retrieved from https://www.adcouncil.org/About-Us

Ad Council. (2019b). *The classics: Drunk driving prevention*. Retrieved from https://www.adcouncil.org/Our-Campaigns/The-Classics/Drunk-Driving-Prevention

Al-Fuzai, M. (2016). $1 million spent on chocolate daily. *Kuwaiti Times*. Retrieved from http://news.kuwaittimes.net/website/1million-spent-on-chocolate-daily

Alpen Capital Investment Banking. (2015, April 28). *GCC food industry report*. Dubai, United Arab Emirates: Author.

American Express. (2019a). *About us*. Retrieved from https://about.americanexpress.com/?inav=footer_about_american_express

American Express. (2019b). *Corporate responsibility*. Retrieved from https://about.americanexpress.com/?inav=footer_about_american_express#four

Ang, K. (2018, July 26). *A new career and house with the help of over 1 million Instagram fans*. Retrieved from https://www.wsj.com/articles/a-new-career-and-house-with-the-help-of-over-1-million-instagram-fans-1532628849

Ansel, D. (n.d.). *The cronut*. Retrieved from https://www.dominiqueansel.com/the-creations/

Artistia Website. (n.d.). Retrieved from https://artistia.com/

Artyfactos. Retrieved from https://artyfactos.com

Asimov, I. (1988). *Understanding physics*. New York, NY: Dorset Press.

BBC News. (2018). *KFC's apology for running out of chicken is pretty cheeky*. Retrieved from https://www.bbc.com/news/newsbeat-43169625

Babson College. (2018). Retrieved from http://www.babson.edu/about/at-a-glance/rankings/

The BalanceSmall Business. (2019). Retrieved from https://www.thebalancesmb.com/what-very-nonprofit-should-know-about-cause-marketing-2502005

Berman, A. (2015). *Don't guess, learn: Rapid prototyping with Tom Chi*. Retrieved from https://singularityhub.com/2015/10/16/dont-guess-learn-rapid-prototyping-with-tom-chi-video/#sm.0001dmtdcn91cfimzfy27sbrta5rw

Burry, M. (2014). *5 successful businesses that got huge by starting small*. Retrieved from https://generalassemb.ly/blog/businesses-that-started-as-a-minimum-viable-product/

The Business Channel. (2016). *The Business Model Canvas: 9 steps to creating a successful business model: Startup tips*. Retrieved from https://www.youtube.com/watch?v=IP0cUBWTgpY

Campaign. (2018). *Plucky PR counters chicken FCK-up*. Retrieved from https://www.campaignlive.com/article/plucky-pr-counters-chicken-fck-up/1485750

Campaign Monitor. (2017). *The eye-opening truth about data-driven marketing*. Retrieved from https://www.campaignmonitor.com/resources/infographics/the-eye-opening-truth-about-data-driven-marketing/

Carriage. (n.d.). Retrieved from https://www.trycarriage.com/restaurants/doh

Carter, R. (2019, May 21). *10 Pinterest statistics marketers must know in 2019*. Retrieved from https://sproutsocial.com/insights/pinterest-statistics/

Central Statistics Agency (BPS), Bali Province. (2018). *Number of foreign visitor [sic] to Indonesia and Bali, 1969–2018*. Retrieved from https://bali.bps.go.id/statictable/2018/02/09/28/jumlah-wisatawan-asing-ke-bali-dan-indonesia-1969-2017.html

Collective Campus. (2017). *10 companies that failed to innovate, resulting in business failure*. Retrieved from https://www.collectivecampus.com.au/blog/10-companies-that-were-too-slow-to-respond-to-change

Cone Communications. (2019): http://www.conecomm.com/awards

Cone Communications. (2017). *2017 Cone communications CSR study*. Retrieved from http://www.conecomm.com/research-blog/2017-csr-study

Cook, C. (2019, July 17). *19 of the best landing page design examples you need to see in 2019*. Retrieved from https://blog.hubspot.com/marketing/landing-page-examples-list

Data & Marketing Association. (2017). *2017 Response Rate Report*. Retrieved from https://www.ana.net/mkc

Deloitte. (2019). *The Deloitte Global Millennial Survey 2018*. Retrieved from https://www2.deloitte.com/tr/en/pages/about-deloitte/articles/millennialsurvey-2018.html

Doran, G. T. (1981). There's a S.M.A.R.T. way to write management's goals and objectives. *Management Review*, 70, 35–36.

Earth Day Network. (2019a). *The history of Earth Day*. Retrieved from https://www.earthday.org/about/the-history-of-earth-day

Earth Day Network. (2019b). What is Earth Day, and what is it meant to accomplish? Retrieved from https://www.earthday.org/earthday/

Emerson, M. (2016, November 2). *How to use Snapchat to market your small business*. Retrieved from https://www.huffingtonpost.com/melinda-emerson/how-to-use-snapchat-to-ma_b_12770408.html

Emerson, M. (2019). *Are you ready to start your dream business?* Retrieved from https://succeedasyourownboss.com

Esterl, M. (2014). "Share a Coke" credited with a pop in sales. *Wall Street Journal*. Retrieved from https://www.wsj.com/articles/share-a-coke-credited-with-a-pop-in-sales-1411661519

Ethnography: Ellen Isaacs at TEDxBroadway (2013). Retrieved from https://www.youtube.com/watch?v=nV0jY5VgymI&feature=youtu.be

Facebook. (2011). SunChips Group Page. Retrieved from www.facebook.com/SunChips/posts/10150106871662863

Facebook. (2019a). *Set up a Facebook page*. Retrieved from https://www.facebook.com/business/learn/set-up-facebook-page

Facebook. (2019b). *Newsroom*. Retrieved from https://newsroom.fb.com/company-info/

Facebook Business. (2019). *See how your page is doing and make it even better with page insights*. Retrieved from https://www.facebook.com/business/pages/manage#page_insights

Forbes Middle East. (n.d.). Retrieved from https://www.forbesmiddleeast.com/

Gauss, A. (n.d.). *6 socially responsible companies to applaud*. Retrieved from https://www.classy.org/blog/6-socially-responsible-companies-applaud/

Geisel, T. S. (1960). *Oh, the places you'll go*. New York, NY: Random House.

Gilbert, B. (2018, May 4). *YouTube now has over 1.8 billion users every month, within spitting distance of Facebook's 2 billion*. Retrieved from https://www.businessinsider.com/youtube-user-statistics-2018-5

Homegrown Market. (n.d.). Retrieved from https://www.instagram.com/homegrown_market/?hl=en

Horwitz, Y., & Zimmer, O. (2017). *Think with Google: Beverage trends 2017: Google data reveals what's satisfying consumers' thirst*. Retrieved from www.thinkwithgoogle.com/consumer-insights/2017-beverage-industry-consumer-habits/

Hosain, A. (2014, February 11). *The failures of J. K. Rowling*. Retrieved from https://www.huffpost.com/entry/the-failures-of-jk-rowlin_b_4763301

IDEO. (2019). *Brainstorming rules*. Retrieved from https://www.ideou.com/pages/brainstorming

Ile Website. (n.d.). Retrieved from https://ile.com.ec

Instagram. (n.d.). *Instagram business tools*. Retrieved from https://help.instagram.com/307876842935851

Instagram. (2010, October 6). *Instagram launches*. Retrieved from https://instagram-press.com/blog/2010/10/06/instagram-launches-2/

Instagram. (2016, August 2). *Introducing Instagram stories*. Retrieved from https://instagram-press.com/blog/2016/08/02/introducing-instagram-stories/

Jobs, S. (2005, June 12). *Commencement address at Stanford University*. Retrieved from https://news.stanford.edu/2005/06/14/jobs-061505/

Jones, C., & USA TODAY. (n.d.). *Frito-Lay trashes noisy chip bag* [Video]. Retrieved from https://abcnews.go.com/Business/video/frito-lay-dumps-noisy-sun-chips-bag-11802811

Kees Chic. (2016, September 2). *Canopies*. Retrieved from https://www.youtube.com/watch?v=2Kb8MDkg248

King Abdullah II Award for Youth Innovation & Achievement. (2016, March 23). Retrieved from https://www.youtube.com/watch?v=Q2R3kx33u3s&feature=youtu.be

Kiser, C., & Leipziger, D. (2014). *Creating social value: A guide for leaders and change makers*. New York, NY: Routledge.

Kuligowski, K. (2019, May 21). *YouTube for business: Everything you need to know*. Retrieved from https://www.businessnewsdaily.com/9854-youtube-for-business.html

Lakhiani, V. (2015). *How Tom Chi, co-founder of Google X innovates like crazy*. Retrieved from http://www.mindvalleyinsights.com/how-tom-chi-co-founder-of-google-x-innovates-like-crazy

Levy, S. (2017). *Google Glass 2.0 is a startling second act*. Retrieved from https://www.wired.com/story/google-glass-2-is-here/

Lifehack. (n.d.). *Michael Jordon quote*. Retrieved from https://www.lifehack.org/333244/ive-failed-over-and-over-and-over-again

Marabots. (2017). Retrieved from https://www.Marabots.com/

MarketingSherpa. (n.d.). *Search the MarketingSherpa Library*. Retrieved from https://www.marketingsherpa.com/library?q=email+marketing

MarketingSherpa. (2015, February 3). *MarketingSherpa survey of consumer attitudes towards email marketing reveals strong preference for email compared with all other communications*. Retrieved from https://www.prnewswire.com/news-releases/marketingsherpa-survey-of-consumer-attitudes-towards-email-marketing-reveals-strong-preference-for-email-compared-with-all-other-communications-300029767.html

Martell, K. (n.d.). *Communications, marketing, and unapologetic truth-telling*. Retrieved from https://www.katie-martell.com/

Mehrabian, A. (1981). *Silent messages: Implicit communication of emotions and attitudes* (2nd ed.). Belmont, CA: Wadsworth.

Merriam-Webster Online Dictionary. (2019): https://www.merriam-webster.com/dictionary

Moye, J. (2015). *Share a Coke 2.0: The hit campaign is back, and it's bigger and better than ever*. Retrieved from https://www.coca-colacompany.com/stories/share-a-coke-20-the-hit-campaign-is-back-and-its-bigger-and-better-than-ever

The National Fund for Small and Medium Enterprise Development, Kuwait. (n.d.). Retrieved from https://www.nationalfund.gov.kw/en/

Neck, H., Neck, C., & Murray, E. (2018). *Entrepreneurship: The practice and mindset*. Thousand Oaks, CA: Sage.

Net Marketshare. (2019). *Search engine market share*. Retrieved from https://netmarketshare.com/search-engine-market-share.aspx

NewTV. (2019). *Innovation Showcase: DetraPel*. Retrieved from https://vp.telvue.com/preview?id=T01443&video=336281

Nonprofits Source. (2019). *The ultimate list of charitable giving statistics for 2018: Charitable giving statistics*. Retrieved from https://nonprofitssource.com/online-giving-statistics/

Orwell, G. (1945). *Animal farm*. London, England: Secker and Warburg.

Osterwalder, A. (2017, March 9). *Value proposition canvas: A tool to understand what customers really want* [Weblog post]. Retrieved from https://blog.strategyzer.com/posts/2017/3/9/value-proposition-canvas-a-tool-to-understand-what-customers-really-want

Osterwalder, A., & Pigneur, Y. (2010). *Business model generation: A handbook for visionaries, game changers, and challengers*. Hoboken, NJ: Wiley.

Paakkone, L. (n.d.). Website. Retrieved from http://www.lassepaakkonen.com/

Parasuraman, A., Berry, L. L., & Zeithaml, V. A. (1991). Refinement and Reassessment of the SERVQUAL scale. *Journal of Retailing, 67*(4), 57–67.

Pestle Analysis. (2019). *What is PESTLE analysis? A tool for business analysis*. Retrieved from https://pestleanalysis.com/what-is-pestle-analysis/

Pew Research Center. (2018a). *14% of Americans have changed their mind about an issue because of something they saw on social media*. Retrieved from http://www.pewresearch.org/fact-tank/2018/08/15/14-of-americans-have-changed-their-mind-about-an-issue-because-of-something-they-saw-on-social-media/

Pew Research Center. (2018b). *Internet/Broadband Fact Sheet*. Retrieved from http://www.pewinternet.org/fact-sheet/internet-broadband/

Pew Research Center. (2019a). *Mobile fact sheet*. Retrieved from http://www.pewinternet.org/fact-sheet/mobile

Pew Research Center. (2019b). *Share of U.S. adults using social media, including Facebook, is mostly unchanged since 2018*. Retrieved from https://www.pewresearch.org/fact-tank/2019/04/10/share-of-u-s-adults-using-social-media-including-facebook-is-mostly-unchanged-since-2018/

PhiloSophies. (2018). Retrieved from www.celebratewithsophies.com

PieShell. (2017). *Wanku Campaign*. Retrieved from https://www.pieshell.com/projects/wanku/

Pinkham, R. (2019). *Email marketing best practices: 125 links to help you be a better marketer* [Web log post]. Retrieved from https://blogs.constantcontact.com/email-marketing-best-practices-2/ (Original work published 2015)

Pinterest Business. (n.d.). *Create your account*. Retrieved from https://business.pinterest.com/en/creating-your-account

Podtrac. (2019b). *Welcome to Podtrac*. Retrieved from http://analytics.podtrac.com

Podtrac. (2019a). *Podcast industry audience rankings*. Retrieved from http://analytics.podtrac.com/podcast-rankings

Pulcinella, S. (2017, August 30). *Why direct mail marketing is far from dead*. Retrieved from https://www.forbes.com/sites/forbescommunicationscouncil/2017/08/30/why-direct-mail-marketing-is-far-from-dead/#5068e400311d

The Radicati Group. (2018, June). *Email Market, 2018–2022*. Retrieved from https://www.radicati.com/wp/wp-content/uploads/2018/01/Email_Market,_2018-2022_Executive_Summary.pdf

Ries, E. (2011). How DropBox started as a minimal viable product. *TechCrunch*. Retrieved from https://techcrunch.com/2011/10/19/dropbox-minimal-viable-product/

Satmetrix. (n.d.). *What is net promoter?* Retrieved from https://www.netpromoter.com/know/

Saul, J. (2010). *Social innovation, Inc.: 5 strategies for driving business growth through social change*. San Francisco, CA: Jossey-Bass.

Singer, S., Herrington, M., & Menipaz, E. (2018). *Global entrepreneurship monitor: 2017/18 Global Report*. Babson Park, MA: Babson College/London Business School.

Small Business Administration. (2012). *Small business fact*. Retrieved from https://www.sba.gov/sites/default/files/Business-Survival.pdf

Social Blade. (2019a). *User statistics table for YouTube*. Retrieved from https://socialblade.com/youtube/user/youtube/monthly

Social Blade. (2019b). *YouTube 101: Social Blade EDU course*. Retrieved from https://socialblade.com/youtube/education

Starbucks. (2018a). *How to order at Starbucks*. Retrieved from https://news.starbucks.com/facts/how-to-order-at-starbucks

Starbucks. (2018b). *Starbucks reports record Q3 fiscal 2018 revenues and EPS*. Retrieved from https://stories.starbucks.com/wp-content/uploads/2019/01/Starbucks_Q3_FY18_Earnings_Release.pdf

Statista. (2018). *Netflix continues to grow internationally*. Retrieved from https://www.statista.com/chart/10311/netflix-subscriptions-usa-international/

Statista. (2019, July 26). *Number of smartphone users worldwide from 2016 to 2021 (in billions)*. Retrieved from https://www.statista.com/statistics/330695/number-of-smartphone-users-worldwide/

Sterling, G. (2017). *Survey: More consumers seeking to buy directly from brands vs. retailers: Survey of 1,000 US adults contains lots of findings and implied recommendations for both brands and traditional retailers*. Retrieved from https://marketingland.com/survey-consumers-seeking-buy-directly-brands-vs-retailers-222955

Strategyzer. (n.d.). *The Value Proposition Canvas*. Retrieved from https://strategyzer.com/canvas/value-proposition-canvas

Strategyzer. (2017). *Strategyzer's Value Proposition Canvas explained* [Video]. (2017). Retrieved from https://www.youtube.com/watch?v=ReM1uqmVfP0

Strategyzer. (2018). *Canvases, tools and more*. Retrieved from https://strategyzer.com/canvas

TEDed. (2012). *Rapid prototyping Google Glass: Tom Chi*. Retrieved from https://ed.ted.com/lessons/rapid-prototyping-google-glass-tom-chi

Thomson, W. (1883). *Lecture to the Institution of Civil Engineers*. Retrieved from https://www.goodreads.com/quotes/166961-when-you-can-measure-what-you-are-speaking-about-and

Unilever. (2017). *Report shows a third of consumers prefer sustainable brands*. Retrieved from https://www.unilever.com/news/press-releases/2017/report-shows-a-third-of-consumers-prefer-sustainable-brands.html

U.S. Environmental Protection Agency. (n.d.). *Trash-free waters: Toxicological threats of plastic*. Retrieved from https://www.epa.gov/trash-free-waters/toxicological-threats-plastic

Warby Parker. (n.d.). *History*. Retrieved from https://www.warbyparker.com/history

Warby Parker. (n.d.). *Buy a pair, give a pair*. Retrieved from https://www.warbyparker.com/buy-a-pair-give-a-pair

YouTube. (2010). *Super-noisy sun chips*. Retrieved from https://video.search.yahoo.com/search/video?fr=befhp&p=NBC4+WCMH-TV+Columbus.+Super-Noisy+Sun+Chips#id=1&vid=6280f87a743de75e36b95d8688c62334&action=click

YouTube. (2019a). *About YouTube*. Retrieved from https://www.youtube.com/yt/about/

YouTube. (2019b). *Learn how to use YouTube to engage your audience and grow your impact*. Retrieved from https://socialimpact.youtube.com/how-to/

YouTube. (2019c). *YouTube for press*. Retrieved from https://www.youtube.com/yt/about/press/

YouTube. (2019d). *Social impact*. Retrieved from https://socialimpact.youtube.com/

Welch, J. (2005). *Winning*. New York, NY: HarperCollins.

Whole Foods Market. (n.d.). *Quality standards*. Retrieved from https://www.wholefoodsmarket.com/quality-standards

Worldometers. (2019). *Ecuador population*. Retrieved from http://www.worldometers.info/world-population/ecuador-population/

Zenith Food and Drink Experts. (2017). *Global alternative waters report 2017*. Retrieved from https://www.zenithglobal.com/reports_data/397/Global%20Alternative%20Waters%20Report%202017

INDEX

Abdulrahman, Al Rabah, 129 (box)–132 (box)
Action Creates Triumphs (ACT)
    Canine Connections: Partners in Action, 165 (box)–166 (box)
    Country Entrepreneurship Opportunity Challenge, 45 (box)–47 (box)
    Creating a Networking Plan, 297 (box)
    Creating a Strong Brand: 8 Key Actions to Take, 145 (box)–146 (box)
    Creating Seamless Experiences, 265 (box)
    Creating Your OWN Pitch, 156 (box)
    Customer Discovery Analysis Assignment, 86 (box)–88 (box)
    Designing Customer Profiles, 114 (box)–115 (box)
    Finding Passion Around a Mission, 251 (box)
    Friend or Foe?, 119 (box)
    Idea Generation, 18 (box)–20 (box)
    Interview an Entrepreneur, 16 (box)–17 (box)
    Mission-Focused Brands, 259 (box)–260 (box)
    Now on to Your Prototype, 108 (box)–109 (box)
    Sales and Marketing Collaboration Model, 188 (box)
    Sales Goals, 192 (box)
    Select Your Questions, 72 (box)
    Social Media Critique and Campaign Development, 285 (box)–287
    Step-by-Step Process to Creating Winning Marketing Partnerships, 162 (box)–164 (box)
    Test Your Readiness to Commit to Your Venture, 314 (box)–316 (box)
    What's Your Brand Value?, 143 (box)
    Whom Do You Really Compete With?, 120 (box)
    Your Favorite Brands, 140 (box)
    Your Market, 38 (box)
Active listening, 185, 217
"Actual words" in presentation, 151–152
Ad Council, 245–246
Aimee Bio, 103 (box)–107 (box), 105 (figure)–107 (figure)
Al Aufi, Leena, 173 (box)–175 (box)
Alberti, Joanna, 9 (box)–12 (box)
AlSoudairy, Lulwa, 172 (box)–175 (box)
Amazon Alexa platform, 264
American Express, 247
Apple, 313–314
Artista—Connecting Customers with Artisans, 172 (box)–175 (box)
Asimov, Isaac, 124
Assignable goals. *See* S.M.A.R.T. goals
Associations and publications, as source of data/trends, 33
Assurance, 98

B2B (business-to-business)
    ascending brand, key traits of, 266 (figure)
    difference from B2C sales, 188–189
    profiling, 113–114
    sales/marketing and, 190 (box)–191 (box)
B2C (business-to-consumer)
    difference from B2B sales, 188–189
    profiling, 113–114
    sales and marketing, 190 (box)–191 (box)
    sales example, 201 (box)–202 (box)
Berry, Madeleine, 98, 109
Blockbuster, 31, 185
BMI Research, 46 (box)
Body language, 83, 151, 152, 154 (box)–155 (box)
Borders Books, 31
Bornstein, Dale, 142 (box)–143 (box)
Bottled water company, 20 (box)–21 (box)
Brand, Stephen, 81
Brand loyalty, 78–79
Brands/branding
    ascending brands, 266 (figure)–267
    Bali Banana example, 148 (box)–151 (box), 149 (table), 150 (figure)
    brand position, communicating, 140–141
    brand position example, 157 (box)–158 (box)
    Business Model Canvas, 146–147
    characteristics of positive brands, 141
    communicating brand, 138–140
    components of successful, 144–145
    delivery skills, 151–152
    developing powerful brands example, 142 (box)–143 (box)

elevator pitch, 152–156 (box), 154 (box)–155 (box)
elevator pitch, developing solid, 145 (box)–146 (box)
exercise, 140 (box)
exercise, brand value, 143 (box)
exercise, creating strong brand, 145 (box)–146 (box)
feedback and, 270
lessons and takeaways, 159 (box)
loyalty measurement tool, 78–79
mission-focused brands, 259 (box)–260 (box)
reasons to buy particular brand, 141–142
transparency and, 140
value proposition, 145 (box)
See also Omnichannel marketing approach
Broadcast Yourself, 280
Brochures marketing, 289–290
Buffer, 284
Business Commitment Scorecard, 314 (box)–316 (box)
Business cards, 236, 290, 293, 295
Business Model Canvas, 1, 4
  brands/branding, 146–147
  channels, 5 (box), 73–74, 133, 147
  competition, 132–133
  cost structure, 6 (table)
  customer discovery analysis, 72–74
  customer relationships, 5 (box), 147
  customer segments analysis, 5 (box), 32, 73
  demographics, 32, 38 (box)
  ecosystem, 32
  exercise, 38 (box)
  feasibility, 6 (box)
  key activities, 6 (table)
  key partnerships, 6 (table), 172
  key resources, 6 (table)
  prototype design, 108 (box)–109 (box)
  questions based on, 5 (table)–6 (table), 326 (table)–327 (table)
  revenue streams, 6 (box), 31, 193
  sales, 200
  size of market, 73
  solution selling, 232
  value proposition, 4, 5 (table), 6 (table)
Business success and failure, 12–14, 13 (figure)

C2C (consumer-to-consumer), 189
Callie's Canine Club, 165 (box)–166 (box)
Canva, 284
Channels
  brands/branding and, 147
  Business Model Canvas, 5 (box), 73–74, 133, 147

competition and, 133
customer discovery questions, 73–74
first to market issues/access to, 123
See also Omnichannel marketing approach
Chewie's Colossal Cookie Company Survey, 88 (box)–93 (box)
  sales prospects, 197–200
Chi, Tom, 97, 100
Closed-ended question, 76–77, 226
Coca-Cola, "Share a Coke" campaign, 2
Cold calls, sales and, 218
Competition
  Bali Banana example, 149 (box)–150 (box)
  channels and, 133
  competitive assessment worksheet, 134–135
  competitive differentiator analysis worksheet, 136–137
  data sources for, 121–122
  defining, 117–118
  ethics and, 122
  exercise, 119 (box), 120 (box)
  finding proper perspective on, 119–120
  first mover advantage, myth of, 122–123
  Gonuts example, 129 (box)–132 (box)
  lessons and takeaways, 133 (box)–134 (box)
  sales and, 217
  second mover advantage, 123–124
  survival strategies, 125–126
  value proposition, 120, 123, 132–133
Conferences
  conducting research at, 296
  follow-up, importance of, 296
  networking at, 235–236, 294–296
  as source of data and trends, 33
Confidentiality, 68, 80
Constant Contact, 283
Consulting/research firms, 33
Consumer-product interaction, 97–98
Consumer-services interaction, 98
Content creation
  podcasts, 276–277 (table)
  Snapchat, 279, 281–283
  YouTube, 277–278
Continuum Economics, 46 (box)
Corporate social innovation (CSI), 248–249 (table)
Corporate social responsibility (CSR), 247–248, 249 (table)
Country data sources, 45 (box)–47 (box), 318 (table)–319 (table)

Country Entrepreneurship Opportunity Challenge, 45 (box)–47 (box)
Cover letter, in survey design, 78
CRM (customer relationship management), 194–197
Crowdfunding, 50 (box)–51 (box), 100 (box)–112 (box), 113, 124
Customer discovery analysis
   determining match, 65–67
   e-mail, text, other communication, 68
   ethnographic studies, 68, 80–83, 82 (box)–83 (box)
   exercise, 86 (box)–88 (box)
   focus groups, 68, 83–85
   lessons and takeaways, 93 (box)–94 (box)
   methods for, 67–68
   one-on-one interviews, 68, 85
   question selection for, 72 (box)–74
   social media exchanges, 68
   survey design, 68, 74–80, 88 (box)–93 (box)
   value proposition, 73
   website activity, 68
Customer gains. *See* Pains and gains
Customer inertia, 123, 124–125, 131 (box), 313
Customer lifetime value (LTV), 322–325, 331
Customer loyalty, 125. *See also* Brands/branding
Customer needs. *See* Customer profile development; Customer voice; Value proposition; Value Proposition Canvas framework
Customer pains. *See* Pains and gains
Customer profile development
   B2B and B2C strategies, 112–113
   customer characteristics relating to needs, 68–71, 69 (figure)
   demographics, 69
   ethical issues in, 68, 80
   exercise, 114 (box)–115 (box)
   ideal profile worksheet, 116
   knowledge gathering, importance of, 65–67
   life-cycle events, 71
   methods of discovering, 67–68
   psychographic and behavioral influences, 69–71
   securing prospects for, 112–113
   social media as source of profile prospects, 113
   See also Customer voice
Customer relationship management (CRM), 39–40
Customer relationships, brands/branding and, 147
Customer segments, 5 (box), 32, 73
Customer validation, 97
Customer voice, 115 (box)–116 (box). *See also* Customer profile development; Prototyping

Daniels, Caroline, 18 (box)
Data
   competition, 121–122
   country sources, 45 (box)–47 (box), 318 (table)–319 (table)
   data analysis (*See* Data analysis)
   data capture plan, 325
   data capture plan worksheet, 329
   ecosystem, sources of, 29
   ethics and, 122
   general sources for, 33–34
   importance of application of, 65
   industry association data, 35–36, 121–122
   lifetime value of customers, 322–325
   lifetime value of customers worksheet, 331
   marketing road map and, 325
   online tools for trends, 35
   primary *vs.* secondary data sources, 29–31, 30 (table)
   sales-marketing flow, problems with, 184–185
   secondary market research, 28–29
   tools for collecting market, 317
Data analysis, 319–322
   customer revenue/profit analysis, 321
   employee analysis, 320–321
   market tactics, 321–322
   input/outcome, 320
   input/outcome worksheet, 329–330
   product/service analysis, 321
   sales analysis and projections, 320
   sales cycle analysis, 320
Data bases, as source of data and trends, 33
Data capture plan, 325
   worksheet, 329
Decision making
   knowledge gathering, importance of, 65–67
   social media impact on, 2
Delivery company example, 297 (box)–300 (box)
Demographics
   Business Model Canvas and, 32, 38 (box)
   data sources for, 318 (box)
   of Internet users, 3
   of target audience, 69 (figure), 75, 195, 196, 287 (box)
DetraPel, 201 (box)–202 (box)

Dewobroto, Wisnu, 148 (box)–151 (box)
Digital ecosystems, 264
Direct mail marketing, 290–291
Disruptive brand marketing, 266 (figure)–267
Distribution channels. *See* Channels
Dropbox, 109

Ecosystem, understanding
   Business Model Canvas, 32
   country data, 45 (box)–47 (box)
   digital, 264
   industry association data, 35–36
   industry association data example, 47 (box)–54 (box)
   lessons and takeaways, 264
   market, defining, 31–32
   market trends, 29–31
   market trends, tools for understanding, 35
   PESTLE Analysis, 42 (figure)–43
   positioning map, 44 (figure)–45, 126 (box)–128 (box), 132 (box)
   primary research, 29
   primary *vs.* secondary data sources, 29, 30 (box)
   secondary research, 28–29
   size of market, 36–37 (figure), 38 (box)
   sources of data and trends, 32–33
   SWOT analysis (*See* SWOT analysis)
   target audience, 36–37 (figure), 38 (box)
EIU.com, 46 (box)
Elevator pitch, brands/branding, 152–156
   body language and, 155 (box)
   creating pitch, 145 (box)–146 (box), 156 (box)
   creating pitch worksheet, 159–160
   delivering pitch, 154 (box)–155 (box)
   eye contact and, 155 (box)
   facial expressions and, 155 (box)
   questions for polished pitch, 153–154
   stimulating interest as goal in, 153
   voice issues in, 155 (box)
E-mail marketing, 269 (box), 283–284
Emerging Markets Information Service, 46 (box)
Emerson, Melinda (SmallBiz Lady), 281–282
Empathy, 98
Employee analysis, 320–321
Entrepreneurship
   defining, 2–3
   lessons and takeaways, 21 (box)–22 (box)
Environmental issues, 217
   social entrepreneurs case, 252 (box)–254 (box)

Estrella, Nicolás (Nico). *See* WAKU
Ethics
   in customer research, 68, 80
   in gathering data on competitors, 122
   importance in business practices, 121
Ethnographic study
   customer discovery analysis, 68, 80–82
   idea generation, 18 (box)–20 (box)
   observation activity, 82 (box)–83 (box)
   worksheet, 26–27
Ethnography, definition of, 18 (box)
Euromonitor Passport, 46 (box)
Expert Insight
   Art of the Pitch, 154 (box)–155 (box)
   Becoming a Thought Leader and Influencer—Lisa Murray, 272 (box)–274 (box)
   Developing Powerful Brands, 142 (box)–143 (box)
   Paul Horn: Golden Rules of Networking, 233 (box)–236 (box)
Eye contact, 155 (box)

Facebook
   as marketing tool, 268 (box)–269 (box), 280
   popularity of, 279
   sources for setting up/measuring social media sites, 285
   webinars and, 276
   See also Social media
Facebook for Business, 285
Facebook Insights, 285
Facebook Live, 276
Facial expressions, 155 (box)
Failure
   learning to accept, 313–314
   prototype design example, 99–100
   reasons for, 12–14, 13 (figure), 139
FedEx, 141–142
Feedback
   branding and, 270
   importance of, 103, 139, 170
   MVTs and, 109
   prototypes and, 98–100, 108 (box)–109 (box)
Feghali, Tony, 103 (box)–107 (box)
Focus groups
   customer discovery analysis, 68, 83–85
   rules for running, 84–85
Forbes, Malcom, 313
Frito Lay prototype, 99–100
Funder buy-in, 98

Gates, Bill, 314
Geisel, Theodor Seuss, 328
GEM (Global Entrepreneurship Monitor) Report, 45 (box)–46 (box)
Geographic data on target audience, 287 (box)
Giraldo, Juan. *See* WAKU
Global Competitiveness Report, 46 (box)
Goals
    of elevator pitch, 153
    sales goals, 192 (box)
    See also S.M.A.R.T. goals
Google
    podcasts and, 277
    prototyping and, 100–101
    sources for setting up/measuring social media sites, 100–101
    webinars and, 276
    See also Social media; YouTube
Google Assistant, 264
Google Beverage Trends Report 2017, 55 (box)–56 (box)
Google Forms, 77
Google Glass, 100–101
Google Play, 277
Google Sheet, 203 (box)
Google Trends, 35
Google X, 100
Greeting card company, 9 (box)–12 (box)
Gretsky, Wayne, 314

Hidden obvious, 81
Horn, Paul, 154 (box)–155 (box), 233 (box)–236 (box), 293
Houston, Drew, 109
Hubspot, 35, 284

Idea generation, 18 (box)–20 (box)
IDEO, 19 (box)–20 (box)
Industry association data, 35–36, 121–122
Industry conferences/trade shows, 121–122, 294–296
Industry statistics, as source of data and trends, 33
Inertia, 123, 124–125, 131 (box), 313
Input and outcome, measuring, 320
    worksheet, 329–330
Instagram, 279, 280–281, 285. *See also* Social media
Instagram Business Tools, 285
Intangibles, 98, 101

Internet
    demographics of users, 3
    See also Social media
Interviews
    exercise, 16 (box)–17 (box)
    one-on-one, 68, 75, 85

Jobs, Steve, 313–314
Jones, Charisse, 100
Jordan, Michael, 314

Kees Chic, 252 (box)–254 (box)
KFC (Kentucky Fried Chicken), 139–140
Khan, Muhammad Hassan, 297 (box)–300 (box)
Kiser, Cheryl, 242–243, 245, 248
Kodak, 31

Landing pages, 102–103, 284
Leipziger, Deborah, 242–243
Life-cycle events, customer needs and, 69 (figure), 71, 75
Lifetime value of customers (LTV), 322–325
    worksheet, 331
LinkedIn, 85, 164 (box), 279. *See also* Social media
Listening
    active, 185, 217
    importance in sales, 211, 214, 217
    See also Customer voice
Logos, 105 (figure)

M Booth, 142 (box)–143 (box)
Management buy-in, 98
Marabots Technology Corporation, 47 (box)–50 (box)
    customer alignment and, 52 (box)
    drone market, understanding, 53 (box)
    features desired, 53 (box)
    final recommendations to, 54 (box)
    impact of aerial on submersible drone market, 51 (box)–52 (box)
    marine market, understanding, 53 (box)
    market size and growth sectors, 52 (box)
    research findings, highlights, 50 (box)–53 (box)
    role of price, 51 (box)
Market
    defining, 31–32
    size of, 36–37 (figure), 38 (box), 52 (box), 63, 73
Market research
    data sources for, 46 (box)
    introduction to, 28

lessons and takeaways, 57 (box)
market trends, 35
secondary market, 28–29
Marketing
   B2B (*See* B2B (business-to-business))
   B2C (*See* B2C (business-to-consumer))
   C2C (consumer-to-consumer), 189
   data analysis and, 321–322
   data collection tools, 317
   disruptive brand, 266 (figure)–267
   entrepreneurial approach to, 2–8
   entrepreneurial approach worksheets, 22–27
   multichannel *vs.* omnichannel, 262 (figure)–263
   road map for, 325
   social media tools for, 283–284
   tactics for, 193–194
   See also Brands/branding; Brands/branding; Channels; Old school marketing tactics; Omnichannel marketing approach; Sales and marketing
Marketing road map, 325
MarketingCo, 119–120
MarketingSherpa, 283
Martell, Katie, 265–266 (figure)
Mead, Margaret, 80
Measurable goals. *See* S.M.A.R.T. goals
Mehrabian, Albert, 151
Minimum viable products. *See* MVPs
Mintel Group, 56 (box)
Mission
   engaging others in, 245
   mission-focused brands, 259 (box)–260 (box)
Multichannel *vs.* omnichannel marketing, 262 (figure)–263
Multiple select response question, 76
Murray, Emma, 2–3
Murray, Lisa, 272 (box)–274 (box)
MVPs (minimum viable products), 97, 109–113, 187
   WAKU design example, 110 (box)–112 (box), 110 (figure)
   See also Prototyping

Neck, Christopher, 2–3
Net Promoter Score® (NPS), 78–79
Netflix, 31
Networking, 233–238
   creating networking plan, 296, 297 (box)
   forms of, 294
   golden rules of, 233 (box)–236 (box), 293

identifying events for, 292–294
at industry conferences, 235–236, 294–296
through own seminars and webinars, 237

Old school marketing tactics
   brochures, 289–290
   direct mail, 290–291
   lessons and takeaways, 304 (box)
   postcards, 290, 291
   traditional advertising, 291–292
   vs. new school tactics, 269–270
Omnichannel marketing approach, 262–263 (figure)
   ascending brands, 266 (figure)–267
   brand engagement and buzz-building, 265–266 (figure)
   channel selection, importance of, 271
   content creation and delivery, 275–279
   disruptive brand marketing, 266 (figure)–267
   lessons and takeaways, 288 (box)
   marketing campaign rollout, 303
   marketing campaign strategy outline worksheet, 307–309
   marketing campaign worksheet, 306–307
   marketing channel identification research findings, 267–268, 268 (box)–269 (box)
   marketing channel projections/analysis worksheet, 305–306
   multichannel marketing *vs.*, 262 (figure)–263
   old *vs.* new school marketing, 269–270
   public relations, 272, 272 (box)–274 (box), 274
   Starbuck's seamless experience example, 263–265 (box)
   thought leaders and influencers, 272, 272 (box)–274 (box), 274–275
   Waku application of, 300 (box)–302 (box), 302 (figure)
   Web as communication channel in, 270–271
One-on-one interviews, 68, 75, 85
Open-ended questions, 75, 76, 84–85, 226
Order items question, 77
Orwell, George, 322

Paakkonen, Lasse, 166 (box)–168 (box)
Pains and gains, 71–72, 86 (box)–87 (box), 111 (box), 115 (box)
Parasuraman, A., 98
Partnerships
   benefits of, 164
   Business Model Canvas and, 172

challenges to, 171–172
creating, step-by-step exercise, 162 (box)–164 (box)
examples of, 166 (box)–168 (box)
factors in successful, 170–171
getting partnerships right worksheet, 178–179
individual partnership assessment worksheet, 180–182
lessons and takeaways, 177–178
partner alliance analysis and strategy worksheet, 179–180
partnership checklist worksheet, 183
PESTLE analysis of, 162 (box)–164 (box)
risk-reward balance in, 165
shared values and, 168–170, 175 (box)–177 (box)
strengths and weaknesses of, 165 (box)–166 (box), 169–170
SWOT analysis of, 162 (box)–164 (box)
with thought leaders and influencers, 274–275
Waku, 175 (box)–177 (box)
Passion, 312–313
PESTLE Analysis, 42 (figure)–43
partnerships, 162 (box)–164 (box)
PhiloSophie's®, 9 (box)–12 (box)
PieShell campaign, 100 (box)–112 (box)
Pinterest
as marketing tool, 279, 281, 285
sources for setting up/measuring social media sites, 285
See also Social media
Pinterest for Business, 285
Pitch. *See* Elevator pitch
Podcasts, 276–277 (table)
Point of view (POV), 266
Positioning (perceptual) map, 44 (figure)–45, 126 (box)–128 (box), 132 (box)
Postcard marketing, 290, 291
Primary *vs.* secondary data sources, 29–31, 30 (table)
Product/service analysis, 321
Profile development. *See* Customer profile development
Profits
customer profit/time analysis worksheet, 208–210
customer revenue/profit analysis, 193, 321
first to market issues, 123
Prototyping
Aimee Bio example, 103 (box)–107 (box), 105 (figure)–107 (figure)
design failure example, 99–100
to identify profiles, 97–100
prototype design exercise, 108 (box)–109 (box)
Google example, 100–101

role-plays, 102
services and apps, 101–103, 107
storyboards, 101–102
websites/social media test sites for, 102–103
See also MVPs (minimum viable products)
Psychographic/behavioral influences, 69 (figure)–71, 75, 287 (box)
Public relations (PR), 272 (box)–274 (box), 274–275

Qualtrics, 77
Questions
closed-ended, 76–77, 226
multiple select response, 76
open-ended, 75, 76, 84–85, 226
order items, 77
rank value, 76
single select response, 77
yes or no, 76

Rank value question, 76
Rayyan, Diana, 252 (box)–254 (box)
Realistic goals. *See* S.M.A.R.T. goals
Reliability, 98
Research/consulting firms, as source of data and trends, 33
Responsiveness, 98
Return on investment (ROI), 54 (box), 196, 272, 290, 291, 311
Revenue streams, 6 (box), 31, 193
Risk
reducing, 164, 172
risk-reward balance, 165
Role-play, 102, 221
Roosevelt, Eleanor, 312
Rowling, J. K., 314
Rumson, Kate, 275

Sales
Business Model Canvas, 200
customer profit/time analysis worksheet, 208–210
customer relationship management, 194–197
customer revenue and profit analysis, 193, 321
data capture plan, 194
data capture plan/dashboard worksheet, 210
designing sales processes and systems, 191–197
distribution strategy, B2B *vs.*, B2C, 188–189
increasing customer base example, 201 (box)–202 (box)
lessons and takeaways, 204 (box)

product distribution example, 203 (box)–204 (box)
prospect/sales cycle, 192–193
sales analysis and projections, 192–195, 320
sales analysis projection worksheet, 207–208
sales conversion worksheet, 205
sales cycle, managing, 197
sales goals, 192 (box)
sales prospect calculator worksheet, 206–207
sales stages worksheet, 239–240
sales time analysis worksheet, 206
selling to difficult customers worksheet, 241
trust and relationships, 231 (box)–232 (box)
WAKU process for, 227 (box)–231 (box)
See also Networking; Sales and marketing; Solution selling

Sales and marketing
collaboration model, 186 (figure)–188 (box)
data flow problems, 184–185
roles, sales *vs.* marketing, 185–186
tactics for, 193–194
See also Omnichannel marketing approach; Sales

Sales cycle analysis, 320
Saul, Jason, 248
Scattershot approach to social media, 273 (box)
Sculley, John, 314
Sears, 185
Second is Best (SIB), 268 (box)–269 (box)
Secondary research, 29–31, 30 (table), 67
Self-assessment, 314 (box)–316 (box)
SEMrush, 35
Serpstat, 35
Serviceable Availability Market (SAM), 36–37 (figure)
SERVQUAL MODEL, 98
Share of the Market (SOM), 37 (figure)
Single select response question, 77
Size of market, 36–37 (figure), 38 (box), 52 (box), 63, 73
Slogans, 287 (box)
S.M.A.R.T. goals
business launch plan/road map worksheet, 24–26
characteristics of, 14–16
sample goal worksheet, 23–24
setting goals worksheet, 22–23
Snapchat, 279, 281–283. *See also* Social media
Social Blade, 278, 280
Social entrepreneurs
campaign design example, 245–246
corporate social innovation, 248–249 (table)
corporate social responsibility, 247–248, 249 (table)
defining, 242–243

environmental issues example, 252 (box)–254 (box)
fundamentals for making social impact on YouTube, 246–247
generational giving differences, 250 (table)–251
lessons and takeaways, 260 (box)
mission engagement, 245
mission-focused brands, 259 (box)–260 (box)
passionate entrepreneurs and, 251 (box)–252
social business model example, 258 (box)–259 (box)
sustainable economic opportunities for women example, 255 (box)–258 (box)
Warby Parker example, 243–244

Social media
critique/campaign development exercise, 285 (box)–287
e-mail marketing, 283–284
Facebook (*See* Facebook)
Google (*See* Google)
impact on decision making, 2
Instagram, 279, 280–281, 285
LinkedIn, 85, 164 (box), 279
management resources, 284
Pinterest, 279, 281, 285
podcasts, 276–277 (table)
scattershot approach to, 273 (box)
Snapchat, 279, 281–283
top tools, 279–281
training and advice for setting up sites, 285
Twitter, 268 (box)–269 (box)
using to find customer profile prospects, 113
webinars, 237, 276
YouTube (*See* YouTube)

Solution selling
analytical skills, 214–215
Business Model Canvas, 232
cold calls, 218
comfort level, increasing, 211–214
communication/listening skills, 214
contact times, 225–226
follow-up/servicing account's needs stage, 224
hot buttons, 226
in-person appointment stage, 221–222
introduction stage, 220–221
learning skills, 216
lessons and takeaways, 238 (box)–239 (box)
listening, importance of, 211, 217
meeting stage, 222–223
objections, dealing with, 225
open- *vs.* close-ended questions, 226

organizational skills, 215
passion and, 216
preparation stage, 218–220
relationship tips, 225–226
researching customer needs, 216–217, 218–224
script template, 220–221
self-discipline skills, 215–216
sales skills, 214–216, 237–238
solution selling stage, 223
stages of sales process, 218–224
time management skills, 215
Specific goals. *See* S.M.A.R.T. goals
Squarespace, 284
Starbuck's Omnichannel approach, 263–265
Statue of Liberty, 247
Storyboards, 101–102
Strategyzer, 4, 71–72, 115 (box)
Strategyzer's Value Proposition Canvas framework, 71–72, 115 (box)
Subgroups, 75
Substitute products, 118
Sun Chips® package example, 99–100
Survey design, 68, 74–80
    Chewie's Colossal Cookie Company Survey example, 88 (box)–93 (box)
    introductory cover letter for, 78
    Net Promoter Score®, 78–79
    question format for, 75–77
    resources worksheet, 94–95
    response rate, boosting, 79–80
    as source of data and trends, 33
    tools for launching, 77
    See also Survey design
Sustainable development goals, 251 (box)
Sustainable economic opportunities for women example, 255 (box)–258 (box)
Suvey Monkey, 77
Switching cost, 125
SWOT analysis, 38–42
    analysis worksheet, 58–63
    market size analysis, 63
    opportunities, 41
    opportunities worksheet, 59
    partnerships, 162 (box)–164 (box)
    positioning (perceptual) map, creating, 44 (figure)–45
    strategic plan to address worksheet, 60–63
    strengths, 39–40
    strengths worksheet, 58
    threats, 41–42
    threats worksheet, 60
    weaknesses, 40–41
    weaknesses worksheet, 58–59
    See also PESTLE analysis

Taglines, 287 (box)
TAM-SAM-SOM approach to market size, 36–37 (figure)
Tangibles, 98
Target audience
    demographics of, 69 (figure), 75, 195, 196, 287 (box)
    ecosystem of, 36–37 (figure), 38 (box)
    primary, 75, 86 (box)–88 (box), 287 (box)
    secondary, 75, 86 (box)–88 (box)
Team buy-in, 98
Thomson, William, 317
Thought leaders/influencers, 272, 272 (box)–274 (box)
    partnerships with, 274–275
Time analysis
    customer profit/time analysis worksheet, 208–210
    sales time analysis worksheet, 206
Time management, 195, 215–216
Time-related goals. *See* S.M.A.R.T. goals
Tone of voice, 151, 155 (box)
Total Availability Market (TAM), 36, 37 (figure)
Toys "R" Us, 31, 185
Traditional advertising, 291–292
Trello, 284
Trends
    Google Beverage Trends Report 2017, 55 (box)–56 (box)
    sources for, 33–34
    tools for understanding, 35
Twain, Mark, 152
Twitter, 268 (box)–269 (box), 279
Typeform, 77

UN Sustainable Development goals, 251 (box)
Unilever, 56 (box)
U.S. Dept. of Commerce County Commercial Guides, 46 (box)

VacuumCo example, 65–67
Value priced, 44
Value Proposition Canvas framework, 71–72, 115 (box)
Value proposition, 1, 4
    branding, 144, 145 (box), 147, 287 (box)
    Business Model Canvas framework, 147, 232
    competition, 120, 123, 132–133

customer discovery analysis, 73
lifetime value of customers, 322–325, 331
marketing, 187, 221, 267
partnerships, 176 (box)
prototypes, 109, 111 (box)
role of price in, 51 (box)
sales, 187, 221, 232
as source of data and trends, 33
Waku, 158 (box), 227 (box)

Values, shared, 168–170, 175 (box)–177 (box)
Videos, marketing and delivering content, 277–279
View from the Trenches
    Artista—Connecting Customers with Artisans, 172 (box)–175 (box)
    Artyfactos—Helping Women—One Orange Peel at a Time, 255 (box)–258 (box)
    Bali Banana, 148 (box)–151 (box), 149 (table), 150 (figure)
    Chewie's Colossal Cookie Company Survey, 88 (box)–93 (box)
    Clothing Consignment: Research First—Channels Second, 268 (box)–269 (box)
    DetraPel—Repelling Stains One Customer at a Time, 201 (box)–202 (box)
    Go Nuts for Gonuts Donuts and Coffee, 129 (box)–132 (box), 132 (figure)
    Kees Chic—Saving the Planet . . . One Plastic Bag at a Time, 252 (box)–254 (box)
    Lasse Paakkonen Olympic Story, The, 166 (box)–168 (box)
    Marabots Technology Corporation, 47 (box)–50 (box)
    Meet Aimee: The Aimee Bio Story, 103 (box)–107 (box), 105 (figure)–107 (figure)
    PhiloSophie's®: From Mass Market to Tying the Knot, 9 (box)–12 (box)
    Stallion Deliveries, 297 (box)–300 (box)

WAKU
    brand positioning, 157 (box)–158 (box)
    competition, 126–128, 127 (figure)–128 (figure)
    market research results, 55 (box)–51 (box)
    marketing tactics, 20 (box)–21 (box)
    MVP design, 110 (box)–112 (box), 110 (figure)
    omnichannel marketing approach, 300 (box)–302 (box), 302 (figure)
    partnerships, 175 (box)–177 (box), 300 (box)–302 (box)
    positioning map creation, 126 (box)–128 (box)
    product distribution, 203 (box)–204 (box)
    sales approach, 190 (box)–191 (box)
    sales process, 227 (box)–231 (box)
    social business model, 258 (box)–259 (box)
    substitute products and, 118
    value proposition, 158 (box), 227 (box)
Warby Parker (WP), 243–244
Web/websites
    analysis of customer activity on, 68
    as communication channel, 270–271
    management resources for, 284
    as source of data and trends, 33
    See also Social Media
Webinars, 237, 276
Website Grader, 35, 284
Welch, Jack, 296
WhatsApp, 279, 280
Wingate, Amanda, 45 (box)
Wingate, Jacqueline, 88 (box)–93 (box)
Wix, 284
Woolworth, 31
Wordpress, 284

Yes or no question, 76
YouTube
    influencers on, 55 (box)
    as marketing tool, 277–278
    popularity of, 279
    tips for making social impact on, 246–247
    videos and, 277–279, 280
    webinars and, 276
    See also Social media

Zamarin, David, 201 (box)–202 (box)
Zeithaml, V. A., 98